FEMINIST THEORY AND THE CLASSICS

Thinking Gender
Edited by Linda Nicholson

Also published in the series

FEMINIST THEORY
AND THE
CLASSICS

Edited by
Nancy Sorkin Rabinowitz and Amy Richlin

ROUTLEDGE

NEW YORK   LONDON

Published in 1993 by

Routledge
29 West 35 Street
New York, NY 10001

Published in Great Britain by

Routledge
11 New Fetter Lane
London EC4P 4EE

Library of Congress Cataloging-in-Publication Data

Feminist theory and the classics / edited by Nancy Sorkin Rabinowitz
  and Amy Richlin.
     p. cm.—(Thinking gender)
  Includes bibliographical references and index.
   ISBN 0-415-90645-8. — ISBN 0-415-90646-6 (pbk.)
    1. Classical literature—History and criticism—Theory, etc.
  2. Feminism and literature—Greece. 3. Feminism and literature—
Rome. 4. Women and literature—Greece. 5. Women and literature—
Rome. 6. Sex roles in literature. I. Rabinowitz, Nancy Sorkin.
II. Richlin, Amy, 1951– . III. Series.
PA35.F46 1993
880'.09—dc20   92-40745
                                               CIP

British Library Cataloguing-in-Publication Data also available.

For all our sisters

Contents

Acknowledgments

The co-editors want first to thank each other for many happy hours of co-editing, from the first phone call when we hatched the idea for the original panel to the last spasms of copy-editing and proofreading. To the contributors go our heartfelt thanks for the enthusiasm with which they wrote and rewrote; they have challenged our notions and inspired us to think through the issues posed by the volume in new and creative ways. This volume grows out of long years of struggle in sisterhood and friendship, as well as from thinking, writing, and talking about feminism and classics. In very real ways, our writing has been made possible by this context of activism and by the work of many others in our double field; the chapter bibliographies and appendix show our debt to the rich work on women in antiquity and in feminist thought. We hope our readers will go further.

Institutional backing is always essential in such an undertaking. Hamilton College and the University of Southern California have provided moral and financial support; our work was made possible by the invaluable assistance of our administrative staff, as well as by the availability of copy machines, phones, and express mail (where would we have been without it?). Special thanks to Sandra Westover for her eagle eye.

We came to Routledge having heard of the miracles wrought by our editor, Maureen MacGrogan, and we are now true believers. She has urged us forward at each stage of the process, but was patient when patience was required. We thank her and Linda Nicholson for their boundless confidence in the project.

This last paragraph is the traditional place for rewarding families for having to put up with the foibles of writers. A paragraph seems hardly enough under the circumstances; this one stands for a lot. Nancy Sorkin Rabinowitz thanks Peter for reading (and editing) every word she writes, Michael and Rachel for graciously allowing her to tie up the phone and the computer, and Sophie Sorkin for being such a tough act to follow. Amy Richlin wants to say here how proud she will always be of the shining example of her father, Samuel Richlin, women's studies major and A student; and thanks her mother, Sylvia Richlin, for making sure she keeps doing her homework. We love you all; this book is one result of all your years of help, understanding, and love.

Although we have made every effort to avoid special usages, this book may contain some abbreviations standard in the field of classics but unfamiliar to those outside it; lists of such abbreviations may be found at the beginning of the *Oxford Classical Dictionary*. The Loeb Classical Library series provides a convenient set of translations of most Greek and Latin texts.

1

Introduction

Nancy Sorkin Rabinowitz

Feminist Theory and the Classics: in many ways our title is not surprising, growing out of a decade of feminist examinations of the traditional disciplines, such as *Feminism and Anthropology* (1988) or *Feminism and Philosophy* (1985), or attempts to make connections to other theoretical perspectives, as in "the unhappy marriage of Marxism and feminism," or *Feminism and Foucault*.

Yet the pairing of feminist theory and the classics is also different from these others. The fact is that classics has, with few exceptions, been anti-theory in general and anti-feminist in particular. In the Modern Language Association, feminism may be under attack as not radical enough,[1] but in the American Philological Association, it is still very radical indeed (Richlin 1991).

The "and" in our title attempts, à la Tarzan, to throw a line over a ravine that has blocked many of us who work in both fields. There are discursive differences that have made writing this introduction deeply troublesome for me. For instance, academic feminists tend increasingly to ask who is speaking and for whom, while in classics such questions are taken to be irrelevant (more on this later). Should I speak in the disembodied voice of "the volume," trying to represent the multiple positions of the individual authors, or in my own voice? The former evenhanded approach might seem ideal, but heightened feminist sensitivity to difference among women has made any form of generalization problematic; thus, to say "classicists do x" may ignore many of my good friends who are classicists and who are trying *not* to do x. Simultaneously, other controversies within feminism have raised consciousness about the partiality of subjectivity: If I decide just to "speak for myself," which of my many voices would I adopt? I come up against the multiplicity of my subject positions: I am a white, bourgeois, Jewish woman, who is "married with children," as well as a Hellenist, a member of a Comparative Literature department teaching feminist literary criticism, and an activist feminist. Much of what I say in the rest of the introduction is then partial, based on my

1

own perspective as a double outsider to classics, but I have also tried to describe and represent the points of view of the other contributors.

These differences between the discourses of classics and feminist theory make conversation (let alone "marriage") between them highly problematic (Passman and Brown this volume).[2] Nonetheless, we intend to speak to three audiences at once: classicists unfamiliar with feminist theory, feminists unfamiliar with classical scholarship, and students of both. Using contemporary theory, we hope to press the classics community to question itself; reviewing ancient material from new perspectives, we hope to enter the ongoing dialogue in feminist theory. As feminists working in classics, however, we have often felt doubly marginalized; on the one hand, our work is largely unrecognized as part of the mainstream of the field, and, on the other hand, our affiliation as classicists renders us virtually invisible to feminists in the theoretical avant-garde. Feminist classicists have published extensively, and special issues about women in antiquity have become common; nonetheless, nonclassicists do not tend to read even those progressive classics journals (such as *Helios, Ramus,* or *Arethusa*) that carry our work.[3] While recognition of the need for theory is not new (see Skinner 1986, for instance), in this collection we have explicitly foregrounded it in an attempt to break out of our earlier isolation. Building on the work done before, while adopting critical perspectives that enable us to look at antiquity afresh, we have tried to make our work public in a way that will make feminist theory and classics mutually accessible to one another.

It is easier to see what I mean by the conflict between the discourses if we first sketch in some definitions. Feminist theory is, of course, made up of two words, each of which is itself complex. The adjective "feminist" is derived from "feminism," but what is feminism? By now it is more accurate and more fashionable to speak of feminism*s*; but while there are many different varieties (for instance, third world, radical, bourgeois, Black, lesbian, Native American), we could perhaps agree that all are avowedly political, and that contemporary feminism is a political movement akin to other liberation movements of this century (Evans 1980). Robyn Warhol and Diane Price Herndl put it well in the introduction to their anthology of feminist literary criticism, *Feminisms:* "But even when they focus on such comparatively abstract matters as discourse, aesthetics, or the constitution of subjectivity, feminists are always engaged in an explicitly political enterprise, always working to change existing power structures both inside and outside academia. Its overtly political nature is perhaps the single most distinguishing feature of feminist scholarly work."[4] Feminist *theory* is no more monolithic than feminism, nor is it separable from other bodies of theory; feminist theory has availed itself of burgeoning discourses around race and class as well as Marxist, psychoanalytic, poststructural, and postcolonial theory, to name a few (see individual essays for bibliography). To complicate matters further, feminist theory has close ties to the development of women's studies in the curriculum but is not interchangeable with the academic study of women. It is obviously possible to count women, describe them, even explain women's behavior without taking a feminist perspective (Blok and Mason 1987) or a theoretical one.

Indeed, one might well ask "is theory feminist?" Such questions continue to surface as feminists wonder what an increasingly specialized and often incomprehensible body of writing has to do with a movement for social change. Barbara Christian uses the term "race for theory" to challenge a certain kind of high academic, jargon-laden theory, at the same time that she claims that African-American women have long been engaged in writing theory. Her piece makes it clear that we cannot simply assume the comfortable coherence of those terms feminism and theory. As a feminist, Christian expresses fear of developments in literary theory, for "when theory is not rooted in practice, it becomes prescriptive, exclusive, elitist" (Christian 1988: 74). She asks pointedly, "For whom are we doing what we are doing when we do literary criticism?" (Christian 1988: 77). As we shall see, that question is even more problematic for feminists who are not only academics and theorists but also classicists.

If feminism is a politics of change, the very word "classics" connotes changelessness (on the name, see Hallett this volume; Richlin 1989). Thus, for instance, classics of clothing don't go out of style (check your Lands' End or Talbots catalogues), and enduring canonical works are called classics (for instance, classics of English literature). Classics is also the name of an academic discipline, a misnomer since there are classical periods in any number of different cultures (Haley 1989: 335), but one that confers status by evoking tradition with all its weight. The *New Yorker* recently carried a story about the classics in Malawi; when the new teacher arrived, she was greeted as "the person who has come here to make us a real university" (Alexander 1991: 58).

But the conservatism of classics is not just in the name. To return to the contradiction between feminist theory and the classics: while the conflict would *appear* to be between feminism, which is avowedly a politics, and classics, which claims to be simply the study of the Greek and Latin languages, as well as Greek and Roman culture in the ancient period, the conflict is in fact between two different and even antithetical forms of politics.

In speaking of the politics of the classics, I do not mean simply that classics focuses on certain texts, although that bias is surely there. The classicist's field of study is generally taken to be texts written by male authors, like Homer, Thucydides, Aeschylus, Vergil, Ovid, Horace. But there is more to the politics of classics than this inherited bias—or, rather, there is more to the bias of the discipline than the biases of the Greeks and Romans themselves. Indeed, classics actually *enacts* a conservative politics in several ways that may be familiar to those in similarly traditional disciplines.

The dominant mode of research in classics is in the grip of an almost total empiricism and rooted in a form of textual study that purports to be value free, because it is based on a supposedly neutral philology. Thus, the professional organization of classicists is named the American Philological Association. Philological work, literally love of the *logos* or word, is typically linguistic in the narrowest sense (Hallett 1983). Consequently, much work in our prestigious journals is still devoted to the establishment of texts—we delete or transpose lines, decide what is spurious, what is authentic; therefore, philological training remains the *sine qua non* for entry into the discipline (Gutzwiller and Michelini 1991: 66–68). Consider the statement of the editorial board of the eminent *American Journal of Philology* (*AJP*) in 1987, entitled "*AJP* Today." It announced that the journal was

> still "philological" in the sense that it is centered on languages and texts. It still invites articles which add to our knowledge of the languages and dialects, literatures, history, and culture of the Greco-Roman world. While *AJP* will always have an interest in certain kinds of literary and philosophical interpretation, the emphasis is still on rigorous scholarly methods. . . . *AJP* will be as receptive as possible to new approaches, but the use of innovative methods is, in itself, not sufficient reason for publication (*AJP* 1987: vii–viii).

The *AJP* editorial stakes out its territory in terms of rigor, presenting the journal as simply opposed to trendiness, a position that would seem to be apolitical. There is, however, an ideology implicit in the very opposition it asserts between "rigorous methods" and another, nonrigorous, kind of "literary interpretation." If elsewhere in the academy, the race for theory is on, in the American Philological Association, the race is away *from* theory. What is construed as the avoidance of any special interests in reality reflects one special interest group's attempt to maintain its authority and control.[5] More important, the devaluation of theory goes along with a devaluation of issues of power, race, and gender, which theory would "import" to a consideration of "the text pure and simple." Simultaneously, this philological bent is consistent with a lack of interest in attracting women or people of color to the discipline. If point of view is irrelevant, what difference does it make who is doing the editing, translating, or interpreting?

Classics, even viewed as philology, is not merely a pursuit carried on in the privacy of the study, or in the pages of rarefied journals. The classroom is a political arena as well, and the study of the classics has not only shaped texts and constituted canons, it has also engendered generations of students and scholars, instilling the masculine values of antiquity. I say masculine advisedly since not only were the authors of epic, tragedy, and philosophy men, but the citizenry of antiquity (even of supposedly democratic Athens) was also male.

The community of scholars studying the period has also been almost exclusively male. While all university study was male until quite recently, Greek and Latin were prerequisites for being a "gentleman" and were systematically withheld from women and other outsiders. Furthermore, as Bernal's analysis in *Black Athena* (Bernal 1987) makes clear, classics as a modern discipline developed on the basis of racist paradigms; while the ancient Greeks gave credit to Egypt, in the nineteenth century that interpretation lost out to the view of the Greeks as the originators of civilization. Outsiders, as Shelley Haley's work on African-American women demonstrates, could aspire to become insiders by learning Latin and Greek, but the discipline's self-definition certainly did not include them.

Upper-level classics courses in general continue to be organized by author—although several authors may be treated in a genre course—and the authors continue to be the canonical ones. There is wide variety in the amount of study outside language and literature that classics graduate students undertake, but at the prestigious university programs, philology still predominates over archaeology, art history, papyrology, and other ancillary studies. In this schema, certain questions *tend not to be asked,* for example, questions about social class, gender, ethnicity, the relationship between author and audience, or outside influences on the author, to say nothing of the value and meaning of this material to the reader in the year 2000. To be sure, students or faculty who are reading theory elsewhere can and do raise such issues, but the current organization does not encourage such inquiry.

Nonetheless, there is more to classics than high philology and the study of language. A drop in enrollments in the language courses has undermined the centrality of the study of Latin and Greek in the academy. For those trained as philologists, this trend raises a fundamental problem; what will new Ph.D.s do? One solution has been the development of courses in classical civilization, which typically attract a large number of students, necessary to compensate for the often tiny enrollments in Greek and Latin language courses. Only at the largest and most prestigious graduate schools will classicists teach what they were trained in; but in classics as in other disciplines, women and feminist scholars tend to be in the two-year or four-year colleges, not at the high-status research universities.[6]

The culture courses share some of the elitist politics implicit in the philological model. The language courses no longer serve the dominant order in quite the way they used to, but Bennett, Bloom, D'Souza, et al. (as we can see in the Stanford curriculum debate) would restore the great books curriculum to the position it once held, and translated Greek and Latin classical texts are a major part of that curriculum. Those holding the conservative position on the curriculum argue that Greek literature is "universal," or that it is in some sense the "foundation" of Western culture. When a scholar asserts (Lefkowitz 1986: 9) that what is most enduring is not Greek democracy but Greek mythology, the underlying assumption is that ancient Greece is worth studying for one of those two contributions to Western culture; the only question is whether antiquity is more important as the source of politics or literature.

The discipline of classics has done and continues to do this form of cultural work; perhaps in consequence of its status, its response to feminism and women's studies has been hostile. For instance, Mary Lefkowitz (1983: 19), who had early on identified herself as a feminist, lambastes "feminist theory" along with feminism's political agenda, for supposedly demanding that "women with qualifications inferior to their male competitors should be hired, and their manuscripts published, just because they were women." And in what claimed to be a balanced review essay, Thomas Fleming (1986: 74; but see Skinner 1987c for a response) praised those who, like Lefkowitz, "have written on women and sex roles in the ancient world" only after having "established their credentials by writing on other subjects." What is tolerable to Fleming is a "mainstream scholar who works from time to time on ancient women."

To a certain extent, recent curricular debates have pitted the allied movements for women's studies and multiculturalism against a traditional curriculum. Allan Bloom (1987: 65) named feminism as one face of the enemy. Indeed, if classics is at the heart of that traditional curriculum, there would seem to be no possible space for feminist classicists. Marilyn Skinner (1989a: 199–201) spoke for many of us when she named the feminist's fear that "she will ultimately be confronted with an excruciating choice between her egalitarian ideals and her disciplinary obligations" (Passman, Brown, Hallett, this volume). As women in classics we must ask ourselves what we are being loyal to; after all, in *Three Guineas* Virginia Woolf calls on feminists to constitute themselves a band of "outsiders," and Adrienne Rich calls on us to be "disloyal to civilization."

How can we wear both hats? One way is to make the classicist hat fit more comfortably. The feminists and theorists scattered through the field need to begin a more consistent reclamation project, replacing the politics of classics with a feminist politics.[7] To return to my (overly) simple definition of classics as a discipline, we can start by acknowledging that classics is *interdisciplinary;* it is not the study of language and literature, but the study of cultures, therefore requiring training and reading in anthropology, archaeology, and art history, to name a few (Richlin 1989; cf. McManus 1990). We can challenge the definition of the field chronologically (Hallett this volume). Looking farther back in time, into prehistory and beyond the Rome traditionally studied to the period under Christianity, might change the picture radically; we would then at least acknowledge the arbitrariness of the "period."

And we can challenge the definition of the field geographically. The adoption of a multicultural lens acknowledges that the ancient world was not just made up of Greece and Rome. We can ask about the Egyptian and Near Eastern influences on Greece, instead of taking Greece as the starting point for "civilization" (Haley this volume). We can consider the Roman empire as a colonialist force, and look at the interrelationships between Romans and "barbarians," in northern and central Europe as well as in the Greek east and in North Africa. We should question the racial makeup of those regions, instead of assuming they were like some unproblematized "us." By challenging the traditional definitions of the field, certain questions will immediately become relevant, and it will no longer be possible to say, "But there weren't any women or people of color."

By remaining self-conscious about the history of the discipline and the ideology it implies, it is possible to resist each aspect of the political work that classics performs. First, feminist theory obviously challenges the discipline's claim of philological objectivity. As reader-oriented critics have noted, the text is a meeting place of author and reader, or author/editor and reader; this is particularly true in the case of ancient texts that have suffered literal "deconstruction" at the hands of time before coming into the hands of the critics. In order to restore the text, the editor must have some idea of what an author might have meant, an idea in turn grounded in the editor's assumptions as to what makes sense, assumptions that are in turn grounded in cultural norms.

Second, we can intervene in the classroom. Even if students come to the classics department to escape issues of gender, sexuality, and race, we can refuse to let them be complacent, teaching them in what way these issues are relevant to antiquity, language and culture. Linguistics is after all made up both of semantics and pragmatics, so we can take up seriously what Wittig (1986) calls the mark of gender in language, or analyze the power struggles that cause languages to change, or that determine who will speak which languages. By asking how Latin gained acceptance, questioning the relationship between language and empire, describing Latin and Greek as having changed over time, and as only two languages among a host of others, language courses can help destabilize the static image of "dead" languages.

Third, today's dominant order does not own the ancient culture courses. Such courses can in effect serve a democratic function by making knowledge of this highly esteemed period more generally available, helping to bridge the gap between those traditionally given a liberal education and those destined for some form of vocational training (Haley this volume). One way to counteract the charge of elitism is to take the classics away from the elite and contribute to the cultural literacy of the larger population (Hirsch 1987, Hallett 1985, Skinner 1989a).

As Amy Richlin points out in "The Ethnographer's Dilemma," there are various reasons for returning to the past; even if we agree that we are searching for origins, one must still ask "origins of what?" That is, some will continue to look to antiquity for the origins of the glory of Western civilization, while others will look to antiquity as a formative moment of misogyny. In response to the claim that Greece is the foundation or origin of Western culture, feminists will ask precisely what it founded. Classics has been political by defining the epic and tragic genres as presenting great *human* truths. We continue to ask whose experience is validated by these generalizations, and whose is excluded in order to make antiquity that neat whole it appears to be. What would happen if we took the slaves in the plays of Euripides as the center? What about the workings of class privilege in Homer? What about the women in the audience of tragedy?

What about the women listening to Ovid's tales of rape? What about the lives of lesbians outside of Lesbos? What can we know about the lives of those who wrote no literature—peasants and slaves?

These critiques have been raised before (Culham and Edmunds 1989), but classics changes slowly, and we have not yet succeeded in transforming it. The second way of wearing two hats, then, is by continuing to tend our own acreage within that larger field and transforming ourselves. Feminists in classics have so far succeeded in developing the study of women per se, an area overlooked when the masculinity of classics passed as universal. For the last twenty years, roughly since the founding of the Women's Classical Caucus, there has been consistent attention to women in antiquity, and there is by now a substantial body of work in that subfield. This research has in many ways followed the path of the development of women's studies, and the problems facing feminist classicists are to some extent merely an extreme version of those facing other feminist scholars.

They are extreme, however, and the discipline of classics has clearly disciplined the study of women in antiquity; the very title of the subfield seems to accept the predominantly empiricist assumptions of classics in general, suggesting that what is at stake is merely the study of some pre-existent singular entity "women."[8] The study of women in antiquity has on the whole been hampered by the tendency of classics to avoid theory from the other disciplines except for some forms of structuralism. Then, too, as classicists we begin our study first in the language classroom, where questions of grammar prevail (Hallett 1983: 12–15); mastery is definitely a desired object. The consequences, indoctrination in docility and emphasis on philological accuracy, are in conflict with feminist goals of sweeping social change (Passman this volume). Furthermore, instruction through the literary authors leads to continued focus on texts and the literary even in the research in women's studies. Finally, publication in traditional classics journals requires that we follow the discipline's rules of research, including an exhaustive and exhausting review of everything that has been thought or said about one's subject, which means going back to the (male) Germans of the nineteenth century before moving ahead.[9] The patriarchy is very much in evidence as we diligently cite our forefathers.

Our studies have been conditioned not simply by the discipline, however, but by the field. The exigencies of passing time (we simply don't have the documents available to modernists) and a thoroughgoing suppression of women's subjectivity in antiquity itself (Skinner 1986: 1–3) have combined to impose stringent limits on our study. Considering the conservatism of the discipline, the apparent silence of ancient women, and the dearth of information about them, feminists in classics have accomplished an enormous amount. The strong and exciting early collections—*Women in the Ancient World: The Arethusa Papers* (Peradotto and Sullivan 1978), *Reflections of Women in Antiquity* (Foley 1981), and *Images of Women in Antiquity* (Cameron and Kuhrt 1983)—give a sense of the possibilities, combining essays on the nonliterary sources with discussion of male authors, as well as a sprinkling of pieces on Sappho.

Scholars working on both Greek and Roman women have been very concerned with the problem of evidence, as is clear in several special issues of the journal *Helios* that appeared in the late 1980s. If we separate history and literature, or referential women and representational women, we find that we have many male representations of women but not much "hard" data about women, let alone material written by women. Our questions have much in common with those of other feminist scholars working outside the modern period. How can we get at women's subjective experience? Can we separate it out from the male literary record? What can we assume about women writers? Whose language and conventions do they use when they do manage to speak?

There have been various responses to the situation sketched out above. One strategy has been the attempt to find the "actual women" by turning attention away from the "male icons," the great authors. Problematizing the concept of classics as a literary study, this position puts material remains and nonliterary texts in the place of the sacred authors, asking what information they yield about women's lived existence (Culham 1986, 1990; Richlin this volume). Phyllis Culham poses the two ways of proceeding as antagonists, asking why feminists would want to continue to reflect on these male writers:

> If the study of women in antiquity is to contribute substantively to feminist scholarship or women's studies, it will be in the investigation of the origins and propagation of Western culture, and that would require "directing discussion toward history, society, culture," not the single text or author at all. That is undeniably an intimidating task, and I am embarrassed, as a feminist scholar of antiquity, that it has mainly been left to Gerda Lerner, an Americanist. If we are to reappropriate our own field, we will have to begin by refusing to perpetuate the assignment of privilege to male-authored, canonical texts (Culham 1990: 165, citing W. E. Can, *The Crisis in Critical Theory: Literature and Reform in English Studies* [Baltimore: Johns Hopkins University Press, 1984], p. 263).

Classicists have, then, participated in the project of making women visible, finding the women missing from the history books; we have asked whether women were citizens (Patterson 1986) or whether they could read or write (Cole 1981). Publication and analysis of relevant information, from inscriptions to gynecological writings, have been crucial in this endeavor.

While searching out the historical women via inscriptions and other such sources, we have also been at work recovering and listening to the voices of the women writers of antiquity who did exist, despite the masculinity of the received tradition. This form of classical gynocritics (Showalter 1985) has been associated with a quest for a women's community. Marilyn Arthur (Katz) early hypothesized a women's world on the basis of her reading of Erinna (Arthur 1980); Marilyn Skinner makes a similar claim on the basis of her work on Sappho and other Greek women poets (Skinner 1991, 1989b, 1987a). As we see in Jane Snyder's book, *The Woman and the Lyre* (1989), part of the problem has been the tendency to emphasize Athens at the expense of other locations, the fifth century at the expense of other eras—for there were times and places more hospitable to women writers.

If the silence is not total, however, the voices are nonetheless muted and fragmentary. To the extent that women's artifacts were not pots but weaving, they were also more perishable (Barber 1991); when women are represented on vases and in sculpture or relief, we see them through male eyes. For the most part, then, classics does come back to cultures dominated by men (French 1990, McManus 1990). As a result, feminism in classics has devoted much attention to decoding the images of women in works by men, a study with its own serious problems (cf. the situation in early modern literature, Fisher and Halley 1989). Particularly with respect to fifth-century Athens, there has been a vigorous debate about how to interpret the different representations of women in poetry and prose documents (Gutzwiller and Michelini 1991: 71; Lefkowitz 1986: 10; Culham 1990: 165, 1986; Skinner 1986: 2; Pomeroy 1975: 58–60). Drama seems to give prominence to female characters, while actual historical women (as represented in the extant speeches of male orators speaking in the Athenian courtroom) seem to have been strictly relegated to the private realm. The critics' points of view may determine what they see: those emphasizing the strong women of drama would fall into Amy Richlin's optimist category, while those emphasizing the sequestered women of rhetoric fall into the pessimist camp (Versnel 1987).

Given this silence, it is not surprising that in classics we have also followed the general shift from women's studies or feminist critiques of patriarchy to gender studies (Scott 1988, Showalter 1989, Modleski 1991). Gender theory suggests that "information about women is necessarily information about men" (Scott 1988: 32). In its most energetic form such a study focuses attention on the way the categories of gender have been formed and in turn form us (de Lauretis 1987), and would as a result force disciplines to make fundamental adjustments. In classics the move to gender has been facilitated by the success of a modified structuralism (Rose this volume, Katz 1990), a consanguinity that suggests the risks of both. For structuralism (Culham 1986; Gutzwiller and Michelini 1991; Rose this volume) implies a form of functionalism; that is, structural analyses of a culture tend to describe its functioning, trying to account for *all* details without making any judgments.

Both gender studies and structuralism therefore satisfy classics' longing for apparently value-neutral scholarship. Elaine Showalter notes the danger of depoliticization even as she observes the shift to gender theory (Showalter 1991: 184–

85); Scott (1988: 31) says gender may have replaced women because it appears "to denote the scholarly seriousness of a work, for 'gender' has a more neutral and objective sound than does 'women.' " And indeed Pomeroy's (1991: xv) claim ("the objective stance of most of the authors included in this collection is characteristic of scholars of women in antiquity in the late 1980s") seems to do exactly that.

Structuralism similarly appeals to the classical scholar's desire for objectivity. In simply recounting how the culture works without attention to the implicit power imbalance or the significance of the particular ways in which it works, such analysis may accept more than would be consistent with a feminist program. The turn to the study of sexuality in classics (Konstan and Nussbaum 1990; Halperin, Winkler, and Zeitlin 1990; critiqued by Richlin 1991, and in this volume), if made without attention to gender, feminist theory, and asymmetries of power, can be similarly problematic.

Perhaps more troubling is the fact that studying gender may be more acceptable than studying women because it is safer; by never studying women without men, such studies avoid the specter of lesbianism (de Lauretis 1987: 14–18; 1989: 31–33). At the same time, if such studies isolate gender as a factor from class and race dynamics, they may revert to a stage in feminist theory already challenged by women of color. The point then is to get beyond the heterosexist, racist, and classist paradigms.

As the study of women in antiquity gains respectability, we must ask *which* women are to be studied and make our grasp more comprehensive. Taking the most radical stance of current feminism, we will not only attend to women, we will look for the differences *among* women of different classes, races, ethnicities, and sexualities. We turn to theory in order to make that move forward, for by its deployment we are encouraged to ask new questions of our own material, to see relationships to other fields. Recognizing what was at stake in the ancient world, perhaps we can better understand our own.

Developments growing out of feminism's contact with postmodernism and New Historicism can help us to carry out the critique of male authors with greater sophistication. That work still needs to be done; as Nancy Miller (1986: 42) argues, "the *tradition* of 'great books' has not been systematically reread from a feminist perspective." Some of us, like myself, continue to work on Greek tragedy in new ways: by using reader-response criticism, we can think about the fifth-century Athenian audience and ask how it constructed the meaning of tragedy; or we can think about literary texts as inscribing asymmetrical structures of subjectivity for women and men; or we can employ psychoanalytic theory to help us understand the culturally constructed masculine desire that motivates the texts and their use of female figures (for example, Rabinowitz 1993). Theory can help us out of the seeming impasse presented by the evidence: we need neither accept tragedy's heroines as real women and thus as straightforward evidence of the importance of Athenian women, nor abandon the hope of using literature as evidence of anything at all. By taking the text's literariness into account—its generic conventions, audience, and period—we can better understand and evaluate the information it might transmit. Yes, we must remain cautious about the referential relationship between these texts and women's lived reality, but we can, nonetheless, take them as indicators of cultural understandings of gender and sexuality (Belsey 1985: 5; cf. Richlin 1984; French 1990; Gamel 1990; McManus 1990).

We hope this volume can help promote a change in classics from the vantage point of feminist theory. It would be a mistake for feminists to throw up their hands and abandon the field of classics to the philologists and the protectors of the culture; the right-wing devotion to antiquity demands that feminist classicists enter the fray. If texts from Greek and Roman antiquity are being used to form our youth into a new citizenry, let those of us in the opposition keep our hold on those texts in an effort to redefine that cultural formation—contesting the definition and use made of the field.

At the same time, it is important that feminists in classics enter a more reciprocal relationship with others outside the discipline. Precisely because of its canonical status, classical material has remained inspiring to feminist writers such as Christa Wolf (*Cassandra*), or Catherine Clément and Hélène Cixous (*The Newly Born Woman*), or Marianne Hirsch (*The Mother-Daughter Plot*). Readers and thinkers not trained as classicists can use our work to undermine the control that classical myth and its ideology exerts over their own disciplines, themselves, and their students. As Amy Richlin argues in her essay, we deploy the past strategically depending on our predispositions; it is neither totally the same nor totally different from the present. Those looking to antiquity to test out a theory, be it of patriarchy or of the existence of women's culture, will find here a working out of some of the evidence. On the other hand, those who resist what Amy calls the move to grand theory and who are trying to take up concrete historically located women instead of "woman" can look here for a rich body of material as well.

Skinner (1986: 2) mentions the danger of falling into overspecialization, which she calls "pointillism"; we have tried to avoid that danger by seeking essays that apply or critique a substantial body of feminist theory in relation to some broad aspect of antiquity. Each contributor has thought *both* of how classicists might benefit from her or his approach, *and* how scholars outside the field might benefit from considering the material. We are hardly free of the ways in which the discipline has organized knowledge (the volume shares the literary bias of classics), but we have deliberately avoided the traditional (for classics) organization of Greek/Roman or early/late in order to change those boundaries; we have instead foregrounded critical perspective. The essays take off from the most recent developments in feminist thought, working at the intersections of diverse methods and material: Black feminist thought (Haley), French feminist critique (Gold),

American feminist gynocritics (Skinner), psychoanalytic film criticism (Robin), radical Lesbian feminism (Passman), Native American feminism (Zweig), Marxism (Rose). They draw on different disciplines: history (Hallett), anthropology (Richlin), and archaeology (Brown). Moreover, each author sets the discussion of theory in the context of a major area within classics: Egyptian and African origins (Haley), Greek women writers (Skinner), Greek myth (Passman), Greek women's culture (Zweig), Roman canons/periods (Hallett), Roman elegy (Gold), Roman drama (Robin), Greek and Roman canonical literary authors (Rose), ancient material culture (Brown, Richlin).

The volume begins with two essays that reconceptualize the discipline itself. Shelley Haley's essay, "Black Feminist Thought and Classics: Re-membering, Re-claiming, Re-empowering," uses her placement as a black feminist to push out the geographical borders of antiquity, showing the racism and sexism implicit in the way the field has delimited itself. On the basis of her experience, she challenges others to recognize the blinders we also wear without recognizing them. Were the Egyptians Black? Given the prominence of Egypt in the Greek imaginary, why are the Egyptians not included in courses on antiquity? Why are they not included in courses on women in antiquity? How do we assess what we find if we decide to look at Egypt? As Haley makes clear, teaching is not only a way of doing politics, but also a way of doing theory.

If Haley explodes the definition of classics as an area study, Judith Hallett, in "Feminist Theory, Historical Periods, Literary Canons and the Study of Greco-Roman Antiquity," explodes time. How do we determine a period and what makes it up? Hallett analyzes the term "classics"; eschewing its use for the field as a whole, she confronts its honorific sense. Consideration of the term "classical" in the light of Joan Kelly's essay on the Renaissance leads Hallett to suggest that we read by juxtaposing material from different periods and genres. She embraces a double approach, asking what reading women writers suggests not only about women's experience but also about traditional periodization. Finally, she addresses the question of how to read the constructions of women by male authors and suggests that we broaden our horizons to include noncanonical authors and texts.

The next two essays, Barbara Gold's " 'But Ariadne Was Never There in the First Place': Finding the Female in Roman Poetry" and Diana Robin's "Film Theory and the Gendered Voice in Seneca," utilize two very different critical perspectives from which to examine the representation of women by male authors. Both these essays look backward for ancient examples of modern tropes or theories; in doing so, they demonstrate that these are in some ways very old tricks, indeed.

Gold accepts as a given the overwhelming masculinity of the body of material left us by antiquity (challenged in the next section of the book); she finds the perspective provided by the modernist notion of "gynesis," the putting into play of the feminine, fruitful for analyzing Propertius and other elegists writing in a time of political disintegration. Drawing parallels between Rome and modernity, Gold sees clearly why classicists need feminist theory; it simultaneously behooves feminists to understand antiquity because of its influence on the present.

Gold takes the task of "salvaging" Propertius for feminism by identifying his subversive potential; Diana Robin takes the opposite tack, seeing instead the repressive potential of Seneca. Using contemporary film theory to analyze the place of the feminine in Seneca, Robin argues with Michel Chion that the female voice is coded not only as the site of anxiety and lack, but also of plenitude. Seneca's troublesome female figures are silenced and watched by male choruses. Robin shows how the textual control of the female speaker replicates contemporary events, especially Nero's killing of his own mother, Agrippina. Like Gold, Robin argues that Seneca has a claim on our attention because of his strong influence on later European drama; she sees his representation of women not as idiosyncratic but as symptomatic, with links to the operation of contemporary film.

These two models of "feminist critique," seeing the subversive and the oppressive elements in male authors, could be and have been applied as well to Greek writers (on Euripides, see for instance Zeitlin 1985, versus Rabinowitz 1986, 1989). Because of the paucity of Roman women authors, however, it is not surprising that the portion of the book which is gynocentric deals primarily with Greek material. The three essays here speak to each other and to the examples of feminist critique in productive ways; they seek evidence of a woman's world.

Marilyn Skinner's essay, "Women and Language in Archaic Greece, or, Why Is Sappho a Woman?" urges us not to ignore the women who have actually spoken and most emphatically not to give up looking to them for evidence about the lives of women. Her essay enters into dialogue with the position adopted by Barbara Gold; she resists the French feminist and particularly Irigarayan mode as anti-feminist and suggests that we not accept the masculinity of antiquity as total. In her work on Sappho and oral culture, Skinner gives us a glimpse into the fabric of women's lives. In Skinner's view, things were not always as they are now; attention to language can reveal a woman's subculture.

While Gold and Skinner engage with poststructuralist methodologies and their problematization of the subject, one embracing and the other rejecting the project, Bella Zweig, in her essay "The Primal Mind: Using Native American Models for the Study of Women in Ancient Greece," invokes the work of contemporary women of color and their challenge to the hegemony of first world feminism. Feminist theory grounded in Native American approaches does not take for granted the Western valorization of everything male. Organizing the world around complementarity rather than hierarchy and looking at the background as well as the foreground, Zweig composes a new picture of Greek antiquity, one in which we can find ways to value positively that which our own culture devalues, such as elements of a separate women's culture. Zweig suggests that women were not totally silenced in ancient Greece, and that those currently interested in feminist spirituality may find much material in antiquity that has been excluded by the dominant order's reconstruction of the past.

Tina Passman's essay, "Out of the Closet and into the Field: Matriculture, the Lesbian Perspective, and Feminist Classics," analyzes the radical feminist contemporary quest for origins as it manifests itself in work on matriarchy or matricentric cultures. As Passman points out, the popular feminist discourse on spirituality is in conflict with that of the classics, yet the goddess myth requires classical knowledge for verification. Passman goes back to an early woman classicist, Jane Harrison, to analyze not only the work she did but also what her reception reveals about the institution of classical studies; the example of Jane Harrison has served to prevent many a feminist classicist from making large claims and more generally from writing "like a dyke."

The next three essays address epistemological concerns and the necessity for using material culture. The contribution of Peter Rose, "The Case for Not Ignoring Marx in the Study of Women in Antiquity," most clearly sounds the activist note; seeing feminism as a progressive movement, he looks to it for "allies." Thus, the political situation that grounds Rose's writing relates to the activist roots of feminism while leading to a specific form of theory. Embracing Marxist standpoint theory, Rose is able to critique many of the tendencies in classics, feminist theory, and earlier work on women in antiquity. He explicitly addresses the problem of considering the literary in isolation from social and historical materiality and, using a Marxist hermeneutic, finds evidence to satisfy both the optimist and the pessimist.

Shelby Brown's essay, "Feminist Research in Archaeology: What Does It Mean? Why Is It Taking So Long?" offers a sustained critique of classical archaeology that will resonate with the experience of those of us doing work in the language and literature side of antiquity, as well as with those in other empirically based fields. Brown reveals that the experience of women "*in* the field" is related to the treatment of gender *by* the field. Like others in the collection, Brown too feels intensely the resistance of the discipline and its discourse to feminism. Her analysis of that resistance then forms the basis for understanding the response of archaeology to radical feminism's popular search for the goddess, as articulated by Tina Passman.

Janus-like, Amy Richlin's essay, "The Ethnographer's Dilemma and the Dream of a Lost Golden Age," looks backward over the field and forward to where we need to go; working through the contemporary debates in feminist anthropology and history, she addresses a series of questions that are difficult for classicists and feminists alike. Her essay focuses on the reasons why scholars have looked to other cultures and to the past (the elsewhere and the elsewhen), and on the "dream of a lost golden age" they have found there. Her synthesis of feminist work in anthropology, history, and classics allows her to encompass and illuminate the divisions in the volume and in classics as a whole: Greek/Roman, feminist critique/gynocritics, literature/history, and underlying them all: pessimist/optimist. She argues that feminists can say something meaningful about the present from the past, that intellectual honesty need not paralyze us, and that we can indeed still create responsible "grand theory."

Feminist theory—Native American, African American, lesbian, psychoanalytic, French feminist, gynocentric, historical, anthropological, archaeological, literary—can open up the traditionally hermetic discipline of classics to the outside world. Once it is so transformed, it will be apparent to scholars in other disciplines that there is more to the discipline than the collections of "great myths" and clichés about the traditional values of "Western culture" currently portrayed in the popular press. In the end, then, theory can turn classics from a rarefied study for the leisure class (by means of which others are kept at bay) to a vital arena for multicultural dialogue in the next century.

Notes

This introduction has been difficult to write in part because of the problems I allude to in it; it would not have been possible without the support of Amy Richlin, my co-editor, who has been like an alter ego and co-author. I have benefited by working in a community of scholars and in particular from the generous and acute comments of Linda Nicholson, Patricia Francis Cholakian, Peter J. Rabinowitz, Shelley Haley, and Barbara Gold, all of whom read and commented on early drafts. The essays of the contributors, especially those of Shelley Haley and Tina Passman, have given me the courage to speak at least occasionally in my own voice.

1. The debate in feminist theory over just what we can say in the name of woman or about women has contributed to this sense that feminism (which seemingly must make claims about women) is outmoded (Modleski 1991); for references and attempted solutions, see the contributions of Gold, Skinner, Rose, and Richlin in this volume.

2. The clash in discourses is reminiscent of that between Nietzsche and Wilamowitz that Steve Nimis has analyzed (1984: 110). The scholarly tone is essential in classical philology.

3. See, for instance, *Rescuing Creusa: New Methodological Approaches to Women in Antiquity, Helios* 13.2 (1986), edited by Marilyn Skinner; in 1989 *Helios* published two volumes on Roman women, edited by Eva Stehle and Adele Scafuro (*Helios* 16.1, 2 [1989]), and in 1990 an issue on decentering the text (*Helios* 17.2 [1990]). The latter is organized as a set of responses to Phyllis Culham's position in favor of abandoning the "tribal totems" (Culham 1990: 161); the resulting essays therefore make up a very interesting set of ruminations on the topics that concern us here.

4. Warhol and Herndl 1991: x; for similar working out of the political meanings of feminism, see Addelson and Potter (1991: 259) and Hartman and Messer-Davidow (1991: 1). The connection between activism and theory is not always easy to maintain, however.

5. This problematic can be clearly seen in the brouhaha over the 1991 APA elections; for a convenient collection of the documents, see *Women's Classical Caucus Newsletter* 17 (Spring 1992).

6. On the two-tiered structure of departments, see Culham and Edmunds 1989: xiii–xv. As a further consequence of the structure, women now make up more than 50 percent of the graduate students but are most often not working with women faculty, and they certainly do not take on feminist topics for their dissertations (see the *Women's Classical Caucus Newsletter* 15 [Fall 1990] for an analysis of dissertations completed and in progress 1989–90). Classics graduate students are clearly not trained in feminist theory.

7. I don't share Marilyn Skinner's optimism (1989a); having sketched in the problem, she indicates that she sees change already happening. I think it has yet to take place.

8. As Marilyn Skinner has observed, that study is now somewhat respectable and even enjoys a status as a subfield (Skinner 1987b; but cf. Hallett 1985: 29, on marginality), so long as it does not challenge the field as a whole.

9. See Nimis 1984 on this point; he cites the "Wilamowitz footnote" as "an inevitable concomitant of a discipline which continues to reproduce, without self-reflection and without any clearly defined goals, its own discourse" (Nimis 1984: 117).

Bibliography

Addelson, Kathryn Pyne, and Elizabeth Potter. "Making Knowledge." In Hartman and Messer-Davidow 1991, 259–77.

Alexander, Caroline. 1991. "Personal History: An Ideal State." *The New Yorker* December 16: 53–88.

Arthur, Marylin (Katz). 1980. "The Tortoise and the Mirror: Erinna PSI 1090." *Classical World* 74: 53–65.

Barber, E. J. W. 1991. *Prehistoric Textiles: The Development of Cloth in the Neolithic and Bronze Ages*. Princeton: Princeton University Press.

Belsey, Catherine. 1985. *The Subject of Tragedy*. London and New York: Methuen.

Bernal, Martin. 1987. *Black Athena*. New Brunswick, N.J.: Rutgers University Press.

Blok, Josine, and Peter Mason, eds. 1987. *Sexual Asymmetry: Studies in Ancient Society*. Amsterdam: J. C. Gieben.

Bloom, Allan. 1987. *The Closing of the American Mind*. New York: Simon and Schuster.

Cameron, Averil, and Amélie Kuhrt, eds. 1983. *Images of Women in Antiquity*. London: Croom Helm.

Christian, Barbara. 1988. "The Race for Theory." *Feminist Studies* 14: 67–79.

Cole, Susan. 1981. "Could Greek Women Read and Write?" In Foley 1981, 219–46.

Culham, Phyllis. 1986. "Ten Years after Pomeroy." *Helios* 13.2: 9–30.

———. 1990. "Decentering the Text: The Case of Ovid." *Helios* 17.2: 161–70.

Culham, Phyllis, and Lowell Edmunds, eds. 1989. *Classics: a Discipline and Profession in Crisis?* Lanham, Md.: University Press of America.

de Lauretis, Teresa. 1987. *Technologies of Gender: Essays on Theory, Film, and Fiction*. Bloomington: Indiana University Press.

————. 1989. "The Essence of the Triangle or, Taking the Risk of Essentialism Seriously: Feminist Theory in Italy, the U.S., and Britain." *differences* 1: 3–37.

Evans, Sara. 1980. *Personal Politics: The Roots of Women's Liberation in the Civil Rights Movement and the New Left*. New York: Random House.

Fisher, Sheila, and Janet E. Halley, eds. 1989. *Seeking the Woman in Late Medieval and Renaissance Writings: Essays in Feminist Contextual Criticism*. Knoxville: University of Tennessee Press.

Fleming, Thomas. 1986. "Des dames du temps jadis." *Classical Journal 82:* 73–80.

Foley, Helene P., ed. 1981. *Reflections of Women in Antiquity*. New York: Gordon and Breach Science Publishers.

French, Valerie. 1990. "What Is Central for the Study of Women in Antiquity?" *Helios* 17.2: 213–29.

Gamel, Mary-Kay. 1990. "Reading 'Reality.' " *Helios* 17.2: 171–74.

Gutzwiller, Kathryn J., and Ann Norris Michelini. 1991. "Women and Other Strangers: Feminist Perspectives in Classical Literature." In Hartman and Messer-Davidow 1991, 66–84.

Haley, Shelley. 1989. "Classics and Minorities." In Culham and Edmunds 1989, 333–38.

Hallett, Judith P. 1983. "Classics and Women's Studies." Working Paper 119. Wellesley College Center for Research on Women.

————. 1985. "Response II: Buzzing of a Confirmed Gadfly: *ho de anexetastos bios ou biōtos anthropōi*." *Helios* 12.2: 23–37.

Halperin, David M., John J. Winkler, and Froma I. Zeitlin, eds. 1990. *Before Sexuality*. Princeton: Princeton University Press.

Hartman, Joan, and Ellen Messer-Davidow, eds. 1991. *(En)Gendering Knowledge: Feminists in Academe*. Knoxville: The University of Tennessee Press.

Hirsch, E. D. 1987. *Cultural Literacy*. New York: Random House.

Katz, Marylin A. 1990. "From Patriarchy to Subjectivity: Women in Tragic Drama." Paper presented at the APA Convention, Panel on "Feminist Theory and the Classics."

Konstan, David, and Martha Nussbaum, eds. 1990. *differences* 2.1. "Sexuality in Greek and Roman Society."

Lefkowitz, Mary. 1983. "Feminism in the American University." *The Salisbury Review* Fall 1983: 18–20.

————. 1986. *Women in Greek Myth*. Baltimore: Johns Hopkins University Press.

McManus, Barbara F. 1990. "Multicentering: The Case of the Athenian Bride." *Helios* 17.2: 225–35.

Miller, Nancy K. 1986. "Parables and Politics: Feminist Criticism in 1986." *Paragraph* 8: 40–54.

Modleski, Tania. 1991. *Feminism without Women: Culture and Criticism in a "Postfeminist" Age*. New York: Routledge.

Nimis, Steve. 1984. "Fussnoten: Das Fundament der Wissenschaft." *Arethusa* 17.2: 105–34.

Patterson, Cynthia. 1986. *"Hai Attikai*: The Other Athenians." *Helios* 13.2: 49–67.

Peradotto, John J., and J. P. Sullivan, eds. 1978. *Women in the Ancient World. Arethusa* 11. 1, 2.

Pomeroy, Sarah B. 1975. *Goddesses, Whores, Wives, and Slaves: Women in Classical Antiquity*. New York: Schocken.

———, ed. 1991. *Women's History and Ancient History*. Chapel Hill: University of North Carolina Press.

Rabinowitz, Nancy Sorkin. 1986. "Female Speech and Sexuality: Euripides' *Hippolytos* as Model." *Helios* 13.2: 127–40.

———. 1989. "Renegotiating the Oedipus: Theseus and Hippolytos." In Beth Kowaleski-Wallace and Patricia Yaeger, eds., *Refiguring the Father: New Feminist Readings of Patriarchy*, 58–77. Carbondale: Southern Illinois University Press.

———. 1993. *Anxiety Veiled: Euripides and the Traffic in Women*. Ithaca: Cornell University Press.

Richlin, Amy. 1984. "Invective against Women in Roman Satire." *Arethusa* 17.1: 67–80.

———. 1989. " 'Is Classics Dead?' The 1988 WCC Report." In Culham and Edmunds 1989, 51–65.

———. 1991. "Zeus and Metis: Foucault, Feminism, Classics." *Helios* 18.2: 160–80.

Scott, Joan. 1988. *Gender and the Politics of History*. New York: Columbia University Press.

Showalter, Elaine. 1985. "Toward a Feminist Poetics." Reprinted in Elaine Showalter, ed., *The New Feminist Criticism: Essays on Women, Literature and Theory*, 125–43. New York: Pantheon.

———. 1989. *Speaking of Gender*. New York: Routledge.

———. 1991. "A Criticism of Our Own: Autonomy and Assimilation in Afro-American and Feminist Literary Theory." In Warhol and Herndl 1991, 169–88.

Skinner, Marilyn B., ed. 1986. "Rescuing Creusa: New Methodological Approaches to Women in Antiquity." *Helios* 13.2: 1–8.

———. 1987a. "Greek Women and the Metronymic: A Note on an Epigram by Nossis." *Ancient History Bulletin* 1: 39–42.

———. 1987b. "Classical Studies, Patriarchy and Feminism: The View from 1986." *Women's Studies International Forum* 10: 181–86.

———. 1987c. "Des Bonnes dames et méchantes." In response to Thomas Fleming, "Des dames du temps jadis." *Classical Journal* 83: 69–74.

———. 1989a. "Expecting the Barbarians: Feminism, Nostalgia, and the 'Epistemic Shift' in Classical Studies." In Culham and Edmunds 1989, 199–210.

———. 1989b. "Sapphic Nossis." *Arethusa* 22: 5–18.

————. 1991. "Nossis *Thêlyglôssos:* The Private Text and the Public Book." In Pomeroy 1991, 20–47. Chapel Hill: University of North Carolina Press.

Snyder, Jane. 1989. *The Woman and the Lyre: Women Writers in Classical Greece and Rome.* Carbondale: Southern Illinois University Press.

Versnel, H. S. 1987. "Wife and Helpmate: Women of Ancient Athens in Anthropological Perspective." In Blok and Mason 1987, 59–85.

Warhol, Robyn R., and Diane Price Herndl, eds. 1991. *Feminisms: An Anthology of Literary Theory and Criticism.* Rutgers: Rutgers University Press.

Wittig, Monique. 1986. "The Mark of Gender." In Nancy K. Miller, ed., *The Poetics of Gender,* 68–73. New York: Columbia University Press.

Zeitlin, Froma. 1985. "Playing the Other: Theater, Theatricality, and the Feminine in Greek Drama." *Representations* 11: 63–94.

Redefining the Field

2

Black Feminist Thought and Classics: Re-membering, Re-claiming, Re-empowering

Shelley P. Haley

I. Re-membering

The questions that first occurred to me when I began to think about this volume on feminist theory and classics were whether there is a role for classics in Black feminist thought and whether there is a role for Black feminist thought in classics. Obviously, I believe the answer to each question is yes, since I am a Black feminist and a classicist. A classicist and feminist, Marilyn Skinner (1987), suggests that the "cultural solidarity" among classicists is comparable to the "race solidarity" among Black feminists. Can Black feminism contribute more to classics than the lessons of solidarity? My Black feminist consciousness answers a resounding yes. There are lessons of re-claiming and re-membering, of giving a voice to ancestors whose life experience has been suppressed and distorted.

But I also have the consciousness of a classicist. As a classicist, I realize that I must validate the existence of ancient African women in accordance with the rigid criteria of documentary evidence upon which my discipline insists. I have seen the contempt classicists have for the work of Van Sertima (1984), James (1954), and Diop (1974), and I do not want to suffer that disrespect. Furthermore, I am, at times painfully, aware that classics is emblematic of White privilege, and the contempt for these Black scholars is part and parcel of that. The discipline (the very word conveys rigidity) of classics still follows the model designed for eighteenth- and nineteenth-century White American gentlemen of independent means. The role of classics in the history of European and American education and the prestige attached to it have led to its self-concept as an elite family of true scholars. Skinner (1987) describes this construction and its ramifications for White feminists. She explores the notion that classics is a family and her vision of family is that of a European, patriarchal and nuclear one. While Skinner's view is justified, she never takes into account the standpoint of those of us who consider this type of family dysfunctional. No thought is given to those of us who have experienced woman-centered family structures. The idea that we are one big happy family renders the issue of race virtually invisible. Consequently, like many southern American families—indeed, like the biracial couple which keeps their marriage and children a secret (*New York Times,* December 2, 1991, p. 1)—the classics family has kept its Brown, Black, and biracial ancestors, sisters, and brothers marginalized and invisible.

My experience as a member of a woman-centered family, and as a Black feminist and a classicist, has resulted in what has been expressed best by Patricia Williams (1991). She relates (Williams 1991: 6) how one employer described her being Black and female as at "oxymoronic odds" with the status of a commercial lawyer. She isn't happy with this particular characterization, but she admits that "my attempts to write in my own voice have placed me in the center of a snarl of social tensions and crossed boundaries" (Williams 1991: 6). Think of the possibilities in my case: feminist classicist and woman classicist, Black classicist and Black woman classicist, and Black feminist and Black feminist classicist. If oxymoronic odds came in degrees, I would be somewhere near the high end. How did I come to this location as a Black feminist classicist?

Questions of gender and sexism had never been an issue for me, even within my family. My family has followed our Iroquois and West African heritage: the woman sets policy and shares in decisions. My father, Charles ("Pete") Tracy Haley, turned his pay over to my mother, and after she died, to his mother. This isn't to say my father didn't assimilate certain patriarchal values. He was the first in his family to attend college; he did so during the depression, and racism drove him to alcoholism. He graduated from Syracuse University in 1937, "thank the laudy," as he used to say. He wanted one of his sons to follow him to Syracuse. When I was admitted (neither of my brothers applied), he was proud but refused to pay my expenses. "Women don't need a college education," he said. My reaction was "I'll show him," and I proceeded to get a Ph.D. in classics. I never did disabuse him of the notion that I didn't *need* the education. In many ways, my father's standpoint was framed by what he had experienced. The women in our family had always had jobs: my grandmother was a cook, my mother was a secretary. My aunts (my father's sisters) had office and sales positions. None of these women had had a college education. So, to my father's way of thinking, they didn't need one. However, it was my grandmother who encouraged me to go as far as I could in education. She had always wanted to be a teacher, but had to leave school at the age of twelve to support her family. I don't think my father ever knew how deeply my grandmother had wanted to go to a teacher's training college.

Like my fellow classicists, I was trained in the Anglo-Germanic tradition of the discipline. I took Latin in high school in upstate New York, continued it at Syracuse, never intending it as a major but always finding it a source of strength and wonder: I was good at it. Nowadays when people ask me how I became interested in classics, I always say truthfully that it was the only subject in high school where I did not have to argue with the teacher. I had a social studies teacher who informed our class that Africa and Asia contributed nothing to human civilization. I had an American History teacher who proclaimed to the class that Puerto Rico would never become a state because it wasn't Anglo-Saxon in background. When I challenged him with the example of Hawaii, I was sent to the principal's office for "impertinence." I spent much time in the principal's office, but never for impertinence in Latin class. It seemed so straightforward; there was nothing to argue about. In college, elementary education was my intended goal, but boredom set in, and I was drawn back to Latin and, more and more, to Roman history. I took Greek and French; I applied to graduate schools; and I won a Danforth Fellowship. As an undergraduate taking classics, I wanted to belong, to be part of that select group who studied Latin and Greek. As I look back on it now, I suppose I liked the feeling of being special and exotic. I enjoyed thumbing my nose at my peers who suggested I would do more for my people if I enrolled in journalism or broadcasting. Those were vocational courses; I was an intellectual.

It has only been in the last few years that I have rediscovered the Black feminists of the nineteenth century who could have served as my role models. Frances Jackson Coppin was a slave whose aunt saved the money ($123.00) to buy her freedom. She went on to obtain a B.A. from Oberlin College in 1865 and taught Latin and Greek to African-Americans in Philadelphia. Anna Julia Cooper and Mary Church Terrell were members of the Oberlin class of 1884 and they too received B.A.s. The curriculum for this degree was classical and usually taken by men only; for that reason it was called the "gentlemen's course." Women took the "ladies'" course, a two-year literary curriculum, which led to a certificate. Both Cooper and Terrell went on to teach Latin at the M Street school in Washington, D.C. Terrell highlights the racist assumptions of inferiority prevalent during her life in her autobiography, *A Colored Woman in a White World* (1940). She relates this incident:

> One day Matthew Arnold, the English writer, visited our class and Professor Frost asked me both to read the Greek and then to translate. After leaving the class Mr. Arnold referred to the young lady who read the passage of Greek so well. Thinking it would interest the Englishman, Professor Frost told him I was of African descent. Thereupon Mr. Arnold expressed the greatest surprise imaginable, because, he said, he thought the tongue of the African was so thick he could not be taught to pronounce the Greek correctly (Terrell 1940: 41).[1]

Coppin, Cooper, and Terrell viewed classics as a challenge, a concrete way to disprove the prevailing racist and sexist stereotypes of their times. They were educators, intellectuals, and social activists. Each believed that education was the key to overthrowing the disadvantages that Black women and men faced and still face. Since a classical education was the yardstick for intellectual capability, Coppin, Cooper, and Terrell learned classics, that microcosm of their society where Black women were silenced and thought incapable of intellectual endeavor. That learning, in turn, had a symbolic value for them. Audre Lorde (1984: 112) has written that "the master's tools will never dismantle the master's house."[2] While that may be true, Coppin, Cooper, and Terrell chipped away at the racist and sexist foundation of the master's house. Classics, the measure of intellectual supremacy, was transformed by them into a tool of resistance.

But I, their daughter on a metaphorical level, must face the fact that they did not consider themselves classicists. They studied Latin and Greek and excelled; in this regard they are my foremothers and role models. But the social constraints of their time pushed them out of the academy and strengthened their commitment to social activism.[3] At the same time, their very education made this commitment vulnerable. As Mary Helen Washington has stated (Washington 1988: xxx), "To counteract the prevailing assumptions about black women as immoral and ignorant, Cooper had to construct a narrator who was aware of the plight of uneducated women but was clearly set apart from them in refinement, intelligence and training." The same can be said of Terrell; classics was a key to the construction of this distance. These women's experience has encouraged me to examine the sociology and history of the discipline. Sociologically, my experience with classics mirrors theirs.

It was at the University of Michigan that the structure and implications of patriarchal education struck me. The hierarchy and competition that characterized the program resulted in dehumanizing groveling. The hierarchy was marked by a progression of nomenclature. Entering graduate students were called by their last names; second and third year students who had passed exams were called Miss or Mr. Those admitted to candidacy were called by their first names. Male faculty were always addressed as Mr. ____, after the Harvard model. There was one woman on the faculty when I was there and she was "Mrs." I noticed, though, that while male faculty in conversation with students would refer to their colleagues as "Mr. ____," their female colleague was "Gerda." Humiliation was used to "separate the men from the boys"; the aim of one professor was to reduce female students to tears. I accepted the hierarchical nomenclature but I drew the line at humiliation. When I stood up to the tears-inducing professor, I acquired the reputation of a "militant" and a "tough cookie."

There was racism. One professor at a social function pointedly told other faculty members within my hearing that Black students were "lousy at Latin" and just not smart enough to take classics. The chair asked me why Blacks were afraid of intellectual disciplines and always went into sociology or education. Another announced during a public lecture that there was no such thing as a "Black classicist." I was told in my second year (I was still Haley) that the dean of the graduate school was under the impression that there were no Black graduate students in the department. I was ordered by the chair of the department to attend a departmental colloquium at which the dean would be present so "he could see a brown face." I didn't go, even though the subject was one I was interested in. I tended to internalize the anger; my attempts at official complaints were always met with, "That's a serious accusation; can you prove it?"

What really annoyed me was that the class hierarchy was internalized and perpetuated by the graduate students themselves. First year students could not socialize with doctoral candidates, or second-years or third-years. Likewise, second-years socialized only with second-years and so on. Students who had passed through qualifying exams (taken at the end of the second year) felt themselves superior to those who failed or had not yet taken them. They resorted to a sort of bullying and intimidation.

A group of students established an informal but exclusive discussion group with a selected faculty member; it was held at the University Club. Student participation was by invitation only and not all students were invited. I, two Jewish men, and an Asian-American man never received an invitation. We referred to this discussion group, always highly publicized, but not public, as the "country club." The group ended when a professor learned that not all students were invited and refused to participate until the group was open to all. Significantly, the main organizers of these discussion groups were two White women, who today consider themselves feminists.

Despite this evidence to the contrary, I continued to believe that classics was the great equalizer. In my mind, these instances of racism were committed by individuals; it wasn't the discipline that was racist. I knew stories from my history about slaves, fugitive slaves, and newly emancipated people who learned Latin and Greek and were very successful. My own mother and aunts and father knew Latin and had encouraged me when I started it in high school. Anyone who could master Latin and Greek was equal and was playing on a level and even field. At Michigan when the professor said, "There is no such thing as a Black classicist," I heard, "we're all classicists." Yes, I thought, aren't I lucky to be in such an egalitarian field.

Yet, throughout my college and graduate school experience, buried deep in the recesses of my mind was the voice of my grandmother, Ethel Clemons Haley, saying, "Remember, no matter what you learn in school, Cleopatra was black." Now where did she get an idea like that?[4] Schooled only as far as the seventh grade, never having learned any foreign language, just a domestic servant, a cook, she obviously had no knowledge about Cleopatra or classics or anything else intellectual. So I, the great teacher, used to tell her about the Ptolemies and how they were Greek and how Cleopatra was a Ptolemy and so she was Greek. At one point I even showed her the genealogical tables of the *Cambridge Ancient History*. "See," I said, "Cleopatra was Greek!" "Oh," she said, "and who wrote those books?" I dismissed her question with exasperation and returned to the study of the ancient sources, confident that what I had been taught to see was indeed what was there to be seen.

I was not very enthusiastic about feminism or feminist theory. I was much like the Black women bell hooks (1981) describes in *Ain't I a Woman?* What is the fuss? All the women in my family had worked, had careers, had families, and balanced everything just fine. They were the center of everything. So the "women's movement" left me bored. About this time in the academy, there was a rising interest in women's history. Classics, rather cautiously, established courses on women in the ancient world; the field found some validation when, in 1975, Sarah Pomeroy published *Goddesses, Whores, Wives and Slaves: Women in Classical Antiquity.* As I completed graduate school, I was drawn to this new specialty but investigated it secretly. I still yearned for the approval of classicists and I believed in loyalty to the discipline's traditional limits. I saw how classicists at Michigan spurned Marxist treatments of ancient history and how African and African-American historians like James and Diop were ignored. In fact I never even heard of George James until I went to teach at Howard University in 1978, although *Stolen Legacy* has been published in 1954. I knew the application of any critical theory to "our" discipline was tantamount to betrayal. I remember making a weak vow at the APA, along with rather more vociferous female colleagues and peers, that I would never teach such a course. Classics was a universally relevant discipline; it was timeless and it didn't need to change. Did it?

It was a weak vow, and in my second year at Howard, I found myself teaching "Women in the Ancient World." As I look back at the syllabus now, it was not particularly feminist; it was a classics survey, Homer, the tragedians, Livy, Vergil, with a few women thrown in. The feminist literature I assigned was not particularly current or radical.[5] I didn't relate to it personally but found places for it in my course. The only women in Africa I dealt with were Dido and Cleopatra, but I didn't regard them as Black, or African.

It was Cleopatra who haunted me. In a "Women in the Ancient World" class, we were studying Cleopatra and Octavian's propaganda against her. Ray, a Black male student, asked me to cover again the arguments identifying Cleopatra as a Greek. I sighed and presented all the evidence. I pulled out the *Cambridge Ancient History* (*CAH*), and we pored over the genealogy. I brought in the research of my colleague Frank Snowden (1970). We reviewed other secondary sources: Volkmann (1958), Grant (1972, 1982), and Lindsay (1971). Ray, very politely but intently, repeated the question my grandmother had posed years before: "But Professor Haley, who wrote those books?" I was going through it all again (growing somewhat irate), when I stared at the *CAH* genealogy and saw—for the first time—question marks where Cleopatra's grandmother should be. As I stared, I heard Ray, again politely, say, "I understand, Professor Haley. You believe what you say is true, but you have bought a lie." The other students in the class were divided; some agreed with Ray, some with me, others were totally indifferent. I was shaken; what did those question marks mean? Why didn't all the students see the evidence as I did? What did they know that I didn't? In buying the lie, had I sold out my race?

At that point, I confronted Cleopatra, and I discovered that my Black students and indeed my grandmother read her on a different level. For them and for me, although I suppressed her, Cleopatra was the lost and found window where we could "claim an identity they taught us to despise" (Cliff 1988: 61). I had disliked discussing Cleopatra; I had been uncomfortable and ill at ease. Why? I began to see and still am arriving at seeing that Cleopatra is the crystallization of the tension between my yearning to fit in among classicists and my identity politics. I clouded this tension by professing that the Ptolemies of the first century B.C.E. were Greco-Egyptian. To me, "Egyptian", "Greco-Egyptian," "Greek," "Roman" had been cultural designations. I refused, rather self-righteously, I admit, to colorize the question as my grandmother had done, along with my students, and, most recently, *Newsweek* ("Was Cleopatra Black": September 23, 1991). What I resisted was the fact that my culture is colorized: Black literature, Black music, Black art, Black feminism. Gradually, by reading my history and Black feminist thought, I perceived that Cleopatra was a signifier on two levels.[6] She gives voice to our "anxiety about cultural disinheritance" (Sadoff 1990: 205), and she represents the contemporary Black woman's double history of oppression and survival.

In the Black oral tradition, Cleopatra becomes a symbolic construction voicing our Black African heritage so long suppressed by racism and the ideology of miscegenation. When we say, in general, that the ancient Egyptians were Black and, more specifically, that Cleopatra was Black, we claim them as part of a culture and history that has known oppression and triumph, exploitation and survival. Cleopatra reacted to the phenomena of oppression and exploitation as a Black woman would. Hence we embrace her as sister; she is Black. Alice Walker (1989: 267) employs a similar symbolic construction with Medusa. Here Medusa's decapitation by Perseus represents the rape and cultural suppression of Africa by Europeans.

My grandmother and students were also reading Cleopatra on the level of their experience with miscegenation and the law of miscegenation (Saks 1988). We had been told that if we have one Black ancestor, then we are Black. Films and plays have reinforced this idea. Our family histories and photographs proved this to us. My grandmother was white, had straight black hair, and the nose of her Onondagan grandmother, but she was "colored." Even as a "Greco-Egyptian," Cleopatra was a product of miscegenation.[7] How is it she is not Black? My grandmother and students were being logical; they were applying to Cleopatra the social decoding typically applied to them.

It seemed to me that the Cleopatra I studied as the "true Cleopatra" was a construction of classical scholars and the Greek and Roman authors they consulted.[8] In this particular case, they were willing—eager—to erase the Black ancestor and claim the beautiful Cleopatra for Europe. Like the biracial family cited earlier, classics has kept Cleopatra's Africanity and Blackness a secret and questionable. Many African-Americans did the same for themselves. My family claimed the West Indies as our point of origin. Shame arising from internalized racism never let us go further back until the rise of the Black pride movement. Sadoff's (1990) analysis and critique of misreading led me to apply this theory to classics and Cleopatra.[9] Classicists and historians have misread Cleopatra as a way of furthering ideas of racial purity and hegemony. Martin Bernal's work (1987) on the demise of ancient Egypt in classical scholarship brought him to the conclusion that we classicists still work within racist paradigms.[10]

I applied the same critique to the ancient evidence; I began to wonder how the Romans and Greeks misread Cleopatra. I did research on foreign women and their image in Roman history and literature. Here Cleopatra was the archetype of the temptress and she was transformed into other characters: Dido in poetry and Sophoniba in historiography.[11] The Romans misread these women as exempla of the temptress who distracted men from their "manliness," *virtus*. As strong queens of African kingdoms, they also constituted a grave threat to the Roman concept of empire. Black feminists, especially King (1988) and Collins (1990), discuss in their work the controlling image of the jezebel/seductress and its impact on the perception and treatment of Black women. Palmer (1983) analyzes the symbolism of Black women in America as sexual enticers who could overthrow reason and social order. She relates this to the virgin/whore dualism in cultural imagery for White women, in existence at least since classical Greece (Palmer 1983: 157).

This same symbol-making process has led to a physical stereotype, which has been applied to ancient African women even by twentieth-century scholars. A good example is Frank Snowden's translation of the physical description of Scybale, an African woman who appears in the *Moretum* (a short Augustan poem of unknown authorship):

> Erat unica custos
> Afra genus, tota patriam testante figura,
> torta comam labroque tumens et fusca colore,
> pectore lata iacens mammis, compressior alvo,
> cruribus exilis, spatiosa prodiga planta
> *(Moretum* 31–35).

African in race, her whole figure proof of her country—her hair tightly curled, lips thick, color dark, chest broad, breasts pendulous, belly somewhat pinched, legs thin, and feet broad and ample (translated by Snowden 1970: 6).

Snowden's translation reminds me too much of the physical stereotype of Black women in the nineteenth century. He does not treat this passage elsewhere in his work, nor does he seem aware that his translation is stereotypical. Can we read the Latin another way? It seems to me that here is a place where classicists can use a Black feminist perspective and Black feminism can rehabilitate the reading of a text. What would a Black feminist translation of this passage look like? Still using a standard Latin lexicon, here's what I came up with:

> She was his only companion,
> African in her race, her whole form a testimony to her country:
> her hair twisted into dreads, her lips full, her color dark, her
> chest broad, her breasts flat, her stomach flat and firm, her legs
> slender, her feet broad and ample.

From this translation, it is clearer that the Roman author was relaying somatic differences, but without the racist stigma attached to Snowden's phrases ("thick lips, pendulous breasts, belly somewhat pinched"). The woman is not portrayed as beautiful in Roman terms, but neither is she the object of a racist gaze. She is exotic, as most non-Roman peoples were to the Romans. Black feminist thought encourages us classicists to acknowledge our own racist and sexist attitudes, not just those of the eighteenth and nineteenth centuries. It prompts us to reevaluate our work. This in turn can lead to opening up a space in which to reclaim and reconstruct the lives of Black women who have been silenced through a dearth of evidential voice. Black feminist thought and ideology, with their focus on inclusivity, can provide the theoretical framework to read the silences that classics has to offer.

II. Re-claiming

In this part of the essay, I'd like to continue my journey by giving examples of how I have attempted to follow through the Black feminist model of inclusivity.[12] Here I was, trained in Anglo-German methodology, a product of the Michigan department, a Black feminist classicist. In 1985, I left Howard to take a "Target of Opportunity" (TOP) position in the classics department at University of California, Irvine, a position I held until 1989. The overwhelming Whiteness and conservatism of that department left me isolated; my colleagues never let me forget that I was a TOP hire. To maintain my self-esteem and my sanity, I read and was deeply moved by bell hooks (1981), Audre Lorde (1984), and Elizabeth Spelman (1982; 1988). I was shaken by Lorde's "Open Letter to Mary Daly" (Lorde 1984: 66–71), because it could have been written to me. I didn't at the time know any of the goddesses to whom she refers; I didn't know there were Dahomeian Amazons or women-warriors of Dan; I didn't even know where these places were. I looked again at my course syllabus: there was a passing reference to the Code of Hammurabi. Well, I thought, it's not Greece. But where are the African women: Egyptian, Nubian, Ethiopian? None. But wait, there is

Cleopatra—again. But I wanted to know of women before the coming of the Ptolemies. Could I find out?

I felt overwhelmed by the seeming hopelessness of the task, and reacted like many of my fellow classicists: "I don't have time for this." "I don't know where to look." "I'm not an Egyptologist." "There isn't any evidence." "Why do I have to do this?" But if I don't, who will? I decided it was up to me; I began by incorporating ancient Egyptian women in my "Women in the Ancient World" course.

I approached the subject like a classicist. First I read general surveys and handbooks on ancient Egypt: Erman (1894), Aldred (1961), Emery (1961), James (1979). Through these men, I saw ancient Egypt as a Mediterranean culture whose nature was intrinsically patriarchal. Like a well-trained classicist, I found myself uncritically accepting the interpretation of these experts. I kept overlooking the cultural and patriarchal assumptions of these scholars and their predecessors.

Finally, my Black feminist consciousness got through to me. It nagged me to look critically at these sources. I found that the issue of race was often ignored. Very early works strove to strip the Egyptians of their Black African culture and physical features. They ignored the mixed racial heritage and minimized into invisibility the African features of Egyptian culture. Early Egyptologists often achieved this by employing taxonomic distinctions between Egyptians and "negroes." Punt, a country now identified with Somalia, is often characterized as mysterious and, along with Nubia, is cited as the home of "negroes," implying that no Blacks lived in Egypt.[13] Gender, too, is virtually ignored; when it is not, remarkable comments are made. For example, Erman (1894: 150) has this to say:

> It has often been said that the essential difference between the civilization of the West and of the East consists in the different status of woman. In the West she is the companion of man, in the East his servant and his toy. In the West, at one time, the esteem in which woman was held rose to a cult, while in the East the question has been earnestly discussed whether women really belonged to the human race.

The contrast would come as a surprise to the reader of Aristotle (*Politics* 1254b3–1277b25; 1313b33–39; 1335a8–17), who opposes women, slaves, children, and animals to men, masters, fathers, and human beings.

Were there sources which acknowledged the Africanity and Blackness of the ancient Egyptians? What was the role of gender in the society? I consulted more sources, in which Africanity along with Semitic influence emerged as factors in ancient Egyptian culture.[14] For the role of women and gender, I had to find other works that dealt with these issues. Lesko (1978) provided me with evidence of female pharaohs and led me to the construction of the pharaohship as a partnership. Lesko (1987: 45) remarks in passing that matrilineage was common in

African society. She hints again at this stance in her later work (Lesko 1989: 313). It appears that except in unusual circumstances there were two pharaohs, co-pharaohs, one male and one female, reflecting the androgyny of the Creator. We have the names of many of these female co-pharaohs, especially from the Old Kingdom (Lesko 1978: 32). I learned the names of female pharaohs who ruled alone: Hetepheres II in the Old Kingdom; Hatshepsut, Twosre, and Mutnodjme in the New. Troy (1986) convinced me of the importance of androgyny, of the feminine principle, and of motherhood in Egyptian religion and monarchy.

Here, I thought, was a society where some women enjoyed high status and power and equality. Lesko (1989) reinforced this further. There were still doubts, though. I wondered whether "pharaoh" was a gender specific term. I kept reading about African society but the perspective was European. Even Van Sertima (1984) has a Eurocentric focus. Reading Van Sertima, I reacted very much as a classicist, embarrassed by the lack of evidence and credible references: Cleopatra's Blackness is supported by a citation of "Ripley's Believe It or Not" from 1934. Now I ask myself whether this is "poor" scholarship or support for my thesis that we African Americans misread Cleopatra symbolically.

Throughout my search for ancient African women, I was swayed by Western feminism, which claimed sexism and women's oppression cut beyond all racial and cultural boundaries. This feminist argument reaches back to the fundamental purpose and function of the patriarchal family, which limited women's social roles to being childbearers and homemakers. Certainly ancient Egypt could be viewed through that lens and could be interpreted as a similar patriarchal structure: women stayed at home with children; during the New Kingdom, women were sometimes depicted in art as smaller than men; the titles of ruling women are translated as great royal wife, not pharaoh. There seemed to be a contradiction: were Egyptian women somehow equal at the same time that they were limited to the roles of childbearers and homemakers?

I didn't realize what was wrong until I read further. As I considered Gae Callender's 1984 essay, "The Status of Women in Old and Early Middle Kingdom Egypt," it struck me that she and I had looked at ancient Egypt from a Eurocentric and Western feminist perspective, not an Afrocentric and Black feminist one. For example, Callender has, unfortunately, assimilated the racist attitudes of her sources. My rudimentary knowledge of ancient Egypt tells me that of all the historical periods, the Old Kingdom (3100–2180 B.C.E.) deviates the least from the predynastic people who were Black African. Yet Callender (1984: 34) includes the following in her discussion of the scholarship concerning Queen Nitikrity: "Her colorful story [Hall] divided up between a male ruler (about whom nothing is known by the way) and a Greek courtesan called Rhodopis, together with the *blonde-haired* Queen we looked at earlier, Hetepheres" (my emphasis). My initial reaction to this blonde hair was not as a scholar, but as an African-American woman. "Here we go again, another White scholar telling me the Egyptians were White—and not even being subtle!" In a more scholarly vein, I reflected that

Callender's article is not about the physical anthropology of the Old Kingdom Egyptians; hence the insertion of this physical trait is curious and suspicious, especially since there is no supporting evidence cited. There are racist overtones here. Coming as it does after Callender's praise of Hetepheres as a queen (Callender 1984: 32), Callender seems to make an implicit connection between Hetepheres' "nordic" traits and her success as a queen. This is reminiscent of the racist theory of the dynastic people who came down from the north bringing civilization to the "savage" Egyptians.

It was then I realized how much I had assimilated Western feminism, and how important it was for me to look to Africa and African feminism.[15] It seemed to me that African feminism and the African construction of gender are more applicable to ancient Egypt than is Western feminism, especially if we want to see Egypt as an African society. The fundamental thesis of the Black feminist approach here is in Omolade's words (1980: 240) that "Black women and men in traditional African societies were conscious human beings who designed and constructed their own societies to meet their defined human needs." There is no universal construction of gender to describe this subjectivity.

Obviously, I can't expound here all the similarities between African constructions of gender and those of ancient Egypt. However, as an example I would like to examine briefly the role and status of motherhood and language in the Yoruba and Igbo societies, keeping in mind, of course, the impact of colonialism upon these societies. I can then set these alongside Egypt and show the similarities among them.

Among the Yoruba and Igbo, there is sex role differentiation; people clearly have designated roles and tasks. Women are traders; men are hunters. Women are mothers; men are fathers. But this differentiation is not dichotomized into domestic and public spheres. "To be a good wife and mother, a woman had not only to cook and attend her husband and children, but she also had to farm, trade or otherwise contribute to her household's livelihood" (Sudarkasa 1981: 54). Likewise, men had domestic chores like participating in the socialization of children, as well as a public occupation. Women participated in decision making; they could own property and accumulate wealth from their work. Sudarkasa (1981: 54) states that the "important economic roles of women in traditional West Africa were part and parcel of the overall domestic roles of wife, mother, sister, and daughter." The same was true for women in ancient Egypt (Lesko 1978, 1989).

Yoruba women's greatest authority comes from motherhood, a sign to many Western feminists of oppression. Troy (1986) delineates the importance of the mother in Egyptian society both mythically and historically. Hence Yoruba society, like ancient Egyptian society, is mother centered, and here motherhood is collective. Marriage is organized around production and reproduction, not the control of sexuality. It is important to point out also that among the Yoruba and other peoples of West Africa, "domestic groups are extended families built around segments of matri- or patrilineages" (Sudarkasa 1981: 52). For the Yoruba, it is the lineage which is important, not the individual or even individual families.

This was also true for the ancient Egyptians. As Diop (1978: 34) states: "In those primitive ages when the security of the group was the primary concern, the respect enjoyed by either of the sexes was connected with its contribution to this collective security." In addition, lineage was important, especially in the royal family where matrifocality insured connections with the goddesses (Troy 1986: 56).

For the Yoruba and Igbo, both males and females have roles of authority within the domestic groups or compounds. Both these societies have developed a seniority system based on age as the primary mode of social organization. Consequently within the compound there are an official male head and female head. This is strikingly reminiscent of the ancient Egyptian pharaohship. In ancient Egypt, as in Yoruba society, motherhood was as much a generational role as a gender role. Women and men related to each other as members of one family. Hence the ancient Egyptian women viewed all men as their brothers; men viewed all women as their sisters. The feminine prototype was that of the mother. As such this prototype was the medium of renewal and is given symmetrical expression in the generational roles of mother, wife, sister, and daughter. As Isis says to Osiris: "I am your sister. I am your wife. I am the daughter of your mother who causes your beautiful face to see" (Troy 1986: 50). The double role of mother/daughter is the primary characteristic of the feminine prototype: she creates the very being by whom she herself has been created.

This mother-centered construction can include men and in both ancient Egyptian and Yoruba society the public and private spheres overlap for men just as they do for women. As a result, for example, men are actively involved in the care of children. Some feminists might argue that there is still a patriarchal cast to Yoruba and Igbo society. The chiefs are men and there can be paternal dominance in the family. One has to wonder how much of this is the result of colonialism. Omolade (1980: 249) correctly reminds us, however, that "the crucial aspect here is not an assertion that African women were liberated in the context of industrialized twentieth century societies, but whether they were citizens with political rights and economic freedoms."

Language provides a further key to the Yoruba construction of gender. In the Yoruba language, there are terms for mother, father, wife, husband, sibling, child. There is no equivalent for men, women, sister, brother, daughter, or son. In Igbo, Amadiume (1987: 89) states that there is no distinction made between male and female in subject pronouns, that is, there is no "she"/"he." Her thesis is that there is a greater possibility for men and women to share attributes.

For sources written in hieroglyphics, I have had to rely on translations undertaken by academics trained in languages which are rigidly gendered. I have already raised the question of whether the term "pharaoh" is gender specific. Diop (in Mokhtar 1990: 28–32) attempted to show the linguistic affinity between the hieroglyphics and the Wolof language, but he was not looking specifically at gender construction. Troy (1986: 104) observes that "ancient Egyptian is known for its lack of an extensive kinship terminology." It seems to cover members of the nuclear family: mother, *mwt;* father, *yt;* sister, *snt;* brother, *sn;* daughter, *s3t;* son, *s3*. These terms in turn were used for other family relationships. It is clear these terms were ambiguous and this ambiguity has its background in the structure of the family group. Troy (1986: 105) states further:

> if one posits that the basic socio-economic unit was the extended family, consisting of several generations, the use of the limited kinship terminology makes some sense as the designation, not only of blood relationships, but also of the relative ranking of the individuals within the household unit.

It sounds strikingly like the seniority system of the Yoruba and Igbo.

It is safe to say that our view of ancient Egyptian society would change if we could show that Egyptian was structured closer, in terms of gender, to Yoruba than to Greek or Latin or Hebrew. Isis to Osiris would read: "I am your sibling. I am your wife. I am the child of your mother who causes your beautiful face to see." At this point, I can only speculate, but it appears that this translation is in keeping with the other African features of ancient Egyptian social structures. These connections show that the "Mediterranean basin" really contained a multiplicity of cultures and not just variations on the theme of Graeco-Roman patriarchy. There obviously is still work to be done. A thorough study of ancient Egypt through the lens of African feminism is a promising avenue for collaboration between Black feminists and classicists. To quote Fannie Barrier Williams (Loewenberg and Bogin 1976: 266), "As it is there is much to be unlearned as well as to be learned."

III. Re-empowering through Re-learning

How do we begin? First we classicists have to move away from the notion of discipline. We speak of the discipline of classics; it evokes an image of narrow boundaries and rigid inflexibility and exclusion. The discipline of classics purports to study the ancient world, yet, in fact, only studies Greece and Rome. But Greece and Rome were not the only cultures in the ancient world. We need to think of classics in terms of ethnic studies and leave ourselves open to all possibilities. Likewise, feminists, whether Black or White, need to rethink the preference for theory over thought (Christian 1988; Lugones and Spelman 1983). Central to this relearning and to my foregoing interpretation of ancient Egypt is the acknowledgement of different standpoints. The standpoint of Black women and its validity is in fact fundamental to Black feminist thought and forms; along with reclaiming our foremothers, it is the core of this ideology (Collins 1990:

21–39). Patricia Hill Collins recently elaborated on the construct of standpoint by retelling "The Emperor's New Clothes."[16] The emperor had convinced all the people that his new clothes were wonderful and that his were the only clothes that were wonderful and that that was the only valid comment which could be made about them. The adults were afraid to contradict the emperor because he was the emperor and they never talked to one another. One day, during one of the emperor's parades, when everyone was praising the emperor's new clothes, a little African-American girl said to the adult next to her, "It seems to me that the emperor is naked! Why do you all say the emperor's clothes are wonderful, when he isn't wearing any?" At first, the little girl was silenced by her fellow bystanders, but she didn't give up. She kept nudging and asking. Soon people began to *talk to one another* and compare notes. Before this, the people never talked to one another; they just accepted the emperor's word. But once communication began, the people began to support the African-American girl's standpoint—not as the sole one, or the "correct" one, but as a valid one. Obviously, Collins's version of the story was "read" differently by different people in the audience. For some, the emperor represented White male privilege, or knowledge, or voice. For me, he was the construct of the discipline of classics.

Only recently has the impact of the Anglo-Germanic construction of the discipline of classics upon the evidence of the ancient world been fully investigated (Bernal 1987). Martin Bernal shows the impact of Black slavery, racial science, and Romanticism upon the reading of ancient evidence. Many of the assumptions of the eighteenth, nineteenth, and even twentieth centuries about gender and race are reflected in the discipline. They mean that any signs of culture or intellect found on the continent of Africa must be devalued. Therefore, the Egyptians, when acknowledged as intellectual or civilized, become White. When they are acknowledged to be of "mixed race" or African, then their "culture" is stagnant, passive, or dead.[17] Furthermore, the cultures of sub-Saharan Africa are never mentioned, and this omission implies the nonexistence of culture, or at least its lack of relevance to Greece and Rome. Even the well-documented ethnic and cultural diversity of Roman Africa is not considered an important issue.[18] This kind of exclusion prevails in mainstream scholarship, and results in courses on women in the ancient world that have no African or even Semitic women represented. The same problem has plagued White feminist theories in the past and was poignantly described by bell hooks (1981), Elizabeth Spelman (1982), Elizabeth Hood (1978), and Phyllis Palmer (1983) for White women and Black women, and by Paula Gunn Allen (1988) for White women and Native American women. If the life and experience of Black women in America have been rendered so invisible, it is not surprising to find a deeper invisibility for ancient African women. We need to hear the tension between the ancient African cultures and the culture of the Greek and Roman men who serve as the evidence of their existence. We need to redefine our field so that it includes African languages, African history, African archaeology. We need to hear and acknowledge the silence of African women when we write books about ancient Africa from a Eurocentric standpoint. We need to learn about African feminism so we can restore their voice. We need to recognize that classics was the educational foundation for our Black feminist foremothers. We need to analyze this as we reclaim these feminists. We have already begun; a good example is Hazel Carby's (1985, 1987) analysis of Pauline Hopkins's use of Sappho in her novel *Contending Forces*.

Black feminist thought provides a standpoint from which to re-member, to re-claim, to re-empower the ancient African woman. Through Black feminist thought, classics can be radically transformed from a discipline into a multi-racial, multicultural, multivalent field which better reflects the ancient world it studies. Black feminists, in turn, should view classics, not as the "enemy," but as a source of symbolic value for so many of our foremothers as they struggled against racism and sexism.

Notes

I would like to thank and acknowledge the following: Amy and Nancy, for asking me to contribute to this volume, and for your suggestions and guidance which have been truly helpful and insightful; Barbara Gold, Carl, and Judy, for your warm and empowering friendship; Tina and Melanie, for Maine; Adrian, Iain, Caitlin, Jenny, Jake, and Elroy, for always reminding me of love and reality; June LeRay and Gerda Seligson, for loving Latin and teaching me to do the same; Fanny Jackson Coppin, Anna Julia Cooper, Mary Church Terrell, for doing it first; and to Mommy and Nama for telling me your dreams and letting me fulfill them.

1. Londa Schiebinger (1990) analyzes how eighteenth-century science supported this notion of Black intellectual inferiority. These assumptions of Black intellectual inferiority are still around. In 1982, while I was attending the annual meeting of the American Philological Association, I was chatting with a grants person (White male) from NEH. When he learned that I taught classics at Howard, he said, "Gee, it must be grim teaching classics to black people."

2. Audre Lorde did not have the happy experience I did learning Latin. See Lorde 1982: 60.

3. Even the American Negro Academy, the foremost scholarly organization for African-Americans contemporary with Terrell and Cooper, did not admit women, despite the recognition of some members that there had been "a higher attainment of scholarship by our women than our men" (Moss 1981: 41). Faculty integration at overwhelmingly White institutions of higher education began only in the 1940s when the University of Chicago accepted a grant awarded by the Rosenwald Fund to pay the salary of a Black faculty member.

4. Cleopatra's Blackness is part of Black oral history. My grandmother may have learned from that. She may well have been influenced by images of Josephine Baker. Phyllis Rose (1990) titles her biography of Baker *Jazz Cleopatra*. Peiss (1990) discusses the employment of Cleopatra in marketing cosmetics to Black women.

Other Black women have heard similar stories from their relatives. Compare Golden (1983: 4, her father is speaking): "I don't care *what* they tell you in school, [Cleopatra] was a black woman."

5. Looking at a syllabus from that time I see listed Bullough (1978), de Beauvoir (1974), Putnam (1910), Rogers (1966), and Slater (1968).

6. My ideas were formed by reading Cooper (1892), DuBois collected by Huggins (1986), King (1988), Collins (1990), Moses (1990), hooks (1981), Walker (1983), Hull, Scott, and Smith (1982), and Terrell (1940).

7. The *Cambridge Ancient History* genealogy has "by a concubine" where Cleopatra's grandmother should be; the Greeks took Egyptian and Ethiopian women as mistresses. See Pomeroy (1990: 55); cf. Cameron (1990). I think it is safe to say that Cleopatra had Black ancestors.

8. The construction by scholars and filmmakers struck me as I viewed Pascal's 1945 film version of G. B. Shaw's *Caesar and Cleopatra,* starring Vivien Leigh. The dialogue intends for us to take Cleopatra as darker than the Roman Caesar, but the visual presence of a very White and European Vivien Leigh contradicts the dialogue.

9. The theoretical standpoint I take here has been articulated by Bloom (1973), Gilbert and Gubar (1979), and Sadoff (1990). My use is unusual in that I am applying it to history and historiography rather than literature.

10. This conclusion is one of the most important and overlooked of his work. The American Philological Association Panel (1989) and the subsequent special issue (1989) of *Arethusa,* "The Challenge of Black Athena," concentrate on rather esoteric points of research and interpretation. Lefkowitz (1992) trivializes the ramifications of this conclusion.

11. See Haley (1989, 1990).

12. The Black feminist conception of inclusivity is not that of Kagan, where he states: "We are all familiar with the demand for diversity of representation—one from each color and continent, and so on" (Kagan 1990: 35).

13. The epithet "mysterious" is always applied to Africa, the "dark" continent. It extends further to the people, especially women. Palmer (1983: 158) analyzes it in this way: "Black women, even more than other women forced to labor outside their homes, come to symbolize sexuality, prowess, mysterious power (mysterious, certainly, since it was so at odds with their actual economic, political and social deprivation); they came to embody the 'myth of the superwoman.' "

14. For the African in Egyptian culture, see Trigger (1978), Trigger, Kemp, O'Connor and Lloyd (1983), Adams (1978), and Diop (1974, 1978).

15. I reread Omolade (1980), and consulted Terborg Penn, Harley, and Rushing (1987), Amadiume (1987), and Steady (1981).

16. Conference on "Integrating Class, Race and Gender into the Curriculum," sponsored by Institute for Research on Women at SUNY, Albany at Albany, New York, June 7, 1991.

17. As near as I can tell, proponents of this theory posit an indigenous people of "Caucasian stock" who were "diluted" by mixing with the "negroid" peoples of Nubia and Kush. See Derry 1956.

18. The most recent study of Rome and its ethnic diversity is Thompson (1989). Camps (1960) deals with the ethnic and cultural diversity of Roman Africa; Mokhtar (1990) and Davidson (1959) are two of the few who deal with sub-Saharan Africa. Other sources include Cracco Ruggini (1968, 1974, 1979), Thompson and Ferguson (1969), and Bugner (1976). Gender is only touched upon in these sources and usually is ignored.

Bibliography

Adams, William Y. 1978. "Geography and Population of the Nile Valley." In S. Hochfield and E. Riefstahl, eds., *Africa in Antiquity: The Arts of Ancient Nubia and the Sudan.* Vol. 1: *The Essays,* 16–25. Brooklyn: Brooklyn Museum.

Aldred, Cyril. 1961. *The Egyptians.* London: Thames and Hudson.

Allen, Paula Gunn. 1988. "Who Is Your Mother?: Red Roots of White Feminism." *The Graywolf Annual* 5: 13–27.

Amadiume, Ifi. 1987. *Male Daughters, Female Husbands.* London: Zed Books.

Bernal, Martin. 1987. *Black Athena: The Afroasiatic Roots of Classical Civilization,* Vols. 1 and 2: *The Fabrication of Greece 1785–1985.* New Brunswick: Rutgers University Press.

Bloom, Harold. 1973. *The Anxiety of Influence: A Theory of Poetry.* New York: Oxford University Press.

Bugner, Ladislas, ed. 1976. *The Image of the Black in Western Art: Vol. I.* New York: The Menil Foundation.

Bullough, Vernon. 1978. *The Subordinate Sex.* Athens: The University of Georgia Press.

Callender, Gae. 1984. "The Status of Women in Old and Early Middle Kingdom Egypt." In Suzanne Dixon and Theresa Munford, eds., *Pre-Industrial Women: Interdisciplinary Perspectives,* 30–36. Canberra: A.N.U. Press.

Cameron, Alan. 1990. "Two Mistresses of Ptolemy Philadelphus." *Greek, Roman and Byzantine Studies* 31: 287–311.

Camps, Gabriel. 1960. "Aux origines de la Berberie: Massinissa ou les débuts de l'Histoire." *Libyca: Bulletin du Service des Antiquités Archéologie-Epigraphie,* vol. 8.

Carby, Hazel V. 1985. " 'On the Threshold of Woman's Era': Lynching, Empire and Sexuality in Black Feminist Theory." *Critical Inquiry* 12: 262–77.

———. 1987. *Reconstructing Womanhood: The Emergence of the Afro-American Woman Novelist.* New York: Oxford University Press.

Christian, Barbara. 1988. "The Race for Theory." *Feminist Studies* 14: 67–79.

Cliff, Michelle. 1988. "A Journey into Speech." *The Graywolf Annual* 5: 57–62.

Collins, Patricia Hill. 1990. *Black Feminist Thought: Knowledge, Consciousness and the Politics of Empowerment.* Boston: Unwin Hyman.

Cooper, Anna Julia. 1892. *A Voice from the South.* Xenia, Ohio: Aldine Publishing House. Reprinted as part of the Schomberg Library of Nineteenth Century Black Women Writers, 1988. New York: Oxford University Press.

Cracco Ruggini, Lellia. 1968. "Pregiudizi razziali, ostilità politica e culturale, intoleranza religiosa nell' impero romano." *Athenaeum* 46: 139–52.

———. 1974. "Leggenda e realtà degli Etiopi nella cultura tardoimperiale." In *Atti de IV° Congresso Internazionale di Studi Etiopici: 1*, 141–93. Rome: Accademia nazionale dei Lincei.

———. 1979. "Il negro buono e il negro malvagio nel mondo antico." In Marta Sordi, ed., *Conoscenze etniche e rapporti di convivenza nell' antichità*, 108–33. Milan: Vita e Pensiero.

Davidson, Basil. 1959. *The Lost Cities of Africa*. Boston: Little, Brown and Company.

de Beauvoir, Simone. 1974. *The Second Sex*. New York: Vintage Books.

Derry, D. E. 1956. "The Dynastic Race in Egypt." *Journal of Egyptian Archaeology* 42: 80–85.

Diop, Cheikh Anta. 1974. *The African Origin of Civilization: Myth or Reality*. Westport, Conn.: Lawrence Hill.

———. 1978. *The Cultural Unity of Black Africa*. Chicago: Third World Press.

Emery, W. B. 1961. *Archaic Egypt*. Harmondsworth: Penguin.

Erman, Adolph. 1894. *Life in Ancient Egypt*. London: MacMillan and Company.

Gilbert, Sandra, and Susan Gubar. 1979. *The Madwoman in the Attic: The Woman Writer and the Nineteenth Century Literary Imagination*. New Haven: Yale University Press.

Golden, Marita. 1983. *Migrations of the Heart: A Personal Odyssey*. Garden City, N.Y.: Anchor Press.

Grant, Michael. 1972. *Cleopatra*. New York: Simon and Schuster.

———. 1982. *From Alexander to Cleopatra: The Hellenistic World*. New York: Scribners.

Haley, Shelley P. 1989. "Livy's Sophoniba." *Classica et Mediaevalia* 40: 171–81.

———. 1990. "Livy, Passion and Cultural Stereotypes." *Historia* 39: 375–81.

Hood, Elizabeth F. 1978. "Black Women, White Women: Separate Paths to Liberation." *The Black Scholar* April: 45–55.

hooks, bell. 1981. *Ain't I a Woman: Black Women and Feminism*. Boston: South End Press.

Huggins, Nathan. 1986. *W. E. B. DuBois: Writings*. New York: The Library of America.

Hull, Gloria, T., Patricia Bell Scott, and Barbara Smith, eds. 1982. *All the Women Are White, All the Blacks Are Men, but Some of Us Are Brave: Black Women's Studies*. New York: The Feminist Press.

James, George G. M. 1954. *Stolen Legacy*. New York: Philosophical Library.

James, T. G. H. 1979. *Introduction to Ancient Egypt*. New York: Harper and Row.

Kagan, Donald. 1990. "Yale University: Testing the Limits." *Academic Questions:* 31–37.

King, Deborah K. 1988. "Multiple Jeopardy, Multiple Consciousness: The Context of a Black Feminist Ideology." *Signs* 14: 42–72.

Lefkowitz, Mary. 1992. "Not Out of Africa." *The New Republic* February 10: 29–35.

Lesko, Barbara S. 1978. *The Remarkable Women of Ancient Egypt.* Providence, R.I.: B.C. Scribe Publications.

———. 1987. "Women of Egypt and the Ancient Near East." In Renate Bridenthal, Claudia Koonz, and Susan Stuard, eds., *Becoming Visible,* second edition, 40–77. Boston: Houghton-Mifflin.

———. 1989. *Woman's Earliest Records.* Providence, R.I.: Brown University Press.

Lindsay, Jack. 1971. *Cleopatra.* London: Constable.

Loewenberg, Bert J., and Ruth Bogin. 1976. *Black Women in Nineteenth Century Life.* University Park: The Pennsylvania State University Press.

Lorde, Audre. 1982. *Zami: A New Spelling of My Name.* Watertown, Mass.: Persephone Press.

———. 1984. *Sister Outsider.* Trumansburg: The Crossing Press.

Lugones, María C., and Elizabeth V. Spelman. 1983. "Have We Got A Theory for You!: Feminist Theory, Cultural Imperialism and the Demand for 'the Woman's Voice.' " *Women's Studies International Forum* 6: 573–81.

Mokhtar, G., ed. 1990. *General History of Africa II: Ancient Civilizations of Africa.* Abridged edition. Berkeley: The University of California Press.

Moses, Wilson Jeremiah. 1990. *The Wings of Ethiopia.* Ames: Iowa State University.

Moss, Alfred A., Jr. 1981. *The American Negro Academy: Voice of The Talented Tenth.* Baton Rouge: Louisiana State University Press.

Omolade, Barbara. 1980. "Black Women and Feminism." In Hester Eisenstein and Alice Jardine, eds., *The Future of Difference,* 247–57. Boston: G. K. Hall and Company.

Palmer, Phyllis Marynick. 1983. "White Women/Black Women: the Dualism of Female Identity and Experience in the United States." *Feminist Studies* 9: 151–70.

Peiss, Kathy. 1990. "Making Faces: The Cosmetic Industry and the Cultural Construction of Gender, 1890–1930." *Genders* 7: 143–69.

Peradotto, Jack, and Molly Myerowitz Levine, eds. 1989. "The Challenge of Black Athena." *Arethusa:* special issue.

Pomeroy, Sarah. 1975. *Goddesses, Whores, Wives, and Slaves: Women in Classical Antiquity.* New York: Schocken Books.

———. 1990. *Women in Hellenistic Egypt: From Alexander to Cleopatra.* Detroit: Wayne State University Press.

Putnam, Emily. 1910. *The Lady.* New York: Putnam Publishers.

Rogers, Katherine. 1966. *The Troublesome Helpmate: A History of Misogyny in Literature.* Seattle: The University of Washington Press.

Rose, Phyllis. 1990. *Jazz Cleopatra: Josephine Baker in Her Time.* New York: Vintage Books.

Sadoff, Diane. 1990. "Black Matrilineage: The Case of Alice Walker and Zora Neale Hurston." In Micheline R. Malson, Elisabeth Mudimbe-Boyi, Jean F. O'Barr, and Mary Wyer, eds., *Black Women in America: Social Science Perspectives,* 197–219.

Chicago: The University of Chicago Press. Originally appeared in *Signs* 11 (1985): 4–26.

Saks, Eva. 1988. "Representing Miscegenation Law." *Raritan* 8: 39–69.

Schiebinger, Londa. 1990. "The Anatomy of Difference: Race and Sex in Eighteenth Century Science." *Eighteenth Century Studies* 23: 387–405.

Skinner, Marilyn B. 1987. "Classical Studies, Patriarchy and Feminism: The View from 1986." *Women's Studies International Forum* 10: 181–86.

Slater, Philip. 1968. *The Glory of Hera*. Boston: Beacon Press.

Snowden, Frank. 1970. *Blacks in Antiquity*. Cambridge, Mass.: Harvard University Press.

Spelman, Elizabeth V. 1982. "Theories of Race and Gender: The Erasure of Black Women." *Quest* 5: 36–62.

————. 1988. *Inessential Woman: Problems of Exclusion in Feminist Thought*. Boston: Beacon Press.

Steady, Filomina Chioma, ed. 1981. *The Black Woman Cross-Culturally*. Cambridge, Mass.: Schenkman Publishing Company.

Sudarkasa, Niara. 1981. "Female Employment and Family Organization in West Africa." In Steady 1981, 49–63.

Terborg Penn, Rosalyn, Sharon Harley, and Andrea Benton Rushing, eds. 1987. *Women in Africa and the African Diaspora*. Washington, D.C.: Howard University Press.

Terrell, Mary Church. 1940. *A Colored Woman in a White World*. Washington, D.C.: Ransdell, Inc.

Thompson, Lloyd A. 1989. *Romans and Blacks*. Norman: The University of Oklahoma Press.

Thompson, Lloyd A., and John Ferguson, eds. 1969. *Africa in Classical Antiquity*. Ibadan: Ibadan University Press.

Trigger, Bruce G. 1978. "Nubian, Negro, Black, Nilotic?" In S. Hochfield and E. Riefstahl, eds., *Africa in Antiquity: The Arts of Ancient Nubia and the Sudan*. Vol. 1: *The Essays*, 26–35. Brooklyn: Brooklyn Museum.

Trigger, B. G., B. J. Kemp, D. O'Connor, and A. B. Lloyd, eds. 1983. *Ancient Egypt: A Social History*. Cambridge: Cambridge University Press.

Troy, Lana. 1986. "Patterns of Queenship in Ancient Egyptian Myth and History." *Boreas: Uppsala Studies in Ancient Mediterranean and Near East Civilizations* 14.

Van Sertima, Ivan. 1984. *Black Women in Antiquity*. New Brunswick: Transaction Books.

Volkmann, Hans. 1958. *Cleopatra: A Study in Politics and Propaganda*. Translated by T. J. Cadoux. New York: Sagamore Press.

Walker, Alice. 1983. *In Search of Our Mothers' Gardens*. New York: Harcourt Brace Jovanovich.

————. 1989. *Temple of My Familiar*. New York: Harcourt Brace Jovanovich.

Washington, Mary Helen. 1988. "Introduction." In *A Voice from the South*, by Anna Julia Cooper, xxvii–liv. New York: Oxford University Press.

Williams, Patricia. 1991. *Alchemy of Race and Rights*. Cambridge, Mass.: Harvard University Press.

3

Feminist Theory, Historical Periods, Literary Canons, and the Study of Greco-Roman Antiquity

Judith P. Hallett

"I don't like the words 'classic' or 'classical.' They imply that there's some absolute fixed worth attached to certain works and authors and literatures. Yet they don't acknowledge who attached this worth, or when, or why. While I can only speak for my own field, English, it disturbs me to hear this label categorically applied to a novel that was virtually unknown until the 1920s—when a group of men in New York decided to promote this book on the grounds that it might hold the interest and make attentive future readers of young boys."

These are obviously not my own words, but words spoken by Peggy McIntosh of the Wellesley College Center for Research on Women. The work whose label disturbs her is, of course, *Moby Dick*. The words were her response to my brief attempts at introducing and identifying myself and my field, at the opening session of a year-long faculty development seminar—on integrating the study of women into the humanities disciplines—that she directed in 1982–1983.

Peggy McIntosh's remarks about the words "classic" and "classical," along with similar comments by a number of like-minded seminar participants, prompted me to try using "Greek and Latin literature," "Greek and Roman culture," and "Greco-Roman antiquity"—anything but those elitist and often unthinkingly applied "c" words—both within and outside of that Wellesley faculty seminar. For those occasions when the "c" words would inadvertently trip off my tongue, I prepared a self-defensive strategy: the argument that the "c" words have a major advantage over the alternative labels "philology" and "philological," inasmuch as "classics" and "classical" are more intelligible to ordinary people, or at least to ordinary academics (Hallett 1983: 3–11). But I struggled mightily to avoid such inadvertent tongue trippings. Suddenly made aware that these two words triggered negative responses to our field among feminist scholars in other disciplines, I did not want to risk further alienation from colleagues with whom I was eager to collaborate in creating a more inclusive humanities curriculum.

Peggy McIntosh's remarks also caused me to reflect upon how we, in the field that defines its realm of inquiry by the "c" noun, apply the "c" adjective: both to periods of time within the historical era of Greco-Roman antiquity, and to the most valued, canonical works of literature among the cultural legacies of Greco-Roman civilization. Thus I not only pondered the appropriateness of employing the term "classical period" for fifth- and fourth-century B.C.E. Athens, and for mid-to-late republican and early imperial Rome, but I simultaneously found myself thinking about efforts by classicists to accord "classical" status to ancient Greek and Roman works of literature. I reflected upon these two matters simultaneously because such efforts at designating works of literature as "classical," as canonical, often do not clearly separate the assessment of these literary works from the assessment of the cultural circumstances—the time, place, and political environment—in which these works are produced, or even from the definition of the cultural circumstances in which literary works are produced as constituting a major historical "period."

Consider, for example, the "classical Roman period." I myself was taught to define this chronological construct as extending from the late third century B.C.E. to the early second century C.E. (Hallett 1984: 3). Such a construct, of course, not only excludes important eras of Roman history from which few written documents survive: the seventh and sixth centuries B.C.E., when Rome was an emerging urban settlement subject to Etruscan rule; and the fifth, fourth, and third centuries B.C.E., during the course of which the Roman republic came first to dominate a confederacy extending throughout Italy and then to exert substantial power in the Mediterranean. Less obviously, this construct also excludes eras from which we have abundant testimony: the reigns of Antoninus Pius and Marcus Aurelius in the later second century C.E., that very period which the eighteenth-century historian Edward Gibbon judged "the happiest known to man"; and the two subsequent centuries, by the close of which Rome had adopted Christianity as a state religion (Scullard 1969: 930–32). And even within what is regarded as the "classical" period, scholarly surveys of Roman history traditionally distinguish between the earlier segment—especially the late republican and Augustan portion—and the later segment—the early imperial portion—by privileging the former and devaluing the latter. What has prompted the division of this period into two parts, the second assessed as far inferior to the first?

One of the reasons, we might argue, has to do with the assessment of the literary works produced in each segment. After all, classicists often apply the laudatory label of "golden" to the literature of the earlier, and the less approbatory label of "silver" to the literature of the later period—even though, as we will shortly see for ourselves, scholars who employ these terms do not appear to agree among themselves on exactly when the "golden" age of Latin literature begins and ends (Teuffel 1870: vol. 1, ix–x, 243; Cruttwell 1877: xi–xii, 5, 139; Scullard 1969: 930; Africa 1974: 208–17; Vessey 1982: 1–2). Indeed, what the latest edition of a standard reference work on Greco-Roman antiquity, *The Oxford Classical Dictionary* (*OCD*), calls "the most extensive treatment of Latin literature in English," written by J. Wight Duff in the early part of this century, is divided into two volumes: *Literary History of Rome from the Origins to the Close of the Golden Age* and *Literary History of Rome in the Silver Age, from Tiberius to Hadrian* (Duff 1909 and 1930; Browning 1969).

Yet we could just as easily invoke widely held assessments of Roman temporal and cultural circumstances to help explain why classicists have applied the labels "golden" and "silver" to these bodies of Latin literature. For scholars customarily regard the later years of the Roman republic, along with those of the Augustan principate—when Rome was ruled by an individual who purported to restore the republic—as a distinct and historically more significant period, as a span of time in a specific place that, for political reasons, merits higher esteem than the early imperial era which follows.

Scholarly attempts to justify such categorization and such terminology vividly illustrate this inextricable knotting of aesthetic assessment and historical periodization, the way in which historical classifications are tied to aesthetic judgments and vice versa. For an instance of the former, the use of Roman literary achievements not only as a basis for historical categorization, but also as grounds for according special historical worth to a chronological era, we need only look at the article on "Rome (History)" by the eminent Roman historian H. H. Scullard in the *Oxford Classical Dictionary* itself. Scullard's discussion concludes the section entitled "The Fall of the Republic (133–31 B.C.)" by acknowledging the political chaos and instability of Roman society during these years. Nevertheless, he cites the artistic accomplishments of this period to argue for its superior historical status:

> Despite civil wars, misgovernment, political corruption, the ambitions of the rival dynasts (*principes viri*), and the collapse of the republican constitution, the Roman world still offered a foundation on which a new system could be constructed. Further, the political unification of Italy was reflected in the greater unity of Italian civilization. The whole of this period and especially the Ciceronian age witnessed a steady advance of oratory, art, and letters. If Cicero was the dominant literary figure there were also Lucretius, Catullus, Caesar, Varro and Sallust. Political instability had not undermined all the productive activities of man.

Scullard's subsequent discussion of the Augustan age does much the same thing. As evidence for the superior achievement of this period, he cites Augustus's debt to "writers such as Virgil, Horace and Livy, who made this the Golden Age of Latin literature." Still, although he maintains that Augustus "created a new system which endured . . . within the framework of the Republic," he admits that by this time the republic itself "had collapsed through the attacks of military dictators and the lack of an adequate civil service."

By the same token, contemporary scholarship in Latin studies continues to argue that the historical period, and especially the political events of the historical period, in which works of Roman literature were created, plays a major role in determining their aesthetic value. In viewing political developments as influencing literary merit, such scholars belong to a critical tradition dating back to the Romans themselves, among them men central to the ruling institutions of the Roman state, like Cicero, the elder Seneca, and Tacitus (Williams 1978: 8–9, 21, 24, 31–32, 46–47). We should, however, accord special attention to the arguments of two nineteenth-century scholars, from England and Germany respectively, inasmuch as they appear to have launched the terms "golden" and "silver" in scholarly discourse about Latin literature. In the introduction to an 1877 volume on the history of Roman literature—a work "designed mainly for Students at our Universities and Public Schools, and for such as are preparing for the Indian Civil Service or other advanced Examinations"—the Oxford classicist C. T. Cruttwell accounted for his use of the term "Golden Age" to describe the literature of the period from "80 B.C. to A.D. 14," from "Cicero to Ovid," by making two claims: first, that such divisions of the subject are "naturally suggested by the history of the language"; second, that these divisions were "recently adopted by Teuffel" (Cruttwell 1877: 4). Seven years earlier, in his *Geschichte der Roemischen Literatur,* Wilhelm Sigmund Teuffel had initially offered artistic grounds for so regarding the "Ciceronian and Augustan Age," stating that, "The golden age of Roman literature is that period in which it reached its climax in the perfection of form, and for the most part also in the methodical treatment of the subject-matter" (Teuffel 1870: vol. 1, 243).

But in arguing that the "later and lesser half" of the Augustan age more properly belongs to the "silver" rather than to the "golden age," Teuffel's study subsequently explains that in these years "the original national energies still continued to be active, though weakened and clogged by the new political conditions, owing to which the Monarchy after Augustus rapidly became a thorough despotism. This gradually extinguished all independent intellectual life" (Teuffel 1870: vol. 2, 1). Teuffel's British admirer Cruttwell in fact uses the term "the period of the Decline, from the accession of Tiberius to the death of Marcus Aurelius (14–180 A.D.)" for Teuffel's "silver age," and singles out as its chief characteristic "unreality, arising from the extinction of freedom and consequent interest in public life" (Cruttwell 1877: 5–6). Both the Teuffel and Cruttwell books furnish historical explanations for the term "golden age" as well, which indeed base aesthetic judgments on political factors. Teuffel's does so with such observations as, "The practical tendencies in literature and the influence of a time of great political excitement became conspicuous in the fields now especially selected for literary cultivation" (Teuffel 1870: vol. 1, 246). Cruttwell's asserts that the "celebrated writers" in the era of golden prose "were now mostly men of action and high position in the state," thereby underlining the relevance of his subject matter for future members of the Indian Civil Service (Cruttwell 1877: 5).

My thoughts, then, about the application of the "c" adjective to periods of ancient Greco-Roman political activity and literary production led me to see the close connection between historical periodization and literary canonization in the study of Greek and Roman antiquity. These thoughts then led me to recognize how my realm of inquiry both resembled and differed from that of the other feminist participants in that Wellesley seminar. While our field may be unique in employing the terms "classics" and "classical" to identify itself in totality, it is similar to other humanities fields in applying these terms to valorize some of its literary voices and some of its chronological and geographical parts. By according special status to certain literary figures and diminishing—even ignoring—the contributions of others to Greco-Roman civilization, we engage in a practice that also occurs in fields focusing on cultures outside of Europe and North America. Indeed, when reminding us that "*Classics* is a misnomer. . . . It is the height of ethnocentrism to say *classics* and mean only the antiquity of Greece and Rome," Shelley Haley has recently pointed out that "every culture, every civilization has a classical period: classical Japan, classical China, classical India, classical Nigeria" (Haley 1989: 335).

We can and should, moreover, trace the practice of selective literary valorization back to Greco-Roman antiquity itself, because we continue to deal with the consequences of its ancient manifestations. The efforts in the late first century C.E., by the Roman rhetorical authority Quintilian, to judge Latin literary works by comparing them with earlier Greek models, were redoubled in the nineteenth century by scholars constructing the discipline of American classical studies; this process, which Thomas Habinek has called "the acquiescence of Latinists in their own subordination," has meant latter-day acclaim for Latin authors of recognized achievement in valued Greek literary genres—hence the label of "classic" awarded to the epic poetry of Vergil by T. S. Eliot—and corresponding obscurity for Latin writers without obvious Greek exemplars (Eliot 1944; Habinek 1992). There is such obscurity, in fact, that many are not aware when scholarly projects that purport to deal with Roman society—most obviously and recently Michel Foucault's *History of Sexuality*—neglect the evidence of numerous, highly relevant texts by Roman writers (Foucault 1986; Halperin 1990, Winkler 1990; Richlin 1991b). At least the traditional valorization of certain places in the ancient Mediterranean, and the corresponding neglect of entire geographical regions—particularly Africa and the Near East—by those who have defined "the classical world," have elicited understandable reactions from scholars both in and outside our field (Hallett 1983: 8–9; Haley 1989).

I was enrolled in Peggy McIntosh's Wellesley faculty seminar in order to become more familiar with feminist theoretical approaches in other humanities disciplines. Such theoretical perspectives also proved valuable in my ruminations on the use of the word "classical," particularly on the literature commonly identified by that label written in historical periods customarily accorded that label. As a result of the contributions to our discussions by feminist literary critics such as my fellow seminar participant Lillian Robinson as well as by Peggy McIntosh herself, I better understood how and why feminist literary critics have been challenging the notion of a literary canon, a roster of esteemed, "classical," texts to be scrutinized and "mastered" (whether by generalists such as university undergraduates or by specialists such as graduate students in departments of languages and literatures). I comprehended more fully that this feminist challenge also entails examining the admissions procedures to various canons, generalist or specialist, ancient or modern. I saw how these admissions processes have themselves been affected by developments, particularly political developments, during various historical periods. For that reason, I recognized that any challenge to any literary canon needs to consider both those historical periods in which individual literary works were produced and—as Peggy McIntosh's comments on the reception of *Moby Dick* emphasize—those in which they were promoted (Baym 1985; Eagleton 1983; Lauter 1983; Tompkins 1985; Zagarell 1986; Robinson 1983, 1985, and 1986; Robbins 1992).

This understanding in turn caused me to consider why changes have occurred in the canon of texts prescribed for serious students in our field of Greek and Latin languages and literatures. For example, Cruttwell, writing a little more than a century ago, devotes an entire chapter of his book to a host of authors from "The Age of Tiberius (14–37 A.D.)." Cruttwell prefaces his discussion of individual writers from that era, such as Velleius Paterculus and Valerius Maximus, with a section headed "Great Depression of Literature" (Cruttwell 1877: 343). His low assessment of this entire group of authors, shared, if not as fully articulated, by Teuffel's study, evidently represents a break with earlier critical opinion, at least as regards Valerius Maximus, whose *Facta et Dicta Memorabilia* provides much evidence about the lives and images of Roman women, and often stresses the similarities between men and women in the process.

According to the nineteenth-century German historian Niebuhr, "the Middle Ages considered Valerius Maximus the most important book next to the Bible": the ninth-century humanist Lupus of Ferrières made his own copy of the *Facta et Dicta Memorabilia* to expound to his learned pupils; it is liberally quoted by the most learned classical scholar of the twelfth century, John of Salisbury, in his *Art of Statesmanship*. So, too, Valerius Maximus had a strong impact on the writing and thinking of the Renaissance: in the fourteenth century the Italian humanist Petrarch frequently quoted, praised, and imitated him; in the fifteenth century Valerius Maximus was one of the first authors to appear in print after the development of moveable type (Carter 1975: 26, 48–50).

Whatever its origins, the negative assessment of these "Tiberian" authors by late nineteenth-century scholars has persisted. This assessment presumably helps to explain why, an ocean away and half a century later, not one of these writers figures in another "canon"—the list of "Prescribed Reading" for Ph.D. candidates in classics issued by Columbia University in the 1920s (Columbia University Bulletin of Information, Division of Ancient and Oriental Languages and Litera- tures: 11–12). The low regard in which the authors from the reign of Tiberius have been held for over a century likewise results in their failure to command much scholarly attention today. There is not even a translation of Valerius Maximus's *Facta et Dicta Memorabilia* in the extensive collection of texts "Englished" by the Loeb Classical Library, a series "administered for well over half a century by trustees acting for the Department of Classics [sic] of Harvard University," which advertises itself as giving "access to all that is important in Greek and Latin Literature." A recent explanation for this treatment of Valerius Maximus even represents the survival of his works as disrespectful to standards of literary justice: "Valerius never deserved to survive . . . an author whom modern taste rightly finds one of the most tedious and affected products of the ancient world . . . the survival of only one more book of Livy or Petronius would be a far greater treasure" (Carter 1975: 26, 40).

But Cruttwell's "canon" does differ implicitly from our twentieth-century canon and Cruttwell does provide a political rationale for his choices. That is, he does spend some time discussing these Tiberian authors, even though he distinguishes the writers of Tiberius's reign from their Augustan predecessors by remarking that "the history of literature presents no stronger contrast than between the rich fertility of the last epoch and the barrenness of the present one" (Cruttwell 1977: 341). Cruttwell's approach to Valerius Maximus in particular differs from that found in the volume on the early principate in the current *Cambridge History of Classical Literature*. Whereas Cruttwell treats Valerius as a literary figure in his own right, inserting a page about his work and its later reception between similar treatments of Velleius Paterculus and A. Cornelius Celsus (Cruttwell 1877: 346–47), the Cambridge volume merely mentions Valerius in one paragraph of a brief introduction to the literature of this era, and then merely as an extant example of "the digests and encyclopedias produced in the first century" c.e. (Vessey 1982: 5–6). Perhaps more significantly, the appendix of authors and works for this Cambridge volume contains biographical and bibliographical en- tries not only for a number of authors from this period but even for obscure works of unknown authorship—the *Bucolica Einsidlensia, Laus Pisonis,* and *Aetna.* Yet Valerius Maximus is nowhere to be found in this appendix (Drury 1982).

And Cruttwell introduces the authors of Tiberius's reign, along with their successors in the later Julio-Claudian principate, by commenting about the politi- cal environment in which they wrote. Remarking, "with these literary pretensions it is clear that [Tiberius's] discouragement of letters as emperor was due to political reasons" (Cruttwell 1877: 342), he adds that "in reading the lives of the chief post-Augustan writers we are struck by the fact that many, if not most of them, held offices of state" (Cruttwell 1877: 343). Through such statements

Cruttwell intimates that these authors' involvement in the political activities of their own day should alone render them of some interest, albeit as negative role models from a much less intellectually tolerant age, to the audience at which he targeted his Latin literary survey—a readership he describes as including future administrators of the British Empire.

So participation in that Wellesley seminar helped me to recognize the importance of historical and political factors in the construction of literary canons: the circumstances in which a given work was originally composed; and the way these circumstances were perceived—as having contemporary relevance—by those later assessing the work's claims to special status. Similarly, and no less importantly, from taking part in that seminar I better understood how and why feminist historians, led by the late Joan Kelly, have developed a distinctive theoretical approach which challenges not only the traditional periodization of history but also the privileging of certain historical periods as "classical" solely on the basis of evidence about men's lives. In an influential 1977 essay entitled "Did Women Have a Renaissance?" Kelly called into question the traditional periodization of modern European history. Using the Renaissance as her case in point, she observed that from roughly 1350 to 1530 Italy may have been "well in advance of the rest of Europe" because of its political innovations, new economic structures, and transformation of social relations." Nevertheless, although these developments "reorganized Italian society along modern lines, and opened the possibilities for the social and cultural expression" for which this era is celebrated, at the same time they "affected women adversely, so much so that there was no Renaissance for women—at least, not during the Renaissance" (Kelly 1977: 19).

Kelly's thesis of course contradicts the widely held notion of the Renaissance as a period of expanded rights and opportunities for all of its denizens, and for that reason a high point in the history of Western civilization. To argue, moreover, that women in the Renaissance experienced a relative contraction of their rights, opportunities, and social possibilities, she pointed to numerous phenomena of this period: the regulations imposed on female (as opposed to male) sexuality; the restriction of women's access to work, property, political power, and education; the limited cultural roles available to women for molding the views of their society; and the repressive ideology about women, in particular "the sex-role system displayed or advocated in the symbolic products of the society, its art, literature and philosophy" (Kelly 1976: 20–21). Most important, Kelly herself emphasized that her approach to this particular period, situating it in a larger historical context, and examining it from the perspective of a group other than advantaged males, has a more general analytical value: such an approach may be employed in studying other periods as well.

Even at the time that I was enrolled in that Wellesley seminar, feminist research on Greco-Roman antiquity had started to challenge historical orthodoxy in the way that Joan Kelly's writing both exemplified and recommended: by calling attention to evidence about women's lives which undermines the claims to "classical" status of fifth- and fourth-century B.C.E. Athens, and of republican and Augustan Rome. I would now like to examine this challenge—the application of Kelly's theoretical contribution—and some of its ramifications for the traditional historical periodization of Greco-Roman antiquity. It serves as an excellent illustration of how feminist theory in the area of modern history has already affected and has the potential to transform both research and teaching in our scholarly discipline. Furthermore, the efforts of feminist classicists to rethink historical categories and phenomena in Greco-Roman antiquity can and do connect with projects by feminist scholars in other fields.

This decision to emphasize the issue of periodization demands some justification, inasmuch as feminist work in ancient history has profitably utilized other kinds of theory developed by feminist scholars. Over the past fifteen years, various studies of the Greek and Roman family as well as historically focused analyses of Greek and Roman myth and literature have acknowledged their debt to feminist anthropological theory, and especially to several essays published in the ground-breaking 1974 volume edited by Michelle Rosaldo and Louise Lamphere, *Woman, Culture and Society* (see Bamberger, Ortner, Rosaldo, Sacks, and Tanner in Rosaldo and Lamphere 1974; Hallett 1984; Kunstler 1986; Segal 1978; Zeitlin 1978). Recent work on ancient sexuality has drawn heavily on theoretical writings by feminist anthropologists, philosophers, and literary critics (de Lauretis 1984; Kappeler 1986; Modleski 1986; Riley 1988; Rubin 1975; Silverman 1980; Snitow, Stansell, and Thompson 1983; Halperin 1990; Joshel 1992; Richlin 1991a, 1991b, and 1992a). An important essay by the American historian Linda Gordon expresses some concern over the emphasis in recent women's studies scholarship on the notion of difference, observing that the history of modern feminism may be chronologically schematized as an alternation between "an androgynous and a female-uniqueness view of women's subordination and liberation," between a stress on women's similarity to and a stress on women's otherness from men (Gordon 1986). These different standpoints have informed theoretical studies by feminist classicists of women's representation in Greek and Roman sources, and have in turn been identified by feminist classicists as informing different views of women in Greco-Roman antiquity (Hallett 1989 and 1990a and b; Culham 1990a and b).

As feminist scholars working in modern history have influenced the study of Greco-Roman antiquity, so the contributions of feminist scholarship to the field of ancient Greco-Roman history bear relevance to researchers in other academic specializations, and to theorists in particular. The paucity of evidence which remains from Greco-Roman antiquity in general, and the paucity of ancient Greco-Roman evidence which pertains to women in particular, have made it especially necessary for those of us interested in recovering women's lived reality and even women's cultural image in Greece and Rome to engage in interdisciplinary and ingenious research efforts. We feminist classicists must rely on a wide range of ancient sources in addition to literary texts (such as inscriptions, papyri, coins, and vase paintings), and adopt sensitive and imaginative approaches to synthesizing and analyzing these sources (Hallett 1983; Culham 1986 and 1990a; French 1990). In other words, we must deal with materials that feminist historians working in more modern—and better documented—eras have not needed to use, and we must construct arguments on the basis of far less testimony than other feminist historians ordinarily have at their disposal. Feminist colleagues in other disciplines may, therefore, wish to follow our example: by investigating a more extensive variety of sources than has been their practice; by asking different, and difficult, questions of these sources; by formulating different hypotheses about women's lives and representations as a result of posing these questions.

Furthermore, before examining the feminist challenge to traditional historical periodization and its implications for the study of ancient Greece and Rome, I would like to acknowledge the contributions made to the study of Greco-Roman antiquity by feminist scholars formally trained as historians of more modern periods. Gerda Lerner's *The Creation of Patriarchy,* winner of the 1986 Joan Kelly Prize of the American Historical Association, claims priority in this regard, inasmuch as Lerner has here investigated ancient Greek as well as Near Eastern sources in developing a feminist theory to account for the collective dominance of women by men. Phyllis Culham has recently argued that, "if the study of women in antiquity is to contribute substantively to feminist scholarship or women's studies, it will be in the investigation of the origins and propagation of Western culture, and that will require 'direct[ing] discussion toward history, society, culture,' not the single text or author at all." Culham continues by stating, "that is undeniably an intimidating task, and I am embarrassed, as a feminist scholar of antiquity, that it has been mainly left to Gerda Lerner, an Americanist" (Culham 1990a: 165). Antonia Fraser's recent book on warrior queens has likewise performed a valuable function as yet unfilled by a work of classical scholarship. Although addressing a more general audience than Lerner, Fraser has researched in great detail, providing a cross-cultural as well as historical perspective, several women represented by ancient Greek and Latin literary sources as "leading their nations in war"—Penthesilea, Camilla, Semiramis, Tomyris, Artemisia, Cleopatra, Boudica/Boadicea, and Cartimandua. Without claiming to formulate any theory or theories of her own, Fraser also endeavors to contextualize the behavior attributed to these women by citing contemporary feminist thinkers, including Joan Kelly (Fraser 1988: 7).

But as I hope I have managed to establish, classical scholarship has traditionally employed notions of what constitutes a significant historical period to influence assessments of literature and conversely allowed assessments of literature to inform definitions of significant historical periods: its thinking about Greco-Roman history is inseparable from its thinking about Greek and Latin literature, and vice versa. The feminist study of classical antiquity has in particular demanded an understanding of what Louis Montrose has called "the historicity of

texts"—"the cultural specificity, the social embedment of all modes of writing"—
and "the textuality of history"—that without the "surviving textual traces" of any
society "we can have no access to a full and authentic past" and "a lived material
existence" (Montrose 1989: 20). It is for this reason that I assign pride of place
to the feminist theoretical approach which challenges conventional historical
periodization of Greco-Roman antiquity—or at least the privileged status accorded certain periods of Greek and Roman history—by considering these periods
from the perspective of women. It is for this reason as well that my discussion
of this challenge concentrates on the benefits it promises for feminist study of
Greek and Latin literature. My aim in this discussion is to share my own thoughts
about how we might revise criteria traditionally utilized to construct canons of
major Greek and Latin literary works as we go about examining them, in order
to accord attention to the position and representation of women. I will look at
some implications of this theoretically-based and historically-focused challenge
for several specific projects of a literary nature, among them projects which are
discussed elsewhere in this volume.

The large majority of feminist efforts to challenge historical orthodoxy in
regard to the two great "classical" periods of Greco-Roman antiquity have focused
on the Greco- at the expense of the Roman. Such efforts do not, as well they
might, challenge the irritating practice of using—in a frequently encountered
synecdoche—the terms "classical Greek" and even "Greek" to refer only to
Athens of the fifth century B.C.E. (a practice exemplified by Kitto; for a recent
historical survey which admirably distinguishes Athenian from earlier and later
and non-Athenian evidence on women in ancient Greece, see Frost 1987). But
at least such feminist scholarship has, as Joan Kelly exhorts, adopted a "relational"
approach by comparing women in classical Athens with men in classical Athens,
and considered such factors as social class in comparing women in "democratic"
classical Athens with women in earlier, aristocratic, segments of societies in
other parts of ancient Greece (Kelly 1976: 4).

In a pioneering essay exploring the ancient Greek origins of the Western
attitude toward women, Marylin Arthur (Katz) compared women in fifth-century
B.C.E. Athens with the aristocratic circle of Sappho, on the island of Lesbos, in the
late seventh and early sixth centuries B.C.E. Arthur concluded that the existence of
Sappho's circle is "testimony to the high degree of culture and independence in
the life of aristocratic women, and suggests a favorable contrast with the largely
uncultured and home-keeping life of the fifth-century Athenian woman" (Arthur
1973: 42). Two years later, in her book about women in classical antiquity, Sarah
Pomeroy contrasted the lives of Athenian women during this period unfavorably
to the lives of another group—their own menfolk—rather than to those of other
Greek women; she here observed that the daughters, sisters, wives, and mothers
of citizens in fifth-century B.C.E. Athens were denied virtually all of the opportunities in the realm of public activity and intellectual development that defined their
male kin as possessing citizen status (Pomeroy 1975: 74, 79–82).

Kelly does not footnote either of these studies in an essay, published a year after Pomeroy's book, entitled "The Social Relations of the Sexes: Methodological Implications of Women's History." Nevertheless, early in this discussion Kelly herself invokes "classical Athenian civilization" to illustrate how "our notions of so-called progressive development" can "undergo a startling re-evaluation" if we consider "the emancipation of women" as "an index of the general emancipation of an age": for women, she states, " 'progress' in Athens meant concubinage and confinement of citizen wives in the gynecaeum." Later in this same essay, Kelly critiques H. D. Kitto's defense of what he, and she at times, calls "Greek" society as a prelude to reminding her readers that "our understanding of the Greek contribution to social life and consciousness now demands an adequate representation of the life experience of women" (Kitto 1951: 230, 232, 234; Kelly 1976: 3, 7–8). More recently, Helene Foley has contrasted Athenian women of this era with aristocratic women of earlier generations to make a point about different degrees of female political involvement, noting that "while the aristocratic wife of the archaic period could through her husband have some positive effect on the public life of her society and win her own reputation for virtue, the Attic wife lived isolated from politics . . . and hence from most sources of social prestige" (Foley 1988: 1312). Foley's footnotes to Arthur and Pomeroy but not Kelly in this essay—like Kelly's failure to footnote Arthur and Pomeroy—regrettably testify to a growing and needless gap between feminist scholars in classics and in modern history who embrace shared methods and goals.

Feminist studies such as these do unto the so-called golden age of ancient Greece what Kelly has done for the Renaissance. By engaging in historical inquiry that assigns a central role to the relation of the sexes, and to "the vantage point of women as well as men," by considering Greek periods of time and geographical locales other than the fifth century B.C.E. in Athens, and by making social class a category of analysis as well (although even in these instances women slaves attract little, if any, notice), they establish that fifth-century B.C.E. Athens was anything but golden for women of free birth. This conclusion holds special ironies for Athenian women of citizen family, inasmuch as these women were related by blood to males privileged over other men by virtue of their own bloodlines (pace Patterson 1986).

Granted, then, that feminist scholars have begun to instill an awareness that there occurred, in Kelly's words, "a relative loss of status for women" in "classical Athenian civilization." Granted that, by Kelly's reckoning, this decline in status exemplifies a "fairly regular pattern" also evinced in other "periods of so-called progressive change" (Kelly 1976: 2–3). How can we apply this awareness to our understanding and ultimately our evaluation of ancient Greek literary works? How might this awareness enable us to read, and teach others to read, Greek literature in a more informed, insightful, and contextually engaged manner?

Most obviously, this awareness should assist us in furnishing a historical context for those Greek literary works attributed to women authors by changing

the way in which we construct historical contexts, the way in which we concomitantly define and assign importance to periods of Greek civilization. That women
of Athenian citizen family were denied the intellectual opportunities available to
their male relations does much to explain the apparent absence of Athenian
women's voices from the orally-rooted Greek female poetic tradition recently
illuminated by Jane Snyder and Marilyn Skinner. Sappho and the later women
poets whose works comprise what remains of this literary tradition—Praxilla,
Corinna, Erinna, Anyte, Nossis—are alike in having non-Athenian backgrounds,
and pre- and post-fifth- and fourth-century B.C.E. dates. The backgrounds and
dates of our surviving Greek women poets in themselves validate a number of
Greek times and Greek places, other than the "central" and "mainstream" areas,
other than the conventionally classical, as foci for future feminist research. They
direct our attention not only to another much-studied era—the Archaic period of
the seventh and sixth centuries B.C.E.—but also to two eras much less studied—
the Hellenistic period of the third and second centuries B.C.E., and the "Roman"
period of the first century B.C.E. and the first and second centuries C.E. They
motivate us to look further into the cultural and social milieux of mainland cities
and towns such as Corinna's Thebes, Praxilla's Sicyon and Anyte's Tegea; of
islands such as Sappho's Lesbos and Erinna's Telos; of south Italian colonies
such as Nossis's Locri (Skinner 1991).

Significantly, in her volume surveying ancient women writers, Snyder only
once mentions Athens in her chapters dealing with women poets in classical
Greece and Rome. There she specifically cites the "fifth-century Golden Age" as
well as the fourth century of Athens when she discusses references to Sappho by
the historian Herodotus, by several comic playwrights including Menander, and
by the philosopher Aristotle (Snyder 1989: 8). Indeed, several representations of
Sappho in Athenian art and literature during this period—a group of red-figured
vases elsewhere cited by Snyder; Plato's portrayal of Socrates at *Phaedrus* 235c
as calling Sappho "beautiful" when paying tribute to her lyric poetry—lend
credibility to an intriguing suggestion made by Skinner elsewhere in this volume.
To account for the preservation of Sappho's songs within the male-oriented Greek
literary tradition, Skinner proposes that Greek males, among them Athenian
citizens of the fifth and fourth centuries B.C.E., cherished Sappho's poetry as "a
fleeting but permissible escape from the strict constraints of masculinity," an
entertainment at the symposium which may have allowed men momentarily to
"play the other" and thereby "to release themselves from the necessity of being
at all times publicly competitive and self-controlled" (Skinner 1993: 137).

But the Athenian evidence supporting Skinner's suggestion needs to be viewed
alongside testimony for the denigration of Sappho in Athenian comedy dating
from the very same period (summarized by Dover 1978: 174). The varied images
of Sappho in our surviving ancient sources, many of them either from fifth- and
early-to-mid-fourth-century B.C.E. Athens or ultimately deriving from authorities
of that era, encourage feminist scholars to regard this period of Athenian culture

as teeming with conflicts about the construction of gender, and about the function of imaginative literature in sustaining and undermining prescribed gender roles. In other words, when regarded from a perspective focused on the reception and perpetuation of a major Greek poetic tradition, of an ever-popular and female-centered body of literature, this evidence about Sappho permits us to view fifth- and fourth-century B.C.E. Athens as a problematic and discordant Greek subculture rather than as *the* exemplary and classical period.

A similar view of fifth-century B.C.E. Athens as anomalous in relation to Greco-Roman culture emerges when we focus on the representations of women in the myths which provided the plots for Attic tragedy, and when we look at the forms in which these myths are narrated both in other parts of the Greco-Roman world, and before and after this period. Indeed, feminist scholars have already profited from such an approach to the Athenian dramatic reworking of earlier mythic tradition in an important essay by Froma Zeitlin. Her study of how Aeschylus "matriarchalizes" the *Oresteia* myth previously related by Homer, transforming this story into a monumental Athenian cultural legitimation of misogynistic attitudes, suggests the value of further gynocentric, diachronic, and diatopic investigations which consider the relationship between women's representation in variant versions of the same myth both within and outside of Attic tragedy (Zeitlin 1978).

But Zeitlin's later article on travesties of gender and genre in Aristophanes's *Thesmophoriazusae* additionally suggests the value of looking at the depictions of women in Attic tragedy alongside portrayals of women in the other form of contemporary Athenian drama—comedy—to obtain a better sense of what is distinctive and characteristic about Athenian misogyny, and to compare Athenian misogynistic expression with that of earlier and later Greek writers (Zeitlin 1981). Admittedly, a 1981 study by Helene Foley on the conception of women in Athenian drama stresses the distinction to be made between "the treatment of male-female relations in the comic and tragic genres" (Foley 1981b: 162). Nonetheless, a project, like Zeitlin's article, focused on the similarities between the two genres in this regard has immense heuristic potential. The recent essay by Bella Zweig on Aristophanes's pornographic treatment of nude, mute female characters represents a step in this fruitful direction by prompting us to examine the representation of mute, albeit clothed, female characters (such as Euripides's Alcestis) in tragic drama, and to ascertain whether silence on the stage becomes or demeans such characters (Zweig 1992).

More to the point, in demonstrating that classical Athenian culture occupies an anomalous role in the reception and perpetuation of the Greek mythic tradition, and in furnishing new perspectives on Greek misogynistic expression, such investigations raise important questions. So does the project, inspired by Skinner's suggestion, analyzing the complex Athenian response to Sappho and the Greek female poetic tradition. These questions concern the assessment and pedagogical use of the literary works created in Athens of the fifth century B.C.E.—

a period which, by virtue of its extensive material and cultural legacy, will continue to command the serious attention of scholars and students alike—and their connections with works produced in prior and subsequent periods of Greek history. In so doing, they also concern the past, present, and prospective construction of the Greek literary canon.

Might, for example, those entrusted with selecting representative Athenian dramas for undergraduate and graduate courses and reading lists, for nonclassicists as well as classicists, in future adopt a practice long current in the study of women in classical antiquity and choose tragedies, such as Aeschylus's *Oresteia* or Sophocles's *Oedipus Rex* or Euripides's *Trojan Women,* which can be studied alongside earlier and later literary treatments of the same myths? or choose tragedies and comedies which can be studied alongside each other and in conjunction with earlier and later literary expressions of misogyny? In selecting these prior and subsequent literary treatments, might we make a special effort to include not only the earlier, already canonical texts of Homer and Hesiod but also less celebrated figures from the archaic age such as Semonides and Archilochus and pertinent writings from later Hellenistic and Roman poets, philosophers, historiographers, and geographers?

A multitextual approach to the literary use of myth can, after all, elucidate how the Athenian tragedians, and their Hellenistic and Roman successors, have transformed this material, especially as regards the representation of female characters, for ideological purposes. By so doing, such study helps to reveal the limitations as well as the strengths of *all* relevant literary works that serve as links in the Greek mythographic tradition. A multitextual approach to Greek misogynistic expression would by definition address, and aid in refuting, Mary Lefkowitz's controversial claim that "Greek men" were not misogynists but "pioneers in recognizing and describing with sympathy both the life and central importance to their society of women" (Lefkowitz 1986: 39).

Like the literary remains of our surviving Greek female poets, whose non–fifth-century dates and non-Athenian provenances have already been noted, Greek texts from regions besides Athens, and from periods besides the fifth and fourth centuries B.C.E., provide much of our extant evidence about women's lives and images. Accordingly, they deserve more attention, too—in reading lists for doctoral candidates in classical languages and literatures, and in syllabi of undergraduate, in-translation surveys of Western literary masterpieces. They merit greater prominence primarily as significant works in their own right, and as informed by notions of gender that differ from those expressed by fifth-century B.C.E. Athenian texts (Gutzwiller and Michelini 1991). But at times they may illuminate the representation of women in the culture of fifth-century B.C.E. Athens as well. They may even help explain why Athenian society, awarded pride of place in scholarly inquiry and university curricula, has not bequeathed us any testimony from women themselves. How might we try to integrate texts of this kind?

What survives of Sappho's poetry has come to figure increasingly on lists of both sorts, proof of what has been and can be accomplished by feminist efforts to rethink the construction of the Greek literary canon. All the same, might we make more of an effort to contextualize Sappho's distinctive literary contribution, and to document the female poetic tradition it inspired, by including the even more fragmentary remains of Corinna, Praxilla, Erinna, Nossis, and Anyte in survey courses and reading lists as well? or by including Hellenistic literary papyri and discussions by later Greek and Roman authors that bear witness to both the literary milieu and the ancient literary reception of these later women poets? Findings by Sarah Pomeroy and Susan Cole on women's activities and education in the Hellenistic and Roman periods have considerable relevance for projects of this sort (Pomeroy 1984; Cole 1981). As Kathryn Gutzwiller and Ann Michelini have observed, "The groundwork has been laid for a feminist challenge to the traditional devaluation of Hellenistic literature by recent historical studies that point to increased literacy and power for women in the period following the death of Alexander" (Gutzwiller and Michelini 1991: 73). The work of the late Jack Winkler, among others, has likewise affirmed the value of numerous and diverse Greek and Latin literary texts from the second century C.E. and thereafter as evidence for attitudes about female behavior, particularly sexual behavior (Winkler 1990). These scholars remind us as well that testimony from outside of Greece and Italy—especially from Egypt and other parts of Africa and the Near East—needs to be scrutinized no less than does fifth-century B.C.E. Athenian evidence in any investigation of women's lives in any era of Greco-Roman antiquity.

Lastly, might we also perhaps "re-canonize" a portion of Plutarch, to my mind our most important secondary source on the lives of ancient Greco-Roman women from various periods and locales, an author who enjoyed wide popularity and immense literary influence in Renaissance England? Although Plutarch inhabited the Roman imperial milieu of the late first and early second centuries C.E., he wrote about both Greeks and Romans, in Greek. His *Life of Pericles,* for example, is of particular importance for shedding light on the literary representations of women in fifth-century B.C.E. Athens, inasmuch as its portrayal of Pericles's mistress Aspasia points up that society's negative views toward women of intellect, talent, and political influence (Henry 1990).

But let us turn now to Roman history and Latin literature. As we have observed, scholars unanimously situate the "classical period" of ancient Greece in fifth- (and often early-to-mid-fourth-) century B.C.E. Athens, and identify it as a highly esteemed "golden age" of culture, and particularly of art and literature. But the geographical locale and the chronological limits of "classical Rome" lack clearly agreed-upon boundaries. "Rome" is implicitly defined by some as merely the city of seven hills on the Tiber whose residents spoke the Latin language. Others, however, recognize that by 146 B.C.E. "Rome" includes Sicily, Greece, Asia Minor, and North Africa, and by 14 C.E. Germany, Britain, France, and most of the Near and Mid-East (a vast geographical expanse whose western, but not eastern, part officially adopted Latin). It is this expanded, inclusively defined Rome which provides us with our most recent Latin text written by a woman, a letter dated to approximately 100 C.E. discovered at the British fort of Vindolanda (Bowman and Thomas 1987). As we have seen, Latinists employ the terms "golden" and "silver" age specifically to refer to eras of literary production, and cannot even agree among themselves when this literary golden age starts and finishes. Scholars such as myself who use the "c" word to describe a period of ancient Roman history generally apply it to a span of time that begins before and ends after any of the dates thought to open and to conclude Rome's "golden age."

These inconsistencies occasion a number of queries which demand responses, even if these responses only assume the form of further queries. For the very process of responding to these queries reveals the extent to which present-day political preoccupations permeate scholarly judgments about Latin literature and Roman history. Why, for example, have scholars in recent years increasingly confined the golden age of Latin literature to the political heyday of Augustus, thereby excluding the late republican era, the so-called age of Cicero (Scullard 1969: 930; Vessey 1982: 1–2)? Might the years of Cicero's public prominence—a period dominated by an ancient Roman statesman who is renowned for eloquence in the defense of political liberty—have dimmed in perceived significance after two oratorically gifted leaders in English and American politics, Winston Churchill and John F. Kennedy, passed from the scene in the early 1960s? Some (though not all) authorities claim that the golden age of Latin literature ended at a crucial political moment in the early principate, when the despotic Tiberius succeeded the relatively benevolent Augustus. How do they then reconcile this claim with the content of the poems which Ovid wrote to Augustus from political exile, proof that Augustus himself could repeatedly turn a deaf ear to pleas for clemency? And if literary works from the Roman republic *are* to be judged as products of the golden age, why are they restricted to works of the late republic, thereby excluding the numerous and extremely popular comedies written by Plautus and Terence in the late third and early-to-mid-second centuries B.C.E.?

Furthermore, the privileging of the Roman republic, whether or not one awards golden stature to its literary contributions, is not merely a hobbyhorse of scholars from the Victorian age through the Eisenhower era. Rather, it dates back to the Romans of the later "classical" period themselves. It is closely connected to the ancient Romans' use of political criteria in their assessment of earlier Greek and Latin literature, especially to their view that certain kinds of literary expression had deteriorated in quality owing to the loss of political liberty. The practice of idealizing the Roman republic and its cultural contributions boasts not only an ancient historical pedigree but also a prestigious modern rationale (Habinek 1992). Plentiful and well-known ancient evidence testifies to appalling abuses of power by several of the emperors who succeeded Augustus. As a result, specialists in Roman studies—like Scullard in the *OCD* article quoted earlier—are conditioned by their very training to valorize the republican and republicanizing Augustan periods. Notwithstanding Syme's monumental efforts to expose the darker side of the latter, they habitually accentuate the positive and de-emphasize the negative aspects of both (Syme 1939).

Thus it is difficult to identify feminist efforts to challenge the superior status of the Roman "classical" period, and thereby to raise questions about how scholars conventionally assess certain periods and outcomes of Latin literary production—far more so than to cite the counterparts of such efforts in Hellenic studies. There exists no obvious consensus about precisely which span of Roman time most risks the loss of its reputation as a "progressive" era by a demonstration that women's options and opportunities in that period were far more limited than those available to men of the same family background. Since the entire field of Roman literary and historical studies sorely needs a clearer self-definition, and hence a stronger intellectual identity, its practitioners have undertaken few revisionist projects of any sort (Habinek 1992).

Just as crucially for our purposes, there is much less evidence surviving from Roman women writers than survives from their Greek counterparts. Our more extensive body of testimony on women's contributions to Greek literature, coming as it does from times and places other than fifth-century B.C.E. Athens, encourages feminist scholars to challenge the primacy accorded to the fifth century B.C.E. and to Athenian culture. By way of contrast, our comparable evidence from Roman women writers, six elegies composed by the Augustan poet Sulpicia, has just the opposite effect, since Sulpicia comes from the heart of the Roman social and literary elite, and from the most esteemed era of Roman history. It is meager evidence to be sure, but it does provide us with a woman's voice from "classical Rome," whereas we can claim no such testimony from classical Athens.

Nonetheless, I would maintain that feminist scholarship has issued challenges to the customary, if confusing, subdivisions of Roman historical time, even if they are relatively indirect as scholarly challenges go. A contrast between two books dealing with Roman law supports this claim. The first, written before the resurgence of feminist scholarship, contains much material and discussion on Roman women but focuses widely on "the law and life" of Rome. In the introduction, its author, John Crook, states his intention to examine a period of Roman history extending from 81 B.C.E. to 224 C.E., "from Cicero to Ulpian." Observing that "this stage of Roman law and society . . . corresponds neither to the 'classical' period of Latin literature, which runs roughly from Cicero to Tacitus, nor to the 'classical' period of Roman law, which runs roughly from Augustus to Ulpian," Cook offers an apology for this unorthodox choice: even though the legal institutions of Cicero's age were "significantly different from those of the 'classical' period of law . . . and not to be casually extrapolated from what we know about the 'classical' period," "the evidence of Cicero is too valuable to sacrifice" (Crook 1967: 8–9).

Nineteen years later, however, in the preface to a book which deals solely with the legal position of Roman women, Jane Gardner simply defines—and defines without apology—"the period under consideration" as "roughly the last two centuries B.C. and the first three of our era, that is, the great classical period of Roman law" (Gardner 1986: 3). Not only does Gardner evidently regard an exclusive focus on Roman evidence about legal practices affecting women as necessitating that she examine a longer period of Roman time than what Crook would term the "classical" period of Roman law, she also labels this extended historical purview "the great classical period." Significantly, Gardner concludes her book by providing a negative answer to the question of whether Roman women achieved "a notably high degree of economic and social independence and self-determination . . . during the classical period through any deliberate, traceable process" (Gardner 1986: 257, 263–64). By her calculations, then, women's autonomy and opportunities did not systematically increase during *the* classical period, *her* classical period, of Roman law.

These feminist challenges include several observations of my own about the perceptions of women voiced by elite Roman male authors. I have, for example, maintained that under Augustus's principate, and during the reigns of his successors, more importance was accorded to familial relationships to and through women than had been the case in the republic (Hallett 1984: 304ff.). Along with and presumably as a result of assigning a higher valuation to such ties, several male sources—among them the younger Seneca, the younger Pliny, Tacitus, and, yes, Valerius Maximus—represent individual elite women of the Augustan and early imperial eras as what I have referred to as "same," as in many respects similar and equal to individual men in their families and social circles. While scholars have rightly argued that these authors attribute to such women "difference" of a monstrous and stereotypical sort, it warrants emphasis that this attribution of difference can coexist with a recognition of "sameness" and even of equality (Hallett 1989).

I have contended, too, that Roman authors who pave the way for this later perception of male and female similarity by stressing resemblances between elite women and their male blood relations, even authors who lived during and admired the republican period such as Cicero, Cornelius Nepos, and Livy, are reflecting an earlier aristocratic emphasis on bloodline which transcends gender difference. By way of contrast, I would connect literary efforts to stress gender differences and to emphasize women's role as subservient wives with the ideology of male plebeians and "political newcomers" (*novi homines*) who struggled to obtain greater political representation and social equality in Rome of the mid-republic; the American feminist historian Carroll Smith-Rosenberg has elaborated a parallel to this phenomenon in the emerging democracy of the United States during the early nineteenth century (Hallett 1990b; Culham 1990b).

Yet I initially posed my own challenge to conventional scholarly assessments of Roman historical periods, and of the literature produced in and canonized from these periods, through a project which argued that a group of Latin literary texts—those constituting the late republican and Augustan genre of love elegy—themselves pose a challenge to elite Roman ideological notions about women. I singled out the early Augustan poet Propertius as most obviously taking issue with the prescriptions for acceptable female behavior among the elite of his day through the characterization of his beloved Cynthia and other women—particularly the noble matron Cornelia in 4.11 (Propertius *Elegies*). Somewhat more controversially, I there contended that, within its Augustan Roman cultural context, Propertius's critique of conventional Roman notions about women contains feminist elements (Hallett 1973 and 1974).

To my arguments there I would add the observation that Propertius assigns more attention and attributes more dynamic, independent, and vocal activity to the female characters he portrays (and depicts as contemporary Roman women) than do comparable literary efforts of the Augustan period: Propertius's depiction of Arethusa, Acanthis, and Cornelia in Book 4—as well as his beloved Cynthia—stands in particularly sharp contrast to Horace's representation of women as shadowy, voiceless presences. Propertius's portrayals of these women merit comparison as well to Ovid's frequent and arguably pornographic representations of women as victims of rape in the *Ars Amatoria, Metamorphoses,* and *Fasti,* the topic of a ground-breaking discussion by Amy Richlin (1992b). I should emphasize, however, that in interpreting Propertius's representation of women as feminist within its Augustan cultural context, I distinguish this Roman manifestation of feminism from the late twentieth-century variety, recognizing—as does Linda Gordon—that definitions of feminism are historically relative, changing from time to time, from culture to culture, and from social segment to social segment within the same culture and period.

My own historicist approach to the representation of women and feminism in Latin elegy is, I realize, at variance with that adopted by Barbara Gold elsewhere in this volume. She compellingly contends—much as scholars such as Paul Veyne and Maria Wyke have also maintained of late—that Propertius constructs and defines Cynthia only in relation to his literary representation of the male poet, a.k.a. himself (Gold 1993; Veyne 1983; Wyke 1987a, 1987b, and 1989). But I would emphasize that in his elegies Propertius constructs other women besides Cynthia, female characters meant to be viewed in connection with both Cynthia and one another. These "inscribed women," their relationship to Cynthia, and the relative verisimilitude of their respective characterizations also need to be taken into account when approaching the depiction of Cynthia from contemporary French feminist theoretical perspectives, and when analyzing Propertius's Cynthia as a *varium et mutabile* poetic projection rather than a realistic representation of a contemporary woman. What is more, in extolling, *inter alia,* Cynthia's literary activities and judgment, Propertius does endow Cynthia with traits and qualities which he also assigns to and values in himself, with what I have called "sameness" (Hallett 1989).

Regardless of what position one takes in this debate about the realism of

Propertius's Cynthia, and thus the extent to which Propertius's poetry challenges ideological assumptions about women that prevail in his elite cultural milieu, the very existence of this debate underlines the current importance of Latin elegy as a source on male attitudes about women. So does a separate debate about the worth of feminist scholarship devoted to the works of another elegiac poet, Ovid, a debate now recorded for scholarly posterity in a recent issue of the journal *Helios* (Culham 1990a; French 1990; Gamel 1990; Hallett 1990a). By maintaining that the Latin elegists manipulate the conventions of Hellenistic Greek poetry, which presents a "feminine value system," to reassert male dominance, Gutzwiller and Michelini have raised additional questions about the Greek literary background of gender representations in Roman elegy (Gutzwiller and Michelini 1991). These discussions hence point to the potential value of Latin elegy as both a topic of future feminist scholarly inquiry and a focal point for efforts to revise Latin literary studies and their historical framework.

Now Latin elegy flourished during the so-called Roman classical period and the so-called golden age of Latin literature. Over the past thirty years it has come to occupy a central role in the graduate Latin literary curriculum, and to gain more visibility in undergraduate literature courses, be they in the original language or in translation. The need for feminist research to pay serious heed to Latin elegy is obvious from the mere fact that our sole surviving female voice from Roman antiquity, Sulpicia, composed in this very genre. One might, therefore, argue that increased attention to Latin elegy fails to qualify as an innovative element with the potential to alter the way that Roman literature is assessed, and Roman civilization is viewed.

But I judge it significant that the Augustan elegists have never been ranked with Vergil, Horace, and Livy in authoritative critical discussions. Not even the phenomenally popular Ovid is customarily credited with composing literary efforts that helped to radiate the golden glow of eternal excellence and hence conferred classical status on the period in which he lived (Hallett 1990a). The enhanced status of the elegiac poets ranks as a relatively new as well as an exciting development in Latin literary criticism. Debates over the ideological message of Latin elegy and its suitability for feminist research bode well for transformation of Latin literary studies by directing us to new and more contextually grounded ways of studying the depiction of women in the extensive and varied Latin literature of the esteemed Augustan period. And this different mode of approach to Augustan literature in turn leads to some questions about defining Roman historical periods and about assessing Latin literary works of all periods as we rethink the Latin literary canon.

Let me be specific. By looking at Propertius's poems alongside contemporary literary evidence such as poems by Horace and Ovid's tales of rape—the very evidence that I would marshal in interpreting his elegies as realistic representations of women with a feminist message—we can see how Propertius both resembles and differs from other Roman poets of the Augustan era. While Horace and Ovid, too, were valued for first-person, realistic, and seemingly autobiographical verse, Horace marginalizes rather than idealizes female erotic partners; while both Propertius and Ovid compose poems with mythic and early Roman settings, Ovid seems to relish delineating sexual violence against women more than poetic inspiration by them. But how are we to explain these similarities and differences? Do they allow us to value Propertius's work more highly than we do that of Horace or Ovid? In defense of Ovid's ultimate literary worth, might we also contrast Ovid's fondness for detailing physical violence against fictitious women with the affectionate and respectful elegies which he wrote to actual women— his wife and his poetic protégée Perilla—from exile at the end of his life? And how are we to reconcile these two aspects of Ovid's treatment of women?

More important, re-evaluation of Augustan poetry from the perspective of its ideological messages about women allows us to view, and to value, both earlier and later Latin literature altogether differently from the way in which it is conventionally regarded and assessed. By thinking of Propertius's Augustan setting not as a "golden age," the culmination of the classical period, but rather as part of an evolving Roman cultural context, we can view his representation of Cynthia and other women in terms of an evolving literary discourse, one in which women are increasingly endowed with sameness as well as difference. Such an approach allows us, for example, to connect Propertius's representation of various women from different social backgrounds with fictitious female characters of the same types in earlier, and extremely popular, Plautine comedy. While Plautus's dramatic characters resemble such Propertian poetic creations as Cynthia, Cornelia, and the procuress Acanthis in their speech and attitudes, they are represented as Greek women, were actually played on the stage by male actors, and for those reasons embodied a sameness that was rendered more comprehensible and arguably less threatening to a Roman male audience. Might we better understand this relationship between Plautine and Propertian constructions of women by adopting a new literary approach that crosses literary genres, reading elegiac texts as part of the Roman dramatic literary tradition, and even as scripts for dramatic performance? by adopting a new historicist approach that compares chronological eras, stressing points of commonality between the periods of postwar prosperity, over a century and a half apart, in which both the lowly born Plautus and the more loftily stationed Propertius attained literary prominence (*pace* Luck 1969, who stresses points of difference)?

Even more significant, if we make an effort to see Augustan elegy not as a genre which dies out when Augustus does, but as closely linked with other literary genres of other historical periods, we can see important continuities between the Augustan period and the century that follows. Such an emphasis not only challenges the authority accorded to separate periods owing to what literary theorists have called "chronologically naturalizing" compartmentalization (Robbins 1992: 40; Graff 1987), it also stands in stark contrast to the conventional assumption that the culture and literature of this subsequent era represent a "silver" age, characterized by differences of a totally negative kind—deterioration and decline. What is more, such an emphasis clearly necessitates that we expand our Latin literary canon by devoting greater attention to sources from the post-Augustan period who document the increasing representation of women as the same—first and foremost Valerius Maximus, then the younger Seneca, Statius, the younger Pliny, Tacitus, and (again) Plutarch, along with writers of the later Christian period (fourth to fifth centuries C.E.). If, however, the *Facta et Dicta Memorabilia* are to be studied as a text, how are we to teach a digest, a handbook, as a work of literature in our classrooms? Can we formulate criteria for assessing and appreciating such texts as a distinct genre of literature which happens to instruct in brief, thematically organized, prose paragraphs? Can we apply these criteria to promote wider acquaintance with other Latin prose works which similarly collect material on a variety of topics, rich in references to women's lives—the *Attic Nights* of Aulus Gellius, written in the second century C.E.; the *Saturnalia* of Macrobius, written in the late fourth or early fifth?

As a result of writing this essay I have resolved to make my fellow participants in Peggy McIntosh's Wellesley seminar more aware of the efforts by feminist classicists to challenge historical orthodoxy and rethink our literary canons. Several of them went on to launch and take the helm at *The Women's Review of Books,* and are ideally positioned to raise awareness of our efforts within the larger feminist scholarly community. But even my present colleagues who do feminist work in other disciplines—at the University of Maryland at College Park, an institution with a large, vibrant, and nationally recognized women's studies program—have little idea of the great distance that feminist classicists have voyaged over the past two decades in freeing their crafts from the moorings of traditional classical scholarship. Indeed, I have the impression that many feminist scholars in other disciplines cannot fathom my love of what must seem to them a reactionary, elitist, and unlovable field, and that they regard the term "feminist classicist" as the ultimate oxymoron.

I am often asked, when I identify myself as a "classicist," about the etymology of the terms "classical" and "classic." In response, I note to those who pose the question that the Latin word *classis* means, among other things, a fleet of ships. I am thereby reminded that "classics" is a "c" word in more ways than one, that Peggy McIntosh's association between the "c" words and *Moby Dick* is multiply appropriate.

When feminist scholars who share Peggy McIntosh's feelings about the problematic "c" words then ask how I can call myself both a feminist and a classicist, I am tempted to observe facetiously that I "follow the fleet" in much the way that Ginger Rogers did in the film by that name: with difficulty, "facing the music and dancing," with the same fancy footwork performed by Fred Astaire, only backwards and in high heels (Allen 1991). Yet in such exchanges I suppose I might do better to invoke, in serious tones, the poetry of Sappho. Although acknowledging in fragment 16 Lobel-Page that some judge a fleet of ships the most beautiful thing on earth, she asserts that the most beautiful thing on earth is what one loves. By challenging the "c" words and revising our literary canons accordingly, by continuing to follow the exhortations of scholars like Joan Kelly as well as our fleet, by communicating the results of this challenge to feminist scholars in other fields, we feminist classicists may even make the ancient Greco-Roman world more lovable.

I owe special thanks to Amy Richlin for her efforts beyond the call of duty in generating, nurturing and editing this essay. I am also indebted to Barbara Gold, Erich Gruen, Thomas Habinek, Peggy McIntosh, and Nancy Sorkin Rabinowitz for their helpful comments and criticisms on earlier versions.

Bibliography

Africa, Thomas W. 1974. *The Immense Majesty: A History of Rome and the Roman Empire*. Arlington Heights, Illinois: A. H. M. Publishing.

Allen, Henry. 1991. "Ginger, after the Ball." *The Washington Post*, October 24, 1991: C1 and C13.

Arthur, Marylin (Katz). 1973. "Early Greece: The Origins of the Western Attitude toward Women." *Arethusa* 6.1. Reprinted in Peradotto and Sullivan, *Women in the Ancient World: The Arethusa Papers*, 7–58.

Bamberger, Joan. 1974. "The Myth of Matriarchy: Why Men Rule in Primitive Society." In Rosaldo and Lamphere, *Women, Culture and Society*, 263–80.

Baym, Nina. 1985. "Melodramas of Beset Masculinity: How Histories of American Fiction Exclude Women Authors." In Showalter, *The New Feminist Criticism: Essays on Women, Literature and Theory*, 63–80.

Bowman, Alan K., and J. David Thomas. 1987. "New Texts from Vindolanda." *Britannia* 18: 125–42.

Browning, Robert. 1969. "Literature, Latin." In Hammond and Scullard, *The Oxford Classical Dictionary*, 612–613.

Carter, C. J. 1975. "Valerius Maximus." In T. A. Dorey, ed., *Empire and Aftermath: Silver Latin* vol. 2, 25–56. London and Boston: Routledge and Kegan Paul.

Cole, Susan G. 1981. "Could Greek Women Read and Write?" In Foley, *Reflections of Women in Antiquity*, 219–46.

Columbia University Bulletin of Information, Division of Ancient and Oriental Languages and Literatures. Announcement 1925–1926, 25.2. New York: Columbia University.

Crook, John A. 1967. *Law and Life of Rome*. Ithaca, N.Y.: Cornell University Press.

Cruttwell, Charles Thomas. 1877. *A History of Roman Literature from the Earliest Period to the Death of Marcus Aurelius*. London: Charles Griffin and Company.

Culham, Phyllis. 1986. "Ten Years after Pomeroy: Studies of the Image and Reality of

Women in Antiquity." In Skinner, *Rescuing Creusa: New Methodological Approaches to Women in Antiquity,* 9–30.

———. 1990a. "Decentering the Text: The Case of Ovid." *Helios* 17.2: 161–70.

———. 1990b. "The Ideology of Gender and Status in the Principate." Paper presented at Rutgers University Conference on Roman Women, December 7.

de Lauretis, Teresa. 1984. *Alice Doesn't: Feminism, Semiotics, Cinema.* Bloomington: Indiana University Press.

———, ed. 1986. *Feminist Studies/Critical Studies.* Bloomington: Indiana University Press.

Dover, Kenneth J. 1978. *Greek Homosexuality.* Cambridge, Mass.: Harvard University Press.

Drury, Martin. 1982. "Appendix of Authors and Works." In *The Cambridge History of Classical Literature.* Vol. 2, part 4: *The Early Principate,* 185–223. Cambridge, Eng.: Cambridge University Press, 1982.

Duff, J. Wight. 1909. *Literary History of Rome from the Origins to the Close of the Golden Age.* London: E. Benn.

———. 1930. *Literary History of Rome in the Silver Age, from Tiberius to Hadrian.* London: E. Benn.

Eagleton, Terry. 1983. *Literary Theory: An Introduction.* Minneapolis: University of Minnesota Press.

Eliot, T. S. 1944. *What Is a Classic? Address Delivered before the Vergil Society on the 16th of October 1944.* London: Faber and Faber.

Foucault, Michel. 1986. *The Care of the Self.* Vol. 3 of *The History of Sexuality.* Translated by Robert Hurley. New York: Random House.

Foley, Helene, ed. 1981a. *Reflections of Women in Antiquity.* New York: Gordon and Breach Science Publishers.

———. 1981b. "The Conception of Women in Athenian Drama." In Foley, *Reflections of Women in Antiquity,* 127–68.

———. 1988. "Women in Greece." In Michael Grant and Rachel Kitzinger, eds., *Civilization of the Ancient Mediterranean: Greece and Rome.* Vol. 3, 1301–17. New York: Charles Scribner's Sons, 1988.

Fraser, Antonia. 1988. *The Warrior Queens.* New York: Random House.

French, Valerie. 1990. "What Is Central for the Study of Women in Antiquity?" *Helios* 17.2: 213–19.

Frost, Frank. 1987. *Greek Society.* Third edition, Lexington, Mass.: D.C. Heath and Co.

Gamel, Mary-Kay. 1990. "Reading 'Reality'." *Helios* 17.2: 171–74.

Gardner, Jane F. 1986. *Women in Roman Law and Society.* Bloomington: Indiana University Press.

Gold, Barbara K. 1993. " 'But Ariadne Was Never There in the First Place': Finding the Female in Roman Poetry." Published elsewhere in this volume.

Gordon, Linda. 1986. "What's New in Women's History?" In de Lauretis, *Feminist Studies/Critical Studies*, 20–30.

Graff, Gerald. 1987. *Professing Literature*. Chicago: University of Chicago Press.

Gutzwiller, Kathryn J., and Ann Norris Michelini. 1991. "Women and Other Strangers: Feminist Perspectives in Classical Literature." In Joan E. Hartman and Ellen Messer-Davidow, eds., *(En)Gendering Knowledge*, 66–84. Knoxville: University of Tennessee Press.

Habinek, Thomas N. 1992. "Grecian Wonders and Roman Woe: The Romantic Rejection of Rome and Its Consequences for the Study of Latin Literature." In G. Karl Galinsky, ed., *The Interpretation of Roman Poetry: Empiricism or Hermeneutics?* 227–42. *Studien zur Klassischen Philologie* 67. Frankfurt, Berlin, New York, Paris: Peter Lang Publishers.

Haley, Shelley P. 1989. "Classics and Minorities." In Phyllis Culham and Lowell Edmunds, eds., *Classics: A Discipline and Profession in Crisis?* 333–38. Lanham, Md.: University Press of America.

Hallett, Judith P. 1973. "The Role of Women in Roman Elegy: Counter-Cultural Feminism." *Arethusa* 6.1. Reprinted in Peradotto and Sullivan, *Women in the Ancient World: The Arethusa Papers*, 241–62.

———. 1974. "Women in Roman Elegy: A Reply." "Forum," *Arethusa* 7.2: 211–17.

———. 1983. "Classics and Women's Studies." Working Paper No. 119, Wellesley College Center for Research on Women.

———. 1984. *Fathers and Daughters in Roman Society: Women and the Elite Family*. Princeton: Princeton University Press.

———. 1989. "Women as 'Same' and 'Other' in the Classical Roman Elite." *Helios* 16.1: 59–78.

———. 1990a. "Contextualizing the Text: The Journey to Ovid." *Helios* 17.2: 187–96.

———. 1990b. "Patrician and Plebeian: Ideological Constructions of Women in the Later Roman Republic." Paper presented at the Rutgers University Conference on Roman Women.

Halperin, David. 1990. *One Hundred Years of Homosexuality*. New York: Routledge.

Hammond, N. G. L., and H. H. Scullard, eds. 1969. *The Oxford Classical Dictionary*. Second edition. Oxford: Oxford University Press.

Harvard University Press. "The Loeb Classical Library" 1989–1990. Cambridge, Mass. and London.

Henry, Madeleine. 1990. "Aspasia of Miletus and Her Biographical Tradition." Paper presented at the Berkshire Conference of Women Historians, June 8.

Joshel, Sandra. 1992. "The Body Female and the Body Politic: Livy's Lucretia and Verginia." In Richlin, *Pornography and Representation in Greece and Rome*, 112–30.

Kappeler, Suzanne. 1986. *The Pornography of Representation*. Minneapolis: University of Minnesota Press.

Kelly, Joan. 1976. "The Social Relations of the Sexes: Methodological Implications of Women's History." *Signs: Journal of Women in Culture and Society* 1.4: 809–23.

Reprinted in and cited from *Women, History and Theory: The Essays of Joan Kelly*. Chicago: University of Chicago Press, 1984, 1–18.

Kelly (Kelly-Gadol), Joan. 1977. "Did Women Have a Renaissance?" In Renate Bridenthal and Claudia Koonz, eds., *Becoming Visible: Women in European History*, 137–64. Boston: Houghton Mifflin Company. Reprinted in and cited from *Women, History and Theory: The Essays of Joan Kelly*, 19–50. Chicago: University of Chicago Press, 1984.

Kitto, H. D. F. 1951. *The Greeks*. Harmondsworth: Penguin Books, Ltd.

Kunstler, Barton. 1986. "Family Dynamics and Female Power in Ancient Sparta." In Skinner, *Rescuing Creusa: New Methodological Approaches to Women in Antiquity*, 31–48.

Lauter, Paul. 1983. "Race and Gender in the Shaping of the American Literary Canon: A Case Study from the Twenties." *Feminist Studies* 9.3: 435–563.

Lefkowitz, Mary. 1986. *Women in Greek Myth*. Baltimore: Johns Hopkins University Press.

Lerner, Gerda. 1986. *The Creation of Patriarchy*. New York and Oxford: Oxford University Press.

Luck, Georg. 1969. *The Latin Love Elegy*. Second edition. London: Methuen.

Modleski, Tania. 1986. *The Women Who Knew Too Much*. New York: Routledge.

Montrose, Louis A. 1989. "Professing the Renaissance: The Poetics and Politics of Culture." In H. Aram Veeser, ed., *The New Historicism*, 15–36. New York: Routledge.

Ortner, Sherry. 1974. "Is Female to Male as Nature Is to Culture?" In Rosaldo and Lamphere, *Woman, Culture and Society*, 67–88.

Patterson, Cynthia. 1986. "*Hai Attikai:* The Other Athenians." In Skinner, *Rescuing Creusa: New Methodological Approaches to Women in Antiquity*, 49–68.

Peradotto, John, and Sullivan, J. P., eds. 1984. *Women in the Ancient World: The Arethusa Papers*. Albany: State University of New York Press.

Pomeroy, Sarah B. 1975. *Goddesses, Whores, Wives and Slaves: Women in Classical Antiquity*. New York: Schocken Press.

—————. 1984. *Women in Hellenistic Egypt: From Alexander to Cleopatra*. New York: Schocken Press.

Richlin, Amy. 1991a. "Not Before Homosexuality: The Materiality of the *Cinaedus* and the Roman Law against Love between Men." Paper presented at the American Philological Association Meeting, December 29.

—————. 1991b. "Zeus and Metis: Foucault, Feminism, Classics." *Helios* 18.2 160–80.

—————, ed. 1992a. *Pornography and Representation in Greece and Rome*. New York: Oxford University Press.

—————. 1992b. "Reading Ovid's Rapes." In Richlin, *Pornography and Representation in Greece and Rome*, 158–79.

Riley, Denise. 1988. *"Am I That Name?": Feminism and the Category of "Women" in History*. Minneapolis: University of Minnesota Press.

Robbins, Bruce. 1992. "Death and Vocation: Narrativizing Narrative Theory." *Publications of the Modern Language Association of America* 107.1: 38–50.

Robinson, Lillian. 1983. "Treason Our Text: Feminist Challenges to the Literary Canon." *Tulsa Studies in Women's Literature* 2.1. Reprinted in Showalter, *The New Feminist Criticism: Essays on Women, Literature and Theory*, 105–22.

———. 1985. "Their Canon, Our Arsenal." Working Paper No. 21, Stanford Center for Research on Women.

———. 1986. "*The Norton Anthology of Literature by Women:* Is There Class in this Text?" *Tulsa Studies in Women's Literature* 5.2: 289–302.

Rosaldo, Michelle. 1974. "Woman, Culture and Society: A Theoretical Overview." In Rosaldo and Lamphere, *Woman, Culture and Society*, 18–42.

Rosaldo, Michelle, and Louise Lamphere, eds. 1974. *Woman, Culture and Society*. Stanford: Stanford University Press.

Rubin, Gayle. 1975. "The Traffic in Women: Notes on the 'Political Economy' of Sex." In Rayna Rapp Reiter, ed., *Toward an Anthropology of Women*, 157–210. New York: Monthly Review Press.

Sacks, Karen. 1974. "Engels Revisited: Women, the Organization of Production, and Private Property." In Rosaldo and Lamphere, *Woman, Culture and Society*, 207–22.

Scullard, Howard Hayes. 1969. "Rome." In Hammond and Scullard, eds., *The Oxford Classical Dictionary:* 925–35.

Segal, Charles P. 1978. "The Menace of Dionysus: Sex Roles and Reversals in Euripides' *Bacchae*." *Arethusa* 11.1, 2. Reprinted in Peradotto and Sullivan, *Women in the Ancient World: The Arethusa Papers*, 195–212.

Showalter, Elaine, ed. 1985. *The New Feminist Criticism: Essays on Women, Literature and Theory*. New York: Pantheon Books.

Silverman, Kaja. 1980. "Masochism and Subjectivity." *Frameworks* 12: 2–9.

Skinner, Marilyn B., ed. 1986. *Rescuing Creusa: New Methodological Approaches to Women in Antiquity. Helios* n.s. 13.1: 31–48.

———. 1991. "*Nossis Thêlyglôssos:* The Private Text and the Public Book." In Sarah B. Pomeroy, ed., *Women's History and Ancient History*, 20–47. Chapel Hill and London: University of North Carolina Press.

———. 1993. "Women and Language in Archaic Greece, or, Why is Sappho a Woman?" Published elsewhere in this volume.

Smith-Rosenberg, Carroll. 1986. "Writing History: Language, Class and Gender." In de Lauretis, *Feminist Studies/Critical Studies*, 31–54.

Snitow, Ann, Christine Stansell, and Sharon Thompson, eds. 1983. *Powers of Desire: The Politics of Sexuality*. New York: Monthly Review Press.

Snyder, Jane M. 1989. *The Woman and the Lyre: Women Writers in Classical Greece and Rome*. Carbondale and Edwardsville: Southern Illinois University Press.

Syme, Ronald. 1939. *The Roman Revolution*. Oxford: Oxford University Press.

Tanner, Nancy. 1974. "Matrifocality in Indonesia and Africa and among Black Americans." In Rosaldo and Lamphere, *Woman, Culture and Society*, 129–56.

Teuffel, Wilhelm Sigmund. 1870. *Geschichte der Roemischen Literatur*. Reprinted as Teuffel's *History of Roman Literature*. Revised and enlarged by Ludwig Schwabe, authorised translation from the Fifth German Edition, by George C. W. Warr. New York: Burt Franklin, 1967. 2 vols.

Tompkins, Jane. 1985. *Sensational Designs: The Cultural Work of American Fiction, 1790–1860*. New York: Oxford University Press.

Vessey, D. W. T. C. 1982. "Challenge and Response." In *The Cambridge History of Classical Literature*. Vol. 2, part 4: *The Early Principate*, 1–6. Cambridge, Eng.: Cambridge University Press.

Veyne, Paul. 1983. *Roman Erotic Poetry: Love, Poetry and the West*. Translated by David Pellauer. Chicago: University of Chicago Press.

Williams, Gordon. 1978. *Change and Decline: Roman Literature in the Early Empire*. Berkeley, Los Angeles and London: University of California Press.

Winkler, John J. 1990. *The Constraints of Desire: The Anthropology of Sex and Gender in Ancient Greece*. New York: Routledge.

Wyke, Maria. 1987a. "Written Women: Propertius' *Scripta Puella*." *Journal of Roman Studies* 77: 47–61.

———. 1987b. "The Elegiac Woman at Rome." *Publications of the Cambridge Philological Society* 213, n.s. 33: 153–78.

———. 1989. "Mistress and Metaphor in Augustan Elegy." *Helios* 16.1: 25–48.

Zagarell, Sandra A. 1986. "Review Essay: Conceptualizing Women's Literary History: Reflections on the *Norton Anthology of Literature by Women*." *Tulsa Studies in Women's Literature* 5.2: 273–87.

Zeitlin, Froma. 1978. "The Dynamics of Misogyny: Myth and Mythmaking in the *Oresteia*." *Arethusa* 11.1, 2. Reprinted in Peradotto and Sullivan, *Women in the Ancient World: The Arethusa Papers*, 159–94.

———. 1981. "Travesties of Gender and Genre in Aristophanes' *Thesmophoriazusae*." In Foley, *Reflections of Women in Antiquity*, 169–218.

Zweig, Bella. 1992. "The Mute Nude Female Characters in Aristophanes' Plays." In Richlin, *Pornography and Representation in Greece and Rome*, 73–89.

Male Writing Female

4

"But Ariadne Was Never There in the First Place": Finding the Female in Roman Poetry

Barbara K. Gold

Or, if you prefer, for a culture busy unraveling itself from within an imaginary labyrinth, Ariadne remains just around the corner. But Ariadne, like Truth, was never really there in the first place (Jardine 1985: 47).

"It's a shame that more people don't take an interest in what you people write." "It's a shame that we don't write for you to read" (Richlin 1990: 176).

Feminist literary criticism is currently undergoing an identity crisis. In her 1977 book *A Literature of Their Own* and her 1979 study "Towards a Feminist Poetics," Elaine Showalter distinguished between *feminist critique* (woman as the consumer of male-produced literature) and *gynocritics* (feminist criticism concerned with "woman as writer—woman as the producer of textual meaning, and the history, themes, genres and structures of literature by women"; Showalter 1979: 25). Showalter advocated that feminist criticism should develop "new models based on the study of female experience," and should include among its subjects linguistics and the problem of a female language, and individual or collective literary careers and histories, rather than analyzing male experience in order to try to understand the presentation of women in his texts (Showalter 1977).

Similarly Annette Kolodny attempted to define what feminist literary criticism might mean. She distinguished three types of women readers: women who write about "men's books," women who write about "women's books," and "any criticism written by a woman no matter what the subject" (Kolodny 1975: 75). In her classification of modes of understanding "woman" or "women," there are two broad distinctions to be made: women as readers versus women as writers and women reading male texts versus women reading female texts. We should now add to these distinctions the current focus on plurality in feminism and the need to take account of both white feminists and feminists of color (Lugones 1991).

Recently, Showalter has turned her attention to "gender studies," arguing that feminists should, with considerable caution, consider questions of masculinity and be willing to focus on male texts, "not as documents of sexism and misogyny, but as inscriptions of gender and 'renditions of sexual difference' " (Showalter 1989: 5). Given the fact that nearly all classical texts still extant are male authored, the gender-studies approach would seem to be a fruitful hermeneutic for most classical feminist scholars, but it is important here to note Modleski's observations on the dangers of allowing gender studies to supersede feminist studies (Modleski 1991). If male critics coopt and bury feminist studies or exploit them for their own advantage, feminist studies will be marginalized and increasingly lost to view and, as Modleski points out, feminism will become "a conduit to the more comprehensive field of gender studies" (Modleski 1991: 5).

Except for Sappho (and even most of her poems have come down to us in a fragmentary state), all of the female writers in antiquity such as Corinna, Erinna, Anyte, Nossis, and the two Sulpicias are known to us from short and incomplete snippets or from late or unreliable testimonies about them (Lefkowitz 1981). Classicists have thus tended to focus on male-authored texts (see Hallett's article in this volume for suggestions on how we might broaden our curriculum to include a wider range of noncanonical authors and different combinations of canonical and noncanonical texts). As increasing numbers of feminist scholars attempt to map the female consciousness of antiquity, more and more attention has been paid to using the admittedly scanty remains of female writers such as those mentioned above to learn about how and what women thought from their own words and to try to re-create the social contexts in which they operated (Hallett 1979, 1993; Winkler 1981; Skinner 1989a, 1991a, 1991b, article in this volume; Snyder 1989, 1991; Stehle 1990; Pomeroy 1991a, 1991b).

A serious debate has recently arisen among feminist classical scholars about the validity of using male-authored, canonical texts, which are labeled as "tribal totems for classicists" in Phyllis Culham's "Decentering the Text: The Case of Ovid" (Culham 1990: 161). This article forms the introduction to and basis of a debate on the choice of a male author, Ovid, by the Women's Classical Caucus for its 1985 panel at the annual meeting of the American Philological Association (for the debate, see *Helios* 17 [1990]). Here Culham argues that we would do far better to work at recovering women's lived reality by reading female authors themselves when possible and by paying close attention to the historical, material context which will reveal, as male-authored literary texts do not, the disparity of male and female experience (see also Culham 1987: 9–30; Pomeroy 1991a: 265).[1] The focus on material culture, according to Culham, would reintroduce working women into the picture, highlight the importance of lived reality over ahistorical, constructed texts that are often regarded as transcendent entities, and help us to provide explanations of social phenomena and to investigate the origins and propagation of Western culture (Culham 1990: 165). Other feminists argue that lived reality is always mediated and its representation always textual (Hallett 1973, 1993; Gamel 1989, 1990; Richlin 1990, 1992b). They further maintain that, even in discussing male writers of antiquity, we are not excluding ancient women since all the events depicted and attitudes voiced in canonical texts "bear on the lives of the women who heard [Ovid's] poems and live(d) in the sign system that produced the canon" (Richlin 1992b: 159). They contend as well that reading several male-authored ancient texts about women against other ancient evidence about women can help to illuminate the social, political, artistic, and erotic aspirations of the women pictured there, especially when we have no other evidence (Hallett 1973, 1993).

Since so few female-authored texts are available, classicists who are interested in "retrieving the bones of our foremothers" (Richlin 1990: 177) need to make creative connections and to use the skills developed by feminist researchers operating in other disciplines in order to find sensitive and successful approaches to elucidating women's actions, thoughts, and desires in antiquity from the male-authored texts that have come down to us. Toward this end, I would like to look at what French and Anglo-American criticism of the last twenty years have to offer us and then to move on to a model that I find a useful hermeneutic for reading certain male-authored Roman texts, namely Alice Jardine's concept of "gynesis" (Jardine 1985). Jardine's approach works particularly well for Roman elegy, a genre of poetry written in Rome of the first century B.C.E. as a reaction to the clearly developed but already collapsing moralistic patriarchal value system of that society. The conditions under which the Roman elegists worked parallel the conditions of contemporary Western life that Jardine discusses precisely because of the unsettled political climate, the concomitant shakeup of societal values, and the search for an individual response to the failure of the patriarchal state in Rome at that time.

Before testing Jardine's gynesis on one of the Roman elegists, Propertius (who lived from some time in the early 40s B.C.E. to some time before 2 C.E.), I will give a brief historical survey of two major "schools" of feminist thought which have been important to the development of Jardine's argument: the French feminists/poststructuralists and the Anglo-Americans, many of whom have tended to follow a more empirical approach that is somewhat akin to the historical empiricism characteristic of Anglo-American classical scholarship. It should be made clear at the outset that the French feminist positions that I will outline here were articulated in the 1970s (see bibliography). A great deal of fundamental work was done in that period by critics such as Kristeva, Cixous, and Irigaray, but French feminist thought today has changed and is now quite different. Nonetheless, the ideas of these critics have had an enormous effect on Anglo-American feminists and on Jardine in particular, and they continue to produce reactions in many feminist quarters.

Using the ideas of the French and the Anglo-American feminists, I will try to show what benefit we can gain from each "school," how classics fits into these approaches, and how Jardine's discussion might help us to continue the dialogue on women in Roman elegy started by Hallett, Wyke, et al., by further developing our thinking on the depiction of women in this genre. I am proposing to proceed in this way with the full knowledge that poststructuralism did not exist (or at least was not recognized as a mode of analysis) in antiquity and that Jardine herself is not talking about antiquity but about modernity. Yet what she says about male writers in our own period can help us to understand the place of "woman" in ancient elegy, and to confirm, as I have proposed above, that modern modes of representing the feminine can be seen in antiquity in such writers as Propertius. It is important that we learn to "reread the past from the unavoidable perspective of present cultural influences . . . without denying the specificity and difference of the past," on the one hand, or our preconceptions of the present, on the other (Belsey and Moore 1989: 223; Beer 1989: 67).

Contemporary critical approaches can certainly help us to elucidate classical texts in new ways that will help the feminist/classicist project. But openness to contemporary criticism should work both ways. An understanding of the feminist possibilities in classical texts adds a historical depth to the current feminist debates. Such classical texts are capable of illuminating the contemporary texts they have influenced by showing that contemporary representations of women have close parallels in literatures from the past. To put the alterations of and repetitions of these representations in a historical context is vital if we are to be able to determine which means of challenging texts produced by a heavily patriarchal tradition will be of most use for the feminist approach. Only by examining the long development of attitudes toward language and representation that have limited women's self-knowledge and expression can we shake off the effects of centuries of patriarchal control.

To the uninitiated, feminist theory may seem a monolithic set of ideas designed to interpret the world and its texts in ways which provide an alternative to or undermine the existent male-generated approaches. But nothing could be further from the truth. Feminist critics would appear to agree on only one thing: the importance of dismantling traditionally male ways of seeing. But questions of how to achieve this goal and what the major focal points of debate should be have proliferated with the development of feminist theory over the past twenty years. As feminism has become more developed and more complex, it has naturally spawned different "schools" of thought on such fundamental issues as the definition of gender identity, the role of language in determining or defining gender, the nature and importance of the unconscious, the importance of the speaking subject, and the desirability of an empirical versus a theoretical mode of analysis. Two of the more polarized stands on such issues have been taken by certain Anglo-American and French feminists (see Moi 1985; Jones 1985). As Jardine points out, "any generic description of either French or American feminism would immediately homogenize, colonialize, and neutralize the specificities of struggles that are often of quite epic proportions" (Jardine 1985: 15), so that what I will say here should be regarded as necessarily schematic and not as an attempt to describe with any specificity each individual French or Anglo-American feminist critic or to generalize unfairly about them.

The central dividing line for French and American feminists has been the

French emphasis on the importance of *language* to the exclusion of all else. For the French feminists, there was no world outside of the text; the text was everything, everything was language, and that language was identified with and dominated by the masculine (Marks 1978: 842; Jones 1985). They were therefore interested in seeing women somehow gain control over language or invent a new kind of writing, writing that was not logocentric, that did not contain preestablished, easily accessible meanings, and that liberated women from the repression of phallocentric language. *Phallocentrism* or *phallogocentrism* (or *phallologocentrism*) is the term French feminists have used to describe and critique a cultural framework in which concepts have an independent existence, the truth of an idea is found outside of language in the subjectivity of the individual, and language itself privileges the phallus as the symbol or source of power. In their view, primacy of place has been given to the male and male forms of discourse; women have been forced either to participate in masculine, phallocentric language or to invent their own form of discourse, which is characterized by lack and marginalizes them even further. The French feminists "have reformulated Freud's question 'What does a woman want?' to, 'What does a woman write?' " (Marks 1978: 842).

The three best-known contemporary French feminists are Luce Irigaray, Hélène Cixous, and Julia Kristeva, all deeply influenced by psychoanalytic and poststructuralist thought and heavily indebted to Lacan and Derrida. To this group I would also add Monique Wittig (for a good summary of contemporary French feminism, see Jones 1985; Moi 1985). These French theorists cannot be lumped together into one category since they vary widely in their approaches and orientations, but they do have certain things in common. All have rejected language as a "natural" communicative function and the belief in any specific correspondence of the signifier to the signified. The idea that there can be a self-contained individual characterized by specific attributes, a special historical, cultural, or biological identity, or a separate consciousness is exposed and revealed to be a fiction of earlier humanist discourse.[2] It also follows that we cannot expect to find in the "subject" (or speaker or author) any individual authorial intentions on which we might rely to discover the meaning of the text or discourse because the "subject" is a construct grounded in social discourse beyond any individual control. Instead of hunting for an authentic individual beneath the cultural and ideological overlay, the French feminists would posit a subject constructed by discourse and inscribed in culture through language.

Thus many of the French feminists (Kristeva and Wittig in particular), like other poststructuralists, have insisted that language does not and cannot guarantee identity or meaning and that therefore subjectivity and identity are not fixed but are always in process; further, the long-accepted idea of the unified subject that controls and fixes meaning must be questioned. According to Kristeva, women cannot be defined and should not be defined since the term "woman" is a social, not a natural construct. Wittig quotes de Beauvoir's famous statement: "One is not born, but becomes a woman. No biological, psychological, or economic fate predetermines the figure that the human female presents in society; it is civilization as a whole that produces this creature, intermediate between male and eunuch, which is described as feminine" (Wittig 1981: 47). The poststructuralist feminists thus problematize the whole notion of a historicized or "real" figure in literature who is characterizable by a specific personality and particularities of experience. For them, "woman" and the "feminine" are metaphors, linguistic categories, terms "in process."

Kristeva, Cixous, and Irigaray each take a very different approach to these fundamental issues. One of the main arguments among them concerns the development of a woman's language and the link between anatomy and verbal destiny (Gilbert and Gubar 1988: 227–71). Kristeva has taken a much criticized position, opposing both women's participation in phallocentric discourse and the development of a special woman's language (Kristeva 1974, Marks 1978; see Gauthier 1974 for an insistence that women must develop their own language). She is suspicious of trying to develop a language that only women can use, and she contends that the only power women can have is to disrupt the system from within. She says, "What we must do is to help women to understand that these modern breaks with tradition and the development of new forms of discourse are harmonious with the women's cause. By participation in this activity of subversion (which exists on a linguistic, family, and social level) and in the growth of new epistemes they will be able to see this as well" (Féral 1976: 17). In her eyes, the only possible feminism is a negative feminism; according to her, "A woman cannot be; it is something which does not even belong in the order of being. It follows that a feminist practice can only be negative, at odds with what already exists so that we may say 'that's not it' and 'that's still not it' " (Kristeva 1974: 137).

Cixous and Irigaray are like each other in insisting on a difference in male and female language based on the difference between male and female "libidinal economies," one of which has been allowed to develop culturally (the male) and the other of which has been repressed (the female) (Marks 1978). Both Cixous and Irigaray believe that an essential feminine exists historically and cross culturally and further that language is closely tied to sexuality. But, unlike Kristeva, they move from male theorists (mainly Lacan for Irigaray and Derrida for Cixous) to develop a language peculiarly feminine which women can use to challenge the effects of a patriarchal order. Cixous's *écriture féminine* is a feminist discourse that is accessible to both male and female to use for dismantling phallocentric discourse; women, however, have a more immediate relationship to this language (Cixous and Clément 1975: 85–89, 91–99; Cixous 1976). Indeed, Cixous's own writing at times exemplifies what she must mean by *écriture féminine*: "Writing is the passageway, the entrance, the exit, the dwelling place of the other in me— the other that I am and am not, that I don't know how to be, but that I feel passing, that makes me live—that tears me apart, changes me, who?—a feminine one, a masculine one, some?—several, some unknown, which is indeed what gives me the desire to know and from which all life soars" (Cixous and Clément 1975: 85–86); or "You only have to look at the Medusa straight on to see her. And she's not deadly. She's beautiful and she's laughing" (Cixous 1976: 885).

Irigaray's *parler femme* ("womanspeak") is a female language produced from women's libido, which is fundamentally different from men's. Irigaray defines female sexuality as unfixed and not locatable in one organ; thus female language is nonlinear, irrational, and incomprehensible (to men) (Irigaray 1977: 28–29). Therefore, her *parler femme* belongs largely to women (although certain male writers such as Genêt have been included in this group) (Irigaray 1974, 1977, 1980). Neither Irigaray nor Cixous emphasizes the effects of culture and history; their theory of language as a force which is rooted in sexuality leaves little room for social or political change (Jardine modulates this position by the introduction of the more action-based Anglo-American feminism).

Many Anglo-American feminists, on the other hand, continue to talk about women's reality, women's experience, and women's history as if they were discussing a set of knowable facts rather than verbal constructs that carry with them an overlay of ideologies and values and specific cultural perspectives (Draine 1989: 147). They are often more interested in seeing women freed from political and social oppression than from the repression of phallocentric language. Some have accepted a more biological or essentialist approach, identifying "woman" as a transparent signifier of a biological female in history, not a metaphor of her sex. For them, "woman" does not signify a process that disrupts symbolic structures in male discourse (as the French would have it); rather, women can be defined by their activities and attributes in their cultural milieu. "Woman" would thus signify, for example, a biological person, a bearer of children, someone who worries about child care, who is an object of male sexuality, who speaks in a different voice. Many of the Anglo-American feminists eschew Freud and Lacan, highlighting and valorizing "natural reality" over the unconscious, and privileging the self and empirical evidence of women's "speech-acts" (Jardine 1985: 42, 44, 47; Lakoff 1975). Language is emphasized by them, but only as a communicative, natural function. Anglo-American feminists have not in the past engaged as much in the same kind of radical rethinking of the male and female subjects' relationship to the real, the imaginary, and the symbolic as have the French feminists, who have focused more on psychoanalysis and the role of the unconscious; an increasing number of Anglo-American feminists (for instance Gallop, Miller, Kamuf, Schor, and Jardine) have begun to think in psychoanalytical terms.

In sum, many Anglo-American feminists, in answer to Simone de Beauvoir's question "are there women?" would respond "yes" and try to define women by their cultural attributes and activities, taking a more empirical and activist stance. Most new French feminists and poststructuralists would answer "no" and attack the very category of "woman" by examining language and its effect on the subject (see Wittig, Delphy, and other materialists). As Marks puts it, "where American women cry out 'male chauvinist pig,' the French women inscribe 'phallologocentric' " (Marks 1978).

Problems abound, of course, with each of these two broadly defined approaches, particularly for classicists. The more empirical approach taken by many American feminists emphasizes the truth value of everyday experience and "natural" reality, but does not give enough attention to the importance of cultural determinations and language. The French poststructuralist theorists' insistence on woman as process, social construct, and fiction downplays the biological aspect of the female, discounts individual and experiential intersections with the imprint of history, and deconstructs the feminine subject to such an extent that feminism has little or no meaning and allows no possibility for action (Kristeva 1974: 137; 1979: 33–34). As Martin (1982), Hartsock (1990), Richlin (1991), and others have pointed out, poststructuralism and Foucauldian thought undercut activist feminism by getting rid of subjectivity, making totalizing discourse impossible, and treating sexual identity as a fiction. The question of the oppression of women becomes muted because the emphasis on linguistic and thus symbolic process, on abstractions, and on categories neutralizes sexual difference and constantly denies or defers the importance of everyday experience. We thus face the difficult task of exploding and undermining traditional categories without either losing the particularity of "women" or forfeiting our right to struggle against the oppression of women. As Bordo says, however, poststructuralism is useful for feminism, but more as an interpretive tool and historical critique than as a theoretical framework to be adopted and applied wholesale (Bordo 1990: 153–54).

Some feminists have tried to offer a *tertium quid* that might allow us to take the best from both theoretical stances and to combine the equally valid but conflicting ideas of *"woman as* (linguistic) *process"* and *"woman as* (biological) *sexual identity"* (Jardine 1985: 41). This compromise position gives us a valuable tool with which to analyze the Roman poetry of the first century B.C.E. For example, Teresa de Lauretis tries to bridge the gap between woman as a poststructuralist genderless subject (woman) and woman as a historicized subject (women); such an approach would allow us to look at the figures in Roman poetry both as they are constructed in language and as they intersect with their social/historical contexts. She uses the term "experience," not in "the individualistic, idiosyncratic sense of something belonging to one and exclusively her own," but "in the general sense of a *process* by which, for all social beings, subjectivity is constructed" (de Lauretis 1984: 159). She thus allows for an intersection of women and their positions in relation to shifting interpersonal and political contexts.[3] For her, language is not the sole locus of meaning; she also places importance on the subjective, individual interpretation of social and historical relations through which meaning can be constructed, and she gives the subject an identity (de Lauretis 1987, 1990: 267).

Like de Lauretis, Alice Jardine, in her 1985 study *Gynesis*, tries to maintain the alliance between feminism and postmodernism and to describe the compromise position that has evolved out of the deconstructive and the essentialist positions by introducing a process which she calls "gynesis." Jardine searches for a theory that can combine the American feminist focus on ethics, practice, and sexual identity with the French idea of woman as a process that disrupts symbolic structures. I will maintain that Propertius and other elegiac poets of the first century B.C.E. use women and gender in just this way: to disrupt the structures of their society and to produce in the process a new formulation of gender. Jardine's gynesis involves "the putting into discourse of 'woman' or 'the feminine' "; gynesis is the process of requestioning and destructuring the traditional Western master narratives, the accounts of the world that have attempted to explain to us "Man, the Subject, Truth, History, Meaning" (Jardine 1985: 25).

In her questioning of the foundations of Western critical thought, Jardine examines the texts of some contemporary French male theorists of modernity, who employ the textual image of woman in their quest to denaturalize concepts like "experience," "the Natural," "the Ethical," "the Good," "the True," and to revalorize what the master Western texts have posited as unknown, uncertain, unnatural, unmanageable. Jardine would focus on what has been left out of, deemphasized, or denied articulation in the master texts (Jardine 1985: 36). This lost object, represented so often but almost impossible to represent (Heath 1978), is manifested in texts in the discourse of uncertainty and unfixity that has traditionally connoted femininity and been coded as "woman" in these master texts. But Jardine points out that this "femininity" is a stereotype of traditional male ways of seeing women, "an excess of patriarchal history" (Belsey and Moore 1989: 19), a product of patriarchal control over language, culture, and texts, and it has nothing to do with biological women (Jardine 1985: 25–26, 36–38).

While the male theorists of modernity in many ways simply reinforce stereotypes of women as passive, uncertain, powerless, and devious, their discourse is still useful for feminism because it points to a space in the text, an area of uncertainty that has feminine connotations and is a place of the unknown, a space over which the narratives have lost control (Jardine 1985: 25). This "space" allows us to problematize and to question anew the representations of women in these texts. Jardine demonstrates the need for women to "enter and renovate the discourse of modernity on a nonsexist basis," "to make something utterly new of/in the discourse, theory, and praxis of modernity, as an alternative to the repetition forced on to traditional feminist discourse by the dominant ideology in the West" (Draine 1989: 156; Jardine 1985: 258).

Jardine asks whether both the concept and the practice of feminism might not be productively redefined in light of the new conceptual paths opened up by the texts of modernity. Such male-engendered texts might offer new directions through which women can conceptually rework "male" and "female" and force us to imagine a new kind of hermeneutics "able to give up its quest for truth and capable of self-reflection on its own complicity with inherited systems of representation" (Draine 1989: 158).

Theories like Jardine's that are clearly grounded in contemporary culture can help us to interpret or to understand texts from other periods as well. Feminists are now studying the structuring of gender and the implied female reader in literatures from many different eras (for example, Krueger for the medieval period; Poovey for the Victorian age). So too, the analysis of gender structuring and definition that gynesis supplies can be done in certain classical texts. The "master narratives" that we might examine from antiquity, analogous to Jardine's Western "master narratives," would be any male-authored text that has received, transmitted, and influenced the traditional male-centered system of representation (for example, Homer, Sophocles, Cicero, Vergil). In these master narratives from antiquity, the authors have naturalized and normalized all of our most fundamental concepts (the good, the true, the natural) according to a particular masculine and aristocratic ideology, and they have created and subsequently reinforced all of the stereotypes of women that Jardine finds in the twentieth-century texts she discusses (passivity, treachery, powerlessness, fluidity). In certain authors, however, we can see a "space" in the fabric, where there is an uneasiness in the representation of gender for both the author and reader, where the language seems to have more potentiality to be interpreted from many different perspectives, where the marginalized characters seem to be trying to "speak," and where there are border challengings (voices speaking against the text).[4] Not only Sappho's explicit rereadings of Homer, or Sulpicia's of elegy, but such figures as the women of Aristophanes's *Lysistrata, Thesmophoriazousai*, and *Ekklesiazousai*; the female characters of Euripides; the freed slaves of Petronius's *Satyricon*; Vergil's Dido and Statius's Hypsipyle; the native leader Calgacus who speaks against Rome in Tacitus's *Agricola*—all these have been seen, or could be seen, as places where the mute are pushing through the fabric of the text.[5]

One place where we find such spaces is in Roman elegy, a genre of personalized lyric poetry that owes much to its Greek predecessors but survived in a peculiarly Roman form for less than a century, from about 55 B.C.E., when our first extant Roman elegiac poet Catullus was writing, until about 17 C.E., when Ovid, the last classical practitioner of this genre probably died (Luck 1959). The origins and development of elegy are buried in mystery since there are many missing links in the tradition. Technically defined as poetry written in elegiac couplets, elegy was written by the Greeks at least as far back as the seventh century B.C.E. It may have been used for funeral dirges, but it seems to have accommodated from the beginning a wide variety of topics, themes, and purposes (for example, war, drinking, politics, and mythological stories). It was connected rather closely with love stories from mythology by some of its Hellenistic practitioners in the fourth through first centuries B.C.E., but these love stories, although often addressed to female lovers (for example, Antimachus of Colophon to his wife Lyde in about 400 B.C.E.), were probably about the love affairs of others or at least cast as mythological narratives rather than as personal experiences. The first poets to have used elegy for the purpose of writing a personal account of their own love affairs to their own mistresses were Catullus and perhaps Cornelius Gallus, a figure from the mid-first century B.C.E. who survives in ten lines (nine of which are disputed and the remaining one of which has nothing to do with love at all; Ross 1975; Anderson 1979). Gallus is one of those tantalizing transitional figures whom we suspect is a key link in the tradition but can only recreate with a considerable amount of speculation and guesswork.

The surviving elegists in the first century B.C.E. are Catullus, Propertius, Tibullus, and Ovid. Catullus, more often called a lyric poet because he wrote many of his 116 poems in lyric meters, wrote 52 poems in elegiac meter. Many of these poems focus on love, either Catullus's love for his mistress, whom he calls Lesbia, or someone else's love (whether mythical or contemporary). Catullus is the first extant Roman poet to write ostensibly sincere, intense, passionate outpourings of desire and emotion to his mistress, the first to call his mistress by a poetic pseudonym (Lesbia for Clodia), the first to intermix mythologems of love with his own personal amatory relationship and to let the mythological stories illuminate his own story, the first to question gender roles and to portray himself, the male, as the weak, passive, and helpless member of the duo (Skinner 1989b, Janan forthcoming; see also Fitzgerald 1988, Oliensis 1991 on gender and sexuality in the poet Horace). Catullus combines what would later become many of the standard qualities of Roman elegy, albeit still in vestigial form (his poem 68 is the only poem in which all of the later elegiac traits are combined but they are there in an uneasy mix), and his influence on the three later elegists is enormous. Propertius, Tibullus, and Ovid all follow Catullus in their use of meter (employing elegiac meter exclusively for their love poetry), their overtly personal displays of affection toward their mistresses, who are also the addressees of many of their poems, and their use of poetic pseudonyms for their lovers (Cynthia, Delia, and Corinna, respectively).

I have chosen Roman elegy for my exploration of gynesis in ancient literature because it is here that we find both the ways of questioning gender constructions and the problematic areas in the text that Jardine identifies in contemporary male writers who attempt to denaturalize traditional concepts and to recast the representations of gender. Elegy offers a fertile ground for such an exploration because it combines traditional ways of seeing love and female lovers with a new sense of male/female relationships and gender redefinitions. And, in contrast to authors such as Vergil, the elegists are more self-conscious in their treatment of gender reversals. The redefinitions of gender found in elegy were developed in response to both the heavily moralistic patriarchal value system that had existed in Rome for centuries and the breakdown of societal values at the end of the first century B.C.E. The spaces present in the texts connote uncertainty, the unknown, the unreal—qualities that are traditionally ascribed to women by male authors and that thus might be viewed with distrust by feminist readers looking for new ways to reconceptualize "male" and "female" in our texts. Yet, if we do not fall into the trap of focusing on and being influenced by only the traditional representations of women in our texts, but see these "spaces" as a way of problematizing and reconceptualizing "woman" both as a concept and as an identity, we might be able to reevaluate our idea of what "truth" we are looking for and, without complicity with the representations transmitted by the authors of antiquity, read differently the stories we have been "forced to live" (Jardine 1985: 258).

One problem that we will face is that in such an approach to the texts, "women" cease to be historically identifiable subjects and become surrounded by and buried in quotation marks. Women become "woman," a process that designates the encased word as a rhetorical or ideological construct. Thus women as thinking, writing subjects are left in the position of wondering whether they are seeking to reconceptualize and identify "women" or "woman," their written *bodies* (real, biological entities) or their *written* bodies (cultural constructions).[6] In either case, we are giving up some part of women's/woman's identity. Jardine says that, although "the attempt to analyze, to separate ideological and cultural determinations of the 'feminine' from the 'real woman' " may be the most logical path for a feminist to follow, it may also be the most interminable process, "one in which women become not only figuratively but also literally impossible" (Jardine 1985: 37). Her way out of this trap is to use "gynesis" as it is described above, not the now-traditional male way of reading women but a more controlled, more careful feminist version of this in which the concept of woman will be identified with difference, with incompleteness, with the unknown.[7]

Gynesis allows us to focus on the male-generated texts that comprise a very large percentage of our available evidence, but to look in them for something different. Jardine proposes for modernity—and I propose for antiquity—that we look in our texts for what is hidden, deemphasized, left out, or denied articulation, and try to make evident the spaces produced in these texts over which the writer has no control and in which "woman" can be found. Jardine's description of the process of requestioning and destabilizing of the Western master narratives, of the concern for the incomplete rather than the whole, for different modes of production rather than representation, and for difference rather than identity,[8] and of "the putting into discourse of women" (Jardine 1985: 25, 36), can, I believe, be helpful to feminists who are searching for a new way to "find" the female in ancient texts. Many classicists of course have already read the text against itself and uncovered spaces and new levels of meaning for women by making use of new critical methodologies (see, for example, Skinner 1983 [for Catullus]; Richlin 1983: 32–56; 1984 [for elegy and satire]; 1992b [for Ovid]; Wyke 1987, 1989 [for Propertius]; Hallett 1989a [for Roman literature]; Ancona 1989 [for Horace]; Nugent 1990 [for Ovid]; Janan forthcoming [for Catullus]). My use of French feminist critics to elucidate the elegies of Propertius owes a great debt in many different ways to these ground-breaking studies. Some of them, however, come to quite different conclusions than I do and find no positive evidence for women in these texts; the various readings against the text that are beginning to be done show a multiplicity of voices and attitudes.

While "woman" has long been seen, since the beginnings of Western literature as we know it, as a problematic object and the locus of contradictions (Miller 1980: 74), contemporary feminist critics now see the contradiction operating not only in the referent but also in the signifier "woman" itself. I am concerned with the *language* in these texts and with the ways in which the spaces left in our texts, after we have questioned and destabilized them, can help us to understand these texts differently. We can thus challenge the idea that sexuality and subjectivity are fixed, and we can open up the fixed identities assigned to fictionalized female characters by authors who are burdened with the cultural, historical, and conceptual limitations inherited from their patriarchal history. This is not to say, of course, that a feminist reader does not have her own limitations, but at the very least we can problematize "woman" as both a concept and an identity, shake up representations that have been accepted as givens for such a long time within the dominant tradition, and question our own complicity with these inherited ideas.

How then can we, who are trying to determine something about "women" and "woman" from ancient, male-authored texts, put these insights to work? How can we read "woman" in a text like Propertius's elegiac poetry, which centers on a woman but springs from a male imagination and a patriarchal culture? How can we apply Alice Jardine's theory of gynesis, or the putting into discourse of "woman" or the "feminine" as problematic, to such a text? One potential pitfall in applying such questions to a male-authored text is that articulated by Spivak in "Displacement and the Discourse of Woman" (Spivak 1983): can we ask a male writer who is embedded in such a hegemonic discourse and who is in total control of his subjects (objects) to provide us with concepts and strategies that do not "appropriate or displace the figure of woman" (Spivak 1983: 170)? If the writer can problematize but never fully discard his own subjectivity, can he ever allow to his object her own subjectivity?

Keeping this potential hazard in mind, I would like to suggest some questions that we might ask about Propertius's text and the "Cynthia" which (who) is presented there (taking Cynthia as a "woman" and not as a particular, historicized woman). I hope that these questions will allow us to continue to problematize the female figure, to eschew the belief that language can reproduce reality and that women can have a material and knowable essence, and to avoid the impulse to try to turn characters like Cynthia into historical figures.

I take as a given that "Cynthia" is constructed as a fictional figure and that, if a real Roman woman did exist under the pseudonym, this information would not alter our understanding of the text.[9] In fact, even if Cynthia were called by her real name in Propertius's text, she would still be a fictionalized character.[10] The

Roman writer Apuleius started the hunt for the "real women" underneath the pseudonyms given in Roman elegy by giving a list of the real names corresponding to these pseudonyms (Apuleius *Apology* 10). Taking their cue from Apuleius, readers of these classical texts have tried to historicize the characters in them and to formulate biographies from "historical details" in the poetry. It is interesting to note in this regard that Propertius's first book of elegies has been called the *Cynthia* by both ancient and modern writers.[11] She is identified both by the author himself and by later male critics (ancient and modern) not only *with* his poetry but *as* his poetry. This is quite a deliberate ploy by the poet: her name appears in the first line of the first poem (and thus was used as a title for the book), and, in another book of his elegies, Propertius claims that he was taunted with the fact that his Cynthia "was being read all over the city" (*tua sit toto Cynthia lecta foro*, Prop. 2.24.2), thus producing an image of Cynthia as a sexually passive object (the written woman).

"Cynthia" then is absolutely vital to Propertius's poetry because, according to him, she constitutes his text. She becomes his book that is the "talk of the town" (Prop. 2.24.1), passed around as an object of exchange, and finally lost or destroyed (*ergo tam doctae nobis periere tabellae*, Prop. 3.23.1).[12] But she is also constituted by the text and exists as an object within it. Propertius can manipulate her time, her space, and her attributes. He can project her impossibly into the past (Prop. 3.24) or into the future (Prop. 2.18.19–20; 3.25), even going so far as to resurrect her from the grave (Prop. 4.7). He can place her in Rome (Prop. 1.6), abroad (1.8), back again (1.8.27ff.), at a seaside resort (1.11), or on a journey (1.12; 2.19). She can be portrayed as a faithful Penelope (Prop. 1.3) or a faithless hussy (1.16), made into a categorized "woman" by being cast in a preset role in a mythologem. She is endlessly adaptable by the poet because she is a projection of his desires and anxieties, as unstable and slippery as his thoughts (Prop. 2.1.4: *ingenium nobis ipsa puella facit*). She is—or becomes—what Propertius wants or fears for himself, and her identity in the poetry changes depending upon whether she is the fulfillment of his erotic desires or the embodiment of all the traits that men fear in women (instability, fickleness, violence, inscrutability, wiliness, deception).

She is thus seen as both an internal object (an element in the poetry) and an external object (an objectification of the poetry book and separable from it), forming an important part of Propertius's "plot" (though never getting to write her own), and eventually becoming identified with the book itself. She is called a story (*fabula,* Prop. 2.24.1; *historia,* 2.1.16), a fictionalized object put to the service of the poet so that she may perform a thousand different roles.

How does Jardine's gynesis help us to analyze what a character like Cynthia means to Propertius's poetry? If we examine her roles and destabilize the identity that Propertius has created for her, we might identify a new space in the text by our questioning of Propertius's traditional categories and from this space gain a clearer understanding of what it meant for a "woman" to be the apparent center and anchor of such a male text. We might say that Propertius himself is unwittingly destabilizing the whole question of gender by appearing to lose control of what "Cynthia" represents and by putting his own representation into play as the feminine in a way that gives him a role parallel to Cynthia's (although Spivak's warning about displacement must be considered here). From the outset he makes Cynthia an element of his poetry that is at the same time essential to its meaning but also absent and elusive. At every opportunity Propertius reminds us of her importance, but he also often characterizes her as absolutely powerless. In addition, he cracks open the traditional identifications of "male" and "female" codes of behavior by casting himself frequently in nontraditional male roles, in fact, in roles that we would usually assign to women. A comparison of Cynthia to Vergil's Carthaginian queen Dido or Aeneas's Trojan wife Creusa, for example, or to Livy's self-effacing heroines Lucretia and Verginia, reveals by contrast the unstable, nontraditional character of the place assigned to Cynthia. Such conventional Roman female figures as Dido, Creusa, Lucretia, and Verginia remain imprisoned in their roles: passive, beloved, models of seemly behavior, and willing in the end to kill themselves or let themselves die for their men, their honor (as defined by their men), and the patriarchy (see Perkell 1981 on Dido and Creusa; Hemker 1985, Joplin 1990, and Joshel 1992a on Livy). In the case of Cynthia, however, I believe that we are justified in saying that Propertius, unlike his contemporaries Vergil and Livy, does at least temporarily destabilize the feminine in such a way that his readers can see in his text new possibilities for gender reversals and gender confusions.[13]

Propertius adopts as his major identity the part of hero/lover, and in this role, which is clearly relational, he needs an "other" to complement him.[14] Cynthia's chief purpose is to play the "other" to Propertius's hero. This is not to say that Propertius pretends to give her any independence in her role, but he does make her an essential element in his story. The text depends upon her presence for its meaning, but her presence and identity are not definable in the same way that the poet's character is. He appears to have (or portrays himself as having) a consistency, a completeness, and a fixed identity. Although he plays a number of different parts, they are all variations on the character of hero.

Therefore, as the story unfolds, Propertius's identity is consistent whereas Cynthia is never really given *a* (one) persona. Her position is relational and is defined entirely by the parts he plays; she is a foil to him. She plays the Penelope to his Odysseus (Prop. 1.3), the Ariadne to his Theseus (1.3), the virago to his abandoned lover (1.15), the wronged woman to his faithless rake (4.8). Often her qualities are summarized and categorized by the use of mythological figures, which are in themselves attempted representations of the unrepresentable (woman), but the frequent changes of representation (sometimes several within one poem) call into question the possibility of so easily confining her to a set mythological character.

Further, many of the bewildering number of roles assigned to Cynthia operate in conflict. Propertius calls Cynthia his parents (a term more focused on the paternal than the maternal aspect) and his household, thus perpetuating the traditional connection of the woman to household (Prop. 1.11.23). In this poem, she is said to contain him and to be his source, an extension of the timeworn idea of the woman as mother, first being, nurturer, creator, womb. Although he never explicitly allows her the maternal role (too dangerous?) and in fact sometimes explicitly denies her this role (Prop. 2.7, 2.15), he draws an analogy between his feelings for her and for his mother (1.11.21–22),[15] and elsewhere he pledges himself to her as her brother and son (2.18.33–34). Thus she is, by strong implication, the force who has created him, the woman who is at once dangerous because of her maternal powers, confined to her chaste, matronal role (Prop. 2.18.33–34), and the object of his affection over whom he watches like a guardian.

In other contexts, Propertius moves beyond his Oedipal role and regards Cynthia in nonfamilial roles as both mistress and wife (*semper amica mihi, semper et uxor eris*, Prop. 2.6.42). Further, she is responsible not only for his birth, existence, and sexuality, but also for his identity as a poet. She plays the literary critic (Prop. 2.13.14), the secure voice of reason (*domina iudice tutus ero*) to counterbalance the "babble of the crowd" (*populi confusa fabula*, 2.13.13–14); she is responsible for his poetic genius (*ingenium nobis ipsa puella facit*, 2.1.4; cf. 1.10.19–20), and she even takes on the role of his patron.[16]

Thus the character of Cynthia is almost infinitely open to adaptation; it (she) can expand to play all the parts that Propertius requires and he can exchange them at his will. Cynthia becomes for the reader an interesting and problematic combination of elements of an "essential woman"; she is a familiar figure, defined by the traditional roles and duties of a Roman woman of the first century B.C.E. She is a literary, sexual, and historical construct, shaped by the poet and by the male members and readers of his Roman society to be the kind of "woman" they want to valorize and privilege. By giving Cynthia so many attributes and by questioning the traditional tropes of the feminine used in writers of his time and before him, Propertius seems to create in his text the kind of "space" that Jardine finds in male texts of modernity. While Propertius himself is certainly not valorizing a "new" kind of woman, I suggest that he is destabilizing the traditional roles and qualities assigned to women by casting both her and himself in so many different and conflicting roles and by problematizing his representation of her.

My reading of Propertius relies on earlier work that opened up new approaches to Roman elegy and helped to dismantle traditional interpretations of it. In a 1973 article, Judith Hallett suggested that male Roman love elegists such as Catullus and Propertius adopted a "counter-culture" persona which repudiated the socially prescribed patterns of behavior for males and females of the Roman elite. In this inversion of gender roles, the poet is often presented as subservient, passive, devoted to one lover alone, defiant of orthodox values, uninterested in politics and war, and obsessed instead with love and life's finer pleasures. His lady takes the dominant role; she is self-sufficient, forthright, and frank about her intentions (amorous and otherwise) to the point of becoming a warrior herself at times (see also Hallett's article in this volume).

Since Hallett first set in motion this type of approach to elegy, superseding the older biographical and aesthetic readings, much interesting work has been done (see, for example, Wyke 1987, 1989). Recently Gutzwiller and Michelini, in an article that investigates and supplements from a feminist perspective the traditional interpretations of the gender systems operating in classical Greece, Hellenistic Greece, and first-century B.C.E. Rome, have argued that elegiac poets like Catullus do indeed reverse traditional gender roles, borrowing on an already available Hellenistic tradition in which women were valued more positively than in an earlier time (Gutzwiller and Michelini 1991). However, they contend that the Roman poets used the subversive Hellenistic view to "effect a covert reversion to the masculine ethos" and thus reasserted traditional male dominance over the women in question (Gutzwiller and Michelini 1991: 76). Two strains can therefore be seen in this poetry: the Hellenistic view that presented a female-oriented value system and the Roman manipulation of this system that uses it to persuade and control the female subject, recipient, and reader.

In my reading of the elegists (and specifically of Propertius), I would agree with Hallett's suggestion that Propertius is voicing "an eloquent if subtle critique of . . . 'establishment' Roman cultural and literary values" (Hallett, this volume) and might even agree that Propertius's work could in some ways be characterized as "feminist" or at least have been seen that way by certain sympathetic female readers (see Hallett 1993).[17] Gutzwiller and Michelini are right to point out that the Roman elegists were not, however, really interested in asserting a new gender structure, but rather in reverting to a traditional form of masculine behavior and roles encoded in earlier Greek literature.

I have chosen to focus specifically on Propertius (and not on Roman elegists in general) because I see Propertius as a particularly interesting and unique case of a Roman writer who is not a "feminist" in the modern sense and who is not quite creating a reversal of gender codes or a new kind of gender structure, but who—whether consciously or unconsciously—has left us a text that destabilizes traditionally assigned male and female roles and that is in some ways strikingly feminist in its nature and in its treatment of women.

It is because of Propertius's unparalleled treatment of the feminine in his poetry that we can apply Jardine's gynesis to his work. Propertius seems to me to "use gynesis" in a very special way, putting himself into play as the feminine and himself filling the space that has been created in the text for "woman." Propertius removes from Cynthia traits that would have been traditionally ascribed to females such as devotion, submissiveness, loyalty, subservience, passivity, and procreativity, and he appropriates them for himself. He becomes the loyal and devoted slave (Prop. 1.1; 1.6.25–30; 3.11.1–8; 3.25.1–4), the passive husband waiting at home (1.15; 2.8; 2.9), the faithful lover even after death (3.15.46), the one who gives birth to poetry (1.7; 2.1.1–4; 3.17; 3.24). Cynthia, on the other hand, has attributes that are a mimesis of the values recognized in the classical tradition by and for the male: she is demanding, faithless, hard-hearted, domineering, self-absorbed, and interested in competition and rivalry (Prop. 1.1; 1.7; 1.10.21–30; 3.8). Propertius's fixed identity and consistency thus are problematized in the same way that Cynthia's identity is.

This lack of presence or fixed identity of the feminine and the male writer's putting himself into play as the feminine can of course be read in a number of ways; the double-voiced nature of the text is a major problem for the feminist critique, but not an insurmountable one. As Claudine Herrmann has well pointed out, in literature "women have learned to see women through the eyes of men";[18] we have learned by necessity—and are constantly learning—strategies to cope with the sources we do have (and coping is exactly what many of us do), to move beyond the inherited, traditional systems of representation, and to "recognize the ways in which we surround ourselves with our fictions" (Jardine 1985: 47; Richlin 1992b: 161). Feminist scholars and female readers are looking for new ways to think about sexual difference without resorting to the sets of ideas and assumptions transmitted to us by previous thinkers and writers. We can do this partly by looking more closely at how meanings are produced and organized in language. Women in fact may have the advantage here, because some of us are not burdened so heavily by the inherited traditions of past generations and have, because of our position in two worlds at once (the dominant male tradition and our own "muted" female tradition), an opportunity to subvert the texts and to reread them in a different light (Ardener 1972; Fetterley 1978). As feminists have long been urging, women writers need to be "thieves of language" in order to define a truly female self and to rewrite the history of the world (Cixous and Clément 1975; Herrmann 1976; Ostriker 1985; Showalter 1985: 261).[19] As Marks says, "women have the élan and the energy borrowed from male techniques for demystifying and deconstructing, but they also have somewhere to go, to an unknown place, the place of the woman from which she can now begin to write" (Marks 1978: 835; see also Weedon 1987, Moi 1985, on the political imperative for feminist critics and the need to avoid traditional patriarchal categories).

Alice Jardine's amalgamation of French, poststructuralist and Anglo-American feminist ideas is useful because it allows us to avoid the pitfalls of earlier approaches that lead us into blind alleys and to find in texts like the Roman elegies spaces which are filled by "woman" as put into discourse by a male writer. Although Propertius never really relinquishes control over his material, he opens up spaces in his text in which we can feel and see the presence of "woman" and in which he interacts with her (see Williams 1991: 19, on finding the shape of the woman described by her absence). This is not to say that Propertius is performing a radical act by simply putting into play the female, any more than certain contemporary male authors are (Spivak 1983; Jardine 1985: 257).[20] But he does show us new ways of organizing and reading sexual difference by portraying two characters, male and female, who exchange gender roles and are defined by flexibility, lack of identity (difference), incompleteness, and lack of representation (or overrepresentation since each has characteristics of both genders). The space is created in the text by this indeterminacy of role assignment and by the author casting himself as the other gender.

We are thus forced to rethink our known categories of what "woman" or "the female" might mean in Roman elegy. Traditionally "woman" has been represented or understood as the unknown, the mysterious, the unreal, the unrecognizable, the ever-elusive element. Although the figure of Cynthia seems to start out as the representation of traditional female qualities, she and Propertius soon begin to exchange roles, an act that problematizes these traditional traits and puts into question what definition exactly we might wish to give to "male" and "female" here. Propertius does not seem to valorize one set of traits over another; I question whether we can even say that there are two definable "sets" of traits that can be assigned to the genders. Propertius's figure of the female defies any identification and, at least by that act of defying identification, manages to elude the traditional categories that have been used to describe the female in Western literature. Using Jardine's gynesis as our entry into Roman elegy in general and into Propertius's elegy in particular, we can continue the work of feminist scholars like Hallett and Wyke[21] in order to discover how "woman" or "the feminine" is put into discourse in these texts.

To shift now back to my opening quotation from Richlin: it is indeed a shame that more people, especially more women, do not read what feminist classical scholars have to say about "their" texts; more to the point, it is a shame that up until recently, classicists, even feminists, have not been interested in writing articles and books about ancient texts that have been accessible to nonclassicists. My hope is that this article and the volume in which it appears will be a step in rectifying this situation, will put us in closer touch with our sister scholars in other disciplines, will open up ideas for our epigones to pursue (if it is right to think in such hierarchical or linear terms), and will add a historical depth to current feminist projects, thereby benefiting them as much as we have benefited from them.

Notes

This paper would not have been conceived or written without the help of many friends and colleagues in the Women's Classical Caucus, who have redefined the word "patron." I would like to give special thanks to the editors and to Judith Hallett, Shelley Haley, and Carl Rubino.

1. See Wyke's remark that "realism is not equivalent to reality nor a realistically constructed beloved equivalent to a real woman" (Wyke 1987: 61).

2. For a discussion of the positions taken by the poststructuralists (who have many things in common with the French feminists), see Alcoff 1988: 415–22.

3. de Lauretis 1984, 1987; see also "Feminist Studies/Critical Studies: Issues, Terms, Contexts," in de Lauretis 1986: 8–9; Flax 1986, 1987.

4. Hélène Cixous unsettles the question of gender and speaks about male figures such as Achilles with whom she has identified from the past (1975: 73–74).

5. For work on border challengings, see Zweig this volume, and Rabinowitz 1993, on Euripides; Foley 1982, and Zeitlin 1981, on Aristophanes; Joshel 1992b, on Roman freed slaves' expressions of subjectivity; Perkell 1981, on Dido; Skinner 1987: 1–8.

6. Jardine 1985: 37. Jardine makes a distinction between the metonymic "discourse *about* women" and the metaphoric "discourse *by, through, as* woman" (Jardine 1985: 36–37).

7. See Stephen Heath, who says that "the woman can only be 'the woman,' *different from*" (Heath 1978: 57).

8. Judith Hallett has problematized the concepts of difference and identity for Roman women in an article on "Women as 'Same' and 'Other' in the Classical Roman Elite" (Hallett 1989b).

9. For a discussion of Cynthia as a historical person, see, for example, Butler and Barber 1933: xxi–xxiii; Williams 1968: 526–42.

10. See Maria Wyke, who says that Cynthia "should not be related to the love life of her poet but to the 'grammar' of his poetry" (Wyke 1989: 35).

11. Ancient writers: Ovid *Rem. Am.* 764; Martial 14.189; modern writers: Butler and Barber 1933: xxxiv; Richmond 1928: appendix A.1, 388; Enk 1946: part 1, 77; Richardson 1977: 8 (who refers to Propertius 2.24.2).

12. His books are called *doctae* here; Cynthia is called *docta* in Prop. 2.11.6 and 2.13.11; cf. also 1.7.11; 1.10.19: *Cynthia me docuit.*

13. See Hallett (1993), who, in a discussion of the satirist Sulpicia's possible appropriations of Propertian language and eroticism, proposes not only that this is a feminist gesture on Sulpicia's part but also an implicit characterization by her of Propertius expressing feminist views. Hallett would also compare Propertius's representation of Cynthia to his representation in 4.11 of Cornelia, a stable, elite woman, and she views this contrast as further evidence of his characterization of Cynthia as a feminist gesture (Hallett 1973).

14. In some poems, for example, Prop. 1.1, Propertius is the anti-hero, unable to perform the feats of his mythic model, but even in these poems, he is defined by his relationship to a standard set of heroic traits (whether positively or negatively).

15. Oddly, Propertius takes on a sort of maternal role himself in Prop. 1.11.21–22 when he says that the protection of his dear mother would be of no greater concern to him than the protection of Cynthia. For Cynthia as his source, see Prop. 1.11.26: *Cynthia causa fuit.*

16. I discuss this in an essay (Gold 1993) entitled "The Master Mistress of My Passion: The Lady as Patron in Ancient and Renaissance Literature."

17. Whether or not there were women who read or heard the poems of the elegists and to what extent these poems were intended for the ears of a female audience is a

vexing issue with no easy answers. Various of the Roman poets certainly do address women as if they would hear or read and respond to these poems. See, for example, Propertius 1.11, 1.15, 1.19, 2.13 (where he talks about reading his poetry while lying in the arms of his learned lady [*doctae puellae*, 11] and calls Cynthia the "judge" of his writings in line 14), 3.8, 3.10, and throughout; Ovid *Tristia* 3.7, addressed to Perilla, whose poetry Ovid claims to have fostered; *Amores* 2.1.5, where Ovid says that he wants a young maiden who is inflamed at the sight of her lover (*in sponsi facie non frigida virgo*) to read his love poetry; *Ars Amatoria* 1.31–34, where Ovid warns respectable Roman matrons away from his tales of love; and Book 3, which is dedicated to the "Amazons" of Rome, "Penthesilea and her crowd" (*Ars Amatoria* 3.1–2). Certainly, we can say that a female audience is strongly implied in these works and must have been expected to read, digest, and engage with the poetry.

18. See Herrmann 1976, cited by Jardine 1985: 38.

19. See Cixous: "What would become of logocentrism, of the great philosophical systems, of world order in general if the rock upon which they founded their church were to crumble? If it were to come out in a new day that the logocentric project had been, undeniably, to found (fund) phallocentrism, to insure for masculine order a rationale equal to history itself? Then all the stories would have to be told differently, the future would be incalculable, the historical forces would, will, change hands, bodies, another thinking, as yet not thinkable, will transform the functioning of all society" (Cixous, "Sorties," *La Jeune Née*, as cited by Ostriker 1985: 314).

20. The male writer most often mentioned as writing woman into his text is Jean Genêt; see Cixous and Clément 1975 as discussed by Belsey and Moore 1989: 103.

21. Wyke refers to Propertius and Cynthia as "the Elegiac Man" and "the Elegiac Woman" (Wyke 1987: 48), and she dismantles the idea that Cynthia is meant to be a pseudonym for a real woman, but she still employs the traditional categories by which males and females have traditionally been judged in her assessment of what Propertius meant Cynthia to represent.

Bibliography

Alcoff, Linda. 1988. "Cultural Feminism versus Post-Structuralism: The Identity Crisis in Feminist Theory." *Signs* 13: 405–36.

Ancona, Ronnie. 1989. "The Subterfuge of Reason: Horace, *Odes* 1.23 and the Construction of Male Desire." *Helios* 16: 49–57.

Anderson, R. D., P. J. Parsons, and R. G. M. Nisbet. 1979. "Elegiacs by Gallus from Qasr Ibrîm." *Journal of Roman Studies* 69: 125–55.

Ardener, Edwin. 1972. "Belief and the Problem of Women." In Shirley Ardener, ed., *Perceiving Women*, 1–17. New York: Halsted Press (division of John Wiley and Sons Inc.), 1978.

Beer, Gillian. 1989. "Representing Women: Re-presenting the Past." In Belsey and Moore 1989, 63–80.

Belsey, Catherine, and Jane Moore, eds. 1989. *The Feminist Reader: Essays in Gender and the Politics of Literary Criticism*. New York: Basil Blackwell.

Bordo, Susan. 1990. "Feminism, Postmodernism, and Gender-Scepticism." In Nicholson 1990, 133–56.

Butler, Harold Edgeworth, and Eric Arthur Barber, eds. 1933. *The Elegies of Propertius*. Oxford: Clarendon Press. Reprinted 1969. Hildesheim: Georg Olms.

Butler, Judith. 1990. *Gender Trouble: Feminism and the Subversion of Identity*. New York: Routledge.

Cixous, Hélène. 1976. "The Laugh of the Medusa." Translated by Keith Cohen and Paula Cohen. *Signs* 1: 875–93.

Cixous, Hélène, and Catherine Clément. 1975. *La jeune née*. Paris: Union Générale d'Éditions. Translated by Betsy Wing (1986). *The Newly Born Woman*. Minneapolis: University of Minnesota Press. References are to the translation.

Culham, Phyllis. 1987. "Ten Years after Pomeroy: Studies of the Image and Reality of Women in Antiquity." In Skinner 1987b, 9–30.

———. 1990. "Decentering the Text: The Case of Ovid." *Helios* 17: 161–70.

de Lauretis, Teresa. 1984. *Alice Doesn't: Feminism, Semiotics, Cinema*. Bloomington: Indiana University Press.

———, ed. 1986. *Feminist Studies/Critical Studies*. Bloomington: Indiana University Press.

———. 1987. *Technologies of Gender: Essays on Theory, Film, and Fiction*. Bloomington: Indiana University Press.

———. 1990. "Upping the Anti (sic) in Feminist Theory." In Marianne Hirsch and Evelyn Fox Keller, eds., *Conflicts in Feminism*, 255–70. New York: Routledge.

Derrida, Jacques. 1978. *Éperons: Les styles de Nietzsche*. Paris: Flammarion. Translated by Barbara Harlow (1979). *Spurs: Nietzsche's Styles*. Chicago: University of Chicago Press.

Delphy, Christine. 1984. *Close to Home: A Materialist Analysis of Women's Oppression*. Translated by Diana Leonard. Amherst: University of Massachusetts Press.

Draine, Betsy. 1989. "Refusing the Wisdom of Solomon: Some Recent Feminist Literary Theory." *Signs* 15: 144–70.

Enk, P. J., ed. 1946. *Sexti Propertii Elegiarum. Liber I (Monobiblos)*. Leiden: E. J. Brill.

Féral, Josette. 1976. "China, Women and the Symbolic: An Interview with Julia Kristeva." Translated by Penny Kritzman. *Sub-Stance* 13: 9–18.

Fetterley, Judith. 1978. *The Resisting Reader: A Feminist Approach to American Fiction*. Bloomington: Indiana University Press.

Fitzgerald, William. 1988. "Power and Impotence in Horace's *Epodes*." *Ramus* 17: 176–91.

Flax, Jane. 1986. "Gender as a Problem: In and For Feminist Theory." *American Studies/Amerika Studien* 31: 193–213.

———. 1987. "Postmodernism and Gender Relations in Feminist Theory." *Signs* 12: 621–43.

Foley, Helene P., ed. 1981. *Reflections of Women in Antiquity*. New York: Gordon and Breach Science Publishers.

———. 1982. "The 'Female Intruder' Reconsidered: Women in Aristophanes' *Lysistrata* and *Ecclesiazusae*." *Classical Philology* 77: 1–21.

Foucault, Michel. 1977. "Nietzsche, Genealogy, History." In Donald F. Bouchard, ed., *Language, Counter-Memory, Practice: Selected Essays and Interviews*. Translated by Donald F. Bouchard and Sherry Simon. Ithaca: Cornell University Press. Also found in Paul Rabinow, ed., *The Foucault Reader*, 76–100. New York: Pantheon Books, 1984. (I have cited the Rabinow version in the text.)

Gamel, Mary-Kay. 1989. "*Non sine caede*: Abortion Politics and Poetics in Ovid's *Amores*." *Helios* 16: 183–206.

———. 1990. "Reading 'Reality'." *Helios* 17: 171–74.

Gallop, Jane. 1982. *The Daughter's Seduction: Feminism and Psychoanalysis*. Ithaca: Cornell University Press.

Gauthier, Xavière. 1974. "Is There Such a Thing as Women's Writing?" In Marks and de Courtivron 1980, 161–64.

Gilbert, Sandra M., and Susan Gubar. 1988. *No Man's Land: The Place of the Woman Writer in the Twentieth Century*. Vol. 1. New Haven: Yale University Press.

Gold, Barbara J. 1993. "The Master Mistress of My Passion: The Lady as Patron in Ancient and Renaissance Literature." In Mary DeForest, ed., *Essays in Honor of Joy King*. Chicago: Bolchazy-Carducci.

Gutzwiller, Kathryn J., and Ann N. Michelini. 1991. "Women and Other Strangers: Feminist Perspectives in Classical Literature." In Joan E. Hartman and Ellen Messer-Davidow, eds., *(En)Gendering Knowledge: Feminists in Academe*, 66–84. Knoxville: University of Tennessee Press.

Hallett, Judith P. 1973. "The Role of Women in Roman Elegy: Counter-Cultural Feminism." *Arethusa* 6.1. Reprinted in John Peradotto and J. P. Sullivan, eds., *Women in the Ancient World: The Arethusa Papers*, 241–62. Albany: State University of New York Press.

———. 1979. "Sappho and Her Social Context: Sense and Sensuality." *Signs* 4: 447–64.

———. 1989a. "Female Homoeroticism and the Denial of Roman Reality in Latin Literature." *Yale Journal of Criticism* 3: 209–27.

———. 1989b. "Women as *Same* and *Other* in the Classical Roman Elite." *Helios* 16: 59–78.

———. 1993. "Martial's Sulpicia and Propertius' Cynthia." In Mary DeForest, ed., *Essays in Honor of Joy King*. Chicago: Bolchazy-Carducci.

Hartsock, Nancy. 1990. "Foucault on Power: A Theory for Women?" In Nicholson 1990, 157–75.

Heath, Stephen. 1978. "Difference." *Screen* 19: 51–113.

Hemker, Julie. 1985. "Rape and the Founding of Rome." *Helios* 12: 41–48.

Herrmann, Claudine. 1976. *Les voleuses de langue*. Paris: des Femmes.

Irigaray, Luce. 1974. *Speculum de l'autre femme*. Paris: Éditions de Minuit. Translated by Gillian C. Gill (1985). *Speculum of the Other Woman*. Ithaca: Cornell University Press. References are to the translation.

———. 1977. *Ce sexe qui n'en est pas un*. Paris: Éditions de Minuit. Translated by Catherine Porter with Carolyn Burke (1985). *This Sex Which Is Not One*. Ithaca: Cornell University Press. References are to the translation.

———. 1980. "When Our Lips Speak Together." Translated by Carolyn Burke. *Signs* 6: 69–79.

Jacobus, Mary, ed. 1979. *Women Writing and Writing about Women*. London: Croom Helm.

Janan, Micaela. Forthcoming. *"When the Lamp is Shattered": Desire in the Poetry of Catullus*. Carbondale: Southern Illinois University Press.

———. In process. *Biography and Textual Controversy in Catullus Studies: Re-evaluation and a New Approach*.

Jardine, Alice. 1985. *Gynesis: Configurations of Woman and Modernity*. Ithaca: Cornell University Press.

Jones, Ann Rosalind. 1985. "Writing the Body: Toward an Understanding of *l'Écriture féminine*." In Showalter 1985, 361–77.

Joplin, Patricia K. 1990. "Ritual Work on Human Flesh: Livy's Lucretia and the Rape of the Body Politic." *Helios* 17: 51–70.

Joshel, Sandra R. 1992a. "The Body Female and the Body Politic: Livy's Lucretia and Verginia." In Richlin 1992a, 112–30.

———. 1992b. *Work, Identity, and Legal Status at Rome: A Study of the Occupational Inscriptions*. Norman and London: University of Oklahoma Press.

Kamuf, Peggy. 1980. "Writing Like a Woman." In Sally McConnell-Ginet, Ruth Borker, Nelly Furman, eds., *Women and Language in Literature and Society*, 284–99. New York: Praeger.

Kolodny, Annette. 1975. "Some Notes on Defining a 'Feminist Literary Criticism.' " *Critical Inquiry* 2: 75–92.

Kristeva, Julia. 1974. "La femme, ce n'est jamais ça." *Tel quel*. Translated by Marilyn A. August (1980). "Woman Can Never Be Defined." In Marks and de Courtivron 1980, 137–41.

———. 1979. "Les temps des femmes." *34/44: Cahiers de recherche de sciences des textes et documents* 5. Translated by Alice Jardine and Harry Blake (1981). "Women's Time." *Signs* 7: 13–35.

Krueger, Roberta. 1993. *The Lady in the Frame: Women Readers and the Ideology of Gender in Twelfth- and Thirteenth-Century Old French Romance*. Cambridge: Cambridge University Press.

Lakoff, Robin. 1975. *LANGUAGE and Woman's Place*. New York: Harper and Row.

Lefkowitz, Mary. 1981. *The Lives of the Greek Poets*. Baltimore: Johns Hopkins University Press.

Luck, Georg. 1959. *The Latin Love Elegy*. London: Methuen and Co. Ltd.

Lugones, María C. 1991. "On the Logic of Pluralist Feminism." In Claudia Card, ed., *Feminist Ethics*, 35–44. Lawrence: University Press of Kansas.

Marks, Elaine. 1978. "Women and Literature in France." *Signs* 3: 832–42.

Marks, Elaine, and Isabelle de Courtivron, eds. 1980. *New French Feminisms*. Amherst: University of Massachusetts Press.

Martin, Biddy. 1982. "Feminism, Criticism, and Foucault." *New German Critique* 27: 3–30.

Miller, Nancy. 1980. *The Heroine's Text: Readings in the French and English Novel, 1722–1782*. New York: Columbia University Press.

Modleski, Tania. 1991. *Feminism without Women: Culture and Criticism in a "Postfeminist" Age*. New York: Routledge.

Moi, Toril. 1985. *Sexual/Textual Politics: Feminist Literary Theory*. London: Methuen and Co. Ltd.

Nicholson, Linda, ed. 1990. *Feminism/Postmodernism*. New York: Routledge.

Nugent, Georgia. 1990. "This Sex Which Is Not One: De-Constructing Ovid's Hermaphrodite." *differences* 2.1: 160–85.

Oliensis, Ellen. 1991. "Canidia, Canicula, and the Decorum of Horace's *Epodes*." *Arethusa* 24: 107–38.

Ostriker, Alicia. 1985. "The Thieves of Language: Women Poets and Revisionist Mythmaking." In Showalter 1985, 314–38.

Perkell, Christine. 1981. "On Creusa, Dido, and the Quality of Victory in Virgil's *Aeneid*." In Foley 1981, 355–77.

Pomeroy, Sarah. 1991a. "Brief Mention: The Study of Women in Antiquity: Past, Present, and Future." *American Journal of Philology* 112: 263–68.

———, ed. 1991b. *Women's History and Ancient History*. Chapel Hill: University of North Carolina Press.

Poovey, Mary. 1984. *The Proper Lady and the Woman Writer: Ideology as Style in the Works of Mary Wollstonecraft, Mary Shelley and Jane Austen*. Chicago: University of Chicago Press.

Rabinowitz, Nancy Sorkin. 1993. *Anxiety Veiled: Euripides and the Traffic in Women*. Ithaca: Cornell University Press.

Richardson, Lawrence, Jr., ed. 1977. *Propertius Elegies I–IV*. Norman: University of Oklahoma Press.

Richlin, Amy. 1983. *The Garden of Priapus: Sexuality and Aggression in Roman Humor*. New Haven: Yale University Press.

———. 1984. "Invective against Women in Roman Satire." *Arethusa* 17: 67–80.

———. 1990. "Hijacking the Palladion." *Helios* 17: 175–85.

———. 1991. "Zeus and Metis: Foucault, Feminism, Classics." *Helios* 18: 160–80.

————, ed. 1992a. *Pornography and Representation in Greece and Rome*. New York: Oxford University Press.

————. 1992b. "Reading Ovid's Rapes." In Richlin 1992a, 158–79.

Richmond, O. L., ed. 1928. *Sexti Properti quae supersunt opera*. Cambridge: Cambridge University Press.

Riley, Denise. 1988. *Am I That Name? Feminism and the Category of "Women" in History*. Minneapolis: University of Minnesota Press.

Ross, David O. 1975. *Backgrounds to Augustan Poetry: Gallus, Elegy and Rome*. Cambridge: Cambridge University Press.

Santirocco, Matthew. 1979. "Sulpicia Reconsidered." *Classical Journal* 74: 229–39.

Schor, Naomi. 1989. "This Essentialism Which Is Not One: Coming to Grips with Irigaray." *differences* 1.2: 38–58.

Showalter, Elaine. 1977. *A Literature of Their Own: British Women Novelists from Brontë to Lessing*. Princeton: Princeton University Press.

————. 1979. "Towards a Feminist Poetics." In Jacobus 1979, 22–41.

————, ed. 1985. *The New Feminist Criticism: Essays on Women, Literature and Theory*. New York: Pantheon Books.

————. 1989. "Introduction: The Rise of Gender." In Elaine Showalter, ed., *Speaking of Gender*, 1–13. New York: Routledge.

Skinner, Marilyn B. 1983. "Clodia Metelli." *Transactions of the American Philological Association* 113: 273–87.

————, ed. 1986. *Rescuing Creusa: New Methodological Approaches to Women in Antiquity*. *Helios* 13.

————. 1989a. "Sapphic Nossis." *Arethusa* 22: 5–18.

————. 1989b. "*Ut Decuit Cinaediorem*: Power, Gender, and Urbanity in Catullus 10." *Helios* 16: 7–23.

————. 1991a. "Aphrodite Garlanded: *Erôs* and Poetic Creativity in Sappho and Nossis." In Francesco de Martino, ed., *Rose di Pieria*, 79–96. Bari: Levante Editori.

————. 1991b. "*Nossis Thêlyglôssos*: The Private Text and the Public Book." In Pomeroy 1991b, 20–47.

Snyder, Jane McIntosh. 1989. *The Woman and the Lyre: Women Writers in Classical Greece and Rome*. Carbondale: Southern Illinois University Press.

————. 1991. "Public Occasion and Private Passion in the Lyrics of Sappho of Lesbos." In Pomeroy 1991b, 1–19.

Spivak, Gayatri Chakravorty. 1983. "Displacement and the Discourse of Woman." In Mark Krupnick, ed., *Displacement: Derrida and After*, 169–95. Bloomington: Indiana University Press.

Stehle, Eva. 1990. "Sappho's Gaze: Fantasies of a Goddess and Young Man." *differences* 2: 88–125.

Weedon, Chris. 1987. *Feminist Practice and Poststructuralist Theory*. Oxford: Basil Blackwell Ltd.

Williams, Gordon. 1968. *Tradition and Originality in Roman Poetry*. Oxford: Clarendon Press.

Williams, Patricia. 1991. *The Alchemy of Race and Rights*. Cambridge: Harvard University Press.

Winkler, Jack. 1981. "Gardens of Nymphs: Public and Private in Sappho's Lyrics." *Women's Studies* 8. Reprinted in Foley 1981, 63–89.

Wittig, Monique. 1981. "One Is Not Born a Woman." *Feminist Issues* 1.2: 47–54.

Wyke, Maria. 1987. "Written Women: Propertius' *Scripta Puella*." *Journal of Roman Studies* 77: 47–61.

———. 1989. "Mistress and Metaphor in Augustan Elegy." *Helios* 16: 25–47.

Zeitlin, Froma I. 1981. "Travesties of Gender and Genre in Aristophanes' *Thesmophoria-zousae*." In Foley 1981, 169–217.

5

Film Theory and the Gendered Voice in Seneca

Diana Robin

Oedipus: Who forbids me to enjoy the darkness? Who gives me back my eyes? Listen, it's the sound of my mother's voice—my mother.

Quis frui tenebris vetat?
quis reddit oculos? Matris, en matris sonus!

(Seneca *Oedipus* 1012–13)[1]

Au commencement, dans la nuit utérine, était la voix, celle de la Mère. La mère est pour l'enfant, aprés la naissance, plus un continuum olfactif et vocal qu'une image. On peut l'imaginer, la Mère, tissant autour de lui, avec sa voix qui provient de tous les points de l'éspace, alors que sa forme entre et sort du champ visuel, un réseau de liens auquel nous sommes tentés de donner le nom de *toile ombilicale*. Expression horrifiante puisqu'elle évoque l'araignée, et de fait, ce lien vocal originel restera ambivalent.

(Chion 1982: 57)

Until 1973, films were studied in terms presumed to be universal, without reference to gender. With the delivery of her paper "Visual Pleasure and Narrative Cinema" in 1973, Laura Mulvey exploded the narrow assumptions of the field concerning the universality of its aesthetics, and feminist film theory was born (Mulvey 1989: 14–26).[2] Mulvey's early work on film owed as much to the women's movement of the 1970s—when the female body emerged as the starting point for all debates and issues from abortion rights to pornography—as it did to Freudian theory (Mulvey 1989: vii–xv). Mulvey argued that classic cinema reinforced the culture of male dominance by its strategy of displacement: Hollywood movies characteristically assuaged male fears of deficiency by representing the female body as the site of impotence and lack, and as the appropriate object for the controlling male gaze. Since Mulvey, a number of feminist film critics and filmmakers, all of them committed to the proposition that art and politics are interlocking forms of representation, have continued to seek not only to reconstruct but to transform woman at the level of images, discourses, and subjectivities—at the level, that is, of what Teresa de Lauretis has called "technologies of gender" (de Lauretis 1987). For example, E. Ann Kaplan and Mary Ann Doane theorize more than Mulvey had about the complex, interactive nature of the gaze, as involving, at the very least, actors, audience, and the filmic apparatus itself.

They saw possession of the gaze as oscillating in Hollywood films of the 1940s between male and female subjectivities (Kaplan 1983; Doane 1987). From the early eighties on, both Doane and Kaja Silverman turned away from their prior emphasis on the gendered body as primarily a visual construct in classic cinema to consider aural representations of woman in film (Doane 1980, 1987; Silverman 1988).

The uses of sound in film and fantasies concerning the origins of aural pleasure *in utero* and early infancy have been the focus of a number of recent studies in film theory. The infant experiences the mother, as Michel Chion has noted, more as "a vocal and olfactory continuum than a visual image" (Chion 1982: 57). Other studies have characterized fantasies of the womb as not only utopic but euphonic: as a sonorous envelope, as music in its most pure and primal form, and as a place where the sound of the mother's voice is linked to unending plenitude (Silverman 1988; Doane 1980; Rosolato 1974; Kristeva 1982). Describing the mother's voice as "the first model of auditory pleasure," Doane relates the aural pleasure we experience at the cinema to fantasies of return to the sheltering enclosure of the mother's body:

> The imaginary fusion of the child with the mother is supported by the recognition of common traits characterizing the different voices, and more particularly, of their potential for harmony. . . . At the cinema, the sonorous envelope provided by the theatrical space together with techniques employed in the construction of the soundtrack work to sustain the narcissistic pleasure derived from the image of a certain unity, cohesion, and hence, an identity grounded on the spectator's fantasmatic relation to his/her own body (Doane 1980: 44–45).

Lacan, as Silverman notes (Lacan 1981: 62–63; Silverman 1988: 85), attributes special significance in psychoanalysis to the mother's voice, grouping it with those objects he calls *objets a*—objects such as the mother's breast, the infant's feces, the mother's gaze, all of which the infant once saw as part of himself but which were lost in what amounted to a castration, or shearing away, of that body part. Silverman cites two films, Orson Welles's *Citizen Kane* (1941) and Jean-Jacques Beineix's *Diva* (1981), as particularly obvious manifestations of the voice/womb fantasy (Silverman 1988: 86–87). In *Citizen Kane*, a powerful but alienated millionaire finances the construction of an opera house to contain a voice whose resonant, reverberating plenitude promises to create for him the lost bliss of the womb.[3] Similarly, in *Diva*, the young protagonist, who is obsessed with the voice of a glamorous opera star old enough to be his mother, is shown in one scene wrapping himself in the womblike folds of the satin gown he has stolen from the diva's dressing room and closing his eyes in ecstasy as he basks in the sounds of her voice coming from his hi-fi. Such movies, Silverman argues, exemplify powerful fantasies of the adult subject's re-entry into the plenitude of the womb, fantasies of recovery of a lost paradise, which Kristeva has called the *chora*, an image from Plato's *Timaeus*, signifying "an unnameable, improbable, hybrid [receptacle], anterior to naming, to the One, to the father, and consequently, maternally connoted" (Kristeva 1982: 133; Silverman 1988: 101–40; and see also Rose 1989). More experimental films such as Francis Ford Coppola's *The Conversation* (1974) play openly with displaying not only the desire for, but also the anxiety engendered by, fantasies of a return to the sonorous containment of the womb (Silverman 1988: 87–98).

Chion presents a view of the female voice, both in adult fantasies and in the cinema, that emphasizes its more unsettling resonances. In his essay, "Le lien vocal" ("The Vocal Bond"), he offers an alternate fantasy of the mother's voice as a spiderlike apparition, swinging back and forth above and around the infant, spinning its *toile ombilicale* ("umbilical web") of sound.[4] Calling attention to fantasies of the female voice as subversive, anxiety-inducing, and generally unpleasurable in a long citation from Denis Vasse's study of psychotic children and adults, Chion suggests an interesting analogy between the umbilicus and the mother's voice: both are conduits between infant and mother; both are boundary markers signifying rupture:

> The umbilical zone, like a cicatrice in its opaque materiality . . . inscribes, at the very center of the infant, the desire . . . that it live according to the law of its species; and this desire is necessarily expressed, whether consciously or not, in the act of umbilical closure. This act of closure, accomplished at birth, is the correlative of the significance attached to the opening of the mouth and the emission of the first cry. Thus, the voice is inscribed in the umbilical rupture. At this closure, which marks, at the center of the body, the definitive rupture with another body . . . the newborn of man finds himself assigned to reside in that body there. . . . Henceforth, contact between the bodies of mother and child will be mediated through the voice. The umbilicus and the voice form, then, this pair in which the umbilicus is closure, and the voice is subversion of the closure.[5]

Striking in the Vasse-Chion paradigm is the reversal of the positions of mother and child: the enveloping, structuring, and omnipotent prenatal maternal voice is supplanted at birth by the voice of the infant, here gendered male (*le petit d'homme*), whose first cry asserts its separation from, and prefigures its mastery over, woman.

Silverman argues that, for the very reason that the maternal voice is generally invested with omnipotence in adult fantasy, classic cinema—the apparatus par excellence of the dominant culture—necessarily operates so as to reverse this fantasy.[6] Not only are visual representations of the female (woman, mother, wife, daughter) so constructed in classic cinema as to displace male fears of insufficiency or lack; the voice of the cultural Other (the female), in Silverman's formulation, becomes the "dumping ground" for all that is not assimilable to the culturally dominant position (that of the male). In classic film, that is, the voice of woman is represented as the repository for nonrational speech, emotional or hysterical utterances, uncontrollable weeping, raw imagistic talk, babble, and most important, the cry of ecstasy or terror. Silverman demonstrates how this displacement of lack works in her analysis of Anatole Litvak's *Sorry, Wrong Number* (1948), a film where a powerful female protagonist, Leona—whose very name suggests an ominous coupling of dominance with femininity—is set up for a fall.[7]

The film dramatizes a single day in the life of Leona (Barbara Stanwyck)—a day that ends with her murder. At the start of the film Leona is shown as isolated and bedridden due to an unexplained nervous disorder. In a series of flashbacks, we see Leona as she was before her marriage; she had been a forceful and overbearing woman who pressured her husband (Burt Lancaster) into marriage, into her father's home, and into her father's business as its head. In short, Leona has arrogated the functions of directorship and mastery to herself—a usurpation of the paternal position for which she will pay dearly (Silverman 1988: 78).

In the present tense of the film's story line, Leona has been reduced to help-lessness: her only connection with the world is a telephone during the hours when her husband is away at work. In the beginning of the film, we see her overhearing a telephone conversation about the planning of a murder—her own—though she doesn't recognize it as such. She tries repeatedly to reach the operator in an effort to stop the murder. But because her voice reveals her hysteria, no one takes seriously her urgent pleas for help. Thus gradually, in the course of the film, we see Leona reduced from the dominant figure in the plot to infantile dependency. She neither has the mobility of an adult nor is she able to use her voice or manipulate language in such a way as to enable her to survive. In the final scene, her husband warns her from his office phone to cry out for help; but she, now too paralyzed and frantic to act, is strangled by the killer her husband has hired, who wraps the telephone cord around her neck, at last eliciting from her the piercing scream of an infant. This cry, according to Chion, is the crisis point, or vortex, toward which every action in classic cinema is irresistibly drawn. Film, Chion writes, is like a great animated machine whose purpose is the "accoucher d'un cri"—the birthing of a cry, a provocative metaphor that suggests a resem-blance between film and the female body in labor (Chion 1982: 68).[8]

Seneca and the Roman Theater

In this essay, I will argue that representations of the female voice, chiefly as the site of lability, anxiety, and lack (moral and physical), though occasionally also as the source of plenitude and security, were already full-blown in the ancient theater in general, and most specifically in the tragedies of Lucius Annaeus Seneca

(c. 4 B.C.E. to 65 C.E.). Seneca's tragedies were seminal to the development of the drama in England and on the Continent, since they had far more direct impact on Renaissance theater and subsequent European drama than did Greek tragedy.[9] We tend not to realize this, since in our own era, Aeschylus's *Oresteia*, Sophocles's *Oedipus Rex*, and Euripides's *Medea* are standard fare in high school and undergraduate literature courses, while Seneca's tragedies, seldom studied outside graduate seminars, have languished.

Despite the importance of Seneca to the rise of tragedy in Europe, he comes from a tradition largely lost to us. A substantial body of comedies from the early republican playwrights Plautus and Terence survives, but nothing remains from the great third and second century B.C.E. tragedians—Livius Andronicus, Naevius, Ennius, Accius, and Pacuvius—except scattered fragments. We know little about the evolution of the theater in Italy, except that after the second century B.C.E., comedy and tragedy ceased to flourish; and both genres gave way to more improvisational, dance-oriented performance forms such as farce, mime, and above all pantomime, where a solo dancer performed all the parts in a dramatic narrative. Only two tragedies were produced in Rome during the early imperial period as far as we know: Varius's *Thyestes* and Ovid's *Medea*, neither of which is extant. Of the hundreds of Latin tragedies known to us by title only, Seneca's tragedies alone survive. Ten plays have been attributed to him, including the eight complete tragedies *Hercules Furens, Troades, Medea, Phaedra, Oedipus, Agamemnon, Thyestes, Hercules Oetaeus*; the incomplete *Phoenissae*; and the almost certainly inauthentic *Octavia*.[10]

Seneca's tragedies in some ways mirror the sinister palace intrigues that marked Nero's regency (54–68 C.E.).[11] According to Tacitus, Seneca was a key player in these intrigues. Nero's mother Agrippina, the wife of the late emperor Claudius, recalled Seneca to the imperial court from Corsica, where he had been exiled on a charge of adultery by Claudius (Tacitus *Annals* 12.8). At court, Seneca was to serve as Nero's guardian and teacher, a role that caused the playwright, like the *nutrix* (nurse) character in his own tragedies, to zigzag uncertainly between playing his ward's moral instructor and his accomplice in crime. Seneca's intimacy with the young emperor resulted in increasing tension between him and his former patron Agrippina—a tension that has certain resonances in his portrayals of the queen mother figures in his tragedies (*Annals* 13.14). The many resemblances between Seneca's tragic plots and Tacitus's account of Nero's reign, moreover, cannot be simply coincidental. Agrippina's murder of her husband Claudius has obvious parallels in Seneca's *Agamemnon* and *Hercules Oetaeus*. Nero's executions of his stepbrother, his stepsister (also his wife), and his mother— according to Tacitus, Seneca was involved in the matricide—have their echoes in the *Agamemnon* and the *Thyestes* (*Annals* 14.7). The incestuous relationship between Agrippina and her son Nero, as Tacitus tells it (*Annals* 14.2), bears similarities to the relationships between the queen mothers and their sons (or sons by marriage) in Seneca's *Oedipus* and *Phaedra*; in each case, the sons were responsible, in one way or another, for their mothers' deaths. Some of the details of Agrippina's death in fact so closely resemble Jocasta's suicide in the *Oedipus*, that we can only wonder whether Tacitus used Seneca's *Oedipus* to embellish his history or whether the report of how Agrippina died had caused Seneca to rewrite the end of his *Oedipus*. (See below on *Annals* 14.6 and *Oedipus* 1033–39.)

The tragedies of Seneca may have been produced at the imperial court, perhaps in a small private theater in the palace. Testifying to the emperor's passion for the theater, Suetonius says that Nero himself sang the roles of Orestes, Oedipus, and other tragedies in public (*Nero* 21). Nonetheless, the question of whether Seneca wrote his tragedies for performance in the theater or merely for recitation is still the subject of controversy.[12] The voice, in any case, played a key role in Senecan tragedy; since the actors wore masks in the performance of tragedy, every emotion, shift in feeling, or reaction had to be vocally registered.[13] From Quintilian we know too that certain conventional ideas about the quality and projection of the male versus the female voice existed in the Roman theater (*Institutio Oratoria* 11.3.19, 32). Moreover, since male actors played both the male and female roles, the "effeminate" or "soft" voices of certain male actors were the frequent objects of derision among Roman writers (Richlin 1992a: 92–95).

The Roman theater differed most from its Greek forerunners in its attitude toward the representation of sex and violence on stage. In Greek tragedy, acts most crucial to the plot such as murder, suicide, rape, and other forms of violence were not enacted on stage but were described to the audience after the fact by a messenger or some other witness. During the imperial period, the Romans' demand for ever increasing levels of sex and carnage on stage so escalated that actual executions and sexual acts were presented on stage as entertainment.[14] In keeping with the tastes of his era, Seneca's tragedies contain a number of explicitly bloody scenes: Theseus's recovery and reassembling of the mutilated remains of his son's body in the *Phaedra* (1262–72); Jocasta's perforation of her own uterus with a sword in the *Oedipus* (1038–39); and Medea's slashing of her arm with a knife in the *Medea* (807–11).

The Female Hysteric in Seneca

As in classic cinema, the female voice in Senecan drama is regularly the site of hysteria and paranoia—states not assimilable to the paternal position. Representations of the female body, and more particularly women's reproductive organs, as generative of emotional illness, can be seen both in Greek poetry from the Archaic period on, and in ancient medical texts, from the fifth century B.C.E. physician Hippocrates to the second century C.E. encyclopedists of medicine (Cyrino 1992; Foucault 1988: 114–15). Seneca's contemporary Celsus wrote that catatonia could be induced by diseases of the uterus (Greek *hystera*):

From the womb of a woman, also, there arises a violent malady; and next to the stomach this organ is affected the most by the body, and has the most influence upon it. At times it makes the woman so insensible that it prostrates her as if by epilepsy. The case, however, differs from epilepsy, in that the eyes are not turned nor is there foaming at the mouth or spasm of sinews; there is merely stupor (*De medicina* 6.27; trans. Lefkowitz and Fant 1982: 230–31).

The second century physician Soranus saw uterine dysfunction as causing the fainting spells he observed in normal, non-epileptic women:

Hysterical suffocation . . . [is] caused by some condition of the uterus. . . . When an attack occurs, sufferers from the disease collapse, show aphonia, laboured breathing, a seizure of the senses, clenching of the teeth, stridor . . . bulging of the network of vessels of the face. The whole body is cool, covered with perspiration, the pulse stops or is very small. In the majority of cases [these women] recover quickly from the collapse and usually recall what has happened . . . [but] sometimes they are even deranged . . . (*Gynaecology* 3.26; trans. Lefkowitz and Fant 1982: 228).

Clytemnestra in Seneca's *Agamemnon*, Phaedra in his *Phaedra*, and Medea in his drama of the same name, who respond in different ways to their husbands' sexual dismissal or abandonment of them, are all made nonetheless to display a similar physical and emotional pathology: trembling of the voice, sudden changes in pitch and volume, a tendency to rant, sigh, pant, groan, or sob audibly. Genitally bereft, these women's other orifices—mouths, eyes, noses, skin—bear the marks of their stress: their mouths refuse food and drink, their eyes water and tear, their skin becomes mottled or pale.[15]

In Greek tragedy, men weep, groan, and mourn openly. In Seneca, the ritual practices for mourning in the ancient world—loud weeping, breast beating, and hair tearing—are the peculiar property of women, and more specifically of female choruses, employed in only three of Seneca's plays (*Troades, Agamemnon*, and *Hercules Oetaeus*). Each of these plays has a chorus of captive women; but both the *Agamemnon* and the *Hercules Oetaeus* have, in addition, a second chorus who represent the local inhabitants, and these choruses sing in opposition to the captive women, thus denying the possibility of a unified female choral voice.[16] Unlike Euripides's choruses, which are predominantly female, Seneca's male choruses neither sing dirges nor do they sympathize with the female protagonists in their plays. Jason and Theseus, who can weep over the corpses of their sons, are the exceptional cases. In Seneca, woman alone remains the figure for raw nature, for feeling and emotionality unrepressed by the constraints of philosophy.

The Sounds of the Womb

The voice of the mother is almost always negative in its impact in Seneca. Agave's shrieking dismemberment of her son Pentheus is a recurring reminiscence in the *Oedipus* (441, 484–85, 616–18, 1005–7) and the *Phoenissae* (15, 363). But the most frightening of Seneca's evocations of what Chion has called *la toile ombilicale* are found in the *Medea*, where images of the womb and childbirth are consistently grouped with those of darkness, death, and Hades. In Seneca's tragedy, from her first appearance until the final scene on the battlements of the palace, Medea binds and envelops the space of the theater with the almost unrelieved continuum of her voice, her glance, and her movement back and forth and around the performance space. In the opening scene she invokes a full company of deities associated with the underworld: Hecate, goddess of witchcraft; Dictynna, deity of nets and traps; the Erinyes, the sometime goddesses of childbirth and fertility, whose snake-infested heads suggest supernumerary phalloi; and Lucina, the goddess of women in childbirth, known as "the one who brings to light," who here is linked with the spirits of darkness. In two long arias, we are shown Medea's occult practices (*Medea* 670–848): in the first of these, it is the nurse who describes Medea's preparations and incantations; in the second scene (like the shot/reverse shot device in film) we see Medea herself going through her paces as she invokes the spirits of ghouls from Hades and mixes the poisons she will use against Creon and Creusa, all the while beating time to her verses, her feet bared for the dance. Bathing the audience in the sounds of her hallucinations (as later she will inundate them with the screams of her children), Medea fantasizes that she sees the mutilated body of her brother Absyrtus who now demands the deaths of her sons. Removing poisonous herbs, serpents' venom, the gall of the Medusa, and the hearts and other vital organs of owls from the recesses of various enclosures, vials, and boxes, and finally applying a knife to her own arm to draw blood, in this aria she suggests a horrific sort of birthing.

> To you, [Dictynna], we consecrate this holy rite on blood-stained grass; for you, a torch seized from the midst of a funeral pyre eclipses the nighttime stars; for you, with swaying head and curving neck, I have made speeches; for you I have bound my streaming hair with a garland, as though I were a mourner; for you I wave a sad bough from the Stygian waters; for you I, a bacchante, with bared breasts shall strike my arms with a holy knife. May my blood wet the altar; may you become used, o my hand, to drawing the sword and to being able to bear the shedding of our own blood. Struck, I consecrate this holy draught to you. (*Medea* 797–811)

In Seneca, the womb itself is fastened on as the source of evil in the world—"greater crimes befit me, now that my womb has born fruit," says Medea (*Medea*

50). The characters both of Hecuba in Seneca's *Troades* and Jocasta in the *Oedipus* use words, cries, and gesticulations physically to frame and rivet the gaze of the audience on their wombs—the emblem of their femaleness and status as mothers—as evil. Hecuba informs the audience in the prologue to the *Troades* that her womb produced the torch that ignited the Trojan War (33–40). When Jocasta learns that Oedipus is her son, in a gripping scene—partly because it so closely resembles Tacitus's account of Agrippina's last words—she thrusts a sword into her womb:[17]

> Jocasta: . . . Shall I stab myself in the breast with this weapon, or shall I gouge my bare throat with it, burying it there? Do you not know enough to choose the wound? Here, right hand of mine, seek out this broad womb that bore sons and husband both (*Oedipus* 1036–39).

> (Ioc.: . . . utrumne pectori infigam meo
> telum an patenti conditum iugulo inprimam?
> eligere nescis vulnus? hunc, dextra, hunc pete
> uterum capacem, qui virum et natos tulit.)

> Tacitus: Now when the centurion drew his sword for the kill, [Agrippina] thrust out her belly and cried, "Strike me here—in the womb" (*Annals* 14.6).

> (Iam in mortem centurioni ferrum destringenti protendens uterum "Ventrem feri" exclamavit.)

The superimposition of womb/tomb imagery is also suggested when Andromache in the *Troades* first hides her child from the Greeks in his father's tomb, and later extracts him, drawing him forth from his uterine tomb so that he may be publicly executed (*Troades* 509–707). Likewise it is from the empty, abandoned wombs of Phaedra, Medea, and Clytemnestra, as Seneca makes clear, that destruction is engendered: woman, womb, and tomb in Seneca are correlatives.

In the prologue to the *Oedipus*, the king's description of Thebes and of its arable fields (always metonymic for the female body) evokes Vergil's sterile lower world.[18] Within the city, as in Chion's uterine night (*la nuit utérine*), the ambience is claustrophobic and without light. A menacing quiet seems to hang over the city: the air is windless, and only the crackling of funeral fires ruptures the silence. No mourning cries are heard and even "tears are dead" (*Oedipus* 1–70).

> The Dirce is dry, the Ismenus barely flows and hardly stains the arid shoals with its feeble wave. Phoebus' sister slips dimly through the sky, and the sad world pales under the cloudy day. No star gleams in the silent nights, but a heavy smog lies on the earth. A deathly light

shrouds the citadels and homes of the gods. Ripe Ceres denies her grain, and tawny with her proud ears of corn, she trembles and her sterile crop decays on its withered stalk (*Oedipus* 42–51).

Womb as Primordial Knowledge/Power

But the womb is also a figure for knowledge and revelation. As in Irigaray's repriviledging of the cave/womb in Plato's famous allegory as *itself* the unrepresentable source of all representations and thus the epistemological first principle, so in Seneca's *Oedipus*, the place where Creon must go in order to embark on solving the mystery of his identity turns out to be a place whose landscape is conventionally suggestive of the female genitalia and womb.[19] The seer Creon visits inhabits a grove which, like Calypso's in the *Odyssey*, is overgrown with laurel, lindens, Paphian myrtle, and alders. Beneath the tangled overgrowth is a dark spring surrounded by soft, wet ground (*Oedipus* 530–48):

> At a distance from the city there is a grove shady with ilex trees. . . .
> A cypress raising its crest high above the lofty forest binds together the
> wooded glen with its green trunk. An old oak tree, decaying where it
> stands, extends its twisted boughs. Voracious old age has afflicted the
> flank of one tree; another, now split and torn from its roots and falling,
> hangs there—supported by a bough from still another tree.
>
> . . . Under that tree over there is a pitiful wet place that knows neither
> trees nor sun: it is stagnant and still, and a murky swamp encircles a
> slow-bubbling spring (*Oedipus* 530–37, 545–47).

In its associations with knowledge of a preverbal, precultural sort, then, the content of the choric voice is mantic rather than rational. This is clearly the case in three other personae of women in Seneca: Cassandra in the *Agamemnon*, Manto in the *Oedipus*, and Hecuba in the *Troades*, all three of whom are drawn to some extent from Aeschylus's Cassandra. Each of these women is capable of seeing or dreaming truths to which male characters are denied direct access. But in each instance, it devolves upon a male intercessor or analyst to act as interpreter. As in the classic Hollywood films of the 1940s that focus on the psychoanalysis of a female patient by a male doctor (*The Spiral Staircase, The Snake Pit,* and *The Lady in the Dark*), the female analysand senses, intuits, fantasizes things she cannot articulate; her analyst must reveal to her what, on a subconscious level, she already knows (Silverman 1988: 59–60). Without the authorization of a male priest, no one takes Hecuba's predictions of the future seriously (*Troades* 35). Manto, the seer Tiresias's daughter in Seneca's *Oedipus* (the seer has no daughter in Sophocles), sees what her blind father cannot see, describes what she cannot make sense of or interpret. Her talk is childlike, a babble of puzzling images that her father must translate and order into meanings. She "reads" the entrails of the animals sacrificed to the gods; but she will need her father to enunciate the significance of her rambling, melodic lists of what she sees or has seen. Andromache in Seneca's *Troades* is capable of divining that the Greeks have marked her son for execution, after a dream in which the ghost of her dead husband appears to warn her of the danger facing their son. But in the end she is verbally outmaneuvered by Ulysses, who tricks her into betraying her child.

In Seneca's *Agamemnon*, Cassandra is shown having a series of visions. The chorus provides a full account of the symptoms of her hysteria: as in Soranus's clinical description of hysterical suffocation quoted above, Cassandra's body is shaken by convulsions, her eyes protrude, her pupils are dilated, she grinds her teeth, and her voice becomes high and tremulous:

> The priestess of Apollo is suddenly silent, her cheeks grow pale, and a quaking takes possession of her whole body; her sacred fillets stand on end, her soft tresses bristle, her panting breast heaves and emits a sigh from within; her eyes flicker uncertainly: first they roll back in their sockets, and then they stare frozenly ahead. Now she walks proudly and lifts her head higher in the air than she usually does. Now she prepares to unlock her struggling jaws; and then, like a bacchante impatient with the god, she guards her words—though her mouth remains open (*Agamemnon* 710–19).

In the first of her hallucinatory, prophetic monologues, speaking in apparent riddles, she seems to have a vision of Clytemnestra's murder of Agamemnon, followed by one in which she sees herself and Agamemnon as dead souls, floating down the Phlegethon (*Agamemnon* 734–50ff.). Though a chorus of Trojan women witnesses her wandering, chaotic speeches detailing her visions of the future, they do not listen to her words, discounting them as the ravings of a madwoman. In the second of her hallucinatory speeches (*Agamemnon* 876–909), she is alone on the stage. As though looking through a window in the palace, Cassandra "sees" the wife helping the king as he slips into the heavy cloak that she has woven—like Chion's *mère tissant*—for her husband's entrapment; she sees him struggling within the weblike folds of the garment to escape the blows of his wife and her lover, and finally she envisions the king's mutilated body, the lips of its severed head still moving to form a cry (*Agamemnon* 901–3).

But a utopic, choric fantasy of the mother's voice can also be found in Senecan tragedy. In the extant fragment of the *Phoenissae*, for example, a maternal Antigone, who leads her now sightless father Oedipus by her voice if not her hands, seems indeed to wash and envelop him in the sounds of her speech as she offers a guided tour of the rugged path they have taken, now pointing to the locus of this steep cliff here, now to that boulder or chasm over there (*Phoenissae* 61–72). Similarly, Sophocles's harsh Electra is very changed in Seneca's hands. In

Seneca's *Agamemnon*, she comforts her brother Orestes, here a small child, promising to hide him under the womblike folds of her gown (*vultus veste furabor tuos, Agamemnon* 914) where, no longer able to see, he can nonetheless *hear* the maternal voice. Andromache in Seneca's *Troades*, on the other hand, is advised by her servant to remove her son out of earshot of her voice, lest he *hear* a tremor in her words and lose heart (*Troades* 513–14). In the prologue to the *Troades*, Hecuba gathers her daughters and serving women (who comprise the chorus) together, seeming to enfold them in the caressing, consoling sounds of her voice, and as she philosophizes on the dangers of power and worldly riches, she leads her women in a song of lamentation. In this scene, she plays the role of a mother babbling sense and nonsense to her children, calling on them to imitate her sounds and to follow her lead (*Troades* 83–164). First she tells them to undress so that they can beat their breasts in grief. Then she calls on them to repeat after her. She orders them to begin with a mourning song for Hector, and they repeat her words. She commands them next to grieve for Priam. When they have done so, she asks them to change their chant to "Happy is Priam," and they promptly obey. And thus the litany continues with the young women mimicking their mother in her long catalogue of death and sorrow. The sound of Hecuba's voice— and she is on stage for at least the entire first quarter and last third of the play— seems to wrap around the poem, containing its movement and moods. From her womb may have come Troy's ruin—indeed, that is her claim—but she is also a figure of courage. After the Greeks have taken Troy, only the sight of the queen still causes the men to tremble: "I only am a terror to the Greeks," she says (*Troades* 62).

Silencing Woman

As in Greek tragedy, when women commit suicide or submit willingly to death in Seneca, they are notably silent (Loraux 1987: 20–23). In Seneca's *Oedipus*, Jocasta specifies before her suicide that she will excise the source of evil in Thebes by literally taking a knife to her womb (*Oedipus* 1038–39). These are the last words she speaks, thus figuring Chion and Vasse's associations of womb, wound, and voice. Similarly, Polyxena at the scene of her execution marches wordlessly to her death, her breasts perhaps still bared in obedience to Hecuba's instructions (*Troades* 87–94). But there are Greek models for the scene. In the messenger's account in Euripides's *Hekabe* the ritual murder of Polyxena is performed as a kind of entertainment in front of thousands of Greek soldiers; the princess insists on stripping herself to the waist before she receives the execution- er's deathblow, while the whole Greek army watches:

> Then he seized his gilt sword by its handle and drew it from its sheath
> (543–44) . . . and when she heard her master's words, she took hold
> of her robe and tore it from her shoulder top down to the middle of her

ribs where her navel was, and she revealed her breasts and chest, which were as beautiful as those of a statue; then, kneeling down on the earth, she spoke the most courageous words of all . . . (*Hekabe* 557–62).

Like the (narrated) public throat cuttings of Iphigenia and Polyxena in Aeschylus's *Agamemnon* and Euripides's *Hekabe*—and as in the modern snuff film, for that matter—the point of Polyxena's public execution in the *Troades* is sexual arousal. As in Silverman's and Chion's examples from classic cinema, Seneca's Greek soldiers have come to see the murder of a young girl and to hear her screams. But in the *Troades*, the soldiers are denied these pleasures: Polyxena remains silent; and, keeping her body rigid, she propels her torso forward and downward, striking the mound of Achilles as though to wound and penetrate it, the messenger reports. Like some omnivorous female "organ-hole"—to borrow Ernest Jones's image (Jones 1935: 263–73; Silverman 1988: 66–67)—the mound instantly sucks down into itself the blood from the wound of the woman so that no spillage remains on the ground:

> Nor did she lose heart though she was dying: she fell face forward on the tomb with an angry smack, as though she wanted to make the earth lie heavy on Achilles's shade . . .; and the blood gushing from her wound did not remain where she lay, nor did it flow down from the summit of the funeral mound; but instantaneously the savage tomb drained the mound dry of all the blood that was there (*Troades* 1157–59, 1161–64).

Voice-over and the Male Chorus

The "voice-over" or "voice-off" in film belongs to a character who is not visible within the frame. Mary Ann Doane draws a distinction between the "voice-over" and the "voice-off," defining the voice-over as that belonging to a disembodied, omniscient enunciator who comments on but is not a character inside the fictional space of the film, inside the diegesis (Doane 1980: 37–42). The voice-off, however, is a voice belonging to a specific character *within* the diegesis, who momentarily speaks from beyond the frameline. Whereas the voice-over always occupies a position that is disembodied, exterior, and hence in excess of or superior to the diegesis, the voice-off only temporarily occupies this position. In classic cinema, the voice-over—which assumes an attitude of disinterest though its role is in fact to mold and influence the way that the diegesis is "read"— whether in fiction films or documentaries, is male. Pascal Bonitzer, who in the passage I am about to quote uses "voice-off" to cover both voice-over and voice-off positions, remarks on the politics of such a positioning of the voice:

The voice-off represents a power, that of disposing of the image and of what it reflects, from a space absolutely *other* with respect to that inscribed in the image track. *Absolutely other and absolutely indeterminate.* Because it rises from the field of the Other, the voice-off is assumed to know: this is the essence of its power. . . . The power of the voice is a stolen power, a usurpation (Bonitzer's emphasis, Doane 1980: 42).

The male choruses in Senecan tragedy play a role similar to the voice-over both in classic cinema and documentaries.[20] Like the voice-over in film, the chorus serves the function of binding together the disparate parts of the drama to create a homogeneous texture, an illusion of unity and smoothness; moreover, like the voice-over, the chorus sometimes provides a running commentary on the action, the purpose of which is to guide the audience to form the "correct" opinion about what it has seen. The chorus, like the voice-over, is also, for all practical purposes, disembodied, exceeds the plot, and is unaffected by its outcome. The voice of the chorus in Seneca is privileged, authoritative, and frequently omniscient: "the one," in Lacanian terms, "presumed to know" (as Bonitzer reminds us).

Unlike the choruses in Euripides, who were frequently represented as all-female groups (though these "women" were played by male actors, as were all women's roles in ancient Greek tragedy), Seneca's choruses (for example, in his *Thyestes, Hercules Furens, Phaedra, Oedipus,* and *Medea*) tend to be all-male groups, who remain exterior to and untouched by the permutations of the plot, and who are apt to keep up a running philosophizing critique of the action. Whereas Euripides's and Aeschylus's choruses of women get involved in the action and often play a decisive role *within* the plots of the dramas, Seneca's choruses are without personal, particular, or bodied features. Like the disembodied voice in the voice-over of a classic Hollywood film, the Senecan chorus often takes a very distant stance to the action, commenting disinterestedly in the *Medea* in two long interior odes on the perils of the sea (nature, and human nature by implication: *Medea* 301–79; 579–669). On the other hand, the choral odes that frame the *Medea* urge the audience to be disgusted by Medea's Asian mannerisms and to approve of her dismissal by Jason (*Medea* 65–115; 849–78). Similarly, the choruses of male Athenians in Seneca's *Phaedra* act to contain yet transcend the action of the drama, impersonally moralizing at each crisis point in the diegesis, from Phaedra's first disclosure of her desires and her shame, to the death of Hippolytus. Their message at each juncture is one of resignation. When Phaedra tells the nurse she has begun to think of suicide, the chorus sings only of the cruelty of love and the history of its domination in the world (*Phaedra* 274–357). After Hippolytus has threatened Phaedra at sword's point, the chorus warns against the dangers of physical beauty, of nature's ravages, and foresees Phaedra's accusations against her stepson (*Phaedra* 736–834). When Theseus has doomed his son with a curse, the chorus simply bemoans the indifference of nature and Jove to human suffering, and complains that there is no moral order or meaning in the universe (*Phaedra* 959–88). Once the messenger has reported the grisly details of Hippolytus's death, the chorus again, in reply to no one in particular, sings that fortune and death rule the world, noting at the end of their song—as though from a great moral and physical distance—that Phaedra can be seen (presumably on the stage) waving a sword around (*Phaedra* 1123–55). The Theban elders' choral odes in Seneca's *Oedipus*—and there are five of them in the play—never vary much. They provide a consistent tattoo: Thebes has a history of tragedy; fate is responsible; and all mortals must yield to fate. The second and third choruses respond to Oedipus's desire to find a culprit to blame for the trouble in Thebes. These two choruses taken together (beginning at *Oedipus* 403 and 709, respectively) sketch the history of Thebes and explain why the city and its rulers are a marked family. Choruses one, four, and five tidily wrap around the action (these begin at *Oedipus* 110, 822, and 980, respectively), sanctioning the fall of Thebes and the inevitability of Oedipus's end. The fourth chorus warns irrelevantly that steering a middle course is best; and the final chorus counsels impersonally that all men must accept and not attempt to flee that which in any case is inexorable, one's fate.

Film Theory, Classics, and the *Longue Durée*

The demonstrable applicability of the pioneering work of Mulvey, Doane, Silverman, and other feminist film theorists to the ancient Roman theater documents yet again the cultural implications of "the very *longue durée* of institutionalized oppression of women" (Richlin 1992a: xvii). Feminist film criticism suggests new roads for the study of visual and aural representations of gender across the distances of time and culture, avenues viable whether we are looking backward at Euripidean, Senecan, or Renaissance drama, or forward to recent films. The displacement of fear about lack onto the figure of woman can be seen in this year's most successful Hollywood movies. In *The Prince of Tides*, a successful New York psychiatrist (Barbra Streisand) is at last taught how to be a "good mother" and a "real woman" by one of her clients (Nick Nolte), a high school football coach who, after a few sessions with her, becomes her lover. In *JFK*, Liz (Sissy Spacek), the wife of New Orleans District Attorney Jim Garrison (Kevin Costner) takes her place beside the telephone and the TV, far from the affairs of men. As we have seen, Silverman's model of the female voice in films such as *Sorry, Wrong Number*, as the "dumping ground" for traits not assimilable to the paternal position, works equally well with Senecan tragedy, where irrationality, runaway emotions, or lack of bodily or mental control are attributes only ascribed to women. Silverman's focus on the female voice in film is an approach especially illuminating since, in Senecan drama, the voice and its textures are so important in the constructing of both persona and sexuality. Manto's rambling talk in the *Oedipus* must be translated into reasoned discourse by her father

Tiresias, the way the dreams of female patients in classic Hollywood films must be explained to them by their male psychiatrists. Seneca's Cassandra and Phaedra, like the Barbara Stanwyck character in *Sorry, Wrong Number*, are reduced from powerful protagonists to infant dependency in their tragedies. Psychoanalytic theories of womb fantasies, either as a sonorous envelope (Rosolato, Doane) or as an arachnoid trap (Chion), prove helpful, whether we are analyzing the Chionian *toile* Seneca's Medea seems to spin with her cries and whispers, the swoon of the young opera fan in Jean-Jacques Beineix's *Diva*, or the refuge that Orestes finds under Electra's skirts in Seneca's *Agamemnon*. Doane's and Bonitzer's formulations about the apportioning of aural space in film according to gender, and their observations about the designation of the voice-over in the classic cinema as the province of the male, have made it clear how the male chorus functions in Seneca and why male choruses are the rule in Senecan tragedy. Like the male voice-over in film, Seneca's choruses of men are not only the bearers of reason and moral clarity; they are positioned, as we have seen, within the diegesis so that they wrap around and enclose the rantings of a Medea or a Phaedra, offering prefaces before, and sententious counseling after, these women's speeches.

As a postscript, I want to offer some tentative conclusions regarding the construction of sexual difference in Aeschylean and Euripidean versus Senecan tragedy, focusing in particular on the representation of the gendered voice in the text. The argument I have presented here suggests that there is in Seneca a more monolithic submergence of woman and a more pervasive gynephobia than exists in Seneca's Greek models.[21] In his tragedies—as in classic Hollywood cinema— the female voice must ultimately be circumscribed and repressed. Gone in Seneca's tragedies are the songs of those women's choruses who in Euripides see themselves as united by their shared oppression, who perceive themselves as allied, even with a Medea or a Phaedra. The more fluid gender boundaries so characteristic of the Greek theater in fifth-century B.C.E. Athens (Zeitlin 1981, 1985) are not to be found on the Senecan stage. In Seneca, gender isoglosses are no longer to be transgressed; the fiction that men and women have different and polar "natures" has become canonical. The superiority (intellectual, physical) of Aeschylus's "masculine" queen Clytemnestra or Euripides's Taurian Iphigenia to the "feminized" men who play opposite these women has no parallel in Seneca, where representations of the maternal voice are confined—albeit with some exceptions—to that of the hysteric, the sexually voracious, the madwoman, and the intellectually and morally incompetent.

Notes

I would like to thank Nancy Sorkin Rabinowitz, Amy Richlin, and Ira Jaffe for all their many suggestions and corrections, and for having had the patience (each of them in turn) to talk me through the several revisions this piece needed to go through.

1. Unless otherwise noted, all the translations in this essay are mine and all the Latin texts are from Miller 1979.

2. For the overview that follows and on many other points related to film theory in this paper, I am indebted to Ira Jaffe.

3. Cf. Chion 1982: 77–79, on the voice in *Citizen Kane*.

4. Chion 1982; the relevant passage is quoted in the original under my chapter heading.

5. Chion 1982, 57: "La zone ombilicale, comme cicatrice, 'dans sa materialité opaque . . . inscrit au centre même de l'enfant la marque du désir . . . qu'il vive selon la loi de son espèce' et ce désir se trouve, consciemment ou non, 'nécessairement impliqué dans l'acte de la fermeture ombilicale'. Cet acte de fermer accompli à la naissance, est 'strictement correlatif à l'attention portée à l'ouverture de la bouche et à l'émission du premier cri'. Ainsi, 'la voix s'inscrit dans la rupture ombilicale'. Par cette fermeture 'témoignant au centre du corps de la rupture définitive avec un autre corps . . . le petit d'homme se trouve assigné à résidence dans ce corps-là. . . . Désormais, le corps à corps avec la mère se trouve médiatisé par la voix'. L'ombilic et la voix forment donc ce couple où 'l'ombilic est clôture, la voix est subversion de la clôture.' " In my translation above of a passage that Chion partly paraphrased and partly quoted verbatim from Denis Vasse's *L'Ombilic et la Voix*, Chion's quotation marks and italics are deleted to make the passage more readable; the ellipses, however, from Vasse's text are all Chion's.

6. On the cultural myth of the mother as omnipotent, see Dinnerstein 1976: esp. 28–37, 160–97. See especially Silverman's two brilliant introductory essays on the female voice in Hollywood cinema, "Body Talk," and "The Fantasy of the Maternal Voice," Silverman 1988: 42–100.

7. For the analysis of *Sorry, Wrong Number* that follows, I am indebted to Silverman 1988: 78–79.

8. Cf. Roland Barthes on the point of the female cry in Sade, as quoted in Kappeler 1986: 90–91.

9. For a general introduction to the Roman theater, Beare 1968 and Bieber 1961 are still valuable; on Seneca's Roman predecessors, see Fantham 1982: 3–9.

10. On the inauthenticity of the *Hercules Oetaeus* and the *Octavia*, see Friedrich 1954 and Axelson 1967; on the manuscript tradition, see Tarrant 1976; on the tragedies in general, see Boyle 1983.

11. On Seneca's well-documented life, see Tacitus, *Annals* 12–14; see also Suetonius, *Nero*; Griffin 1974, 1976.

12. For bibliographies on the performance versus recitation debate see Sutton 1986: esp. 1–6, and Ahl 1986: esp. 18–30, who argue for stage performance; contrast Fantham 1982: esp. 34–49, and Segal 1986: 207ff., who argue for recitation or reading. On recitations (public and private) as a means of publication, see the testimony of the younger Pliny, writing in the generation after Seneca (*Epistles* 1.13; 1.15; 4.19).

13. But this is not to dismiss the popularity and expressiveness of pantomime in Neronian Rome; on this see Richlin 1992c: 173–76.

14. Suetonius describes the burning down of an entire house in a play of Afranius (*Nero* 11); and the anal rape of Pasiphaë in a pantomime (*Nero* 12). See also Beare 1968: 238, 275; on startling visual effects, see Ovid, *Ars Am.* 1.102ff.

15. These women's symptoms are described in: *Agamemnon* 234–38; *Phaedra* 360–83; *Medea* 382–91.

16. Seneca does not specify the gender of these opposing choruses of townspeople; in his *Hercules Oetaeus*, the second chorus seems to be a band of Aetolian men sympathetic to Hercules; in Seneca's *Agamemnon*, the alternate chorus begins by singing: "*canite, o pubes inclita*" ("sing, o famous youths"), so they appear to be a band of young men.

17. Since Seneca outlived Agrippina by six years, we can conjecture that either Tacitus got the idea for the womb stabbing (which does not occur in Suetonius's account of Agrippina's execution: *Nero* 34) from Seneca's *Oedipus*; or that Seneca simply chose to use certain details from the report he had heard about Agrippina's execution in his own play about matricide. Either way, the dating of Seneca's play makes no difference; he could easily have made revisions or additions to his text until the day he died.

18. On the trope of the female body or womb as furrow see duBois 1988: 65–85; on place/space (the *chora*) as always connoting the female, see Jardine 1985: 88–89; Kristeva 1980: 238.

19. For the explication of the womb as ur-source in Plato's *Republic* 514a–517b see Irigaray 1985: 243–364. For associations of female body, grove, garden, and glen see duBois 1988: 39–58.

20. For the sake of simplification, I hereafter use the term "voice-over" to cover both voice-over and voice-off.

21. But contrast Rabinowitz 1992: 46–51, who demonstrates a comparable (though different species of) misogyny and gynephobia in Euripides.

Bibliography

Ahl, Frederick. 1986. *Seneca*: Trojan Women. Ithaca and London: Cornell University Press.

Axelson, Bertil. 1967. *Korruptelenkult: Studien zur Textcritik der unechten Seneca-Tragoedie "Hercules Oetaeus."* Lund.

Beare, William. 1968. *The Roman Stage: A Short History of Latin Drama in the Time of the Late Republic*. London: Methuen.

Bieber, Margarete. 1961. *The History of the Greek and Roman Theatre*. Princeton: Princeton University Press.

Boyle, A. J., ed. 1983. *Seneca Tragicus: Ramus Essays on Senecan Drama*. Berwick, Australia: Aureole.

Chion, Michel. 1982. *La Voix au Cinema*. Paris: Éditions de L'Étoile.

Costa, C. D. N., ed. 1974. *Seneca*. London: Routledge & Kegan Paul.

Cyrino, Monica. 1992. "In the Pithos of Pandora: Images of Disease and Madness for Erotic Experience in Early Greek Poetry." Dissertation, Yale.

Dinnerstein, Dorothy. 1976. *The Mermaid and the Minotaur*. New York: Harper & Row.

Doane, Mary Ann. 1987. *The Desire to Desire: The Woman's Film of the 1940s*. Bloomington: Indiana University Press.

———. 1980. "The Voice in the Cinema: The Articulation of Body and Space." *Yale French Studies* 60: 33–50.

de Lauretis, Teresa. 1987. *Technologies of Gender: Essays on Theory, Film, and Fiction*. Bloomington: Indiana University Press.

duBois, Page. 1988. *Sowing the Body: Psychoanalysis and Ancient Representations of Women*. Chicago: University of Chicago Press.

Fantham, Elaine. 1982. *Seneca's* Troades: *A Literary Introduction with Text, Translation, and Commentary*. Princeton: Princeton University Press.

Foucault, Michel. 1988. *The Care of the Self*. Vol. 3 of *The History of Sexuality*. Translated by Robert Hurley. New York: Vintage Books.

Friedrich, Wolf-Hartmut. 1954. "Sprach und Stil des *Hercules Oetaeus*." *Hermes* 82: 51–84.

Griffin, Miriam. 1974. "Imago Vitae Suae." In Costa 1974, 1–38.

———. 1976. *Seneca, a Philosopher in Politics*. Oxford: Oxford University Press.

Hay, Arthur S., trans. 1925. *Euripides*, 4 vols. Loeb Classical Library, vol. 1. London: William Heinemann.

Irigaray, Luce. 1985. *Speculum of the Other Woman*. Translated by G. C. Gill. Ithaca: Cornell University Press.

Jardine, Alice A. 1985. *Gynesis: Configurations of Woman and Modernity*. Ithaca: Cornell University Press.

Jones, Ernest. 1935. "The Early Development of Female Sexuality." *International Journal of Psycho-analysis* 16.3: 263–73.

Kaplan, E. Ann. 1983. *Women and Film: Both Sides of the Camera*. New York: Methuen.

Kappeler, Susanne. 1986. *The Pornography of Representation*. Minneapolis: University of Minnesota Press.

Kristeva, Julia. 1982. *Desire in Language: A Semiotic Approach to Literature and Art*. Translated by T. Gora, A. Jardine, and L. S. Roudiez. New York: Columbia University Press.

Lacan, Jacques. 1981. *The Four Fundamental Concepts of Psychoanalysis*. Translated by Alan Sheridan. New York: W. W. Norton & Co.

Lefkowitz, Mary R., and Maureen B. Fant, eds. 1982. *Women's Life in Greece and Rome: A Sourcebook in Translation*. Baltimore: Johns Hopkins University Press.

Loraux, Nicole. 1987. *Tragic Ways of Killing a Woman*. Translated by Anthony Forster. Cambridge, Mass.: Harvard University Press.

Miller, Frank Justus, ed. and trans. 1979. *Seneca: Tragedies*. Loeb Classical Library, 2 vols. Cambridge: Harvard University Press.

Mulvey, Laura. 1989. *Visual and Other Pleasures*. Bloomington: Indiana University Press.

Rabinowitz, Nancy Sorkin. 1992. "Tragedy and the Politics of Containment." In Richlin 1992b, 36–52.

Richlin, Amy. 1992a. *The Garden of Priapus*. New York: Oxford University Press.

———, ed. 1992b. *Pornography and Representation in Greece and Rome*. New York: Oxford University Press.

———. 1992c. "Reading Ovid's Rapes." In Richlin 1992b, 158–79.

Rose, Jacqueline. 1989. "Julia Kristeva: Take Two." In Elizabeth Weed, ed., *Coming to Terms: Feminism, Theory, Politics*, 17–33. New York: Routledge.

Rosolato, Guy. 1974. "La Voix: entre corps et langage." *Revue française de psychanalyse* 37.1: 79–86.

Segal, Charles. 1986. *Language and Desire in Seneca's* Phaedra. Princeton: Princeton University Press.

Silverman, Kaja. 1988. *The Acoustic Mirror: The Female Voice in Psychoanalysis and Cinema*. Bloomington: Indiana University Press.

Sutton, Dana. 1986. *Seneca on the Stage*. Leiden: E. J. Brill.

Tarrant, R. J., ed. 1976. *Seneca* Agamemnon. Cambridge: Cambridge University Press.

Zeitlin, Froma. 1981. "Travesties of Gender and Genre in Aristophanes' *Thesmophoria-zousae*." In Helene P. Foley, ed., *Reflections of Women in Antiquity*, 169–217. New York and London: Gordon and Breach Science Publishers.

———. 1985. "Playing the Other: Theatre, Theatricality, and the Feminine in Greek Drama." *Representations* 11.3: 63–94.

Gynocentrics

6

Woman and Language in Archaic Greece, or, Why Is Sappho a Woman?

Marilyn B. Skinner

The challenge posed by French theory to received ideas of female consciousness and self-representation has emerged during the past decade as the most urgent intellectual problem confronting feminist literary critics on this side of the Atlantic (Alcoff 1988; Draine 1989). Historically, American feminist criticism has been based on an empirical notion of authorship and a concomitant view of literary texts as repositories of gender ideology (Todd 1988). During its earliest phases, then, practitioners sought to expose the misogyny of male-authored literature and to posit an alternative female poetics, as contained in a new canon of recovered women writers. Emanating from the Continent, radical attacks on the liberal humanist creed now seem to call that "fundamental feminist gesture" into question (Jardine 1985: 50–64). The threat is all the more insidious for being incorporated in critiques of patriarchal discourse undertaken by Hélène Cixous, Luce Irigaray, and Julia Kristeva—thinkers who, insofar as they themselves are reckoned as "feminists," might be presumed sympathetic to an engaged feminist enterprise.[1]

Although Cixous, Irigaray, and Kristeva differ considerably with respect to other issues, they jointly insist that woman is excluded from dominant structures of representation (Moi 1985). Taking Lacanian psychoanalysis as their methodological point of departure, all three contend that sexual difference is inscribed into Western symbolic systems at the most rudimentary level. Language in a patriarchal culture originates with man, who locates himself as discursive subject and positive reference point of thought; woman is relegated simultaneously to the negative pole of any conceptual antithesis and to a subordinate object position. She can be defined only in terms of her alterity, named in a way that inevitably reduces itself to "not-man." Linguistic transgression, then, must necessarily precede and facilitate her political resistance.

What shape female linguistic transgression might take is, however, a contested matter. Kristeva's formulation is the least oppositional. Rejecting the possibility of a biologically based female identity, she argues instead that subversion of the

125

rational symbolic process occurs only through irruption of a repressed linguistic core, the "semiotic"—affiliated, though not explicitly identified, with the cultural category of the feminine (Moi 1985: 163–67; cf. Hekman 1990: 87–90). Cixous, for her part, advocates the active production of *écriture féminine,* a mode of writing informed by sexual difference yet not absolutely restricted to women. Characterized by a lyric openness and a lack of conventional, logical organization—qualities also imputed to the tender utterances of the lost pre-Oedipal mother—the texts of *écriture féminine* are intended to challenge the "phallogocentric" symbolic order directly (Jones 1981). Lastly, Irigaray postulates an exclusively female discourse (*parler femme*) grounded in women's specific libidinal economy. Only by speaking (as) woman, in a language that, like female sexual pleasure itself, is "plural, autoerotic, diffuse, and undefinable within the familiar rules of (masculine) logic" (Burke 1981: 289) can women affirm a bodily desire excluded from standard patriarchal speech.

Of the three positions summarized above, Irigaray's is obviously the most immediately vulnerable to charges of "essentialism," that is, the questionable presupposition of an ontological essence or nature in which all women participate by virtue of their sex (Fuss 1989: 56–58; Butler 1990: 9–13). Leading exponents of feminist theory are consequently more and more inclined to treat her assertions nonreferentially, not as factual pronouncements but as rhetorical ploys for displacement of fixed conceptual schemes (Gallop 1988: 92–99; Fuss 1989: 71–72; Schor 1989). Due, however, to her polemic interrogation of Platonic epistemology, which we will examine below, Irigaray has won an unexpected following among feminist students of Greco-Roman culture. With classicists her declarations tend to take on literal force. Adopted as investigative premises, they in turn give rise to tediously homogeneous readings of the Greco-Roman literary tradition, readings whose consequences for the study of women in antiquity are potentially disastrous. In this essay, I attempt to alert my colleagues to the danger of arriving, via Irigaray, at such a theoretical impasse and to outline a more positive way of conceptualizing the ancient literary record, using Sappho as my exemplary text.

Alone among Continental feminists, Irigaray glances back to the temporal origins of patriarchal discourse, seeking to expose its roots as well as its controlling principles. In *Speculum of the Other Woman* (Irigaray 1985a: 243–364), she grapples with the foundation legend of male linguistic hegemony. Western cultural erasure of woman as speaking subject commences, according to her, in fourth-century B.C.E. Greece, receiving primary metaphysical expression in Plato's "Myth of the Cave" (*Republic* 7.514a–517a). In that authoritative text the cave is a "metaphor of the inner space, of the den, the womb or *hystera,* sometimes of the earth" (Irigaray 1985a: 243) and thus linked, by extension, to infancy and prelogical symbiosis with the mother. In Socrates's eyes, it is the prison from which one escapes in order to ascend to the full light of masculine Being and Truth, the abode of the Father. That initiatory pilgrimage once accomplished, return to the dark female abyss is unthinkable: in future, the sole licit relationships will be those between father and son, or philosopher and pupil. "But what becomes of the mother from now on?" asks Irigaray (1985a: 315). She vanishes from sight, for "man has become blind by dint of projecting (himself) into the brilliance of that Good, into the purity of that Being, into that mirage of the Absolute" (362). Obsession with the abstract ideal banishes woman's specificity to the void of the unintelligible.

What results from male abolition of female presence is an underlying "sexual indifference" in the putative representation of gender relations (Gallop 1982: 58; de Lauretis 1988). In a second treatise, *This Sex Which Is Not One* (1985b), Irigaray elucidates that notion. Statements purporting to describe an encounter between male and female subjects in fact record the mere interaction of a male subject with externalized and objectified aspects of himself projected onto "woman," a counterfeit token of dissimilarity. Woman's actual subjectivity is ineffable, since in the male "sexual imaginary" she can be no more than "a more or less obliging prop for the enactment of man's fantasies" (25). Later it is stated categorically that *"the feminine occurs only within models and laws devised by male subjects.* Which implies that there are not really two sexes, but only one. A single practice and representation of the sexual" (1985b: 86; Irigaray's italics). Irigaray's perception of an intrinsic uniformity underlying representations of pseudo-heterosexual congress between man and his manufactured "opposite" is encapsulated in her well-known pun *hom(m)osexualité*. As Gallop (1982: 84) concludes: "Irigaray has discovered that phallic sexual theory, male sexual science, is homosexual, a sexuality of sames, of identities, excluding otherness."

Irigaray's portrayal of Platonic idealism, and post-Platonic Greek discourse in general, as a unitary thought system from which the female is summarily excluded resonates powerfully with the misgivings of feminist classical scholars, long accustomed to apologize for the "male-centeredness" of surviving primary sources (Culham 1986: 15–17; cf. Culham 1990, and responses). It should come as no surprise, then, that recent important work on Greco-Roman gender ideology betrays a deep indebtedness to her ideas. Page duBois, although undertaking what she herself labels "a critique of psychoanalytic theory and its ahistorical, universal claims about gendering" (duBois 1988: 3), finally revamps Irigaray's contentions into a quasi-historical scenario in which Plato's texts become the instrument whereby woman's distinct metaphorical role in pre-Socratic discourse is usurped by masculinity (169–83). Similarly, Georgia Nugent discovers beneath Ovid's facile play with the titillating figure of the hermaphrodite a hom(m)o-sexual "reflection of the (masculine) Same" (Nugent 1990: 176). As the most conspicuous application of Irigaray's ideas by a trained classicist, though, David Halperin's essay "Why Is Diotima a Woman?" (Halperin 1990: 113–51) merits lengthier consideration.

The Diotima of Plato's *Symposium* is, Halperin argues, a rhetorical trope. Plato puts the Socratic model of philosophical intercourse into the mouth of a prophetess in order to call attention to this model's novel qualities of reciprocity and procreativity. Within the male-structured Greek gender system, those elements had formerly been excluded from masculine eroticism and subsumed wholly under female sexuality. In the *Symposium,* that culturally prescribed feminine "difference" is reappropriated, in an intellectualized and sanitized form, for males. What is true for Diotima, Halperin concludes, also obtains for any other Greek inscription of "woman": in the ancient representational economy the female serves as "an alternate male identity whose constant accessibility to men lends men a fullness and a totality that enables them to dispense (supposedly) with otherness altogether" (1990: 151). For Halperin, then, as for anyone else who takes Irigaray's account of Plato's myth literally, it is impossible to find any hint of authentic female reality in the Greek signifier "woman." When an Athenian man speaks to his fellow symposiasts, *Woman,* the universal, does not exist—as Irigaray's mentor Lacan disquietingly asserted (Lacan 1982: 144).

One dubious effect of this line of reasoning about language is that studies of female literary production are rendered otiose. *Gynocritics,* defined by Elaine Showalter as the investigation of the "history, themes, genres, and structures of literature by women" (1985a: 128), was, as I have previously stated, a driving preoccupation of Anglo-American feminist criticism in its earlier developmental stage, during the middle to late 1970s. What energized and justified that sociohistorically based method of inquiry was the assumption that texts composed by women reflect the peculiar conditions of women's lived experience within given cultures, ordinarily the shared experience of a "subculture" marginal to the male public world (Showalter 1985a: 131–32). According to this hypothesis, female subcultures, especially in pre-industrial societies, are wholly occupied with the vital activities customarily assigned to women by a cultural division of labor— the tasks of domesticity, including sexuality, reproduction, and nurturing, and the ceremonies surrounding the human life cycle. On an emotional level, the energies of participants are meanwhile channeled into female bonding networks, primarily ties among blood and marriage kin, and into attachments, sometimes passionate, between friends (Smith-Rosenberg 1975). Discourses originating in the female subculture address such concerns, which are separate and distinct from those of males in the same society. Real life female experience therefore engenders a "female perspective" encapsulated in women's texts. This entire set of common-sense propositions has now been called into question by apostles of French theory (Jardine 1985: 40–41; Moi 1985: 75–80). If the Western symbolic system is a male-ordered construct, as they believe, the feminine specificity putatively contained in women's writing must be an illusion.

Let us consider a practical application of that skeptical postulate. Despite its patriarchal bent, Greek society nurtured a lively and continuous tradition of female authorship, extending from the Archaic age well into the Hellenistic period (Snyder 1989). A canonical roster of major women poets, arguably compiled by the learned scholars of Alexandria, was in circulation by Augustan times (Antipater of Thessalonica *Anth. Pal.* 9.26; cf. Baale 1903: 7–9). Sappho of Lesbos, who flourished approximately 600 B.C.E., headed the list as Homer's counterpart, a complementary model of excellence for her sex (*Anth. Pal.* 7.15). Hellenistic women writers like Erinna and Nossis expressly looked back to Sappho as their exemplar (Rauk 1989; Skinner 1989). Applying gynocritic methods to these texts readily illustrates how books by women "continue each other" (Woolf 1957: 84).

Feminist classical scholars have just begun to direct intense critical attention toward Sappho's neglected followers. Continuing that scholarly project would help to validate the creative ventures of contemporary women. It is no secret that texts signed by females are habitually targeted for ideologically motivated suppression (Russ 1983). To contemplate the numbers of women thus far silenced is utterly disheartening (Olsen 1989). But if ancient female poets did sustain a distinct creative tradition, no matter how minor, within such a male-dominated society as that of ancient Greece, patriarchal discourses evidently do not always succeed in drowning women out. Conversely, if the Greek conceptual system is construed as inherently masculine, one must necessarily concede that no Greek woman, not even Sappho, was ever able to transcend androcentric cultural categories (duBois 1988: 29). The "female voice" in antiquity would turn out to be a male voice with a slight foreign inflection. Under such circumstances, work on the female literary tradition might well be abandoned as useless, insofar as women's texts could no longer claim to reflect a separate, gender-specific sensibility. This would surely be a discouraging outcome for a feminist scholar seeking to uncover scanty traces of ancient women's subjectivity. For the aspiring woman writer, its corollary implications are even more disturbing.

Before acquiescing in such methodological injunctions, however, we ought to scrutinize French feminist theory more intently. First of all, readers otherwise favorably disposed to a psychoanalytic approach are increasingly troubled by its resolute ahistoricism. Despite her ostensible recourse to origins in setting up Plato as the *ktistês* of Western metaphysics, Irigaray elsewhere repudiates history as just another hom(m)o-sexual construct (1985b: 126, 171–72), a move harshly criticized by Moi (1985: 147–49). In more sweeping terms, Weedon (1987: 166) protests that an investigation of gender confined to the level of textual analysis, "irrespective of the discursive context and the power/knowledge relations of the discursive field within which textual relations are located," is simply inadequate as feminist practice. Similarly, Todd (1988: 84) charges that French theory's abstraction of sexual difference from historical flux and change entails a *de facto* "erasing of the history of women which we have only just begun to glimpse." The argument is taken one step further by Jane Flax, who contends that women's obvious exclusion from public discourse is actually the pragmatic result of a political inequality shaped by material conditions: "culture *is* masculine, not as the effect of language but as the consequence of actual power relations to which men have far more access than women" (Flax 1990: 103).

Under pressure of these critiques, the denial of history implicit in French feminist theory emerges as both reductionist and perverse. We classical scholars ought to ask ourselves, then, whether adoption of such a timeless model of linguistic gender asymmetry is not so much at odds with our own disciplinary mission as to involve us in embarrassing self-contradiction. For we are students of Greco-Roman civilization, that is, of a given sociotemporal milieu; and we are consequently bound to address the issue of language and gender (or any other issue, for that matter), with proper attention to the conditions of life in particular ancient environments, as far as we are able to ascertain them. History is, by definition, what we are mandated to do.

Second, even within that psychoanalytic model, language itself is not entirely monolithic. Though they place control of logic and normative discourse on the side of the male, Kristeva, Cixous, and Irigaray all make some provision for a disruptive impulse stemming from the female—or from whatever passes for "female" within their respective systems. We have seen that for Kristeva "woman" can be reintroduced into language as that which escapes signification, while for Cixous she resurfaces as the pre-Oedipal mother making fond inarticulate noises. For Irigaray, at least in one chapter of *This Sex Which Is Not One*, she materializes in a surprisingly familiar form: as embodied women speaking among themselves.[2] Responding to an interviewer's question about the possibility of evolution within the masculine cultural and political realm, Irigaray cites the new discourses— marginal, to be sure—created by women's liberation movements: "Something is being elaborated there that has to do with the 'feminine,' with what women- among-themselves might be, what a 'women's society' might mean" (1985b: 127). At a slightly later point in the interview (1985b: 135), she expands on that suggestion:

> There may be a speaking-among-women that is still a speaking (as) man but that may also be the place where a speaking (as) woman may dare to express itself. It is certain that with women-among-themselves . . . in these places of women-among-themselves, something of a speaking (as) woman is heard. This accounts for the desire or the necessity of sexual nonintegration: the dominant language is so power- ful that women do not dare to speak (as) woman outside the context of nonintegration.

Tentative as this formulation may be, Irigaray in my opinion has cleared a space within her own Lacanian cosmos for real-life women interacting as speaking subjects. And though she has contemporary liberation movements in mind, her notion of "places of women-among-themselves" can surely be extended to other communities of women, especially those sheltered to some degree, as a result of unusual cultural circumstances, from patriarchal modes of thought.

I therefore propose to negotiate the restoration of "woman" into the Greek literary tradition as the historical consequence of "women-among-themselves speaking (as) woman," that is, producing woman-specific discourses. In the poetry of Sappho, semiotic analysis has uncovered an elaborate complex of coding strategies differing perceptibly from those of the dominant symbolic order ([Stehle] Stigers 1981; Burnett 1983; Rissman 1983; Stehle 1990; Winkler 1990: 162–87). Open, fluid, and polysemous—and hence conspicuously nonphallic—those strategies are employed to convey the passionate sexual longing felt by a woman—the first-person speaker designated as "Sappho"—for a female companion, who is often but not always physically absent ([Stehle] Stigers 1981: 47–48; Snyder 1991). To me they supply fragmentary but nevertheless arresting evidence that on archaic Lesbos a socially segregated group of girls and women devised its own symbolic system and set of discursive conventions, formally adapted to the expression of female homoerotic desire and exercised in the composition and delivery of oral poetry.

That repertory of poetic discourses has been assumed throughout antiquity and down to the present day to be wholly Sappho's own invention, designed to articulate private feelings; for convenience's sake, it may even yet be termed a "Sapphic" voice.[3] One need not deny the poetic genius of the flesh-and-blood singer capable of handling her material with such artistic economy that it rapidly passed from mouth to mouth throughout the Greek world and survived intact for many centuries. Yet, given the normal function of the archaic Greek poet as appointed spokesperson for his or her community, it is far more likely that Sappho's self-stylization as desiring *ego,* along with her extensive stock of themes, verse forms and melodies, tropes and imagery, was largely traditional, a product of many generations of local creative endeavor. Thus Sappho would have inherited both her social role and her craft from a long line of female predecessors.[4]

By approaching these songs as social discourses, we avoid the sticky problems of representation involved in treating a text as the faithful mirror of an author's unique subjectivity. To redeploy Showalter's concept, then, Sappho's poetry will here be presumed to distill the shared impressions of a historically contextualized "subculture," refracting to some degree women's lived realities, their confrontations with experience, albeit only in synthetic and highly idealized form. Yet in affording us insights into patterns of social ideology promulgated among a group of elite Greek women on sixth-century B.C.E. Lesbos, this body of texts may still prove immeasurably valuable for feminist historical inquiry.[5]

Sappho's friends were able to "speak (as) woman among themselves" precisely because they were not readers. In contemporary postindustrial societies, where males are educationally advantaged, control of electronically based information systems is guarded, and writing is still the primary mode of communication, the ordination of "man" as unmarked subject of discourse is probably inevitable. In predominantly oral societies, on the other hand, women do have readier access to the cultural tradition insofar as it is conveyed by word of mouth. The nucleus of a cultural heritage is, according to Goody and Watt, "the particular range of meanings and attitudes which members of any society attach to their verbal symbols" (Goody and Watt 1968: 28). But that collection of meanings is always open to modification. Within tightly integrated nonliterate societies, then, women can verbally intervene in dominant symbolic systems and append additional "feminine" values to signifiers, provided they have first had occasion to invent their own ways of encoding those values. Given a culture endowed with the custom of female musical performance before same-sex audiences, such occasions do arise: having positioned herself as speaking subject, the singer will tailor her presentation to her listeners' interests, imbuing it, as Showalter has argued, with "women's experience," as that is commonly understood by her society.[6]

Now if, within the oral tradition, a female perspective has thus secured a claim to validity, that perspective could well assume a legitimate, albeit subordinate, place in a subsequent written tradition, so as ultimately to provide readers with an alternative subject position available to either sex. By "subject position" I mean an organized way of seeing the world, constituted through language, that permits the individual to impose a coherent meaning on the circumstances and events of his or her life, simultaneously enjoining practices based on that meaning (Weedon 1987: 21–27). Once incorporated into a discursive system, a subject position may be adapted to various ends, long-term or immediate, serious or playful—utilized as a set of practical strategies for living in the world or, in contrast, appropriated as a vehicle for escapist fantasy. In the ancient literary tradition, the "Sapphic voice" seems to have become just such an alternative subject position.

From the Archaic period to the early Hellenistic era, the Greek world experienced a slow transition from orality to literacy (Havelock 1963, 1977; Harris 1989). Available evidence, chiefly from Athens, indicates that the capacity to write, with a corollary dependence on written records, spread through the population only gradually, coexisting for a long time with the time-honored mnemonic skills of a nonliterate society (Thomas 1989). Though women are decoratively shown as readers on fifth-century B.C.E. Athenian vases, in practice they remained disproportionately illiterate, not only in Greece but in all parts of the ancient world and at all historical periods (Cole 1981; Harris 1989: 106–8). On the other hand, women storytellers perhaps contributed a great deal to preserving and handing on oral traditions, even after the dissemination of literacy (Thomas 1989: 109).

Though this societal transformation was already well advanced in his lifetime, Plato in his last treatise still singles out song and dance, rather than books, as the basic medium for transmitting an awareness of cultural values to the young (Plato *Laws* 2.653c–656c). From time immemorial, oral instruction in the knowledge necessary to survive in Greek society—including an understanding of theology, history, politics, law, and even agriculture, as well as practical training in poetry, music, and rhythmic movement—had been made available to all upper-class youth, girls as well as boys, through their attendance at public festivals and their own parts in cult and ritual. For girls in particular, socialization was achieved by membership in a chorus composed of age-mates, beginning in childhood and continuing until marriage (Calame 1977). The anomalous phenomenon of women poets in a rigidly gender-stratified society is plausibly explained by their function as poet-educators for adolescent groups of female initiates (Dowden 1989: 103). Sappho, it is widely believed, was just such an educator, composing cult songs for the young women enrolled in her sodality or *thiasos* and training them in oral performance (Merkelbach 1957; Calame 1977: 385–420; Gentili 1988: 72–89).

Responsibility for instructing Greek girls in music and dance was not, however, confined to women. The genre of *partheneia,* or "maiden songs," was extremely popular, and a number of famous male poets—Alcman, Pindar, Simonides, Bacchylides—are credited with producing such works ([Plutarch] *De Musica* 17.1136f). Lengthy fragments of two *partheneia* by Alcman, active in Sparta in the mid-seventh century B.C.E., are frequently compared to Sappho's verses because his speakers, like hers, express a strong homoerotic attraction to the beauty of their companions (Calame 1977: 420–39; Dover 1978: 179–82; Rissman 1983: 119–21). This generic resemblance has prompted the suggestion that Sappho was herself a follower of Alcman (Hallett 1979: 461–64). At the very least, it proves that her function as socializer of young female initiates could elsewhere be undertaken by men, and thus leads us to wonder about the authenticity of her female perspective. Could Sappho be imposing upon her young charges a cognitive structure derived from, and intended to reinforce, patriarchy? If so, this would be but one more instance of women choosing "to inhabit the space to which they are already assigned" by a male "logic of domination" (duBois 1988: 29).

I do not believe, though, that that is the case. While Sappho's manipulation of verbal devices like diction, figures of speech, and imagery is clearly indebted to the mainstream tradition (Fowler 1984), her modes of subjectivity differentiate her to an extraordinary degree from her male counterparts—particularly those working within the same genre, whether *partheneion* or erotic monody. Specifically, her model of homoerotic relations is bilateral and egalitarian ([Stehle] Stigers 1981), in marked contrast to the rigid patterns of pursuit and physical mastery inscribed into the role of the adult male *erastês,* whatever the sex of his love object (Foucault 1986: 38–93). The distinction between these two ways of constituting homoerotic passion can be illustrated by juxtaposing Alcman's representations of girls in love with the desiring speakers portrayed in numerous Sapphic texts, most notably her fr. 31.[7] The chorus's admiration of their leaders Hagesichora and Agido in Alcman fr. 1 is permeated with a spirit of eager rivalry, since they are competing with another chorus (Page 1951: 52–57). Such agonistic tensions emulate the mindset of a male warrior society. Meanwhile, the yearning for Astymeloisa expressed in Alcman fr. 3 betrays an abject dependency quite foreign to Sappho herself ([Stehle] Stigers 1979: 469–71). In contrast, Sappho's declarations of passion are a subtle means of awakening the beloved to the mutual pleasures of sexuality. Thus fr. 31 is no anguished confession, but instead a virtuoso display of seductive poetic control: by making her vividly conscious of her own power to captivate others, the speaker draws the addressee into a dense web of sensual self-awareness and so encourages in her a reciprocal erotic response (O'Higgins 1990).

There are corresponding differences, too, in each poet's stance toward members of the opposite sex and concomitant portrayal of gender relations. Though Alcman's singing girls are center stage, the gaze fixed upon them is unmistakably male, for in their sweet naivety and emotional vulnerability they present themselves as unsuspecting objects of heterosexual desire. In Sappho's poetic universe, however, men are hardly a focus of female interest; as Joan DeJean deflatingly remarks, they are "relegated to a peripheral, if not an intrusive, role" (DeJean 1987: 790). Masculine ideology, on the other hand, is present as inescapable background noise, representing both the power of the cultural system to enforce its demands on women (Stehle 1990: 111–12) and a privileged conceptual framework to which Sappho counterposes her own antithetical outlook. For example, in rebuking the transgressions of her errant brother Charaxus and his mistress Doricha (fr. 5, 7, and 15), she seems to be censuring a male economy of desire: erotic obsession, the impulse to possess the object undividedly, has brought public disgrace upon Charaxus himself and provoked unseemly arrogance in his paramour (fr. 15.9–12). Again, the first stanza of fr. 16 confirms the speaker's superior insight into what is "the most beautiful" (*to kalliston*) by opposing her comprehensive and relativisitic definition of beauty to a series of overtly male, and patently limited, foils. Lastly, the violence of Sappho's reaction to the sight of her beloved in fr. 31 is enhanced by an indirect contrast with masculine impassivity. While the man sitting opposite the girl must be taken as a hypothetical, rather than a concrete, figure (Winkler 1990: 179), his intrusion into this intimate conversation warns of the crass indifference of the great world outside the *thiasos,* less inclined to appreciate the addressee's singular loveliness.

In none of these texts does Sappho close her eyes to the ontological reality of the masculine order. She recognizes it, instead, as a prior and controlling presence, but still avows the ethical superiority of her nonnormative subject position, her radically woman-centered approach to existence. Whenever her texts trope difference by an appeal to gender, then, the female stance affords a posture of resistance to prevailing male attitudes and practices. But the resulting polarity is not inversely "hom(m)o-sexual," in Irigaray's sense: rather than conjuring up male alterity as the mere negative projection of itself, the speaker's perspective defiantly locates itself against patriarchy, the pre-extant condition. One might state, paradoxically, that Sappho's poetry is literally "heterosexual," for it affirms the availability of distinct, gender-specific modes of subjectivity and directs its audience to choose what is identified as the better, though less advantaged, of two real alternatives.

It appears, then, that the subject position extracted from Sappho's monodies and choral compositions does not replicate patriarchal modes of awareness but rather affords a substitute basis for organizing female experience. Through imaginative identification with the first-person speaker, a girl would have absorbed survival tricks for living within a patriarchal culture: formulas for resisting misogynistic assumptions and so protecting self-esteem, for expressing active female erotic desire, for bonding deeply with other women, and for accepting the underlying ambiguities and absences of full closure inherent in both human discourse and human life. Consequently, she would be, in her adult years, an energetic and wholly socialized participant in female communities—those into which she was born and those she would join upon her marriage. The ultimate purpose of Sapphic song, we may conclude, was to encode strategies for perpetuating women's culture.

But would it really have been possible for a girl who internalized a female subject position to preserve it after leaving the *thiasos* and reentering a patriarchal milieu? Again, let us observe the peculiar epistemic processes of oral cultures. In passing information from one generation to the next, nonliterate societies exhibit "structural amnesia": aspects of the past no longer relevant to present concerns are sloughed off from the record and forgotten (Ong 1982: 46–49). Susan Schibanoff (1986: 87–91) suggests that illiterate women respond to directives from the dominant culture in similar fashion. With no concept of a fixed, unyielding written text to deter them, they can "mishear" utterances in conflict with their own values and thereby resist immasculation. If Schibanoff is right, it follows that adult women in Archaic and early Classical Greece, segregated from the larger public sphere except on ritual occasions and having little or no exposure to reading or writing, could easily have retained a woman-centered perspective— more easily, no doubt, than their literate great-granddaughters.[8] At separate cult gatherings such as the Adonia and the Thesmophoria, to say nothing of daily private interaction in their own homes, these women had abundant opportunities to speak and joke among themselves, to chant and dance, to adapt a flexible mythic heritage to their purposes—in short, to propagate their own discourses in relative isolation (Winkler 1990: 188–209). We know, for example, that women sang folk songs, because scraps of them have been preserved, including one (*Poetae Melici Graeci* 869) that may have originated on Lesbos in Sappho's own lifetime: its reference to Pittacus, a ruling tyrant, is suspiciously familiar and quite possibly obscene (Campbell 1967: 448–49). It is reasonable to surmise, then, that compositions of Sappho and other women poets also formed part of a widespread female oral tradition handed down from mother to daughter, and that those compositions served, in effect, as a mechanism for opposing patriarchy.

Considered in such a way, Sappho's poetry offers an intriguing parallel to Luce Irigaray's own demonstration of *parler femme,* "speaking (as) woman," in "When Our Lips Speak Together," the essay that concludes *This Sex Which Is Not One* (Irigaray 1985b: 205–18). There, troping speech as lesbian erotic play, Irigaray gives substance to her conception of a polysemous feminine language enacted through the female body. Communication between her lovers takes place on a timeless, almost wordless plane beyond patriarchal "compartments" and "schemas" (1985b: 212), where only the body's truths are valid. "You," the addressee, and "I," the speaker, meld into one composite being through simultaneous *jouissance*, and this interchange of inexhaustible orgasmic pleasure constitutes a sharing of consciousness. Because Irigaray's model of female language depends upon corporeal contact, however, the subject is forced to seek a way of embracing across distances and can only appeal, in the end, to a vague notion of mystical somatic fusion (1985b: 215–16). Yet it seems obvious that a connection with the absent partner cannot be sustained, in practice, without recourse to writing— which poses the danger of reinscription as object within a prefabricated patriarchal account.

Song, Sappho's medium of communication, avoids this pitfall because it is memory based. In oral societies, memory is the repository of all knowledge and the matrix of the collective as well as the individual consciousness. Thus an idealized experience captured in song and committed to memory can surmount the physical limitations of space and time. Meanwhile, song as performance art also provides scope for idiosyncratic self-expression by prescribing that every successive rendition will be unique, produced by one singer at a particular moment in time. The song text is both infinitely repeatable and infinitely varied.[9] Patterns of intimacy forged by erotic encounters within the Sapphic *thiasos* would consequently have survived a patriarchially enforced separation by marriage, for the searing intensity of the love affair could be rekindled through verses associated with that affair and later performed over and over again during the singer's lifetime (Burnett 1983: 277–313). By the same means, the moving lessons learned from her adolescent experience of desire might be imparted to outsiders—women of another community, or her own children and grandchildren (Segal 1974). Long after the composer's death and long after the death of her last companion, then, this poetry would have continued to offer generations of women an authentic female subject position. That in turn explains the emergence, century after century, of yet other Greek women poets, for whom their archaic foremother served as enabling prototype and fount of inspiration.

But we should not forget that Sappho's songs would not have gained fame in the wider world, or eventually circulated as written texts, had they not offered something to men as well as to women. Divorced from their primary cultural context, artistic works produced by female communities are subject to marginalization or distortion precisely because they exhibit disturbing deviations from normal social ideology. Thus, to cite an already familiar example, Alcman in his maiden songs is most likely appropriating a Spartan female initiatory discourse akin to the one Sappho herself inherited and making it conform to a masculine symbolic order. Sappho's poetry is, as we have seen, undeniably deviant; yet it was still preserved, transcribed, and ultimately enshrined within the androcentric literary tradition as a special category of discourse. Had men used it solely for voyeuristic gratification, converting its female subjects into erotic objects, they would have drastically modified its content, as we have observed Alcman doing, and excised in the process its woman-oriented elements. Clearly, then, Greek male listeners must have found another, peculiar application for it, one that required its survival intact and unchanged.

Sappho's great poetic achievement, I believe, was to articulate a female desire so compellingly as to make it at once emotionally accessible to men as well as women—although men's responses to it were shaped by far different relations of gender and power. The diffused eroticism that taught female auditors in the sheltered atmosphere of the *thiasos* how to transcend linear symbolic systems was perceived within the masculine sphere as delightfully idyllic and romantic. Consequently, as we learn from ancient critical pronouncements, anecdotal evidence, and visual representations of the poet as cultural icon, male listeners and readers cherished Sappho's works as a socially permissible escape from the strict constraints of masculinity.[10] In the symposium, singing one of these compositions—songs charged with the comforting presence of benign divinity and flooded with aching but sweet reciprocal desire—would have allowed men momentarily to "play the other," in Zeitlin's phrase, and so to release themselves from the necessity of being at all times publicly competitive and self-controlled.[11]

By logical extension, allusion to Sappho became an obvious tactic for projecting metaphoric "difference" upon one of two antithetical male-structured categories, particularly during the long process of conversion to a writing based system of literary production. Yet the Sapphic texts still stayed in play as a locus of real differentiation, continually reinscribing into mainstream Greek discourse a set of gender assumptions radically free from male bias. *Pace* Irigaray, woman accordingly maintained a toehold in the Western symbolic order for as long as those texts remained intact. *Pace* Halperin, there is a dash of actual female subjectivity even in Diotima: when he argues persuasively that the Platonic image of reciprocal intellectual eroticism is derived from earlier ideas of female homoerotic relations (1990: 126–37), Halperin overlooks the fact that Plato's audience would have obtained its artistic impressions of female homoeroticism chiefly from the poetry of Sappho.

If meganarratives like Irigaray's are to serve as frameworks for profitable scholarly inquiry, they must be pliant enough to admit a blurring of polarities, to incorporate pronounced exceptions to their rules. Confronting a gargantuan heap of male-authored texts, feminist classical scholars have understandably perceived sexual/textual oppression everywhere and so written off the Greco-Roman literary tradition as a blank page of canonical female silence. But, as Cicero informs us, silenced voices do cry out (*Cat.* 1.21) and, according to Susan Gubar, blank pages can tell tales (Gubar 1985). While we may accurately describe Western culture as masculine in orientation, we must refrain from subscribing to paradigms of cultural construction that obliterate women's historical contributions to art and learning, for to do so is to do patriarchy's work.

In conclusion, then, I submit that the female-specific discourse known as Sappho's poetry is not so marginal to the Greek, or to the Western European, literary tradition as to be readily excluded from consideration as an influential cultural factor, no matter how absolute and totalitarian the grip of the patriarchal symbolic system might appear. As many honorific allusions by later women writers suggest, this discourse did provide generations of ancient women with a (m)other tongue and a basis for constructing a positive account of their own experiences. More important for its perpetuation (and, one might add, for the overall mental health of the culture), Greco-Roman males benefited from the opportunity afforded by Sappho's texts to enact a woman's part, if only in play, and so to enter imaginatively into states of awareness foreign to them. In the innovative Hellenistic period, literary representation itself gained new vitality from incorporating additional elements of the female perspective preserved in Sapphic poetry. Finally, we should not forget that, exactly like their predecessors in antiquity, women taking up the pen at the beginning of the modern era invoked Sappho as a heroic authorizing presence (Kolodny 1987). Thus all contemporary women who write, within the Western tradition at least, may call themselves daughters of Sappho. As we reread her scanty fragments, we consequently do much more than rediscover the woman's voice in ancient literature. We are hearing, though brokenly, the missing half of the Greco-Roman gender dialectic, glimpsing the other shattered surface of what was once a two-sided glass. That no comparable glass has existed until recently for modern man has been his loss, no less than woman's.

Notes

An oral version of this essay was delivered at the "Feminist Theory and the Classics" panel presented on December 30, 1990, at the one hundred and twenty-second annual meeting of the American Philological Association in San Francisco, California. I wish to thank the panel co-organizers Nancy Sorkin Rabinowitz and Amy Richlin, my fellow presenters Marilyn A. Katz and Barbara K. Gold, the two respondents Judith Hallett and Kristina Passman, as well as many members of the audience, for a wealth of stimulating suggestions. Subsequently, in her role as editor, Nancy Rabinowitz carefully assisted me in blocking out a tighter, more linear argument. I also owe a great debt to Eva Stehle and Jane Snyder, who read draft versions of the paper and commented extensively on them. Lastly, my special thanks to David Halperin, whose painstaking efforts to help improve a paper disputing his position manifest an exceptional scholarly generosity, feminist in every sense.

1. Key passages from the writings of Cixous, Irigaray, and Kristeva were conveniently selected and translated by Marks and de Courtivron 1980. The difficulties French feminist theory poses for an Anglo-American feminist criticism that regards the text as the representation of an author's personal subjectivity and experience are explored in the classic debate between Kamuf 1982 and Miller 1982. For subsequent elaborations, see, among others, Weedon 1987: 165–66; Butler 1990: 1–34; Flax 1990:

168–78; and Hekman 1990: 144–51. Strategies for transcending the ensuing dilemma are put forward by Homans 1987; Alcoff 1988; and de Lauretis 1984, 1989, and 1990. For further insight into the relevance of French feminist theory to feminist criticism of classical texts, the reader is directed to Gold 1993 in this volume.

2. For an excellent analysis of the scheme of practical politics outlined in this passage, see Fuss 1989: 66–70.

3. For an important reading of Sappho as spokesperson for a group, rather than an individual, consciousness, see Hallett 1979. In a new study (Hallett, in progress), subsequent Roman appropriations of Sappho's mode of homoerotic discourse are surveyed and comprehensively identified as a "Sapphic tradition." While I am deeply indebted to Hallett for the concept of an ancient gender-specific style of literary expression capable of articulating female desire, my purpose here is not primarily to defend her revisionist approach to Sappho nor to trace out the poet's impact on later literature, but rather to urge my colleagues to forgo constructions of ancient literary history that eradicate Sappho's achievement and its continuing influence.

4. Plausible arguments for a continuous Greek lyric tradition extending as far back as the eighth century B.C.E. are supplied by Fowler 1987: 9–13. It is worth recalling Virginia Woolf's observation that, "if you consider any great figure of the past, like Sappho, like the Lady Murasaki, like Emily Brontë, you will find that she is an inheritor as well as an originator, and has come into existence because women have come to have the habit of writing naturally" (Woolf 1957: 113). Though I would question the use of the term "writing" in Sappho's case, I believe Woolf's intuitive perception of her as heir to a female poetic tradition is probably accurate.

5. Here I follow the lead of Homans 1987: 173, who holds out to feminist critics a possible route of escape from the liberal humanist/poststructuralist quarrel over individual subjectivity: turning one's attention to collective female discourses.

6. In contemporary sex-segregated Middle Eastern cultures, women still create oral poetry and employ it for precisely this purpose: see Joseph 1980; Abu-Lughod 1986: 171–271. The overall effectiveness of female poetic discourse as a power tool depends on its acceptance by men: when memorized and quoted by males, women's songs indirectly provide their composers with a strong voice in the larger community (Joseph 1980: 427). As we will see, this modern parallel illuminates the reception of Sappho's songs in antiquity.

7. For the convenience of nonspecialists, the numeration of the fragments (fr.) of both Sappho's and Alcman's poems is that found in the most recent Loeb editions (Campbell 1982, and 1988, respectively).

8. On the increased availability of formal education for women from the fourth century B.C.E. onward, see Pomeroy 1977.

9. For a theoretical analogy, compare de Lauretis's several arguments for redefining personal subjectivity as an ongoing "process of engagement" with externally formulated social discourses. According to de Lauretis, the agent exercises a considerable degree of self-determination in adapting those discourses to serve her private needs and even combining them into more complex vehicles of consciousness that escape conventional categories (de Lauretis 1984: 182–86, cf. 1986: 8–10, and 1990: 144–45).

10. The psychological spell Sappho exerted over a male listener's imagination is implied at [Longinus] *On the Sublime* 10.1–3, where the author marvels at her ability to select and combine "the most extreme and intense" (*ta akra . . . kai hypertetamena*) emotions in her descriptions of love. Praise of the charm (*charis*) and pleasure (*hêdonê*) of her subject matter points to a general perception of her poetry as emotionally enthralling; see Demetrius *Eloc.* 132 and Hermogenes *Id.* 2.4 (p. 331 Rabe). Portrayals of Sappho on red-figure pottery (for example, the kalathos by Brygos on which she appears with Alcaeus [Munich 2416, *ARV*² 385/228] and the hydria [Athens 1260, *ARV*² 1060/145] showing her reading in the presence of three female companions, one of whom crowns her with a wreath) hint at widespread use of her songs as entertainment at symposia in fifth-century B.C.E. Athens; cf. the apocryphal tale of Solon's reaction to one such performance (Aelian *ap.* Stobaeus *Flor.* 3.29.58; Campbell 1982: 13, no. 10), which, though admittedly late, nevertheless provides insight into how male listeners responded to Sappho and how her songs were transmitted orally. That cultural image of Sappho explains why the musical theorist Aristoxenus attributed to her the invention of the poignant and affecting mixolydian mode ([Plutarch] *Mus.* 16.1136d; for its character, see Plato *Republic* 3.398e).

11. On Greek mimesis of the female as a theatrical device for affirming elements excluded from ordinary male experience, consult Zeitlin 1985. For the pattern of "the Greek male's fascination with and gradual appropriation of the socially suppressed female other," see duBois 1988: 176–77; and, on the symposium as privileged space for the assumption of a "tempered alterity," see Frontisi-Ducroux and Lissarrague 1990.

Bibliography

Abu-Lughod, Lila. 1986. *Veiled Sentiments: Honor and Poetry in a Bedouin Society.* Berkeley and Los Angeles: University of California Press.

Alcoff, Linda. 1988. "Cultural Feminism versus Post-Structuralism: The Identity Crisis in Feminist Theory." *Signs* 13: 405–36.

Baale, Maria Joanna. 1903. *Studia in Anytes poetriae vitam et carminum reliquias.* Dissertation, Amsterdam.

Burke, Carolyn. 1981. "Irigaray through the Looking Glass." *Feminist Studies* 7: 288–306.

Burnett, Anne Pippin. 1983. *Three Archaic Poets: Archilochus, Alcaeus, Sappho.* Cambridge, Mass.: Harvard University Press.

Butler, Judith. 1990. *Gender Trouble: Feminism and the Subversion of Identity.* New York: Routledge.

Calame, Claude. 1977. *Les chœurs de jeunes filles en Grèce archaïque* I: *Morphologie, fonction religieuse et sociale.* Rome: Edizioni dell'Ateneo & Bizzarri.

Campbell, David A. 1967. *Greek Lyric Poetry.* London: Macmillan.

———. 1982. *Greek Lyric* I. Loeb Classical Library. Cambridge, Mass.: Harvard University Press.

———. 1988. *Greek Lyric* II. Loeb Classical Library. Cambridge, Mass.: Harvard University Press.

Cole, Susan Guettel. 1981. "Could Greek Women Read and Write?" In Foley 1981, 219–45.

Culham, Phyllis. 1986. "Ten Years after Pomeroy: Studies of the Image and Reality of Women in Antiquity." *Helios* 13: 9–30.

———. 1990. "Decentering the Text: The Case of Ovid." *Helios* 17: 161–70.

DeJean, Joan. 1987. "Fictions of Sappho." *Critical Inquiry* 13: 787–805.

de Lauretis, Teresa. 1984. *Alice Doesn't: Feminism, Semiotics, Cinema.* Bloomington: Indiana University Press.

———. 1986. "Feminist Studies/Critical Studies: Issues, Terms, and Contexts." In Teresa de Lauretis, ed., *Feminist Studies/Critical Studies,* 1–19. Bloomington: Indiana University Press.

———. 1988. "Sexual Indifference and Lesbian Representation." *Theatre Journal* 40: 155–77.

———. 1989. "The Essence of the Triangle or, Taking the Risk of Essentialism Seriously: Feminist Theory in Italy, the U.S., and Britain." *differences* 1: 3–37.

———. 1990. "Eccentric Subjects: Feminist Theory and Historical Consciousness." *Feminist Studies* 16: 115–50.

Dover, K. J. 1978. *Greek Homosexuality.* London: Duckworth.

Dowden, Ken. 1989. *Death and the Maiden: Girls' Initiation Rites in Greek Mythology.* London: Routledge.

Draine, Betsy. 1989. "Refusing the Wisdom of Solomon: Some Recent Feminist Literary Theory." *Signs* 15: 144–70.

duBois, Page. 1988. *Sowing the Body: Psychoanalysis and Ancient Representations of Women.* Chicago: The University of Chicago Press.

Flax, Jane. 1990. *Thinking Fragments: Psychoanalysis, Feminism, and Postmodernism in the Contemporary West.* Berkeley and Los Angeles: University of California Press.

Foley, Helene P., ed. 1981. *Reflections of Women in Antiquity.* New York: Gordon and Breach Science Publishers.

Foucault, Michel. 1986 [1984]. *The Use of Pleasure.* Translated by Robert Hurley. New York: Vintage.

Fowler, Barbara Hughes. 1984. "The Archaic Aesthetic." *American Journal of Philology* 105: 119–49.

Fowler, R. L. 1987. *The Nature of Early Greek Lyric: Three Preliminary Studies.* Toronto: University of Toronto Press.

Frontisi-Ducroux, François, and François Lissarrague. 1990 [1983]. "From Ambiguity to Ambivalence: A Dionysiac Excursion through the 'Anakreontic' Vases." Translated by Robert Lamberton. In David M. Halperin, John J. Winkler, and Froma I. Zeitlin, eds., *Before Sexuality: The Construction of Erotic Experience in the Ancient Greek World,* 211–56. Princeton: Princeton University Press.

Fuss, Diana. 1989. *Essentially Speaking: Feminism, Nature and Difference*. New York: Routledge.

Gallop, Jane. 1982. *The Daughter's Seduction: Feminism and Psychoanalysis*. Ithaca: Cornell University Press.

———. 1988. *Thinking through the Body*. New York: Columbia University Press.

Gentili, Bruno. 1988 [1985]. *Poetry and Its Public in Ancient Greece: From Homer to the Fifth Century*. Translated by A. Thomas Cole. Baltimore: Johns Hopkins University Press.

Gold, Barbara. 1993. " 'But Ariadne Was Never There in the First Place': Finding the Female in Roman Poetry." In Nancy Sorkin Rabinowitz and Amy Richlin, eds., *Feminist Theory and the Classics*, 75–101. New York: Routledge.

Goody, Jack, and Ian Watt. 1968. "The Consequences of Literacy." In Jack Goody, ed., *Literacy in Traditional Societies*, 27–68. Cambridge: Cambridge University Press.

Gubar, Susan. 1985 [1982]. " 'The Blank Page' and the Issues of Female Creativity." In Showalter 1985b, 292–313.

Hallett, Judith P. 1979. "Sappho and Her Social Context: Sense and Sensuality." *Signs* 4: 447–64.

———. In progress. *Breathing Beneath the Images: Latin Literary Texts and the Recovery of Elite Roman Women*.

Halperin, David M. 1990. *One Hundred Years of Homosexuality*. New York: Routledge.

Harris, William V. 1989. *Ancient Literacy*. Cambridge, Mass.: Harvard University Press.

Havelock, Eric A. 1963. *Preface to Plato*. Cambridge, Mass.: Harvard University Press.

———. 1977. "The Preliteracy of the Greeks." *New Literary History* 8: 369–91.

Hekman, Susan J. 1990. *Gender and Knowledge: Elements of a Postmodern Feminism*. Boston: Northeastern University Press.

Homans, Margaret. 1987. "Feminist Criticism and Theory: The Ghost of Creusa." *Yale Journal of Criticism* 1: 153–82.

Irigaray, Luce. 1985a [1974]. *Speculum of the Other Woman*. Translated by Gillian C. Gill. Ithaca: Cornell University Press.

———. 1985b [1977]. *This Sex Which Is Not One*. Translated by Catherine Porter, with Carolyn Burke. Ithaca: Cornell University Press.

Jardine, Alice. 1985. *Gynesis: Configurations of Woman and Modernity*. Ithaca: Cornell University Press.

Jones, Ann Rosalind. 1981. "Writing the Body: Toward an Understanding of *l'écriture féminine*." *Feminist Studies* 7: 247–63.

Joseph, Terri Brint. 1980. "Poetry as a Strategy of Power: The Case of Riffian Berber Women." *Signs* 5: 418–34.

Kamuf, Peggy. 1982. "Replacing Feminist Criticism." *Diacritics* 12: 42–47.

Kolodny, Annette. 1987 [1985]. "The Influence of Anxiety: Prolegomena to a Study of the Production of Poetry by Women." In Marie Harris and Kathleen Aguero, eds., *A Gift* *of Tongues: Critical Challenges in Contemporary American Poetry,*112–41. Athens: University of Georgia Press.

Lacan, Jacques. 1982 [1975]. "God and the *Jouissance* of The Woman." In Juliet Mitchell and Jacqueline Rose, eds., *Feminine Sexuality: Jacques Lacan and the* école freudienne, 137–48. Translated by Jacqueline Rose. New York: W. W. Norton.

Marks, Elaine, and Isabelle de Courtivron, eds. 1980. *New French Feminisms.* Amherst: University of Massachusetts Press.

Merkelbach, Reinhold. 1957. "Sappho und ihr Kreis." *Philologus* 101: 1–29.

Miller, Nancy K. 1982. "The Text's Heroine: A Feminist Critic and Her Fictions." *Diacritics* 12: 48–53.

Moi, Toril. 1985. *Sexual/Textual Politics: Feminist Literary Theory.* London: Methuen.

Nugent, Georgia. 1990. "This Sex Which Is Not One: De-Constructing Ovid's Hermaphrodite." *differences* 2: 160–85.

O'Higgins, Dolores. 1990. "Sappho's Splintered Tongue: Silence in Sappho 31 and Catullus 51." *American Journal of Philology* 111: 156–67.

Olsen, Tillie. 1989 [1978]. *Silences.* New York: Delta/Seymour Lawrence.

Ong, Walter J. 1982. *Orality and Literacy: The Technologizing of the Word.* London: Methuen.

Page, Denys L. 1951. *Alcman: The Partheneion.* Oxford: Oxford University Press.

Pomeroy, S. B. 1977. "ΤΕCΗΝΙΚΑΙ ΚΑΙ ΜΟUSΙΚΑΙ: The Education of Women in the Fourth Century and in the Hellenistic Period." *American Journal of Ancient History* 2: 51–68.

Rauk, John. 1989. "Erinna's *Distaff* and Sappho Fr. 94." *Greek, Roman and Byzantine Studies* 30: 101–16.

Rissman, Leah. 1983. *Love as War: Homeric Allusion in the Poetry of Sappho.* Beiträge zur klassischen Philologie, Heft 157. Königstein/Ts.: Verlag Anton Hain.

Russ, Joanna. 1983. *How to Suppress Women's Writing.* Austin: University of Texas Press.

Schibanoff, Susan. 1986. "Taking the Gold out of Egypt: The Art of Reading as a Woman." In Elizabeth A. Flynn and Patrocinio P. Schweickart, eds., *Gender and Reading: Essays on Readers, Texts and Contexts,* 83–106. Baltimore: Johns Hopkins University Press.

Schor, Naomi. 1989. "This Essentialism Which Is Not One: Coming to Grips with Irigaray." *differences* 1: 38–58.

Segal, Charles. 1974. "Eros and Incantation: Sappho and Oral Poetry." *Arethusa* 7: 139–60.

Showalter, Elaine. 1985a [1979]. "Toward a Feminist Poetics." In Showalter 1985b, 125–43.

Showalter, Elaine, ed. 1985b. *The New Feminist Criticism: Essays on Women, Literature and Theory.* New York: Pantheon.

Skinner, Marilyn B. 1989. "Sapphic Nossis." *Arethusa* 22: 5–18.

Smith-Rosenberg, Carroll. 1975. "The Female World of Love and Ritual: Relations between Women in Nineteenth Century America." *Signs* 1: 1–29.

Snyder, Jane McIntosh. 1989. *The Woman and the Lyre: Women Writers in Classical Greece and Rome*. Carbondale: Southern Illinois University Press.

———. 1991. "Public Occasion and Private Passion in the Lyrics of Sappho of Lesbos." In Sarah B. Pomeroy, ed., *Women's History and Ancient History*, 1–19. Chapel Hill: The University of North Carolina Press.

Stehle, Eva. 1990. "Sappho's Gaze: Fantasies of a Goddess and a Young Man." *differences* 2: 88–125.

Stigers, Eva [Stehle]. 1979. "Romantic Sensuality, Poetic Sense: A Response to Hallett on Sappho." *Signs* 4: 465–71.

———. 1981. "Sappho's Private World." In Foley 1981, 219–45.

Thomas, Rosalind. 1989. *Oral Tradition and Written Record in Classical Athens*. Cambridge: Cambridge University Press.

Todd, Janet. 1988. *Feminist Literary History*. New York: Routledge.

Weedon, Chris. 1987. *Feminist Practice and Poststructuralist Theory*. Oxford: Basil Blackwell.

Winkler, John J. 1990. *The Constraints of Desire: The Anthropology of Sex and Gender in Ancient Greece*. New York: Routledge.

Woolf, Virginia. 1957 [1929]. *A Room of One's Own*. San Diego: Harcourt Brace Jovanovich.

Zeitlin, Froma I. 1985. "Playing the Other: Theater, Theatricality, and the Feminine in Greek Drama." *Representations* 11: 63–94.

7

The Primal Mind: Using Native American Models for the Study of Women in Ancient Greece[1]

Bella Zweig

> If the women shake their heads
> the men must begin again.
> —Norman H. Russell, "Two Circles" (1991)

My purpose in this study is to provide models for approaching the study of women in ancient Greece that derive from non-Western, in particular, Native American, modes of perception and discourse. This cross-cultural approach is doubly formed: accentuating the non-Western dimensions of ancient Greek culture and incorporating non-Western modes into our analysis. As will become evident, this cross-cultural approach has particular relevance for understanding the significance of women's activities, the status women gained from these activities, and the images created of women in ancient Greece. I focus on the so-called Archaic (eighth to sixth centuries B.C.E.) and Classical periods (fifth to fourth centuries).[2]

Subject of This Inquiry: Identifying the Problem

In approaching the field designated as "women in ancient Greece," the researcher soon finds the subject to be in many ways elusive. Most obvious, and of course most noted, is the paucity of female voices directly expressing women's thoughts, beliefs, concerns, and lives. Although the few women's voices that do exist, and which have been largely ignored in traditional classical scholarship, comprise an extremely small fraction of the corpus of material extant from antiquity, they are essential for helping us understand women's lives in the ancient Greek world. The methodological approach presented here will provide a contextual framework for better appreciating the value and meanings of these primary texts. However, since the vast majority of evidence comes from literary, documentary, artistic, and archaeological sources known or presumed to be the work of men, and in which male bias intrudes to varying degrees, scholarly selection and interpretation of this evidence crucially shapes the picture we might draw.

A double helix of male biases seriously circumscribes what we may infer about women's lives in ancient Greece: that of the ancient evidence, and that of modern scholars of antiquity, who seem both to inherit and to be continually refashioning the male bias of these ancient Greek forebears. Thus, for instance, while the evidence points to male domination at different times, in different locales and spheres of activity, and to differing degrees in the ancient Greek world, modern scholars tend to assume that contemporary forms of male domination in Western society similarly characterized the nature and extent of male domination throughout all areas and periods in ancient Greece. At the same time that Just (1989) critiques the problems that have resulted from this white-male ethnocentrism in the scholarship, he acknowledges that his analysis of women in ancient Athens still reflects a male, British-oriented point of view. One sphere of activity where the shortsightedness of this approach has become especially salient is in the realm of ancient Greek religious practices, where scholars are increasingly recognizing that women may have enjoyed powers and esteem in ways unmatched by any comparable activity in the contemporary Western world (Calame 1977; Burkert 1985; Winkler 1990: 188–209), and where practices in modern Greece (Hirschon 1978) and in other cultures (Lincoln 1981) may provide closer analogies for those in ancient Greek times.

Almost inextricable from this double bind of androcentric biases is the additional constraining complex of ethnocentric ones, also evident in a double helix of ancient and modern strands. Page duBois (1982) has shown that some early Greek mythology and art manifests parallel oppositions—of Greeks to barbarians, of Greek men to women and beasts—thereby establishing a hierarchy, with Greek males at the top conquering and ruling women, foreigners, and animals. Aristotle's theoretical encoding of these views (*Politics* I and II) became over time the ideological justification for Christian and subsequent white-male, Western discriminatory attitudes and practices. In classical scholarship these views have become manifest in the intense Germano- and Anglocentrism permeating much of the literature, marked in its extreme form by the claims of British and German scholars of the nineteenth and early twentieth centuries to be the direct descendants racially and intellectually of the superior men of fifth- and fourth-century B.C.E. Athens.

Exacerbating these ethnocentric views is the Athenocentrism of many of our sources, especially from the fifth century B.C.E. on, and maintained to a large extent by modern scholars. In this regard, too, until recently, scholars uncritically assumed that conditions in ancient Athens typified those throughout the Hellenic world, so that use of the term "ancient Greek" frequently referred only to practices in ancient Athens. Often little attempt was made to distinguish among the different ancient communities, except when drawing gross contrasts between the "advanced, democratic Athenians" and the old-fashioned oligarchy of their archrival Sparta, or between an "enlightened" Athens and the backwater Macedonia that was to conquer her. This Athenocentric focus in the ancient evidence and in the scholarly literature is critical to our study of women because the extreme male domination of ancient Athenian society was largely unparalleled in the ancient Greek world (Pomeroy 1975; Schaps 1979; Kunstler 1986). Thus, the use of

Athens as foundation and justification for the male, ethnic, and racial oppressions that were to characterize Western society needs to be problematized, for Athens was only one of many social, political, economic, and gender systems functioning in the ancient Greek world.

Even where extreme forms of white-male ethnocentrism have been challenged or abandoned,[3] the combined double complex of ancient and modern andro- and ethnocentrisms has led to two crucial methodological weaknesses in studies of the ancient Greek world in general, and in studies of women in ancient Greece in particular. Both derive from the assumption that modern Western modes of perception are appropriate for examining ancient Greek society. The first assumes a number of similarities between ancient Greek and modern Western society: that ancient Greek—in particular, Athenian—society was structured according to a hierarchical model comprised of categories of social activity—religion, politics, economics, family—that are congruent with the definitions, forms, and valuations assigned these categories by contemporary Western society; that those features of ancient Greek society that parallel or provide the source for similar features in modern Western society are uniformly similar in meaning and function; that other aspects of ancient society are also fundamentally like those of the modern Western world; and that any of these issues may be studied in isolation, without considering the entire context in order to appreciate the meaning of its discrete parts. Increasingly, anthropological analyses (Schlegel 1977a; Sanday and Goodenough 1990), including those focused on the study of ancient Greece (Humphreys 1978), have addressed the limitations of such an approach. These anthropologists urge instead that we examine features of any society within the total context of that society.

Seeing ancient Greek male writers as the source for many of the ideas of modern society contributes to the problem. To take one example: in the sixth century B.C.E., Pythagoras developed lists of hierarchically ranked oppositions, such as positive/negative, male/female, day/night, hot/cold, that influenced the Athenian Plato almost two centuries later and subsequently the development of Western philosophy. Interpretations assume these concepts must have had the same ideological and social meanings for Pythagoras as for modern commentators, without taking into account that these ideas developed in the community he founded in Croton, Italy, where women and men lived according to the same strict rules of behavior, studying and discussing matters of a theological, metaphysical, mathematical, and scientific nature (Ward 1992). Thus, the relationship between these oppositions and their meaning for forms of interaction between actual women and men needs to be examined.

The other methodological shortcoming, according primacy to men's activities and values as the only ones of importance to the ancient community, and simultaneously devaluing women's roles and concerns as of no import, has repeatedly produced one-sided discussions of antiquity that rarely examine women and that sometimes display a willful blindness to potential interpretations of the evidence that diverge from models familiar within Western constructs. This complex of biases has resulted in: (1) neglect of works by women—except, at times, for Sappho—in the critical literature, and their omission from anthologies; (2) the misreading of ancient texts, for example accepting Apollo's biological argument that gives full parentage only to the father (Aeschylus, *Eumenides* 665ff.) as a straightforward reflection of Athenian belief, when this argument, in fact, directly contravenes contemporary Athenian practices (Harrison 1968; see Zweig 1982: 169; Halperin 1990: 139); (3) ignoring or refusing to accept the evident meaning of some of the sources, for example selectively denying the validity of Herodotus's ethnography when it portrays the strong roles of women in non-Greek societies; and (4) deliberate falsification of ancient material, for example changing the gender endings in editions of Sappho's poetry to make it appear that her love objects are male.

Just as the problem confronting the researcher is multiply formed, so does any correcting solution require an approach where the dual strands of better ethnic and gendered understanding are more tightly interwoven. That is, we must both give greater attention to women's activities, roles, images, and forms of power, authority, and status in the ancient world, and we must also see the Greeks as "desperately foreign" (Humphreys 1978: 26) to avoid the misconceptions that result from a false sense of overfamiliarity. Classical scholarship of the last twenty years has explored both areas. To cite only a few recent examples: in gender studies, Keuls (1985) examines the role of phallocentricity in ancient Athenian ritual, social, sexual, and artistic activities and the implications for attitudes toward women and the shaping of women's roles; duBois (1988) presents an analysis of the positive and often self-sufficient images of woman's body in ancient Greece prior to Aristotle, which contrast sharply with modern psychological imagery that characterizes women as "lacking" in some essential properties; and the essays in Richlin (1992) analyze how the representation of women in a variety of ancient Greek and Roman artistic, literary, and documentary sources shape the construction of gender in those societies. Other studies employ cross-cultural resources to elucidate those features of ancient Greek society that are manifestly non-Western and that remain enigmatic and ill-understood by Western-based analyses, requiring us, therefore, to look to non-Western models for interpretation (see Humphreys 1978: chap. 1, for overview). Notably these studies concentrate on particular activities that are strikingly non-Western in form and function: the role of male, same-sex practices for ritual, social, political, and military purposes in the ancient Greek world (Dover 1978; Sergent 1986; Halperin 1990; Winkler 1990); the role of ritual and religion in the lives of the ancient Greeks (Burkert 1985); or more particularly, the significance of female ritual initiation practices (Lincoln 1981).

As they reshape the lenses by which we view our subject, these and many other works illuminate important aspects of the ancient world. However, studies focusing on women's lives rarely give consideration to potential non-Western dimensions, both how these might have affected the dynamics of gender roles in antiquity as well as how we perceive them today; and those that depend on a comparative, cross-cultural approach rarely employ feminist analysis to aid in their interpretations. To differing degrees, many still show the limitations of a Western-conscribed approach. Thus the theme of a doubled duality arises again, both in the double focus of our subject and in the dual analytical tools we employ.

My goal is to bring together these doubled, double helices of awareness. For the cross-cultural approach I employ models from Native American societies to establish certain correspondences in metaphysical constructs and modes of perception between Native American and ancient Greek societies. In this regard my use of cross-cultural material differs significantly from that of many other researchers, who have concentrated rather on the similarity of certain discrete features across cultures, without examining fully the meaning of these features within the context of the underlying cultural precepts.[4] The dual intent here is to highlight the ways in which ancient Greek society parallels non-Western societies in some fundamental areas of perception and discourse, and, in order to enable us to perceive and appreciate these ancient non-Western dimensions, to approach the study of ancient Greece through forms of perception and models of analysis that also derive from non-Western sources.

Establishing these correspondences forms the foundation for this study's focus on women's roles. A key aspect that will emerge from the overview of Native American perceptual constructs is the recognition by native peoples themselves of the distinctively feminine source and dimensions of their perceptions. Although this strong feminine focus in Native American thought has generally not been acknowledged in modern feminist discourse (Medicine 1978: 4; Green 1980: 264), I hope both that my analytic use of it in this study will generate better appreciation of aspects of ancient Greek culture, and also that it may serve as a model for better inclusion of some of these distinctively feminine, Native American perceptions into a broader scope of feminist theory and analysis.

Native American Models I: General

> Or, she would be looking at the field of vision itself, refusing to favor a central form, such as a water tower, but concentrating instead on the zone surrounding the tower, finding pattern and substance in areas our eyes tend to regard as secondary, vacant, vague.
> —Tom Robbins, *Skinny Legs and All* (1990: 17–18)

My use of Native American resources divides into two groups: first, works by Native American scholars (Allen, Deloria, Green, Medicine, Momaday, Ortiz), who express directly from their own perspectives the modes of perception, description, and epistemology characteristic of Native American peoples; second, research by non-Indian observers on aspects of Native American culture, which provides support for the views presented by Native American scholars, in the framework of Western disciplines—anthropology, artistic and literary analyses, linguistics, and comparative religion. While significantly different approaches characterize these two categories, together they reinforce each other, sometimes combined into one text (Albers and Medicine 1983b; Underhill 1985), and they suggest compelling models for the possible shapes, definitions, and social and economic structures assigned to women's power and exercise of authority.[5]

In addition, I bring to this study my own decade-plus contact with Native American peoples, which began in 1980 with my participation for six months on the Long Walk for Survival, a cross-country, spiritual walk for world peace and the preservation of Mother Earth, organized and led by Native Americans. From this, my first direct interaction with the native peoples of this land, their languages, cultures, values, and ways of thinking and acting, I have maintained continuous contact with many Native American peoples for personal, social, political, and educational reasons. All these contacts provide me with the foundation for the ideas I discuss in this paper, and have allowed me to corroborate from my own direct experiences the points raised in the ethnographic analyses.

While hundreds of Native American tribes with distinct languages and cultural constructions exist, certain attitudes and modes of perception appear common to Native American peoples regardless of surface differences in customs. Highwater (1981: xviii) calls this common indigenous mentality "primal" and Allen (1986: 3) calls it "tribal"; both believe that the indigenous peoples of the Americas share this mentality with indigenous peoples around the world. It is with this understanding that one may speak of "Native American" views or perceptions, while relying at the same time on examples from particular Native American cultures (Momaday 1988). The range of Native American peoples discussed in this study well illustrates this point, for they represent varied geographical regions and culturally distinct groups: Hopi and Rio Grande Pueblos (Puebloan)—high desert Southwest; Tohono O'odham (Papago)[6]—low desert Southwest; Navajo (Apachean)—mountainous Southwest, with affinities with Athabaskan peoples of Canada; Yurok—central California; Blackfoot, Lakota (Sioux)—the Plains; Seneca (Iroquoian)—Northeast forests (Kehoe 1981). The commonality of certain features under consideration here among these culturally and linguistically varied groups demonstrates that these features are not isolated phenomena, and it further reinforces the value of their use as potential models in our study of antiquity. In order to place the discussion of women's roles and images within the ideological and social context of the culture, it is important first to establish some correspondences between Native American and early Greek thought.

Basic to a Native American worldview is a spiritually oriented perception: the universe is alive, aware, and supernaturally ordered; primary value is accorded relations with the spiritual world; and sacred, metaphysical principles, not political, economic, or other social constructions, underlie the society's functioning (Allen 1986: 80, 247). Ritual language and practices are only one means of expressing this sense of the sacred, which permeates every aspect of life: speech and the use of language (Witherspoon 1977: 34; Highwater 1981: 55; Bataille and Sands 1984: 3; Allen 1986: 56; Momaday 1988); belief in the reality of dreams, visions, and supernatural beings (Highwater 1981: 89; Allen 1986: 2–3); artistic and creative activities (Highwater 1976; Albers and Medicine 1983b: 134; Schneider 1983: 115; Parezo, Hays, and Slivac 1987); daily activities (Schlegel 1977b: 264); and the social structure and rhythm of society (Ortiz 1969: 98; Schlegel 1977b: 254–55; Buckley 1982; Allen 1986: 3). This sacred sense informs the metaphysical constructs governing one's role in life and the way one relates with another person, with other forms of life, and with the natural environment (Highwater 1981: 69, 180; DeMallie 1983: 255; Medicine 1983a: 71, 1983b: 269; Schlegel 1990: 32); and it shapes the formulation of one's relationship to such abstract notions as "time," regarded as a sacred and extraordinary "dreamtime" (as Highwater uses the Australian-aboriginal term) of subconscious activities, which is distinguished from the time/space of everyday, pragmatic activities (Highwater 1981: 89; Allen 1986: 147). This profoundly spiritual sense reflects an active interrelationship with one's world, which is not seen as a collection of objects, animate or inanimate, available merely for human use, but which has a vitality and life of its own in its various, manifest forms.

Allied with this sense of the sacred is the power of the inner consciousness, and all the activities that take place there, to shape the outer world through thought, speech, and action (Witherspoon 1977: 9, 47; Highwater 1981: 56, 90–91; Allen 1986: 68). This subjective realm, which includes dreams and all that we envision, and is thus associated with the "dreamtime" noted above, is regarded as more important and potent than what Westerners call "objective," external reality. Correlative with this emphasis on the subjective is the perception that the "heart," however broadly that may be defined (Highwater 1981: 107), rather than the mind, is the instrumental source for human activities. Allen (1986: 22) notes that for the Laguna the heart is associated with the womb, as the center of power within woman and within the universe. In this way women's procreative and creative abilities are interwoven and seen to form the central matrix of human thought and action. Whereas Native American metaphysics affirms the power of this inner, intuitive, feminized realm, Western metaphysics has discounted its validity, devaluing both its subjective and feminine dimensions (Highwater 1981: 66, 91).

Reflecting their central spiritual orientation, Native Americans describe their world in mythic terms (Highwater 1981: 12; Kehoe 1981: 1–2), via a mythological form of discourse, in contrast to the modern scientific mode. Linguistically, Native American languages representing distinctly varied language groups emphasize event, relationship, process, or action, that is, the verb, rather than the product of any of these activities, or the noun (Hallowell on Ojibwa, Lee on Wintu, and Whorf on Hopi, all in Tedlock and Tedlock 1975; Schlegel 1977b, 1990 on Hopi; Witherspoon 1977 on Navajo). Natonabah (1978) illustrates the sacred nature of the activity of motion, especially walking, as he first chants the sacred song for walking and then tells a story that illustrates the importance of the song, of walking, of the Holy People, of life, of the human being's place in the large order of life. Both the emphasis on process and motion and the differing notions of time are reflected grammatically. Hopi language has no reference to time (Highwater 1981: 104), and motion, not time, is the significant aspect of Navajo verbs (Witherspoon 1977: 48–49), where the principal verb is not "to be" as in many other languages, but "to go," for which Witherspoon "conservatively estimate[s] . . . some 356,200 distinct conjugations" (1977: 49).

This central importance of a sense of the sacred for both ideology and social practice fundamentally differentiates Native American perceptions from those of the highly secularized modern Western society. In many respects, closer parallels exist between the perceptual orientations of Native Americans and those of ancient Greeks than between either and the modes of perception and discourse of the modern West. The ancient Greek evidence shows numerous similarities:

(1) Sense of the sacred: the extensive ritual life in all ancient Greek communities marking moments in the calendrical year and stages in a person's life; the sacralized dimension of activities we consider secular, such as athletic, dramatic, and poetic competitions; the cleansing necessary after battle—compare Odysseus's command to purify the halls (*Odyssey* 22.485ff.) with the purification of the warrior described by Underhill (1985: 41ff.); the belief that a range of human activities is governed by supernatural inspiration, guidance, or sanction—speech, perceived as the power of Peitho (Gorgias, *Helen*), poetry and artistic activity (Homer; Plato, *Apology, Ion*), political and military endeavors (Thucydides).

(2) The power of the subjective consciousness to effect manifestations in external reality: the importance of dreams as guides for practical activities and as a major part of cures (Edelstein and Edelstein 1945; Winkler 1990); Homeric *phrên*, "heart," versus the later privileging of the brain or mind; and—ironic because of his importance in the development of Western philosophy—Socrates's reliance upon his *daimôn*, his divinely inspired inner voice, enigmatic and even an embarrassment to a long line of rationalizing philosophers, beginning with his most admiring yet nonunderstanding pupil, Plato, who firmly fixed the supremacy of a detached, "objective" mind for the future course of Western ideologies.

(3) Language: Some of the similarities in language use may be attributed to the oral orientation of Native American and ancient Greek cultures in contrast to that of literate societies, notably the mythological, metaphorical modes of expression seen in the circular structures, the manner of moving between and use of themes, that generically align the Homeric poems, hymns, the epinician odes of Bacchylides and Pindar, and the choral lyrics of ancient tragedies with creative verbal expressions in Native American societies (Natonabah 1978; Momaday 1988). But orality does not account for other similarities of language use, such as concepts of time and motion. Recalling Native American rather than modern Western conceptualizations, aspect in ancient Greek grammar carries greater importance than tense, in a verb system that is far more elaborated and expressive than those of modern European languages. In particular, Homeric language of

the Archaic age depicts notions of time and movement that differ from those of classical Attic as well as from modern Western ones. The Homeric verb *pelomai,* whose meaning seems to be "I go," baffles translators who find it in contexts where English requires the verb "to be." The implication of movement underlying notions of "being" highlights an emphasis on relationships as noted in Native American languages. Analogously, the movability of the past-marking verbal prefix "*e-*" emphasizes the separate conceptualization of the notion of time from the other aspects conveyed by the particular verbal form.

These spiritual modes of perception and forms of discourse began to be challenged in the Archaic period by the demythologizing questionings of a few early thinkers, who were seeking descriptions of the natural world and its functioning that approximate the "naturalistic," "rationalistic" explanations familiar to modern Western thinking. The demythologizing premises advanced by these early philosophers, which predominated in the subsequent development of Western ideologies, supplanted radically different forms of perception, thought, and articulation among the early Greeks. At least in the areas considered here—sense of the sacred, the power of the heart and the inner consciousness, and linguistic expressions—early Greek epistemological modes demonstrate significant affinities with Native American epistemologies.

Native American Models II: Gynocentric

A nation is not conquered until the hearts of the women are on the ground.
—Cheyenne proverb

These correspondences between Native American and ancient Greek modes of perception are critical for the study of women. For Native American societies, these essentially sacralized perceptions are expressed through spiritual, social, and metaphysical constructs featuring the primacy of feminine dimensions. Spiritual life is often closely interwoven with concepts of femaleness, expressed in numerous ways, beginning with belief in a primary female deity. For the Laguna, Thought Woman is the original creatrix whose spirit informs everything (Allen 1986: 14–15). To call her a "fertility goddess" demeans and limits the power inherent in femininity, since as thinker and bearer, she brings into being both material and nonmaterial reality (Allen 1986: 15). For both the Tewa- and Keresan-speaking Puebloans, Ortiz (1969: 13) and Allen (1986: 17), respectively, note the crucial role of the Corn Mother deities in communications between individuals and the tribe and between the tribe and supernaturals. Changing Woman is regarded as the supreme mother of the Navajo, most blessed and revered of all the Holy People (Witherspoon 1977: 201).

Besides the belief in a primary female deity, many cultures hold that a female spirit brought important ceremonies to the people—White Buffalo Calf Woman to the Cheyenne and Lakota—or that she enables the continuous functioning of the society—Yellow Woman to the Laguna (Allen 1986: 238). Actual women also embody the sacredness of female spirits in various ways. Many Native American societies believe that women by the very process of menstruation are naturally endowed with a sacred power that men do not have—Laguna (Allen 1986: 47, 253); Lakota (DeMallie 1983: 256; Medicine 1983a: 68); Tohono O'odham (Underhill 1985: 92); Yurok (Buckley 1982)—or that a woman is capable of being imbued with the special power of femaleness for which no comparable sacralized conceptualization of maleness exists for men—Apache (Perry 1977: 104); Cheyenne (Medicine 1978: 43–44). Woman's innate association with the spiritual enables her to effect a ritual transfer of sacred power between men—Blackfoot (Kehoe 1983: 67).

Central to this sacralized image of woman is her primary role as childbearer (Schlegel 1977b: 245; Leacock 1978: 248; Medicine 1983a: 65). Witherspoon (1977: 85) notes that the most important bond in Navajo society is the mother-child bond, which symbolizes giving life and sharing sustenance. It is the ideal pattern for all social interaction, and leads to the major emphasis on generosity, caring, and helping one another as central values in the society—Pueblo (Ortiz 1969: 49); Navajo (Lamphere 1977); Lakota (Albers 1983b: 189). In Iroquoian and Hopi societies, the mother-daughter dyad is the dominant social pattern, and daughters are more highly valued than sons (Brown 1975: 241; McCall 1980: 228; Schlegel 1990: 32).

The primacy of women's values and concerns forms the central matrix for community and social action. Regarding childrearing as the most important activity of the community leads to men's socialization into childrearers and nurturers, their activities often formed to support women's fundamental roles. Generally, women's centrality is seen to bring about the spiritual well-being of the tribe (Bataille and Sands 1984: 18). Thus, it is Hopi men's responsibility to insure that women enjoy the physical and spiritual safety to carry out their roles with an untroubled mind (Schlegel 1977b: 264). Lakota women's activities sustain the society spiritually and literally, while the men's activities are regarded as secondary to the women's. For the benefit of the children, Cheyenne and Lakota men must curb their sexual desires (Medicine 1978: 52–53; DeMallie 1983: 256, 261). The title of "Mother" can indicate the highest degree of status as a social and not a biologically based designation (Allen 1986: 28); thus one can appreciate the significance among the Tewa Puebloans of calling the male chiefs of the village "Mother" at appropriate times (Ortiz 1969: 36).[7]

Closely tied to the sanctified power of women's procreativity are women's creative abilities, which are also highly esteemed by the society (Kehoe 1983: 69; Schneider 1983: 109; Parezo, Hays, and Slivac 1987). Although Western observers tend to view women's lives as being filled with drudgery, the research literature repeatedly affirms that women in many cultures take great pride in their work in bearing and raising children, processing food, feeding their families, displaying their generosity by feeding guests, and excelling in creative work—

basketry, beading, poetry, pottery, quilting, singing, weaving—for both economic and ceremonial purposes for both family and community (Schlegel 1977b; Albers 1983a: 4; Schneider 1983: 102; Weist 1983: 31, 36–40; and many occasions which I have witnessed).

Materially, women are also esteemed for their economic contributions to both daily sustenance and ceremonial occasions (Albers and Medicine 1983b). They control their own labor, resources, making of necessary tools, products, and distribution (McCall 1980: 250; Spector 1983: 93–94). As frequently noted in the ethnographic literature, those societies where women's economic contribution to the society is recognized and where women control their own economic role are generally characterized by women's important roles in the decision-making process for the society (Brown 1975: 237; Leacock 1978: 248; Jensen 1990: 51). However, economic power alone cannot account for the social and political power of women in Native American societies (Brown 1975: 251), and as Schlegel (1977a: 14, 31) remarks, one must also consider the role ideology plays in determining actual roles and status in the society.

We may thus see the recognition of women's economic role as a material support for the sacralized centrality of femaleness, of motherhood, and of woman, which all together translate into women's actual status and roles in a number of ways. Women are in charge of the distribution of all goods, both the products of their own labor and those of men's labor as well, and the distribution itself is usually equitable among all members of the society (Hopi—Schlegel 1990: 28; Iroquois—Brown 1975: 247, McCall 1980: 249; Lakota—Albers 1983b: 213; Tohono O'odham—Underhill 1985: 12). Women are regarded as autonomous individuals with their own inherent rights, duties, and privileges—Iroquois (Leacock 1978: 252)—reflective of the general notion of respect for individual autonomy among different Native American societies—Navajo (Lamphere 1977: 41–42). This respect for individual autonomy means that social and political activities are engaged in through negotiation and consensus, not coercion (Lamphere 1977: 41; Schlegel 1977b: 253; Witherspoon 1977: 83; Leacock 1978: 249). This respect also permits great latitude in individual behavior, where behavioral deviations from ideologized social norms are accepted because everyone is a part of the whole (Highwater 1981: 172; Underhill 1985: 64), nor are deviations regarded as a social threat, but rather as manifestations of great power and spirituality (Highwater 1981: 180). Thus, a range of socially accepted roles is open to women in Plains societies (Medicine 1983b: 273–76), and movement between social categories of gender, which may or may not entail homosexuality, is both possible (Schlegel 1977a: 4) and often divinely sanctioned (Allen 1986: 200; Medicine 1983b: 269; Williams 1986).

Women's influence on societal matters cannot be well appreciated if one is seeking women's participation in formal economic or political structures which may not exist according to Western ideas of social organization (Schlegel 1977b: 254). To counter the frequent use of a priori notions of dominance and subordination, Schlegel (1977a: 355) notes that in no society, however asymmetrical the roles between women and men may be, does one gender have complete domination or control over the other. Rather, spheres of activity are divided between the two genders in such a way that each has primary control over certain activities. Furthermore, Sanday (1981: 113) notes that it is Western bias that equates dominance with public leadership, and Moore (1988: 134) expresses the need to differentiate between notions of power and authority. Hierarchization of areas of activity, reflecting the tendency to view one's topic within a dominating/subordinate polarity, obscures the nature of women's activity, and the actual power, prestige, or authority women may derive from it. Similarly, to consider that women's political activity is expressed only as "informal" influence as compared with men's formally organized mechanisms of authoritative action may again undermine the real value of women's authority (Friedl 1962, 1967; Hirschon 1978). In some cases men function as representatives *of* the women's views in the roles they play out in the "formal" structures recognizable to Western observers, and not necessarily as spokesmen *for* women's views.

Thus, we must be open to varied forms of influence and decisionmaking in the society by both women and men, and examine the relative importance of the roles of each gender. The construction in recent scholarship of domestic and public realms as the appropriate key to understanding women's and men's roles in society has come to exemplify the limitations entailed in approaching another culture with preconceived categories. Presented by Rosaldo (1974) as a universal, polarized opposition, this construct has been rejected by a long list of researchers as an inadequate way to perceive women's and men's realms in a society, since for many societies a sharp division does not exist between what the West defines as domestic and public spheres, which tend rather to be interactive or which may even coincide (Reiter 1975; Lamphere 1977; Schlegel 1977a: 15–17; Leacock 1978; Allen 1986; Dubisch 1986; Moore 1988: 21–22; and Sanday and Goodenough 1990; cf. Rosaldo's later remarks [1980]). Kelly (1984: 57) proposes that we regard woman's place not as a separate domain of existence, but rather as a position within social existence generally.

In Native American societies, women's activities *are* community activities. Women exert their influence and authority on the society by speaking out and acting directly in any situations affecting their lives and the well-being of the community, by taking charge as they deem necessary (Schlegel 1977b: 254; Albers 1983b: 190–91), and by controlling essential goods and services, thereby controlling the behavior of anyone who requires them (Schneider 1983: 117). The female principle is pivotal for the social organization of the Athabaskans (Perry 1977: 103), and women's biological and ritual cycles establish the pattern for the social and ceremonial rhythm of Yurok society (Buckley 1982). In the Iroquoian societies in particular all these elements translate into women's formal control through the leadership of the clan grandmothers who make the important decisions for the community, who appoint the men they empower to execute their decisions, and who maintain the authority to remove from his duties any man not carrying out his assigned tasks (Brown 1975: 238–44; Schlegel 1977a: 30; Jensen 1990: 52–54).

Although McCall (1980: 252) is virtually unique among modern scholars in calling Iroquois society a matriarchy,[8] Native American peoples describe their societies that accord primacy to women's activities as matriarchal, but the conceptualization of matriarchy differs markedly from modern Western notions (Green 1980: 254; Allen 1986: 40, 223).[9] Expressed not as a hierarchical domination of one gender by the other (Schlegel 1977b: 264; Albers 1983b: 190; Allen 1986: 243–44), that is, as the mirror-reverse image of modern patriarchy, the metaphysical constructs and the social formations underlying the native traditional concept of matriarchy tend rather toward notions of balance and complementarity within which both genders are seen as essential to the continuity of life and to the ongoing, harmonious functioning of the society (Schlegel 1977b: 246). Both the Native American and outside researchers emphasize the complementary balance in Native American societies between the spheres of activities engaged in by women and men, each gender having its appropriate realm whose activities, products, and proceeds they each control (Schlegel 1977a: 32–33, 1990: 28; Leacock 1978: 249, 252; Green 1980: 260, 264; Albers 1983b: 188–89; Allen 1986: 82), and one gender not taking precedence over the other (Deloria 1945: 39–40; Medicine 1983a: 68; Spector 1983).

This notion of complementarity and balance does not imply similarity or equality (Schlegel 1977b: 264; Witherspoon 1977: 196–97), an elision that Highwater (1981: 10) regards as a definitional pitfall of modern Western liberal thought, which transforms notions of political democracy into concepts of psychological, cultural, and individual sameness. Each sex is recognized as fundamentally different in biology and in its function in society (Medicine 1983a: 63). Thus, the primacy accorded the female realm spiritually and socially acknowledges the very different demands on women and men in their biological roles in child production, in which, beyond the dual-sex participation in conception, the balance accrues to the female—pregnancy, childbirth, lactation. Because women are regarded as being imbued naturally with great spiritual power, they are often exempt from particular spiritual ceremonies in which the men must participate in order to develop ritually some of the spiritual power that women possess naturally (Underhill 1985: 92; Allen 1986: 87). Or a greater emphasis may be placed on men's symbolic achievements (Kehoe 1983: 69; Schneider 1983: 115), which does not thereby equate with male dominance socially, since symbolic importance may have little to do with or even be contradicted by actual societal roles (DeMallie 1983). Moreover, ideological precepts regarding female and male roles may not always coincide with actual activities that women and men engage in within the society (Schlegel 1990: 24).

For many of these Native American societies, the complementarity between women's and men's roles may be seen as the societal manifestations of the culture's metaphysical conceptualizations and mythological expressions. Just as human beings are dimorphous as female and male sexes, metaphysical concepts of duality seem to be prominent in many Native American cultures. These dualities are perceived as balanced pairs, not the polarized or hierarchical oppositions characteristic of modern Western thinking. At this crucial level of thought and verbal expression, the importance of the female role establishes the ideological ground for the importance accorded to women's actual roles in the society. I present in some detail examples from two distinctively different Native American societies. Witherspoon (1977: 48, 141, 196) describes the principal dualism of Navajo metaphysical thought as between activity, a dynamic, creative, productive, and reproductive female principle, and stasis, a period of rest, of withdrawal of movement, that is static, fixed, unchanging, and associated with the male principle. Areas of male prerogative, notably rituals, expressed principally through songs and sandpaintings, are characterized by their fixed, unchanging nature, whereas areas of female concern, such as weaving and social and economic life, are characterized by innovation and change, activity and productivity. This latter area is concerned with the generation of new conditions and beings, thus suitable to the actual bearers of life, while the ceremonial area is concerned with restoring prior states of being that have gotten out of balance (Witherspoon 1977: 142, 160). While female and male are seen as complementary and both necessary, they are not equal. The greater importance of women than men to the community grows out of their far greater role in generation, manifested metaphysically by their association with the more important active, vital, creative, productive, and procreative principle, and manifested materially by their dominant role in the social and economic life of the community, and which my own observations have seen manifested in political leadership and decision making. The women's role in these areas is balanced by the ritual role engaged in by the men (196–97).

Thus, parallels may be observed for the Navajo whereby linguistically verbs predominate over nouns, metaphysically movement carries greater weight than stasis, and socially women hold greater authority than men. While the parallels between these realms seem evident, it must also be noted that specific forms of metaphysically conceived realms of primacy do not translate into identical realms of social activity. Thus, at the same time that spiritual primacy is accorded to a female deity and to concepts of femaleness, principal ritual activity in the society is engaged in by men, regarded as an important part of men's role in maintaining the balance in the society, and as necessary for men to obtain the kind of sacred power women possess by the fact of their biology.

Allen (1986: 226ff.) discusses from various perspectives one of the Kochinnenako (Yellow Woman) stories of Laguna culture, where Kochinnenako plays a crucial role in the battle between Sh-ah-cock, male spirit of winter, and Miochin, male spirit of summer.[10] A traditional Laguna interpretation, founded on spiritual perceptions, recognizes the ritual and social elements basic to the meaning of the narrative, whereby woman's centrality maintains the fundamental principles and order of society. Through woman's agency, balance and harmony are preserved both in the alternation of the seasons and in the exchange of village leadership between the two moieties also called summer and winter, whereby each portion of the community takes responsibility in turn for the prosperity and well-being of the people. The story is thus satisfying to the traditional Laguna because it affirms their ritual understandings and can be visualized ritually (Allen 1986: 232–34).

Allen also notes (1986: 234–35) that the narrative level of the story is dissatisfying to modern Western feminists who see in it a repetition of abusive, hierarchical gender and social dynamics characteristic of Western narratives. Not only is the sacred, ritual dimension significant for countering this misinterpretation from the outside, but Allen (1986: 243–44) also points out the varying emphases given to foreground and background in Native American and Western forms of perception. She argues that Westerners overemphasize the foreground and whatever exists or takes place there to the virtual exclusion of the background and whatever exists or takes place there.[11] In Native American perception, women and the earth form the background, perceived not as a shadowy realm whose existence only serves to highlight the foreground, but rather as the essential foundation that enables all other activity and life to exist.

In addition to these analyses, Perry (1977), Buckley (1982), Medicine (1983a), and Schlegel (1990) demonstrate similar correspondences between metaphysical constructions of femaleness and the actual roles of women in the societies they study. These examples all demonstrate the centrality and high valuation of the female in Native American metaphysics. Not only do descriptions of the cultures reveal a strong woman-centered orientation, but discussions by Native American researchers themselves emphatically associate Native American modes of perception with specific feminine modes, describing their own modes as feminine and regarding both primal and feminine modes as having long been subordinated to the domination of male thinking in Western thought (Highwater 1981: 205). Thus, Allen (1986: 26–28) notes that the features discussed here for many Native American societies are distinctively feminine in character: the primacy of spiritual values, the recognition of women's elemental power, the equitable distribution of goods, the interacting notions of consensus and autonomy, the respect for all individuals within the society according to both age and gender, the flexibility in societal roles permitted each individual. The feminine modes of perception that underlie these social manifestations emphasize the qualities of care, respect, and value for life in its many forms. Allen calls this feminine orientation in perception and action by the etymologically Greek term, "gynocentric."

A brief look at the feminist literature across disciplinary and ethnic lines reveals two points about the gynocentrism here described. First, regardless of cultural, ideological, or individual differences, certain attitudes, values, and modes of action emerge as characteristically female: the significance of spirituality and of metaphysical concepts to women's and men's self-conceptualizations (Daly 1978;

160 / BELLA ZWEIG

Christ and Plaskow 1979; Saiving 1979; Reuther 1983; Cannon 1988); the importance of motherhood and the maternal activities derived from it such as caring, concern with individual respect, and desire for balance and consensus (Gilligan 1982; Ruddick 1989; Cole and Coultrap-McQuin 1992); circular, nonlinear modes of thinking that recognize the importance of the subjective realm (Kristeva 1981); and inclusive, balanced, egalitarian social tendencies (Sanday 1981). Linguistic innovations—"feminist," "gynocentric," "womanist"—testify to a distinctive woman's consciousness that merits recognition and respect within the range of human perceptions.[12] At the same time that some fundamental "female" commonalities arise, cultural, ethnic, religious, or other factors can significantly differentiate constructions of gender ideals and activities, a point emphasized in the literature by women of color and by women marginalized because of class, sexuality, or other factors (Walker 1983; hooks 1989; DuBois and Ruiz 1990; Lorber and Farrell 1991). These studies draw attention to the interweaving of gender and ethnic identities, emphasizing the inseparability of the conceptualization of gender from the culture in which it arises.

The very existence of these similarities between Native American and Western-based woman-centered modes of thought confirms the likelihood that these commonalities also existed in ancient Greece, thus reinforcing the value for the study of Greece of the gynocentric Native American models here proposed. Moreover, if we want to see gender identity within distinct cultural contexts, the Native American cultures are especially relevant; they can provide a view of women both within a full cultural context and seen from the woman-oriented perspectives of the women and men of those cultures, perspectives not as readily available for ancient Greece.

In summation, the Native American models described here show the centrality of women in Native American cultures, manifested in the modes of thinking and expression, social constructions, and symbolic representations of each society. This centrality of women is closely interwoven with a fundamental spiritual orientation which also finds expression at numerous levels in the society. Metaphysical constructs, rituals, and social interactions reinforce each other, but not necessarily in unidimensional ways. In essence, women's centrality shapes the values and behavior of all members of the society. Furthermore, the various cultural forms of expression are critical in helping to shape women's sense of value and self-esteem, and these various cultural arenas underscore in public, recognizable ways woman's importance to the society.

Women in Ancient Greece

> "Daddy's come around to Mommy's way of thinking."
> —Contemporary Country-and-Western song by Paul Overstreet

This comprehensive overview of women in Native American societies—their modes of perception and articulation, their activities and standings within their societies, symbolic representations of them, and Native American gynocentric ways of approach—serves as our model for looking at women in ancient Greece. In this section I will first look at texts by women to establish the validity of examining women's distinctive voices and activities in ancient Greece. I will then examine women's roles in the spiritual and ritual spheres, with implications for social roles, and conclude with suggestions for approaching literary and cultural analysis.

In her interpretation and analysis of the Kochinnenako story from her own Laguna tradition and from her own perspective as a Laguna woman, Allen (1986: 226ff.) presents highly instructive paradigms for seeing into cultural forms of expression. Significantly, the story and its meanings are rooted in the spiritual, relate to ritual and social constructions of Laguna society, and provide satisfactory symbolic and narratological self-expressions for the members of that culture. At the center background of the story, representing woman's fundamental centrality in the culture, is Kochinnenako. By indicating how this same story approached from a Western epistemological framework yields a mistaken and denigrating picture of women's roles, Allen shows clearly how crucial it is to stretch beyond Western epistemological boundaries and attempt to see another culture and its constructs through the eyes of that culture's members. Since for ancient Greece, this directness is impossible, the model Allen provides from a non-Western culture shown to have significant perceptual and expressive similarities with those of ancient Greece is invaluable for our study. It provides the very epistemological strategies to overcome the limitations of Western patriarchal discourses that researchers in classics as well as other disciplines are calling for (de Lauretis 1987; duBois 1988; Winkler 1990).

The few extant poetic and philosophical texts known to be by women writers demonstrate ways of thinking about oneself and the world that differ from the ancient Greek male views, sharing instead the gynocentric features noted by Native American and other researchers. Recent scholarship underscores the distinctive women's perceptions given voice in the poetry by women, which echo the strong sense of ritual, female deity, women's associations, female creativity, and that assured sense of self and of woman's place characteristic of a gynocentric, Native American outlook. Dover (1978: chap. 3) and Stigers (1981) note that Sappho's love poetry is distinguished from that of male poets not only in the fact of the female gender of her lovers. Instead of the hierarchical games according to fixed rules characterizing love between men, Sappho and other female poets describe the love between women as mutual, complementary, and tender. In two articles, Winkler (1981, 1990: 162–87) discusses how Sappho transforms Homer's epic, male poetry into her feminine vision, emphasizing in the latter the distinctive woman's consciousness Sappho presents, while Snyder (1989) brings out the multiple approaches Sappho employs in her creative expressions. And Judith Hallett (1982) shows how Sappho (fr. 123) employs language otherwise used of a cherished only son to describe the intensity of her love for her daughter, matching the intensity of the mother-daughter bond portrayed in the *Homeric Hymn to Demeter*. Finally, Marilyn Skinner's several articles (see this volume, with bibliography) bring out the distinctive women's themes expressed in the poetic fragments of Anyte, Corinna, Erinna, and Nossis.

The few fragments extant from the writings of early women philosophers, which are just now receiving scholarly attention (Waithe 1987; Ward 1992), address concerns of special importance to women—women's virtues, childrearing, household management—as well as transcendental concepts of mathematical and cosmic harmonies, universal laws of nature and physics, and the immortality and transmigration of the soul (Waithe 1987: chaps. 2–4).[13] Ancient chroniclers attribute some of Pythagoras's "sacred discourses" to his mother Theano of Croton and his daughter Arignote, and his ethical doctrines to Themistoclea, a priestess at Delphi (Waithe 1987: 11–14). Aesara of Lucana, who may have lived anywhere from the late fifth to the first century B.C.E., in her *Book on Human Nature,* presents theories on the soul remarkably similar to those expressed by Plato in his *Republic.* She sets forth the premise that introspection into the nature of the human soul establishes the philosophical foundation of all human "laws" evidenced in the individual, in the family, and in social institutions. And she discusses a tripartite division of the soul into mind, spirit, and desire, with mind ruling and desire being ruled, the three parts functioning together according to a rational principle of appropriate proportion (Waithe 1987: 19–22). These striking correspondences render it especially frustrating not to know the dates of Aesara's life, making it impossible to know which philosopher influenced the other. Given the recognized influence of women philosophers as noted above, and the propensity for male appropriation of women's ideas, it is certainly possible, and tantalizing, to consider that Plato derived his ideas on the nature of the soul from Aesara much as his Socrates claims to have learned all he knows from the old wise woman Diotima (Plato, *Symposium* 201d ff.; see Waithe 1987: chap. 6, and Halperin 1990: chap. 6).

While these ideas reflect the cosmic concerns of ancient philosophers, other writings focus on issues of particular interest to women. Myia, another daughter of Theano and Pythagoras, notes that the different tasks and social realities of women's and men's lives reflect their essentially different natures. Acknowledging that it is the task of women philosophers to teach other women what they must know to lead harmonious lives, she states that both women and men must strive to achieve justice and harmony in their souls so they can actualize these qualities in their respective realms of the household (*oikos*) and the community (*polis*) (Waithe 1987: 15–17). Aesara of Lucana unmistakably notes the complementarity between women and men in her claims that women's responsibility for maintaining law and justice (*harmonia*) in the home functions as a microcosm of and foundation for the existence of *harmonia* in the state. Women's work in the home is the moral equivalent to men's work in the state. Thus, women's concerns are not peripheral but central to concepts of social justice (Waithe 1987: 14, 25).

The extant writings of Myia in a letter to Phyllis, and of later philosophers—
Phintys of Sparta, an older contemporary of Plato, in *On the Moderation of
Women;* Perictione I, perhaps Plato's mother, in *On the Harmony of Women;* and
the Hellenistic philosophers Theano II, in several letters, and Perictione II—
provide specific advice on applying the principles of a universal *harmonia* to the
realities of women's daily lives in the areas of childcare (Waithe 1987: 15–16,
41–44), relations to one's husband (Waithe 1987: 32–33, 44–47), and household
management, especially the treatment of slaves (Waithe 1987: 47–50; Ward
1992). Grounded in pragmatic rather than idealizing theory, so that, ironically,
Aristotle would find himself in familiar theoretical company, they stress moderation as a key principle. By accepting and not challenging the status quo of social
realities, in the area of conjugal relations they stress the wife's role in serving
and being morally superior to her husband. At the same time, Theano II notes
that as soon as she is married, authority is granted to a woman *by law* (my
emphasis) to govern her household, and that the young wife would do well to
seek and respect the advice of older women continually. Finally, Theano II's
advocation of moderation in childrearing leads her to argue against luxurious
indulgence; rather, children above a certain age should be allowed to endure
hunger and thirst, cold and heat, and shame, a hardening-up process by which
virtue is perfected, and a process of childrearing quite similar to the practices in
ancient Sparta (Waithe 1987: 33, 43, 47).

Both through discussion of transcendental, cosmic themes and through their
focus on appropriate women's activities, these women thinkers show clearly that
their ethical ideas are no less significant, "universal," and critical to the good and
well-being of the society than those treated by male philosophers and that their
intellectual discourses are as much a part of philosophic dialogue as the men's. At
the very least, recognizing the existence of these women's philosophic discourses
requires us to question why it is that the most extreme of male-focused, misogynistic writers, namely Plato and Aristotle, set the standard for Western intellectual
discourse. Fundamentally, accepting the validity of these women's voices within
the discipline of philosophy challenges how we define areas of importance for
society, and how we define the very nature of intellectual thinking and of philosophy.

These and a scant few other women's texts (Skinner 1986 directs our attention
also to the women epigrammatists) remain the only direct sources by women
from ancient Greece—that other voice longed for by the chorus of Euripides's
Medea (420 ff.). Providing a strong balance to the predominantly male sources
and to the tendency to find in any text that which replicates the epistemological
modes with which one is familiar, these women's voices demonstrate the distinctiveness of ancient Greek women's perceptions and forms of expression that
correspond in fundamental ways with the gynocentric, Native American perceptions described above. These correspondences in turn affirm the validity of the
present approach to the study of women in ancient Greece from a gynocentric,

Native American perspective. This doubled use of these models, both recognizing them within our subject of study and engaging them in our approach, rights the balance of the double helix of biases outlined at the beginning and permits us to look with refreshened hearts, eyes, and minds at the indirect evidence concerning women in ancient Greece.

Since the spiritual dimension—at the core of Native American perceptions and values—is the locus for women's central place within the society, and since spirituality is to a great extent at the core of ancient Greek societies, allying them more closely with a Native American than a modern Western secular outlook, it is fitting to start with ancient Greek women's place in spirituality. The ancient Greeks believed in the primacy of female deities for various functions: material abundance and female fertility—Demeter, Gaia; spiritual blessedness—Persephone; growth and maturation of the young—Artemis, Helen; creative and intellectual activity—Aphrodite, Athena; love, sexuality, marriage—Aphrodite, Hera, Hestia; providing law and the basis for civilized society—Themis. These and many other female deities, their attributes overlapping in different regions, had shrines to which individual prayers and offerings were made, and most were celebrated in rites that set the ritual cycles—of the agricultural and seasonal year, of the various stages in a woman's life, and of the community—in annual or periodic public ceremonies. Many of the rites for female deities were celebrated by women only, their success measured in part by the well-maintained secrecy that prevented their divulgence to the noninitiated, remaining hidden also from the view of the men of their culture, and consequently left unrecorded by and for outsiders. Yet extant sources demonstrate the centrality of female deities in the thoughts and perceptions, and in the ritual, procreative, social, familial, and creative areas of activity in ancient Greece (Deubner 1956; Calame 1977; Simon 1983; Kraemer 1992).

An overview of the rituals that women engaged in annually throughout the calendar year and periodically throughout their lives will demonstrate the major role ritual activities played in the lives of women in ancient Greece. Extensive studies on the rites in the regions of Athens and Sparta, confirmed by sources from throughout the ancient Hellenic world, show evidence of rituals for girls that often began at about age six and lasted throughout a woman's life. The most significant rites were those marking the two passages from childhood into adolescence and from adolescent to adult woman, and those celebrating adult women's continued fertility. The first transition from girlhood into puberty, celebrating the onset of menstruation and a girl's reproductive potential, was symbolized by myths of death or transformation (King 1983; Dowden 1989). Frequently, these rites occurred prior to the actual onset of menarche, so that the girls participating in the rituals, whether directly or by proxy of group leaders, ranged from six to ten years of age. Actual rites could differ greatly, as indicated by two rituals of Athenian girls, both remembered by the protagonist Lysistrata in Aristophanes's comedy of the same name (*Lysistrata* 641–43). In the Arrephoria, two girls resident in Athena's sanctuary situated below her most prominent temple on the acropolis—the central outcropping overlooking Athens—solemnly exchange *hiera,* "holy things," with others in a pit located in a grove sacred to Aphrodite. This ritual passage from one state to another, signified also by the transfer from one goddess to another, emphasizes the awesome quality of this time of transition (Deubner 1956: 9–17; Simon 1983: 39–46). The rites of the Brauronia, celebrated on the eastern coast of Attica in honor of Artemis, the goddess of the young par excellence, seem to have added joy to awe as the girls "played the bear" as part of the festivities (Deubner 1956: 207–8; Simon 1983: 83–88; Kraemer 1992: 22–23). While the myths symbolically characterized the transformation of the child into a fertile woman, actual rites ritualized this period of transition by spiritually preparing the child for the physical changes that would eventually take place and that would signal her entry into adolescence.[14]

Attitudes varied toward this period of adolescence, known as *partheneia,* "maidenhood," and toward the pubescent girl, called a *parthenos,* "maiden." Many myths reveal concepts of the danger of this time, when the adolescent girl is perceived as biologically capable of having a child, but not yet under the control of—in Greek, literally "tamed by"—a husband to legitimate any children she might have. Thus the myths of Kallisto and Io depict the ostracism of the pregnant adolescent, and the practice in Athens was to keep this period of latent danger brief by marrying off young girls shortly after menarche. By contrast, adolescent girls in Sparta were encouraged to mature more fully before getting married at about age eighteen.

The next transition from adolescent into adult woman was also celebrated by major rites and rituals. Many communities, equating adult woman with married woman, celebrated this transition with marriage ceremonies. In others, public celebrations separate from weddings marked a woman's social status as an adult of the community, thus recognizing an adult woman's integral role in the community, independent of her marital status. Thus, the Spartan Hyakinthia celebrated the entry into adult status of both Spartan women and men, and Calame (1977: vol. 1, 39) believes it demonstrated the greater importance to the community of the women.[15]

While wedding celebrations tend to be especially joyous for both women and men, many myths associated with this stage of transition entail stories of rape and many marriage ceremonies are marked by actual or mock rituals of abduction or rape. A symbolic reading of these myths and this aspect of marriage ritual suggests that this transition from *parthenos* to woman, especially married woman, both denoted by the word *gynê,* entails a violent wrenching from one state to the next.[16] At the same time, the celebratory nature of many wedding ceremonies emphasizes woman's potential role in the community as a mother and the rewards to be gained from her new status as *gynê.*

Then, for mature women, the cycle of rituals for several goddesses throughout the year engaged in by Athenian women repeatedly emphasizes woman's importance in connection with the cycles and fertility of the earth, the continued well-being of the community, and blessedness in this life and the next. Demeter was celebrated by fertility and agricultural women-only festivals in the spring (Skiria), fall (Thesmophoria), and winter (Haloa), and her summer festival evolved into the transcendental Eleusinian Mysteries for both women and men. Based on archaeological, historical, and literary documents, these last appear to have been the most important religious ceremonies in the ancient Greek and Roman worlds for a good two thousand years (Deubner 1956: chap. 2; Simon 1983: chap. 2). Athenian women celebrated both Aphrodite and Athena by an annual Plynteria, when the goddesses' temples were cleaned and their cult statues taken down to the sea to be washed. Athena's Plynteria is known to have been a dangerous holy day when the spiritually unprepared were not permitted out along the processional route because they would not be able to withstand the power emanating from the cult statue (Deubner 1956: 17–22; Simon 1983: 46–48). Like Athena, the city's patron deity, Aphrodite Pandemos ("Of the People") was honored in an annual civic festival, the Aphrodisia. And Athenian women played a central, honored role in the Panathenaia, weaving a new ceremonial robe, the *peplos,* for Athena's cult statute in the Parthenon. Thus even at Athens, where women's roles were more circumscribed than almost anywhere else in the ancient Hellenic world, women engaged in extensive ritual activities in the performance of public rites, other lesser known rites, and many private ones for personal and family reasons throughout the year and throughout their lives. Phintys of Sparta acknowledged that women carry out their public, ritual activity "on behalf of themselves, their husbands, and their entire households" (Waithe 1987: 30).

To appreciate the fuller cultural context, it bears noting that rites for male deities were also of importance, some representing realms of masculinity or male activities comparable to those for women: male fertility and vegetation—Dionysos, Poseidon; creative and intellectual activity—Dionysos, Orpheus; growth and maturation of young men—Apollo. The rituals for these male deities, some of which were men-only celebrations, were also important for setting annual and periodic community celebrations. However, in other ways they differ significantly from the rites for female deities, who remain central and of primary importance in ritual life, in matters associated with life, with fertility of women and of the earth, and with blessedness after death. The primacy of female deities in belief is echoed by the far greater numbers of rituals marking girls' and women's lives than men's. Many of the celebrations of male deities came to be associated with the public aspect of the community, and especially the man's role as citizen—Zeus, Apollo (Deubner 1956; Simon 1983; Dowden 1989). This greater public aspect of the male deities and many of the men's rituals for them, exacerbated by the lack of knowledge about the women-only rituals, has often resulted in an inflated perception of the significance to the culture of the men's rites, and a concomitant devaluation of the fundamental role of the women's.

Despite the greater public visibility of many of the men's rites for male deities, female deities—and frequently the women's rites for them—endowed Greek society with some of its most important spiritual and ritual meanings, and studies of ancient religion underscore the importance of women's religious activity for themselves, for the community, and for the cosmos (Calame 1977; Lincoln 1981; Burkert 1985; Winkler 1990: 188–209).

The Native American, gynocentric model enables us to appreciate more fully the significance of female deities and of women's rituals for the community and to counter several modern, Western assumptions concerning both women and the realm of ritual activity: (1) that assume the centrality, normalcy, and primacy of men's activities, which are also believed to form the model or even the rationale for the existence of women's activities; (2) that regard political activity as the most important for the society, relegating ritual activity to a subordinate value; and (3) that generally fail to appreciate the implications of spiritual belief and ritual action upon the thinking of the members of a society. Thus, dominating the scholarly literature is the view that women's ritual roles function essentially or merely as a mechanism of release for women from their lives otherwise filled with drudgery and restraint (Kraemer 1979, 1992: 46–49; Zeitlin 1982; Bremmer 1984), and that women's rituals are little other than an opiate to keep women in their societal secondary place (Lincoln 1981: 107–9; Kraemer 1992: 29).

Without denying this possible function of women's rituals at some periods and in some locales, and rather than minimizing the significance of women's ritual role, our model also allows us to see other possible dimensions of the female, and women's central place in the spiritual conceptions and the ritual activities of the community. First, for women's sense of self, the work of Western feminist theologians also reminds us how critical the religious sphere is for framing our metaphysical and epistemological approaches. Besides taking seriously the spiritual basis of much of ancient Greek society, studies of women in ancient religion need to address the following questions: What does it mean for women's concept of self to live in a culture that expresses its notions of divinity in poly- rather than monotheistic form? where many of the deities most important in a woman's life and often for the life of the community are female? where stages of a woman's life are celebrated with numerous rituals in honor of several, mostly female deities? where many of women's rituals are women oriented and for women only? where notions of women's power, value, and worth are perceived in different ways and are culturally validated by publicly recognized and financed women's activities? where women's roles as mothers are given community recognition and importance? These aspects of ancient Greek society must have shaped women's and men's self-perceptions, perceptions of each other, and of their respective roles in their communities. To differing degrees, women in ancient Greek societies must have enjoyed the positive sense of self and self-worth produced by comparable aspects of Native American societies.

Furthermore, the answers to these questions affect both the manner and extent of women's participation in other areas of society and how these activities are regarded. As in Native American cultures, female procreative and creative powers are intertwined in narrative expressions—for example, the stories of Aphrodite, Helen, Penelope. Similarly, women's roles as mothers establish their standing within the community, honored in ancient Sparta by public ceremonies celebrating mothers and reflected in the proud assertion of their identity as mothers by Spartan women (Plutarch, *Sayings of the Spartan Women;* Zweig 1993). This focus on motherhood with the accompanying primacy accorded to childrearing also generates men's and the public's concerns with these areas, evident in the laws relating to child-production (*teknopoiia*) in Athens and Sparta, the injunction on Spartan men to curb their sexual desires, and the emphasis in Homer's *Iliad* and *Odyssey* and in Euripides's *Herakles* on the man's role as a father to his children.

Using the concept of complementarity between women's and men's activities helps us better to situate women's ritual roles within the entire cultural context. As long as women's activities are believed to be confined to a privatized, secluded sector, the *oikos*,[17] believed to be controlled by the all-important activities of men in the public sector of the *polis,* women's religious activities in the ancient world have appeared anomalous (Zeitlin 1982). Hirschon (1978) notes that women's religious activities in a modern Greek urbanized community, in a manner perhaps similar to ancient practices, provide women with an important and legitimate reason to move about outside the home autonomously. Women's activity in the realm of ritual forces us to redefine the contours and interactions of different realms of activity in ancient Greece. Foley (1981: 148–62) and Just (1989: 28) show that far from being isomorphic categories, the modern domestic/public dichotomy limits understanding of the *oikos/polis* complex in ancient Athenian life; they demonstrate instead that the *oikos* forms the very foundation enabling the *polis* to exist, and that the concerns of the *oikos* and the women who inhabit and run it are fundamental to the men's deliberations and concerns within the activities of the *polis.* Even more so for ancient Sparta: Kunstler (1986) describes the *oikos/polis* nexus as a dynamic interaction between complementary spheres, and not as an entrenched opposition. Of particular interest for this analysis, ethnographic studies of modern rural Greece describe the fluid and active interplay between these two realms (Dubisch 1986).

It appears, therefore, that women's centrality in carrying on the essential activities of the community through their childrearing and religious activities provides the foundation for their activities within the *oikos,* and for influencing their husbands' activities in the *polis,* thereby offsetting the male political and legal lenses by which we tend to judge women's roles. This approach to women's roles does not deny the rising importance of men's activities and the increasing subordination of women and their activities in many parts of ancient Greece, especially Athens. It permits us, however, to recognize the forms and extent of women's powers that are being so subordinated in the establishment of patriarchal structures, and it encourages us to remain alert to possibilities of women's roles and status that have historically been overlooked in descriptions that see only total subordination.

This last is a critical point in studies of women in ancient Greece, many of which react to false notions of some mirror-reverse "matriarchy" rather than examining the evidence for women's roles in true scholarly fashion.[18] Pivotal for this trend are Pembroke's two articles (1965, 1967), which set out to disprove any possibility of woman's power in the ancient Mediterranean world, but which are filled with polemical assertions, misconstructions of the data, and conclusions that gloss over the illogic of his argumentation. Despite these serious critical flaws in Pembroke's "proofs," both articles have been cited frequently to argue the impossibility of any positive social, political, or prestige roles for women in antiquity,[19] while scholarship that suggests positive possibilities has been summarily dismissed (Mellaart 1967; Thomas 1973; Gimbutas 1974; see Webster 1975 and Barstow 1978 on this issue). Removing expectations of total domination, subordination, and control, and removing expectations of hierarchical social structures derived from contemporary models, we become open to the possibility of positive interpretations of women's roles. The concept of complementary spheres characteristic of Native American cultures and the recognition of the extensive significance of women's spiritual and ritual roles will enable us to see women as interactive agents in their societies, and to describe both the social arenas for women's activities and the status and prestige they held. This is not to say that we will not find evidence of women's subordination, but that when we do, we can more accurately identify the context and note in what areas women may be subordinate and in which ones they may have primary or complete authority and control. This approach not only provides us with a truer picture of the roles of both women and men in ancient Greece, but it also enables us better to perceive the formation of the male-dominating ideologies that have proved so destructive in Western society.

Finally, this gynocentric, Native American model enables us to counter interpretations that automatically ascribe to women and to female spheres only negative valuations, a tendency that undermines scholarly inquiry, circumscribing analyses even by feminist classicists.[20] Instead, this model can be highly illuminating in our interpretations of the early literature, enabling us to find numerous examples of esteem for women's activities. The symbolic and economic importance of women's creative endeavors, notably weaving, is seen throughout the *Odyssey* in the association of all important mortal and immortal female characters with weaving, and in particular in Penelope's pride in her weaving and in men's esteem for it (*Od.* 2.104–5, 117, 19.241–42). It is also reflected in the careful and intricate attention paid to depiction of clothing for women and for men in archaic and classical vase painting and sculpture. As in the case of the star quilt made by Lakota women (described by Albers and Medicine 1983b), the ceremonial importance of weaving dovetails with women's gift giving: the ritual presentation of the *peplos* to Athena and other deities; Helen's gift of her own woven robe to Telemakhos (*Od*. 15.124); and the destructive distortion of women's productive and gift-giving actions instanced by Deianeira's and Medea's fatal giving of robes in Sophocles's *The Women of Trachis* and Euripides's *Medea,* respectively. Women's economic role may also underlie women's role in hospitality, a crucial aspect of ancient Greek as of Native American societies: the necessity of Arete's initial acceptance of Odysseus (*Od*. 6.305 ff., 7.142 ff.), Metaneira's of the old nurse (*Homeric Hymn to Demeter*), Clytemnestra's of Orestes (*Choephoroi*). This role is also supported by fundamental similarities observed in women's activities in modern rural Greece (Dubisch 1986).

The concept of complementary female and male spheres, each esteemed for fulfilling their respective roles, now unmistakably emerges in the early literature, best illustrated in Homer's *Odyssey*. While the themes of the narrative illustrate this complementarity throughout the poem, two passages bring it out explicitly. At 6.182–84, Odysseus tells the Phaeacian princess Nausikaa that "there is nothing greater or finer than when a man and woman [or husband and wife] who are harmonious in their thinking (*homophroneonte noêmasin*) together hold their home." And after their reunion, Odysseus acknowledges to his wife Penelope the comparability of the trials each has endured (*Od*. 23.350–53).

Not only are the genders and their spheres seen to be complementary, but Odysseus's journey is in part a quest for understanding of the feminine dimensions within himself and in the world (Austin 1975; Foley 1978; Winkler 1990: 129–61; and see Heilbrun 1973). In this respect, it is interesting to note that while Odysseus must achieve this perceived gender balance within himself, Penelope needs only to be herself, a woman. Ortiz (1969: 36) notes a similar feature for Tewa society, where men, who are deemed to possess also the qualities of women, are enjoined on ceremonial occasions to "be a woman, be a man," whereas women, who are "only women," are enjoined "to be a woman." Although Ortiz offers no interpretation, Schlegel (1977b: 260–62, 1990: 33), discussing a similar conceptualization for the culturally related Hopi, notes that women are perceived to have a single nature as the givers and keepers of life. But since men's roles as germinators and hunters entail both life-productive and life-destructive activities, they are considered to be of a dual nature. Far from marking woman as lacking some essential qualities, these concepts seem rather to reflect women's positive, self-sufficient, and central role for the community. I believe such concepts of gender balance and roles are significant for the interpretation of Homer's *Odyssey,* which acknowledges and respects the distinctiveness of women's perceptions and the comparability of women's and men's spheres of activity. These very brief illustrations may point the direction for expanding analyses of the vast corpus of ancient Greek literary, artistic, documentary, and material sources.

Conclusion

I hope this analysis has shown the value of employing Native American, gynocentric perspectives in our study of women in ancient Greece, for they provide both new ways of looking at the roles and the imagery of women, and, because of these novel perceptions, they also enable us to appreciate aspects of women's lives not considered before. The extent to which many ancient Greek communities were patriarchal or misogynistic necessarily circumscribed both the real roles women may have held as well as the images projected of women and the female spheres; however, given the fundamental non-Western character of much of ancient Greek society, manifestations of these patriarchal and misogynistic features will differ in form, kind, degree, and meaning from those of contemporary Western society. Approaching antiquity from the radically different perspective of a non-Western society permits us to see these masculinist traits within the context of the larger society. We thereby gain in our understanding of antiquity and in our comprehension of the development of those features that may have originated in antiquity, evolved throughout the course of Western history, and are still having an impact on our current and future lives. Conscientiously applying gynocentric and cross-cultural perspectives concretely provides us with new vantage points, different lenses, even different cameras, that will permit us to see our field in new ways, and to perceive areas, objects, relations that may have been completely veiled before. These perspectives can greatly illuminate aspects of antiquity that touch upon the lives, images, and societal structures of all—women and men.

Notes

I dedicate this study to all the Native American people I have met over the years from whose respectful ways and teachings I have learned invaluable lessons, in the hopes of achieving better understanding and respect among all peoples.

I wish to express my deepest appreciation to both editors of this volume: Amy Richlin, who has supported my development of these ideas since their inception over a decade ago; and Nancy Rabinowitz, whose challenging comments have helped me shape these ideas into the present, critical analysis.

1. The title of my analysis recognizes the value for Western thinking of the issues Highwater raises in his 1981 study, at the same time that I am aware of his false representations of his Native American status.

2. I use these terms for convenience of historical reference, recognizing that this periodization presents certain problems obstructing the study of women in antiquity (Arthur 1973), and without accepting thereby the valuations frequently ascribed to them in classical scholarship.

3. Richlin (1991) shows how little feminist analyses have influenced large areas of classical scholarship (and compare, for example, Dowden 1989). Even more disturbing, she demonstrates the unacknowledged appropriation of classical feminist criticism, in particular by scholars otherwise producing significant work on gender studies and even feminist analyses of antiquity, such as, sadly, Halperin (1990), Halperin, Winkler, and Zeitlin (1990), and Winkler (1990).

Bernal's challenge (1987) to the white, Western ethnocentricity in classical scholarship has sparked a controversial, sometimes contentious debate (special issue of
Arethusa [Fall 1989, and Winter 1992]). While I find that Bernal often errs toward
another extreme in the details of his analysis, I agree with the fundamental need to
recognize the multiculturalism of the ancient Mediterranean world (for example,
Haley, this volume).

4.   While differing methodologically from my analysis, by exploring the underlying
dyadic dynamics of gender relations in ancient Spartan society, Kunstler (1986)
also makes use of cross-cultural material at a more fundamental level than other
researchers.

5.   See Green (1980: *passim*) for a survey of these two categories of scholarship up to
the late 1970s.

6.   A few years ago the Tohono O'odham received official recognition from the United
States government for their own name rather than the Spanish designation. Although
the indigenous name Lakota (Sioux) does not have the same official status, many
researchers, both Lakota and others, commonly refer to the Lakota people by their
own name.

7.   Interestingly, Green (1975) shows that the first images of Native American women
to enter white lore were as "Mothers," and that over time these images shifted to the
"Princess" and the "squaw" as Anglo-American attitudes toward the native peoples
changed.

8.   See also Rohrlich-Leavitt et al. in Reiter 1975, 110–26.

9.   I have personally heard women and men from virtually every native nation describe
their society as matriarchal, most recently a female Apache and a male Hopi educator,
both speaking as part of the University of Arizona 1991 Summer Series on Native
American Education.

10.   Silko (1981) is an excellent, imaginative, modern rendering of some of these traditional tales. See Ortiz (1969) for a detailed discussion of the social and religious
functioning of the moieties in Pueblo society.

11.   This idea was the subject of a public presentation given by Dr. N. Scott Momaday,
University of Arizona, March 1989. Both Witherspoon (1977: 166, 174ff.) and
Highwater (1981: 119ff.) note the influence of this equalizing concept as expressed
in Navajo sandpaintings on the "field" painting style developed by Jackson Pollock;
see Alberto Busignani *Pollock* (Feltham, Middlesex: The Hamlyn Publishing Group,
Ltd., 1971).

12.   Because of the specific historic implications drawn in Western ideology from the
concept of distinctive feminine perceptions, some social scientists challenge its
validity, noting on the one hand the female-subordinating application made of the
concept "biology is destiny" (Lowe and Hubbard 1983: introduction), on the other
that these perceptual differences result from the sex/gender inequities in Western
society (Hartsock 1983; Kelly 1984). Epistemologically, de Lauretis (1987: 1–2)
finds this concept of feminine perceptions inhibiting to feminist thought by keeping
it bound to the conceptual terms of patriarchal discourse. Yet the radical feminist
epistemology she envisions appears rooted in a conception of self for which the

gynocentric, Native American modes provide excellent examples. The essays in Cole and Coultrap-McQuin (1992) address this issue from an ethical standpoint.

13. I find it puzzling that even though these women-authored philosophical texts have been available at least since Thesleff (1965), Waithe's primary source, they are not fully addressed in the early standard works on women in antiquity. But see now Snyder 1989: 99–121.

14. This analysis is developed more fully in a paper I presented at the 1992 annual meeting of the Classical Association of the Midwest and South in Austin, Texas, entitled *"The Homeric Hymn to Demeter:* The Rape of Persephone and the Experience of the Kore," and is part of my work in progress on women in ancient Greek religion.

15. Even in communities that do recognize adult women's importance independent of marriage, motherhood remains a major factor in determining women's community status. Although a *parthenos* ("maiden") in Sparta might be a mother, it may be that her status as such is not formally recognized until she is also a married woman, the basis for her social standing in other communities. Hence the focus in the remainder of this discussion is on married women.

16. This symbolic interpretation does not deny the social implications of rape stories and actions, as discussed by Keuls (1985) and Richlin (1992).

17. *Oikos* may be understood as comprising the family and household interests, that would include a wide range of childrearing, food and clothing preparation, religious, economic, and kin-related activities. The *polis* represents the community as a civic entity, actualized by the activities of its citizens. Although ancient Athens had no word for a female citizen, ancient Sparta did.

18. Reputedly inspired by Lewis Morgan's description of the Iroquoian matriarchate, J. J. Bachofen, in his 1860 *Motherright,* advanced a theory of ancient matriarchy that is instead an exact reverse image of Victorian-European patriarchy in every respect. In tune with the then-prevalent notion of the progression of civilizations through three stages, Bachofen's matriarchy is characterized by an earth-bound, materialist existence that naturally evolves over time to the more advanced, lofty, spiritual stage of patriarchy. Thus, despite the supposed influence of Iroquoian society, Bachofen's description simply reiterates in the language of his day the more imaginative and poetic allusions to an early, mirror-reverse matriarchy found in Hesiod's *Theogony* and Aeschylus's *Oresteia.* Harrison (1922) and Thomson (1941) represent the very few classical scholars who have seriously entertained the possibility of ancient matriarchy. In the lay scholarly literature of interest to women, Bachofen's theories continue to be influential.

19. Bamberger's discussion of the myths of mirror-reverse matriarchy in two South American cultures, from which she concludes that matriarchy everywhere, always, and only functions as a fictive myth to justify the converse current status quo (in Rosaldo and Lamphere 1974, 263–80), has further complicated the issue, often seen as reinforcing Pembroke's position. The weaknesses in Bamberger's methodology and analysis have been criticized along with the other reductionist, universalist claims made in that anthology, and in an analysis of these same myths by these same tribes, Sanday (1981: 180–81) draws conclusions radically different from Bamberger's.

20. Thus, Carson and Loraux, both in Halperin et al. (1990), find only negative associations for women in their analyses, and restricted by her psychoanalytic lens, duBois
(1988) does not draw out the implications of the positive analogies she finds between
images of women and of the earth.

Bibliography

Albers, Patricia. 1983a. "Introduction: New Perspectives on Plains Indian Women." In
Albers and Medicine 1983a, 1–26.

———. 1983b. "Sioux Women in Transition." In Albers and Medicine 1983a, 175–234.

Albers, Patricia, and Beatrice Medicine, eds. 1983a. *The Hidden Half: Studies of Plains
Indian Women*. Lanham, Md.: University Press of America.

Albers, Patricia, and Beatrice Medicine. 1983b. "The Role of Sioux Women in the
Production of Ceremonial Objects: The Case of the Star Quilt." In Albers and Medicine
1983a, 123–40.

Allen, Paula Gunn. 1986. *The Sacred Hoop: Recovering the Feminine in American Indian
Traditions*. Boston: Beacon Press.

Arthur, Marylin. 1973. "Early Greece: The Origins of the Western Attitude towards
Women." *Arethusa* 6: 7–58.

Austin, Norman. 1975. *Archery at the Dark of the Moon*. Berkeley: University of California Press.

Barstow, Anne. 1978. "The Uses of Archaeology for Women's History: James Mellaart's
Work on the Neolithic Goddess at Çatal Hüyük." *Feminist Studies* 4: 7–18.

Bataille, Gretchen M., and Kathleen M. Sands. 1984. *American Indian Women: Telling
Their Lives*. Lincoln and London: University of Nebraska Press.

Bernal, Martin. 1987. *Black Athena: The Afroasiatic Roots of Classical Civilization*, vol.
1. New Brunswick, N.J.: Rutgers University Press.

Bremmer, Jan N. 1984. "Greek Maenadism Reconsidered." *Zeitschrift für Papyrologie
und Epigraphik* 55: 267–86.

Brown, Judith K. 1975. "Iroquois Women: An Ethnohistoric Note." In Reiter 1975, 235–
51.

Buckley, Thomas. 1982. "Menstruation and the Power of Yurok Women: Methods in
Cultural Reconstruction." *American Ethnologist* 9: 47–60.

Burkert, Walter. 1985. *Greek Religion*. Translated by J. Raffan. Cambridge, Mass.:
Harvard University Press.

Calame, Claude. 1977. *Les chœurs de jeunes filles en Grèce archaïque*. 2 vols. Rome:
Edizioni dell'Ateneo & Bizzarri.

Cannon, Katie G. 1988. *Black Womanist Ethics*. Atlanta, Ga.: Scholars Press.

Christ, Carol, and Judith Plaskow, eds. 1979. *Womanspirit Rising: A Feminist Reader in
Religion*. New York: Harper and Row.

Cole, Eve Browning, and Susan Coultrap-McQuin, eds. 1992. *Explorations in Feminist
Ethics: Theory and Practice*. Bloomington and Indianapolis: Indiana University Press.

Daly, Mary. 1978. *Gyn/Ecology: The Metaethics of Radical Feminism*. Boston: Beacon Press.

de Lauretis, Teresa. 1987. *Technologies of Gender: Essays on Theory, Film, and Fiction*. Bloomington: Indiana University Press.

Deloria, Ella. 1945. *Speaking of Indians*. New York: Friendship Press.

DeMallie, Raymond J. 1983. "Male and Female in Traditional Lakota Culture." In Albers and Medicine 1983a, 237–65.

Deubner, Ludwig. 1956. *Attische Feste*. Berlin: Akademie Verlag.

Dover, Kenneth J. 1978. *Greek Homosexuality*. Cambridge, Mass.: Harvard University Press.

Dowden, Ken. 1989. *Death and the Maiden: Girls' Initiation Rites in Greek Mythology*. London and New York: Routledge.

Dubisch, Jill, ed. 1986. *Gender & Power in Rural Greece*. Princeton: Princeton University Press.

DuBois, Ellen Carol, and Vicki L. Ruiz, eds. 1990. *Unequal Sisters: A Multi-Cultural Reader in U.S. Women's History*. New York and London: Routledge.

duBois, Page. 1982. *Centaurs and Amazons*. Ann Arbor: The University of Michigan Press.

———. 1988. *Sowing the Body: Psychoanalysis and Ancient Representations of Women*. Chicago: The University of Chicago Press.

Edelstein, Emma J., and Ludwig Edelstein. 1945. *Asclepius: A Collection and Interpretation of the Testimonies*. Baltimore: The Johns Hopkins University Press.

Foley, Helene P. 1978. " 'Reverse Similes' and Sex Roles in the *Odyssey*." *Arethusa* 11: 7–26.

———, ed. 1981. *Reflections of Women in Antiquity*. New York, London, Paris: Gordon and Breach Science Publishers.

Friedl, Ernestine. 1962. *Vasilika: A Village in Modern Greece*. New York: Holt, Rinehart, and Winston.

———. 1967. "The Position of Women: Appearance and Reality." *Anthropological Quarterly* 40: 97–108.

Gilligan, Carol. 1982. *In a Different Voice: Psychological Theory and Women's Development*. Cambridge, Mass.: Harvard University Press.

Gimbutas, Marija. 1974. *The Gods and Goddesses of Old Europe*. Berkeley: University of California Press.

Green, Rayna. 1975. "The Pocahontas Perplex: The Image of Indian Women in American Culture." *The Massachusetts Review* 16: 698–714. Reprinted in DuBois and Ruiz 1990, 15–21.

———. 1980. "Native American Women." *Signs* 6: 248–67.

Hallett, Judith P. 1982. "Beloved Cleis." *Quaderni Urbinati di Cultura Classica* n.s. 10: 21–31.

Halperin, David M. 1990. *One Hundred Years of Homosexuality*. New York and London: Routledge.

Halperin, David M., John J. Winkler, and Froma I. Zeitlin, eds. 1990. *Before Sexuality: The Construction of Erotic Experience in the Ancient Greek World*. Princeton: Princeton University Press.

Harrison, A. R. W. 1968. *The Law of Athens: The Family and Property*. Oxford: Oxford University Press.

Harrison, Jane Ellen. 1922. *Prolegomena to the Study of Greek Religion*. Cambridge: Cambridge University Press.

Hartsock, Nancy C. M. 1983. "The Feminist Standpoint: Developing the Ground for a Specifically Feminist Historical Materialism." In Sandra Harding and M. B. Hintikka, eds., *Discovering Reality: Feminist Perspectives on Epistemology, Metaphysics, Methodology, and Philosophy of Science*, 283–310. Dordrecht and Boston: D. Reidel.

Heilbrun, Carolyn. 1973. *Toward a Recognition of Androgyny*. New York: Columbia University Press.

Highwater, Jamake. 1976. *Song from the Earth: American Indian Painting*. Boston: New York Graphic Society.

————. 1981. *The Primal Mind: Vision and Reality in Indian America*. New York: Harper and Row.

Hirschon, Renee. 1978. "Open Body/Closed Space: The Transformation of Female Sexuality." In Shirley Ardener, ed., *Defining Females: The Nature of Women in Society*, 66–88. London: Croom Helm.

hooks, bell. 1989. *Talking Back: Thinking Feminist, Thinking Black*. Boston: South End Press.

Humphreys, S. C. 1978. *Anthropology and the Greeks*. London and Boston: Routledge & Kegan Paul.

Jensen, Joan M. 1990. "Native American Women and Agriculture: A Seneca Case Study." In DuBois and Ruiz 1990, 51–65.

Just, Roger. 1989. *Women in Athenian Law and Life*. London and New York: Routledge.

Kehoe, Alice. 1981. *North American Indians*. Englewood Cliffs, N.J.: Prentice-Hall.

————. 1983. "The Shackles of Tradition." In Albers and Medicine 1983a, 53–73.

Kelly, Joan. 1984. *Women, History and Theory*. Chicago: The University of Chicago Press.

Keuls, Eva C. 1985. *The Reign of the Phallus: Sexual Politics in Ancient Athens*. New York: Harper and Row.

King, Helen. 1983. "Bound to Bleed: Artemis and Greek Women." In Averil Cameron and Amélie Kuhrt, eds., *Images of Women in Antiquity*, 109–27. Detroit: Wayne State University Press.

Kraemer, Ross. 1979. "Ecstasy and Possession: The Attraction of Women to the Cult of Dionysus." *Harvard Theological Review* 72: 55–80.

————. 1992. *Her Share of the Blessings: Women's Religions Among Pagans, Jews, and Christians in the Greco-Roman World*. New York and Oxford: Oxford University Press.

Kristeva, Julia. 1981. "Women's Time." Translated by Alice Jardine and Harry Blake. In Nannerl O. Keohane, Michelle Z. Rosaldo, and Barbara C. Gelpi, eds., *Feminist Theory: A Critique of Ideology*, 31–53. Chicago: The University of Chicago Press.

Kunstler, Barton. 1986. "Family Dynamics and Female Power in Ancient Sparta." In Skinner 1986, 31–48.

Lamphere, Louise. 1977. *To Run after Them: Cultural and Social Bases of Cooperation in a Navajo Community*. Tucson: University of Arizona Press.

Leacock, Eleanor. 1978. "Women's Status in Egalitarian Societies: Implications for Social Evolution." *Current Anthropology* 19: 247–75.

Lincoln, Bruce. 1981. *Emerging from the Chrysalis: Studies in Rituals of Women's Initiation*. Cambridge, Mass.: Harvard University Press.

Lorber, Judy, and Susan A. Farrell, eds. 1991. *The Social Construction of Gender*. Newbury Park, Calif.: Sage Publications.

Lowe, Marian, and Ruth Hubbard, eds. 1983. *Woman's Nature: Rationalizations of Inequality*. New York: Pergamon Press.

McCall, Dan. 1980. "The Dominant Dyad: Mother Right and the Iroquois Case." In Stanley Diamond, ed., *Theory and Practice: Essays Presented to Gene Weltfish*, 221–62. The Hague, Paris, New York: Mouton Publishers.

Medicine, Beatrice. 1978. *The Native American Woman: A Perspective*. Austin, Tex.: National Educational Laboratory Publishers.

————. 1983a. "Indian Women: Tribal Identity as Status Quo." In Lowe and Hubbard 1983, 63–73.

————. 1983b. " 'Warrior Women': Sex Role Alternatives for Plains Indian Women." In Albers and Medicine 1983a, 267–80.

Mellaart, James. 1967. *Çatal Hüyük*. London: Thames and Hudson.

Momaday, N. Scott. 1988. "The Native Voice." In E. Elliott, ed., *The Columbia Literary History of the United States*, 5–15. New York: Columbia University Press.

Moore, Henrietta L. 1988. *Feminism and Anthropology*. Cambridge, U.K.: Polity Press.

Natonabah, Andrew. 1978. *By This Song I Walk*. Tucson, Ariz.: Sun Tracks Productions.

Ortiz, Alfonso. 1969. *The Tewa World: Space, Time, Being, and Becoming in a Pueblo Society*. Chicago: The University of Chicago Press.

Parezo, Nancy J., Kelley A. Hays, and Barbara F. Slivac. 1987. "The Mind's Road: Southwestern Indian Women's Art." In Vera Norwood and Jan Monk, eds., *The Desert Is No Lady*, 146–73. New Haven: Yale University Press.

Pembroke, Simon. 1965. "Last of the Matriarchs: A Study in the Inscriptions of Lycia." *Journal of the Economic and Social History of the Orient* 8: 217–47.

————. 1967. "Women in Charge: The Function of Alternatives in Early Greek Tradition and the Ancient Idea of Matriarchy." *Journal of the Warburg and Courtauld Institutes* 30: 1–35.

Perry, Richard J. 1977. "Variations on the Female Referent in Athabaskan Cultures." *Journal of Anthropological Research* 33: 99–119.

Pomeroy, Sarah B. 1975. *Goddesses, Whores, Wives, and Slaves: Women in Classical Antiquity*. New York: Schocken Books.

Reiter, Rayna, ed. 1975. *Toward an Anthropology of Women*. New York and London: Monthly Review Press.

Reuther, Rosemary R. 1983. *Sexism and God-Talk: Toward a Feminist Theology*. Boston: Beacon Press.

Richlin, Amy. 1991. "Zeus and Metis: Foucault, Feminism, Classics." *Helios* 18: 160–80.

———, ed. 1992. *Pornography and Representation in Greece and Rome*. New York and Oxford: Oxford University Press.

Robbins, Tom. 1990. *Skinny Legs and All*. New York: Bantam Books.

Rosaldo, Michelle. 1974. "Woman, Culture, and Society: A Theoretical Overview." In Rosaldo and Lamphere 1974, 17–42.

———. 1980. "The Use and Abuse of Anthropology: Reflections on Feminism and Cross-Cultural Understanding." *Signs* 5.3: 389–417.

Rosaldo, Michelle, and Louise Lamphere, eds. 1974. *Woman, Culture and Society*. Stanford, Calif.: Stanford University Press.

Ruddick, Sara. 1989. *Maternal Thinking: Toward a Politics of Peace*. Boston: Beacon Press.

Russell, Norman H. 1991. "Two Circles." In Geary Hobson, ed., *The Remembered Earth*, 123. Albuquerque: University of New Mexico Press.

Saiving, Valerie. 1979. "The Human Situation: A Feminine View." In Christ and Plaskow 1979, 25–42.

Sanday, Peggy. 1981. *Female Power and Male Dominance: On the Origin of Sexual Inequality*. Cambridge: Cambridge University Press.

Sanday, Peggy R., and R. G. Goodenough, eds. 1990. *Beyond the Second Sex: New Directions in the Anthropology of Gender*. Philadelphia: University of Pennsylvania Press.

Schaps, David M. 1979. *Economic Rights of Women in Ancient Greece*. Edinburgh: Edinburgh University Press.

Schlegel, Alice, ed. 1977a. *Sexual Stratification: A Cross-Cultural View*. New York: Columbia University Press.

———. 1977b. "Male and Female in Hopi Thought and Action." In Schlegel 1977a, 245–69.

———. 1990. "Gender Meanings: General and Specific." In Sanday and Goodenough 1990, 21–41.

Schneider, Mary Jane. 1983. "Women's Work: An Examination of Women's Roles in Plains Indian Arts and Crafts." In Albers and Medicine 1983a, 101–21.

Sergent, Bernard. 1986. *Homosexuality in Greek Myth*. Translated by Arthur Goldhammer. Boston: Beacon Press.

Silko, Leslie Marmon. 1981. *Storyteller*. New York: Little, Brown and Company.

Simon, Erika. 1983. *Festivals of the Athenians*. Madison: University of Wisconsin Press.

Skinner, Marilyn, ed. 1986. *Rescuing Creusa: New Methodological Approaches to Women in Antiquity*. Lubbock: Texas Tech University Press. (=*Helios* 13.2 [Fall 1986].)

Snyder, Jane McIntosh. 1989. *The Woman and the Lyre: Women Writers in Classical Greece and Rome*. Carbondale: Southern Illinois University Press.

Spector, Janet. "Male/Female Task Differentiation among the Hidatsa: Toward the Development of an Archaeological Approach to the Study of Gender." In Albers and Medicine 1983a, 77–99.

Stigers, Eva S. 1981. "Sappho's Private World." In Foley 1981, 45–61.

Tedlock, Dan, and Barbara Tedlock, eds. 1975. *Teachings from the American Earth: Indian Religion and Philosophy*. New York: Liveright.

Thesleff, Holger. 1965. *Pythagorean Texts of the Hellenistic Period*. Acta Academiae Aboensis Humaniora. Ser. A, v. 30.1.

Thomas, Carol G. 1973. "Matriarchy in Early Greece: The Bronze and Dark Ages." *Arethusa* 6: 173–95.

Thomson, George. 1941. *Aeschylus and Athens*. London: Methuen.

Underhill, Ruth M. 1985. *Papago Woman*. Prospect Heights, Ill.: Waveland Press, Inc.

Waithe, Mary Ellen, ed. 1987. *A History of Women Philosophers: Ancient Women Philosophers, 600 B.C.–500 A.D.*, vol. 1. Dordrecht, Boston, Lancaster: Martinus Nijhoff.

Walker, Alice. 1983. *In Search of Our Mothers' Gardens: Womanist Prose*. New York: Harcourt Brace Jovanovich.

Ward, Julie K. 1992. "*Harmonia* and *Koinonia:* Moral Values for Pythagorean Women." In Cole and Coultrap-McQuin 1992, 57–68.

Webster, Paula. 1975. "Matriarchy: A Vision of Power." In Reiter 1975, 141–56.

Weist, Katherine M. 1983. "Beasts of Burden and Menial Slaves: 19th Century Observations of Northern Plains Indian Women." In Albers and Medicine 1983a, 29–52.

Williams, Walter L. 1986. *The Spirit and the Flesh: Sexual Diversity in American Indian Culture*. Boston: Beacon Press.

Winkler, John J. 1981. "Gardens of Nymphs: Public and Private in Sappho's Lyrics." In Foley 1981, 63–89.

———. 1990. *The Constraints of Desire: The Anthropology of Sex and Gender in Ancient Greece*. New York and London: Routledge.

Witherspoon, Gary. 1977. *Language and Art in the Navajo Universe*. Ann Arbor: The University of Michigan Press.

Zeitlin, Froma I. 1982. "Cultic Models of the Female: Rites of Dionysus and Demeter." *Arethusa* 15: 129–57.

180 / BELLA ZWEIG

Zweig, Bella. 1982. *Personifications in the Oresteia: Motivating Agents for the Dramatic Action*. Dissertation, Stanford University.

———. 1993. "The Only Women Who Give Birth to Men: A Gynocentric, Cross-Cultural View of Women in Ancient Sparta." In Mary DeForest, ed., *Essays in Honor of Joy King*, 40–60. Chicago: Bolchazy-Carducci Publishers.

8

Out of the Closet and into the Field: Matriculture, the Lesbian Perspective, and Feminist Classics

Tina Passman

"Don't pay any attention to Jane Harrison. She was a fanatic who had nothing to say of any importance." I was an undergraduate Greek major sitting in a mythology class taught by a stimulating and beloved (male) professor. It took me eighteen years to read Jane Harrison, and when I did, I felt robbed, cheated, lied to. By then I understood that the real problem was that Jane Harrison wrote like a dyke and lived like a dyke, as any Lesbian could see. As the first woman with classical training and the status of an authority to indict patriarchy as a step backward in human development, she was also a foremother who used what would now be termed a "Lesbian Perspective" to challenge the consensus reality of Western heteropatriarchy in her analysis of ancient (and modern) culture (Harrison 1915, 1926). In so doing Harrison provided the perspective, background, and language that radical contemporary feminisms have employed in reconstructing the early history of the Mediterranean.[1]

In this paper, I question the objection of traditional contemporary classics to the possibility of the existence of early matricentric culture. This denial within the classics profession is an aspect of a broad heteropatriarchal attitude that opposes the ultimate goal of feminism: the dismantling of patriarchy for an egalitarian, nonhierarchical ethic of self-governance and interaction between persons, groups, and nations. At stake are two views of humanity: one that insists upon a hierarchy of values and persons, and sees the world in terms of dichotomous, "either/or" thinking, and one that asserts that all persons and opinions have value, conceiving of the world in terms of "both/and" thinking (Goldenberg 1979, 1990; Göttner-Abendroth 1991; Spelman 1988).

The patriarchal denial of the possibility of early matriculture found in traditional classics is elitist, (hetero)sexist, and insidiously racist and anti-Semitic, since it dismisses academic discussion—i.e., the production and dissemination of knowledge—of a matricentric and egalitarian early culture and discounts African influence on the cultural development of the West (Bernal 1987). Ancient Africa, including Egypt, was matricentric. The work of Cheikh Anta Diop (1974) and Martin Bernal, especially volume 1 of Bernal's *Black Athena* (1987), illustrates this issue particularly well.Thus, although I use the situation of the feminist classicist in this paper as illustrative of difficulties encountered by those involved in non-"mainstream" pursuits in classical studies, I am hopeful that my remarks can be generalized to the experiences of others involved in nontraditional classics.[2]

The concept of a "feminist classicist" was oxymoronic until the work and experience of Jane Ellen Harrison, who first introduced a feminist—indeed, a radical feminist—perspective to classics. Due to the construction of the field itself and the attitudes of those within it, classics historically reflects the hierarchical structures and assumptions of heteropatriarchy (Bernal 1987; Skinner 1987). Traditional classicists characteristically seek to provide information about the world of the ancient text through cultural, historical, and philological analysis, an approach that militates against the use of modern theories. The truth value of traditional research (and the accompanying respect and status attached to those who engage in that research) is measured conservatively and in masculinist terms within the discipline of classics; that the assumptions behind these measures or "standards" are inherently racist, sexist, and heterosexist is seldom acknowledged within the field.

In this particular cultural moment when many of us cry for a revolution in human thought and action, some feminisms have anchored their visionary work firmly to the past, linking the notions "ancient" and "future." By this means a step into an uncertain unknown may be guided by a richly figured heritage, one that humanity once lived, then lost, and now may live again. The unearthing of evidence for early matriculture in the West—Europe, Asia Minor, and Africa— furnishes the seed for this feminist re-visioning and re-construction of a matristic past and carries with it a web of ethics, aesthetics, history, and spirituality. The journey and quest become a return; in this way we may reconcile the idea of progress with the idea of cycle, embracing the notion of spiraling time (Eisler 1987; Orenstein 1990; Sjöö and Mor 1987; Stein 1991). This feminist myth of a matricultural origin for the West proposes a view of cultural history that challenges the basic values and assumptions of Western patriarchy.

In their discussions of feminist philosophy, spirituality, history, and aesthetics, Lesbians and radical feminists increasingly use the myth of an original matricentric culture for Western Europe, Africa, and the Mediterranean basin as a core assumption. Among feminists, especially non-classically trained feminists, this interpretation of a matricultural heritage has a growing number of adherents within and, significantly, outside of the academy.[3]

The matrix of ideas associated with the matricentric ideal and with the issues the concept of Mediterranean matriculture raises for radical/Lesbian feminism, mainstream feminism, and feminist classics forms the basis for my discussion. The great interest in this mythic representation of women's past among feminists offers a special opportunity for feminist classicists to contribute to the larger feminist discourse on academic and nonacademic levels. The matricentric myth is a feature of our academic heritage as classicists. Developed with specific reference to classics by Bachofen in 1861 and embraced by Harrison, Murray, Cornford, Cook, and other philologists, it has entered, in one form or another, into the initiatory assumptions of those involved in many aspects of classical studies. Like theories of the Ionian or Dorian invasion, the theory of indigenous matricentric culture is implicit in the work of many scholars studying ancient religious practices, archaeology, cultural studies, and literary archaeology (Ackerman 1991: 118–200; Calder 1991: *passim*).[4]

Feminism has a variety of forms, and each is unique in its history and assumptions. I discuss the difficulties several communities (radical/Lesbian, mainstream or academic, feminist classical) have with the approaches and methods of the others, drawing attention to the areas of tension through the use of anecdote and quotation. I elaborate the myth of matriculture as an originary myth for feminism, and its importance for feminist classics, attributing its development to the pioneering work of the classicist Jane Ellen Harrison. The focus of Harrison's most significant work was on the original matricentric culture of early Greek culture, and its survivals into the historical period. It was Harrison's articulation and interpretation of this material that make her consequential for mainstream and radical/Lesbian feminisms. Harrison's work and important position have undergone a *damnatio memoriae*—an erasure from the historic record—at the hands of traditional classicists. As a result, few feminist classicists consider her contributions when engaged in their own research. Classics adopted neo-conservative methodologies and ideologies after the Cambridge Ritual School, with Harrison as its center and motive force, had embarrassed the discipline at large through its promotion of interdisciplinary approaches to the study of ancient Western cultures (Ackerman 1991: 159–200).

Finally, the character of the matricultural myth is important for feminism as offering a paradigm for coalitions between radical/Lesbian feminisms and academic or mainstream feminism in their common goal of social change. It is essential for all groups involved to practice the kind of discourse-pluralism that the matricultural ideal requires in order to circumvent the claims of unilinear patriarchal and academic discourse that serve to polarize and divide us from each other. Such pluralism furthers the notion of consensus revolution within and outside of academe.

The Lesbian Perspective and Classics

What I call the "Lesbian Perspective" is a "turn of mind," a stance in the world, that asks unpopular questions, that can be comfortable only when it confronts the sources of its discomfort, a frame of mind that refuses to accept what most people believe to be "true." This turn of mind I identify as "Lesbian." It is what enabled us to reject heterosexual bribery. It is a mind that must have its own integrity on its own terms. Just as being a living, breathing Lesbian exposes the lie of heterosexuality as "normal" and "natural," the Lesbian Perspective challenges *every* lie on which male society is founded (Penelope 1992a: 39–40; 1990: 90).

Those of us who are Lesbians and in academia struggle constantly with vast dissonances in the realities of our lives. Although, as Nancy Sorkin Rabinowitz points out in her introduction (and this collection makes clear), it is now possible for a scholar to name herself a feminist classicist, the definition offered above attests to the paradox of living as a Lesbian in an academic institution and doing academic research, since our entire way of being-in-the-world challenges the assumptions and goals of traditional academe.

However, there *are* Lesbians in the academy, just as there are Lesbians everywhere. Radical/Lesbian theory and methodology are critical to all discussions purporting to be feminist. Lesbian voices are especially necessary. However, in order to survive in a hostile world we have historically participated in our own silencing (Penelope 1992a: 23–36). Under patriarchy, we have all internalized homophobia and mistrust autonomous women; it is therefore not entirely the fault of mainstream academic feminists that the concerns and interests of Lesbians are often glossed over. Many Lesbians no longer identify as feminists or even as women, since both notions have tended to reduce us to a "subset" rather than valuing us as a whole.[5]

Even the concept "Lesbian" is problematic for academic discourse, since the notion eludes the Aristotelian categorization so dear to academics. Lesbians, unlike heteropatriarchal theorists who strive to produce a consensus reality, do not accept a single definition of Lesbian identity.[6] This is due mainly to the (vocal) refusal of Lesbians to accept any one definition of our identities.

Contemporary Lesbian scholars address the question, "Who is a Lesbian?" in provocative and creative ways. Lesbian identity is not limited to or defined by affectional orientation, although that orientation and all it implies are basic to contemporary Lesbian identity: being a Lesbian is a way of being-in-the-world that defies all assumptions of the heteropatriarchy (Allen 1990; Penelope 1992a; Phelan 1989).

At the core of Lesbian theory is the fact of lived Lesbian reality. Ever aware of class, ethnic, racial, and ableist issues, the Lesbian theorist speaks from the position that is uniquely her own in her critique of heteropatriarchy and of other ideological positions (Allen 1990; Anzaldúa 1990; Lorde 1984). Unless co-opted by the patriarchal academic process, those of us who engage in Lesbian theory utilize no theoretical position unless it can be converted to praxis.[7] Our theory shifts and unfolds as the experiences of Lesbians living and writing our lives shift and unfold, in a continuous spiral. Although there may be a modicum of consensus around a position, no one Lesbian speaks for all Lesbians, or even for any other

Lesbian (Penelope 1992a; Trebilcot 1990).[8] Lesbian theory is a theory of *process* and is always grounded in the notion of *resistance* to and *questioning* of the heteropatriarchy. As such, Lesbian theory has much in common with the theory emerging from the myth of matriculture and its implications for contemporary praxis. Julia Penelope, in discussing the innate quality of the Lesbian Perspective (1992a: 51), makes clear the ways in which being a Lesbian in patriarchal culture challenges that culture. In an academic discipline as patriarchal as classics, to embody this challenge can be quite discouraging.[9]

I did not enter the field of classics as an angry dyke storming the great bastion of patriarchy. A bright, reserved young woman, I yearned after the golden world classics promised if I could become fluent enough in Greek and Latin and know the culture and literature these languages revealed. I sought this world believing that the price of entry and acceptance was only that one love it, learn to teach it, and spark others to embrace it. For me, classics represented *our* sacred past, a country that existed only within *ourselves* as classicists; early on I thought of myself as a high priestess who would keep the flame burning within my heart and mind, and pass it to those like-minded individuals I encountered in my teaching career. I still believe—and live—this idea, only the "truth" I now carry conjures up Hecuba with the firebrand in her heart and at times Apollo's co-opted priestess Cassandra.

My experience as an undergraduate and graduate student at the University of Iowa did nothing to dissuade me from my dream of classics, although there were discrepancies I tried not to notice. One of these was the warning against Jane Ellen Harrison with which I began this essay. This experience has haunted me for years; it represented the only mention of a female classicist I recall from my undergraduate and graduate academic career. As I have gone on in my career as a Lesbian, radical feminist, and classicist, conflicts have arisen for me that I trace back to my first hearing of Jane Harrison's name. Writing this piece has been an arduous task, one which has required me to grapple with each of my own fragmented identities in a struggle toward some resolution.[10]

The Feminist Myth of Origins

The feminist myth of origins presents one challenge to male consensus reality. It also defines the perspective, values, and expectations of Lesbian feminists and mainstream feminists in opposition to those of traditional classicists.

The terms "matricentric" and "matriculture" describe a matrilinear culture with women as the focus; in such a culture, there is usually an extended clan structure, with goods and status passed through the motherline. This culture does not presume the subordination of men, but rather a partnership between the sexes, with the expected division of labor determined by gender (French 1985: 25–64). Several authors, particularly those writing from Europe (Göttner-Abendroth 1991, 1987; Sjöö and Mor 1987), use the term "matriarchy" to denote the same idea, as do earlier writers on the topic (Bachofen 1967; Harrison 1913, 1926, 1927, 1991 [1922]; Reed 1975). They are taking a patriarchal term and rewriting it; like Alice Walker (1984) in her use of the term "womanist" to denote a particular quality of a woman's relationship to the world, I prefer to use a less value-laden term in my discussion. For a succinct vision of what a matricentric culture (or matriculture) would be, see Stein (1991: 3–5).

The myth holds that there was an earth- or nature-centered culture in Old Europe and the Mediterranean prior to the imposition of patriarchy by bands of roving Indo-Europeans (called "Kurgans" by Gimbutas 1982, 1989; taken up by Eisler 1987). The culture was woman-centered and woman-valuing (Sjöö and Mor 1987; Orenstein 1990; Stein 1991; Stone 1976), with women as the spiritual leaders and conscience of the culture, and men as their respectful companions and helpmeets. Women represented the source of life, healing, and wisdom.

Göttner-Abendroth (1991: x–xi) distinguishes matriarchal and patriarchal cultures in this way:

> In patriarchal societies all social spheres are strictly separated and isolated in various institutions. That in turn creates elite groups and serves to enforce power interests. All of society is hierarchically ordered according to these power interests. The result is domination and oppression—not only *within* but *among* the individual institutions. . . . Matriarchal societies did not recognize such hierarchies and consequently knew neither dominance on the one hand nor oppression and exploitation on the other. Matriarchal societies did not split consciousness into "art," "science," "religion," "economics," and "politics."

According to this model, women invented culture (Bachofen 1967; Bleier 1984; Reed 1975). It was either through male invasion and conquest (Gimbutas 1982; Eisler 1987) or women abusing power, forcing men to overpower them (Bachofen 1967; Stein 1991) that patriarchy was imposed. The most popular myth in contemporary feminism is that this imposition was effected through centuries of strife, in which the peaceful followers of the earth/nature-centric culture were forced into the patriarchal mold. Vestiges of the original state of balance and harmony were retained in myth and legend, but heavily coded. Beginning with Harrison (1991 [1922]), feminists and feminist classicists have sought to decode these vestiges of women's early history.

The story of the descent of women into patriarchy contains significant assumptions for feminism. This secular version of the Edenic Fall, in some ways analogous to the Lacanian Fall into language, assumes an original prepatriarchal state, characterized by peace, balance, and harmony. Women in this culture are wise and all-knowing; they regulate themselves and the world of nature, which is a mirror of themselves, and they are further mirrors of the symbol of this power, the Goddess.

In nonradical circles, there is confusion over what is meant by the Goddess. Göttner-Abendroth (1991: 217) offers the following definition:

> When matriarchal spirituality speaks of the "Goddess," it does not mean an omnipotent, omniscient supreme Mother in Heaven, a counterpart to God the Father. On the contrary, this concept signifies nothing more—and nothing less—than the *inherent spiritual capacity in every individual,* which harmoniously expresses itself *together with* the totality of the intellectual, emotional, and physical capacities of the person. The Goddess does not exist independent of those capacities; she is something like the unifying thread, the vitality, the energy of life. In this sense, the Goddess is present in every person and in all creatures and elements that possess or impart the vital energy.

The characteristics of these original, "whole" women were autonomy, integration, self-knowledge, and an intuitive consciousness transcending linear reason. The cultures themselves were superior to later cultures in that war was nonexistent, with conflict resolved as it arose. Violence and aggression had negative social value and were suppressed (Eisler 1987; Stein 1991). Several writers cite remains from Old Europe, Çatal Hüyük, early Egypt, and Minoan Crete (Diop 1974; Eisler 1987; Gimbutas 1982, 1989; Lerner 1986; Mellaart 1967) as indicating a lack of defensive fortifications, therefore attesting to a peaceful culture.

Those reconstructing early matriculture do not agree that this culture was completely life-affirming. As noted above, some feel that it was often women's own abuse or misuse of power, or their complicity in their disempowerment (Lerner 1986) that accounted for the destruction of matricentric culture (see especially Stein 1991: 32–48). Although some authors acknowledge the disturbing (for them) implications of blood sacrifice and other attested or suggested violent practices (George 1992; Göttner-Abendroth 1991; Graves 1948; Harrison 1922, 1927; Wolkstein and Kramer 1983), others discount the possibility of violence in early matriculture, even to the point of suggesting a norm of universal vegetarianism (Reed 1975; Sjöö and Mor 1987; Stein 1991). The question of violence in early matriculture has yet to be confronted, especially in the face of the spiritual ideology developed by radical/Lesbian feminists and ecofeminists who adopt the myth.

This mythic history defines the preeminent features of feminism's originary myth: harmony and oneness with the natural world; a valuation of the intuitive and nonrational in balance with the rational/linear; emphasis on peace, wholeness, and autonomy; respect for women and their sacred knowledge; the "rightness" of women's self-determination. Finally, many feminists feel that if we can establish that our originary myth has some objective, historical reality, the restoration of women's power and the culture the prepatriarchal world enjoyed becomes possible, resulting in the dismantling of patriarchy. Stein (1991) and Orenstein (1990), for example, see the myth of early matriculture as an important model for envisioning and bringing about utopia.[11]

The myth of an early, egalitarian culture thus can legitimate the women's movement much in the same way that filling in the gaps of women's history and experience does when applied to other eras. Harrison, a woman with a complete knowledge of classics as well as a feminist sensibility, began the task that others, mostly outside of classics and often outside of academe, are busily carrying forward as a primary emancipatory task. It is here that feminist classics can be most helpful to the women's movement: our specialized knowledge and research tools could propel this project further once we gain clarity as to our own identities as feminist classicists.

Feminism, Feminist Classics, and the Lesbian Perspective

The feminist classicist is in a difficult position. The lens she wishes to turn upon the ancient world—a feminist perspective—along with her desire to select methodologies acceptable to classics *and* feminism, are viewed with suspicion by the discipline at large. Feminist classicists, by virtue of their very existence within the patriarchal discipline which has claimed to supply the source and rationale for Western patriarchal culture, are rightly viewed as subverting the traditional discourse of classics, regardless of their own attempts to legitimate their experience (Skinner 1987). Harsh punishment is meted out to those who stray from the methodological fold, and to maintain credibility, feminist classicists, like the co-opted Amazon goddess Athena, must be "dutiful daughters" in academic research goals and presentations, emphasizing a "rationalist," "objective" perspective.

At the same time, however, feminist classicists are regarded with suspicion by radical/Lesbian feminists. Mary Daly (1987) sees academic feminism as heteropatriarchy's solution to female participation in the academy. The following definitions from her *Wickedary* encapsulate the radical/Lesbian view of the academic feminist, and are, I feel, especially applicable to the position in which the feminist classicist finds herself:

> *plastic feminism:* elementary substitute/replacement for Original Woman-identified bonding and movement; manmade pseudofeminism; rageless, humorless product of Boredom; fashionable, feminine "feminism" (Daly 1987: 217)

> *abominable snowmen of androcratic academia:* freezers and packagers of learning; chilling throng of frigid fellows, specialists in verbigeration and refrigeration of knowledge (Daly 1987: 183)

> *re-search:* a function of patriarchal scholarship (including pseudofeminist scholarship); circular academented game of hide-and-seek; pseu-

dosearch for information which, in fact, has been systematically hidden by previous re-searchers, and which, when found, is then ritually re-covered by succeeding investigators, only to be re-discovered and re-covered endlessly; syndrome often described . . . as the "kitty litter box syndrome of patriarchal scholarship" (Daly 1987: 222)

Applied to the discipline of classics, Daly's words show how the constraints of traditional methodology and the ideological assumptions behind this methodology situate classics outside of, and in opposition to, feminisms that lie outside the academy. Ironically, feminists outside academe use classical sources often and to great effect. Marcia Dobson (1992: 42) points out that,

Feminists . . . tend to use classical sources and scholarship as a medium for social, spiritual, psychological, and political inquiries and transformations of a Western patriarchy that began with these very sources. I do not mean to imply that there are no feminist classical philologists; however, our critical methodologies often conflict, and we deal with these conflicts constantly.

Another difficulty that feminist classicists face arises from the proliferation of feminist theoretical constructs and the valuation of these constructs by mainstream academic feminisms (see this volume). The discipline of classics is not receptive to modern theory, and, although feminist theory purports to derive from common experience, much of feminist theory does not arise from the feminist classicist's experience of her own discipline. Feminist classicists often feel inferior for their lack of knowledge of or interest in feminist theory, a situation that certainly alienates many potential feminist classicists from radical/Lesbian feminism and mainstream feminism, dividing us from our sisters.

Very often, the phenomenon of "horizontal hostility" is involved. Horizontal hostility functions "to insure our ongoing victimization within our own groups, and it keeps us silent when we want to speak out" (Penelope 1992a: 60). Horizontal hostility comes from our insecurity, frustration, anger, and fear as women struggling to survive in patriarchal institutions and culture, and keeps women from working together. It is thus "one of patriarchy's most successful weapons in its self-perpetuation because it maintains our internalized oppression" (Penelope 1992a: 60). This is a difficult and submerged phenomenon, and one that promotes exclusionary politics and good old-fashioned "trashing" of our sisters (Penelope 1992a: 60–77). It involves an internalized feeling of inferiority/superiority between individual feminists or groups of feminists, which creates a perceived power differential. The result is (self-) silencing. The way to overcome the phenomenon of horizontal hostility is not to avoid discussion of issues over which feminists disagree, but to engage them honestly, learning to face conflict as it arises and to examine our motives in implied or overt silencing activities as well as in our feelings of being silenced.

I experienced horizontal hostility recently at a professional conference. A dear friend—a radical feminist—began to quiz me about my knowledge of feminist theory. She barraged me with concepts, jargon, and bibliography, and I became first defensive, then silent. The situation might have been humorous; however, it obviously reflected our internalized perception of a power differential. She was a (heterosexual) full professor at a large land-grant institution. I was a (Lesbian) assistant professor up for promotion and tenure, at a very small, impoverished land-grant institution. Together we were effectively doing the work of patriarchy. My self-esteem was diminished, my self-confidence and feeling of participation as a feminist classicist destroyed. I returned to Maine feeling even more marginalized and isolated, having anticipated this meeting with other feminist classicists as safe and affirming. Since then, I hesitate to participate in panels and events for feminist classicists. This was not the first time I had felt silenced and inferior to other feminist classicists; my feelings at the time were that it would be the last.[12]

The issue of the position of theory in feminism is complex for academic and nonacademic feminisms. Privileging theory for the sake of theory (or, perhaps, as an act of horizontal hostility, for the sake of feeling superior to other feminists) in one sense is privileging Aristotelian, patriarchal fragmentation of self and discipline. It also represents an understandable and admirable attempt to assimilate and legitimate feminism within the academy (Cocks 1989: 3–11, 63–81; O'Barr 1989: 5–7; Spelman 1988: 160–87). However, many feminists, within and outside of the academy, especially those who are not white, middle-class (heterosexual) ("Christian") women, believe that if theory does not arise from the lived experience of a diverse group of women, the use of such theory is exclusionary and elitist and plays into the patriarchal agenda (Anzaldúa 1990: xv–xvii; Cocks 1989; Daly 1987; Spelman 1988).

Feminist interpretations of classical antiquity, especially radical feminist interpretations, in turn, present a difficulty to feminist classicists. The feminist who is not a classicist relies on translations of ancient material and secondary information; she is often unaware of or unconcerned with the nuances of language and of culture as conveyed through language, a central concern to the classical philologist.[13] Her interpretations of the ancient world and her motives for those interpretations are often considered nonrigorous by academics and dismissed as intuitive and ungrounded in history, reason, and methodology. Marcia Dobson (1992: 42) reminds us that there are two "worlds" at stake here—the constrained world of classics and academic feminism, and the larger world of women.

The Lesbian Perspective would require the feminist classicist to question all assumptions regarding the field of classics as traditionally defined. It is a perspective I feel can no longer be avoided, given the inherent patriarchal bias in the field and the ideological pressures we face from two fronts: feminism and the discipline of traditional classics. Turning now to the work of Jane Ellen Harrison, we can see how these pressures—the pressures of the "two worlds" we as feminist classicists confront—conspire.

The Foremother of the Originary Myth

Nor Hall (1988: 18–19) reviews Harrison's significance for feminism:

> She called up the emotions of recognition, the feeling that you are seeing and hearing something you can identify from your own experience. . . . [S]he recognized the significance of the artifact and was the first professor to include archaeological field material in lectures on classical literature. Her critics accused her of "dragging in" everything: psychology, anthropology, philosophy—apparently even feeling. When she said . . . "our hearts are sore for the outrage done to the order of ancient goddesses," she sent out a distress signal that still resonates in our atmosphere.

When we compare Hall's remarks with the view of Harrison by traditional classicists, the difficulty feminist classicists face becomes clear. A 1991 classics publication contains the following:

> Popular books about "the Goddess" and attempts to "revive" female cults in the modern world sometimes invoke the name of Jane Harrison as a venerable (if unread) Wise Woman. Given her feel for the authentic and love of antiquity, she would not feel honored by such attention (Africa 1991: 34).

> Her critics blasted her earlier works for their emphasis on the irrational and the emotional. Many of her theories have been proven wrong, and much of her work stands in danger of being misinterpreted in the current revival of interest in her, particularly by feminist scholars (Peacock 1991: 184).

These remarks appear in *The Cambridge Ritualists Reconsidered* (1991), edited by William Calder III. They indicate the ambiguous position Harrison holds among traditional classicists. The remarks also reflect the devaluation, dismissal, and snobbery many traditional classicists accord to interpretations that occur outside the discipline. On the other hand, anthropologists, historians of ideas, feminist historians, psychoanalysts and myth theorists do not attempt to take over the discourse on Harrison's place in the history of ideas (Ackerman 1991; Hall 1988; Segal 1980a, 1980b). Beyond a voyeuristic attitude toward Harrison's personal life ("She was a Lesbian, wasn't she? She was always with a female companion or student"), or a need to "explain away" the fact that she lived independently, I have detected little interest in Harrison's achievements or contributions to classics from colleagues. This attitude is significant, for it indicates an effective erasure of Harrison's presence from the discourse of classics.[14]

The quotations from Calder's collection reflect the complex attitudes of traditional scholars who wish to retain an orthodox interpretation of Harrison's work and its significance; the quotations also underscore the importance of an alliance between feminist scholarship and classics. Jane Harrison bequeaths to us a critical feminist legacy; her fate makes it imperative to articulate the goals of feminist scholarship and feminist classical scholarship. Feminist scholarship must become aware of the particular gifts that feminist classicists bring to their work; feminist classicists must appreciate the importance of their work for the unfolding of feminism as a whole. Together we can find a resolution of the obstructions to our common purpose of midwifing social change through the production and dissemination of knowledge about women's lives and achievements. We can begin from a re-collection of Harrison's example.

Method

It is in the *Prolegomena* (1991 [1922]) that Harrison sounds the first salvo in her critique of patriarchy. Her methodology is first accumulative, then interpretive, a methodology which remains standard (for example, Gimbutas 1982, 1989). Harrison demonstrated the historical existence of matriarchy by connecting matriliny and matriarchy, a nexus previously described by Bachofen, the Swiss specialist in Roman law. Bachofen's best known work, *Das Mutterrecht: Eine Untersuchung über die Gynaikocratie der alten Welt nach ihrer religiösen und rechtlichen Natur,* first published in 1861, demonstrated through the use of classical mythology, history, and ethnography the existence of a matriarchal culture previous to the Indo-European invasions of the Mediterranean basin. Bachofen believed that patriarchal culture was superior to matriarchal culture, because it made possible the development of civilization (Bachofen 1967: 116–19). Harrison footnotes *Mutterrecht* twice: in the *Prolegomena* (1991, from the third edition of 1922: 262n.1) as a work that "in spite of the wildness of its theories, remains of value as the fullest existing collection of ancient fact"; and in *Themis* (1912, 1927: 35n.1).

Bachofen's connection of matriliny and matriarchy was in error; attempts to establish that matriliny implies matriarchy have proven inconclusive, although they may point to a matriculture in existence at one time (see the discussion in Lerner 1986: 21–31). Harrison understood the difference between matriliny and matriarchy (1927: 492).

Survivals of Matricentric Culture

Two important assumptions that Harrison developed in her work form the basis for radical feminist scholarship dealing with the myth of matriculture and the development of patriarchy, the most compelling example of which is in Göttner-Abendroth 1987. This set of assumptions requires a modified euhemerism (defined as the notion that events and persons in mythology refer to actual historical occurrences and figures), to be linked with Harrison's use of Durkheim. Following Durkheim, Harrison posited that the pantheon acts as a group projection of cultural values and ideologies (discussed in Harrison 1927: xiii).

Thus, by looking at mythology and art, Harrison argued that a harmonious matriarchal/matrilinear culture indigenous to the Mediterranean basin had been displaced by the conquering patriarchal invaders from the north (Harrison 1927: 490–92, 1913: 27–34). This accounts for the subsequent emergence of the Olympian pantheon. Simply put, Harrison believed that classical Greek mythology contains traces, or "survivals," of the earlier woman-centered culture (Ackerman 1991: 36–39). Even the most benign rituals of traditional Greek cultural practices contained a deeper layer that revealed pre-Olympian customs and beliefs that retained power over the psyches of Greeks in the classical period. These basic beliefs were enacted unconsciously, simultaneously with those contemporary rituals that had won out or had been established (Harrison 1927: 480–535; Murray, in Harrison 1927: 341–63; Peacock 1988: 188 and *passim*).

Harrison expanded her idea of "survivals" from the work of E. B. Tylor, who introduced the concept in *Primitive Culture* (1924 [1871]). In the *Prolegomena* (1991 [1922]) and *Themis* (1927) she accumulates data from mythology, art, and literature to demonstrate that this lower stratum always existed in Greek culture and undergirded literature, art, and religious practices during the classical period of ancient Greek society. Harrison's method and attitude are apparent in her description of Pandora (Harrison 1991 [1922]: 285):

> Zeus the Father will have no great Earth-goddess, Mother and Maid in one, in his man-fashioned Olympus, but her figure *is* from the beginning, so he remakes it; woman, who was the inspirer, becomes the temptress; she who made all things, gods and mortals alike, is become their plaything, their slave, dowered only with personal beauty, and with a slave's tricks and blandishments. To Zeus, the archpatriarchal *bourgeois*, the birth of the first woman is but a huge Olympian jest.

Harrison points out that Pandora was an important pre-Hellenic goddess, noting her reduction as a result of the projection of the dominant group into the patriarchal concept(ion) of woman.[15]

Non-rational and Rational

Jane Harrison felt that the irrational or the "Dionysian" was an important part of humanity on both the individual and collective levels, and as such must not be denied. Other contemporary scholars viewed the "Apollonian" or the development and emphasis on linearity and rationality as a step forward in the progressive, evolutionary development of humanity—classical Greek culture being the prime example (Bachofen 1967; Freud 1950; Morgan 1963; Nietzsche 1967). Harrison did not believe that linear development alone indicated worthwhile progress for humanity. Instead, she argued for a recognition of "archaeological" development, where what has gone before becomes the basis of what exists now.

Harrison applied a psychoanalytic model to questions of religion, and maintained that the irrational was the site of the religious impulse, acting as the subconscious of the culture (see especially Harrison 1921). Thus, the triumph of the Olympians over the Titans represents the denial of the subconscious; this victory is therefore dangerous to the "mental health" of the collectivity (Harrison 1927: 445–79). The irrational must break out if repressed, and will either erupt in seemingly horrendous fashion (from the standpoint of patriarchy), as in Euripides's *Bacchae,* or in orderly and channeled fashion, as in the Orphic religion. Harrison sees the latter as the intersection of and agreement between the irrational and the rational in Greek religion (first articulated in the *Prolegomena,* 1922; a basic argument of *Themis,* 1927).

Many contemporary feminists, such as those in the collection edited by Lauter and Rupprecht (1985), Goldenberg (1979, 1990), and Reis (1991), have taken up this position in their development of a feminist psychology of women, discussing the complex ways in which the psychoanalytic process and the religious impulse are intertwined. Since religion is a normative institution in culture, Harrison's ideas also provide a working model for the analysis of the workings of patriarchal religious ideologies in internalized sexism, racism, and homophobia (Goldenberg 1979, 1990).

Ritual, Emotion, and Authentic Being

Harrison agreed with Nietzsche's concepts of the Apollonian and Dionysian, concepts which he adapted from Bachofen, and expressed in his early work, *The Birth of Tragedy.* Nietzsche identified a terrifying (for him) substratum of irrationality beneath the veneer of contemporary and ancient civilization (Nietzsche 1967: 36–38). He believed that the Greeks were aware of this element, and created the Apollonian as a balance or a "dream-world" to superimpose upon this stratum (Ackerman 1991: 97). Ackerman (1991: 97–100) and Peacock (1988: 186–87) discuss the similarities between the Cambridge Ritualists and Nietzsche in their conceptions of the origins and social function (or meaning) of tragedy. For the general influence of *The Birth of Tragedy,* see Silk and Stern (1981).

Harrison, as she had with the work of Bachofen, agreed with Nietzsche's premise but disagreed with his interpretation. Where Nietzsche felt it was impossible for the Greeks (i.e., human beings) to live with the truth of the irrational within them and remain sane, Harrison felt that acknowledgement of and living with the irrational was the only means the Greeks (and by extension, all human beings) had to achieve psychic balance and what we today would call authentic being. She notes in *Themis* (1927: 476),

> We touch here on the very heart and secret of the difference between the Olympian and the mystery-god, between Apollo and Zeus on the one hand and Dionysos on the other: a difference the real significance of which was long ago, with the instinct of genius, divined by Nietzsche. The Olympian has clear form, he is the *principium individuationis* incarnate; he can be thought, hence his calm, his *sophrosyne*. The mystery-god is the life of the whole of things, he can only be felt—as soon as he is thought and individualized he passes, as Dionysos had to pass, into the thin, rare ether of the Olympian. The Olympians are of conscious thinking, divided, distinct, departmental; the mystery-god is the impulse of life through all things, perennial, indivisible.

In her extended discussion of the characteristics of the Olympic gods, Harrison notes, "Still less must we assume off-hand that the shift from nature-god to human-nature god is necessarily an advance" (1927: 447). Indeed, in following Harrison's argument, we find that the denial of the Dionysian and the elevation of the Olympian resulted in the desacralization of religion and the marginalization of the irrational and what it contained to the borders of consciousness, and, concomitantly, to the borders of the known world—ideas that duBois (1982, 1988), Passman (1991), Passman and March (forthcoming 1993), and Tyrrell (1984) have developed further in discussions of Amazons and "Others" in Greek thought. Harrison felt there was great psychic danger in the dichotomization of intellect and emotion (1927: 478).

This danger would be described today as the loss of immanence and the distancing of humanity from active participation in the sacred. Göttner-Abendroth (1991) and Goldenberg (1979, 1990) articulately address this as the central issue of feminist or matriarchal spirituality. Writers who underscore ecofeminist principles in their discussions of feminist spirituality hail the return or reemergence of the Goddess in Western consciousness as indicative of a nascent, transformative inclination toward spiritual and psychic wholeness that will result in the healing of the planet and the peace that the vision of matriculture offers (Christ 1987; Plaskow and Christ 1989; Sjöö and Mor 1987; Starhawk 1982; Stein 1991). Orenstein (1990: 187), for example, writes:

> This rebirth of ecological and matristic values . . . has announced a paradigm shift away from the cosmogony of the Father God to that of the Mother Goddess as the symbol system of the sacred. . . . Our contemporary feminist matristic journeys and cycles . . . have reconnected us with our lost history, with a female cosmogonic mythos,

with nature, with the spirit world, with the oral tradition, and with the other worlds of dream, psyche, and prehistory. . . . The flourishing of a feminist matristic vision today is a sign that it might not be too late to save our Mother's life.

Understanding what the irrational and the Dionysian meant for Harrison yields further recognition of the ways in which her theories presage many assumptions in contemporary feminism. Harrison investigated the unconscious motives behind the religious impulse, which she situated in its most pure form in ancient ritual. The root of her work has to do with her belief in the primacy of emotion as a motive impulse for human behavior. Emotion arises from tension, created through unsatisfied desire. The locus of unsatisfied desire occurred for early humankind in the tensions surrounding the acquisition of food and sexual gratification, and resulted in the development of ritual.

Thus, in her discussion of the *drômenon,* the sacred "thing done," Harrison notes that *mimesis,* "imitation," lies at its heart. "In all religion, as in all art, there is this element of make-believe. Not the attempt to deceive, but a desire to *re*-live, to *re*-present" (Harrison 1927: 43). This idea is basic to the matristic aesthetics developed by Göttner-Abendroth (1991: 2–30) and Orenstein (1990), principles derived from contemporary artistic and spiritual practice among women artists. Göttner-Abendroth argues that it is the fact of representation that marks the decline of matristic art from the authenticity of lived ritual expression and the inception of patriarchal, "dead" art, for representation is a distancing from actual experience (Göttner-Abendroth 1991: 2–8). She thus takes Harrison's hypothesis regarding the development of art and ritual one step further.

The Loss of Connection with Nature

The victory of the Olympians meant for the Greeks and subsequent Western culture the loss of connection with nature and of those areas associated with nature—the intuitive, the mysterious, the nonrational. For Harrison, the loss of the animal and plant world resulted in the psychic distancing of human beings from this world, and was a true and lamentable Fall. Harrison does not pretend that the earlier, archaic worship did not sacrifice animals, and she is horrified by the proof for this; she does, however, mourn a religious and philosophic impulse that removes humanity completely from sympathy with and appreciation for plant and animal life (Harrison 1927: 449–50).

This view of the importance of the relationship of humanity to the natural world is a significant contribution of Harrison to feminism, for she emphasizes that it is through Dionysos, the "god of women," that women retained their connection to nature and the nonrational even after the Olympian ascendancy. Harrison's historical perspective, along with her complex explanation of the identification of women with nature as a result of cultural phenomena, make her a true foremother of the symbolic anthropology of duBois, for example, as well as illuminating and enlarging assumptions found in ecofeminism and goddess-centered feminist spirituality (Orenstein 1990; Sjöö and Mor 1987; Stein 1991; Zweig in this volume). Harrison refused to accept that patriarchal society marked an improvement over nature; indeed, she implies at the end of *Themis* that the cycle of human culture is only partially completed. This statement left feminist scholars with a clear challenge—one taken up by radical thinkers—to envision a world beyond patriarchy (Harrison 1927: 534–35):

> To any rational thinker it is at once clear that Dike, Natural Order, and Themis, Social Order, are not the same, nay even that they are not mother and daughter; they stand at two poles remote and even alien. Natural Law is from the beginning; from the first pulse of life, nay even before the beginning of that specialized movement which we know as life, it rules over what we call the inorganic. Social order, morality, "goodness" is not in nature at the outset; it only appears with "man her last work." . . . to say that Alpha is Omega, the end is the beginning, that life and force are the same as moral good, and to name the mystical marriage of the two "God," is to darken counsel. It is to deny that very change and movement which *is* life. . . .

The Feminist Myth of Origins Revisited

Underlying the interconnected worlds of radical/Lesbian feminism, academic feminism, and feminist classics are the preeminent assumptions that history is nonlinear and that the early status of Western society was matricultural. These premises are also closely connected to a familiar Western notion: matricentric society represents an Edenic condition of ecological balance, mutual respect and egalitarian relations, with the (positive) power of the feminine being revered. Patriarchal development becomes equivalent to the Fall. Feminism today manifests the millennialism the West has often experienced at the end of a century. However, one hundred years after the "Death of God," the expectation of either ecological disaster or a return to the original matristic Garden has replaced the anticipation of Armageddon and the Second Coming (Kermode 1967). For feminism, the myth of matriculture provides a vision of origin and return.

Thus, Orenstein (1990: 4) can suggest that

> contemporary feminist scholars, writing on the subject of the Goddess from any number of disciplines (archeology, religion, history, art, anthropology, etc.), are actually reliving and reversing a patriarchal biblical story, the story of Eve in the Garden of Eden, and as they taste of the forbidden fruit of the tree of knowledge, they are discovering a knowledge that is taboo in their culture.

It is not the myth of Eve alone that holds meaning for contemporary feminism(s). The fruits of the forbidden tree of knowledge involve more than the biblical myth. They include the access of women to education, specifically classical education, and the means, through collegial support, job security, and income, to interpret the legacy of the past through our own eyes and voices.

It is the question of access and interpretation that imbues this consideration of Harrison's pioneering work and its reception with significance for feminist classicists today. She leaves a legacy that reminds the feminist classicist of the difficulty of her task. Harrison was the first feminist classicist to apply a transformational critique to the "received wisdom" of antiquity, providing us with a topography of what is mostly *terra incognita*—the status of women in the pre-Hellenic ancient world before and in the early stages of patriarchy. Among her other legacies, she provides feminism with the justification for a myth of origins that later thinkers have developed into a positive vision affirming the feminist project of social change (Richlin, in this volume). At the same time, there is the negative example of the reception of her life and theories. The *damnatio memoriae* Harrison experienced at the end of her life persists today in her silencing by traditional classicists. Many of us, many in this volume, have experienced similar contempt, deprecation of our areas of inquiry, and constraints on the publication of our research (see Nancy Rabinowitz's introduction to this volume). It is past time to break the silences we have been disciplined into.

Calling the Question

> The kinds of answers we receive always depend on the kinds of questions we ask, and the kinds of questions we ask always depend on our particular personal and cultural needs and perspectives (Dobson 1992: 42).

The issues surrounding the acceptance within classics of the notion of an ancient matricentric culture for the Mediterranean basin, Europe, and Africa are complex. Gimbutas (1982, 1989) and others have presented evidence from material remains, art, and architecture that strongly indicates the existence of such a culture. Acceptance, however, raises crucial questions about the field of classics. For example, where and when does the ancient world begin? The work now being done on the African influence upon ancient cultures is essential here. In 1974 Cheikh Anta Diop (142) declared: "The matriarchal system is the base of the social organization in Egypt and throughout Black Africa." Diop, who had first published his ground-breaking work in 1955 and 1967, next spends several pages refuting the possibility of matricentric culture in white culture, due to its misogynistic characteristics (Diop 1974: 142–45). Since then, the work of Gimbutas and others has suggested the existence of a prepatriarchal matriculture in the West. African and feminist scholars working together could begin to piece together a view of matriculture extending throughout the Mediterranean basin and the African continent that would radically challenge existing assumptions regarding the development of patriarchy as human progress, a position that Reed (1975) developed using anthropology and modified Marxist history.

Denying ancient African influence on the development of classical civilization is as suggestive of prejudice as denying ancient Semitic cultural influence on that development (Bernal 1987: 337ff.). If these cultures were also matricentric, what does rejection of the importance of these ancient matricultures and valuation of Indo-European patriculture by classicists mean? Speaking for myself, the devaluation of the work of Diop, Bernal, Gimbutas, and others indicates a serious racist/(hetero)sexist sentiment inherent in the discipline of classics.

And so I return to my initial discussion. The feminist classicist is faced with embracing heterodox ideas at the cost of jeopardizing her hard-won standing in the field. Additionally, she must ask what position she will take in the world(s) of feminism. With her training in ancient languages and her ability to interpret ancient culture, she has much to contribute to mainstream and radical/Lesbian feminism. This opportunity should pull her out of her paralyzing dilemma.

In her book on matriarchal aesthetics, Göttner-Abendroth (1991) reminds us that our greatest challenge is to step beyond patriarchy and create our own reality. Echoing other writers on the subject, she points out that the termination of patriarchy may be our only means to survival as a species. One guide we have is the myth of matricentric culture and all it requires and implies. The perspective of matriculture, like Julia Penelope's Lesbian Perspective, provides a means to "think beyond" heteropatriarchy. These complementary perspectives allow the various feminisms to move beyond a hierarchy of values, compulsive competition, and horizontal hostility to a pluralistic vision, a vision that will accommodate as many points of view, as many theoretical positions simultaneously, as may be necessary. The underlying implication of the matricultural perspective is political, according to Göttner-Abendroth. It offers, first and foremost, a politics that esteems "diversity, change, vitality, and a dynamism that admits of no strictures or encrustation . . . [it] negates and neutralizes all types of dualism used by patriarchal politics throughout the millennia to secure domination" (Göttner-Abendroth 1991: 229).

This encourages us, as radical/Lesbian feminists, academic feminists, and feminist classicists, to renew ourselves as complementary agents of social change. As feminists, we take an ideological position. If we are academic or mainstream feminists, we are seeking to reform the institutions in which we participate, finding ways to "work within the system" to effect change without compromising our values. If we are radical/Lesbian feminists, we work to transform the very structure and existence of Western patriarchal culture. Both groups can make good use of the myth and vision of ancient matricentric culture in differing, although linked, ways, since the myth allows a multiple approach to the dismantling of patriarchy.

Reform movements are ideologically based and presume a social critique linked to the call for change; moreover, to be taken seriously, Western ideologies must establish legitimacy. "Legitimacy" requires a foundational lineage (patriarchy being linear and passed through a "father-line" of ideas) for credibility (Foucault 1970, 1972). The feminist myth of matriculture gives mainstream feminists the legitimacy the system demands, and a useful means to challenge patriarchal assumptions about the shape of history.[16] The myth of origins provides a needful lineage, creating a "mother-line" that links women with their own kind in historical succession. Additionally, it offers feminists exemplary ethics and spiritual practice that are alternative to those of patriarchy.

Radical/Lesbian feminisms call for complete social transformation, an uprooting of all patriarchal institutions. Adoption of matricultural principles would clarify what we mean by this social transformation. The myth and its assumptions affirm radical/Lesbian ethics and philosophies, and name the web of practice and being-in-the-world that those of us who have been marginalized, disenfranchised, and excluded from mainstream culture and from mainstream feminism have sought to realize in our ongoing struggle to live with pride and dignity. In addition, the myth of early matriculture gives to radical feminists a utopian vision to strive for, a blueprint of the unknown land that is the aftermath of transformation.

In either case, we are, as Tracy Chapman says, "talkin' 'bout a revolution." This revolution, based on matricultural principles, is a revolution of consensus, not the revolution of conquest that is the model bequeathed to us by patriarchal politics.[17] The essence of consensus revolution is that the necessity and responsibility to change rest with each one of us individually. Göttner-Abendroth (1991: 233) states,

> This means that not only the goal but also the path to it, the continuous process, are valued in order to do justice to that which we have become—whatever we are. . . . This requires us to follow circuitous paths with patience, since overt, direct opposition merely revives old antagonisms and various types of dualism. . . . The decisive aspect of the consensus revolution is the absence of . . . a select group with the correct vision, the correct utopia, the correct consciousness; they would only re-create the old patriarchal hierarchy, in essence changing nothing.

It is clearly in the interest of those invested in maintaining the status quo to keep us divided from each other through maintenance of the academic hierarchy of values. I suggest that the adoption of the principles of the Lesbian Perspective and the matricultural myth and values by feminist classicists is a way of both furthering our understanding of antiquity, and of negotiating our more active participation within the process of transformation.

All of this requires that we inventively question our resistances from wherever we stand, be we radical feminists, Lesbians, academic feminists, mainstream feminists, classical feminists, or traditional classicists. This process of honest questioning will go a long way toward casting down the barriers that internalized heteropatriarchal assumptions have erected to divide us and keep us from building coalitions based on trust and mutual respect. In this way, we can share our various knowledge and perspectives to further our particular visions, whether they are for reformation or transformation. Feminist classicists can aid their nonclassicist sisters by sharing their particular expertise and insight into the ancient world in accessible and inclusive ways; feminist classicists can learn from other academic feminists and nonacademic, radical/Lesbian feminists who bring a different but complementary perspective to the questions we ask. The result would be a solidarity that is pluralistic, valuing, and ultimately healing. I envision this healing as not only filling the gaps in our common history, but also filling the gaps between our lives. As a Lesbian, as a feminist, as a classicist, I have worked in physical, emotional, spiritual, and psychic isolation, relying upon the voices of other women who share many parts of my dream of a world and a language welcoming and common to women. This volume seems to me to be a good point from which feminist classicists can begin to break their silence and isolation and enter that world, which we are helping to create. We have so much to learn from each other; we must never forget that it was only a little over a hundred years ago that the child Jane Harrison dreamed of learning Greek (Harrison 1915: 117):

> Some half-century ago a very happy little girl secretly possessed herself of a Greek grammar. A much-adored aunt swiftly stripped the gilt from the gingerbread with these chill, cutting words: "I do not see how Greek grammar is to help little Jane to keep house when she has a home of her own." . . . The child understood: she was a little girl, and thereby damned to eternal domesticity; she heard the gates of the Temple of Learning clang as they closed.

Notes

I wish to thank my sisters: Shelley Haley provided courage, honesty, and inspiration for this work. Nancy Sorkin Rabinowitz affirmed and mentored me in every phase of this process. Amy Richlin gave enthusiastic support and acknowledgement. Christina Baker discussed Jane Ellen Harrison at length and with much insight. The anonymous reader for the manuscript offered solid suggestions for improvement. Most especially, this work owes its uncompromising spirit to my teacher, partner and friend, Melanie K. Noyes, *sine qua non*.

1. For Harrison's social context, see Vicinus (1977, 1985); McWilliams-Tullberg (1977). For Harrison's place in the history of the development of the social sciences and her treatment of myth, Ackerman's work (1991) is essential. Renate Schlesier

(1991) begins to place her as a classicist. I am currently working on an evaluation of Harrison's contributions to radical feminism and feminist classics.

2. On the question of women and traditional scholarship within the academy, see Elizabeth Spelman's (1988: 37–56) discussion of women and categories of thought, found in her chapter "Who's Who in the Polis?" See also the special issue of *differences* (2: Fall 1990), "Notes from the Beehive: Feminism and the Institution."

3. The works to which I will be referring throughout this essay are predicated upon this notion. They are only intended as representative; the list is by no means inclusive. What they all have in common is that they are extraordinarily popular works, used as textbooks in women's studies courses and read eagerly by nonacademic women in reading groups and individually. The extent to which this is taking place is attested to by the number of large publishing houses offering such material (see bibliography). This phenomenon indicates that the myth of original matriculture has become a true modern myth for many women, both those who identify as feminists and those to whom feminism is an amorphous term attached to the academy or the middle class. Although I cannot here provide statistics, anecdotal evidence suggests that classicists, both feminist and nonfeminist, need to be aware of the number of women for whom this myth contains important psychic "truth."

4. Many of these points are addressed below.

5. Penelope (1992a: 48–49; also 1990: 103) discusses the idea of "Lesbian" as a "subset" identity:

> Because we're biologically categorized as female, it seems meaningful to say that, by inclusion with heterosexual women, we're oppressed as "women," and our experience of socialization confirms this category overlap. Likewise, because we aren't hetero, we're also oppressed as "homosexuals," so some Lesbians identify with gay men, in which case they call themselves "gay women." . . . Our invisibility, even to ourselves, is at least partially due to the fact that our identity is subsumed by two groups: women and gays. As a result, Lesbian issues seem to find their way, by neglect or elimination, to the bottom of both liberation agendas. The liberation of Lesbians is supposed to wait for the liberation of all women, or be absorbed and evaporate into the agenda created by gay men. . . . The issue here is making explicit the basis of our prioritizing, which has been the idea that we are "sub-" somebody else.

6. Julia Penelope (1992b) describes the linguistic and psychological "field" of heteropatriarchy in relation to Lesbian identity. This article has relevance for all women, for it engages the heteropatriarchal notion of the boundaries of the "feminine."

7. Just as aspects of feminism have been partially co-opted by academia, there is the danger of Lesbian theory becoming co-opted by women, such as myself, situated within academia, trying to legitimate such studies through production of an "acceptable" academic body of knowledge. Such a body of knowledge is increasingly found under the rubric of "Lesbian and Gay Studies." Also, just as we had/have men claiming to be feminists when this became academically chic, we are also beginning to find straight women calling themselves "Lesbians" or, more offensively, "Dykes." In a recent conversation with a woman of color, she likened this situation to that of a person who has enjoyed all the privileges of white society deciding to identify herself as "Black" out of well-intended solidarity. As a Lesbian who has struggled

with issues of identity and survival, I thank my straight and bisexual sisters for their support, but also request that that support not extend itself to my fought-for identity.

8. These ideas are expressed in Joyce Trebilcot, "Dyke Methods" (1990: 15):

    First principle: I speak only for myself.
    Second principle: I do not try to get other wimmin to accept my beliefs in place of their own.
    Third principle: There is no given.

9. Penelope (1992a: 51) further articulates these tensions:

    The Lesbian Perspective challenges what heterosexuals choose to believe is "fact." As our joy in being outcasts expands, so does our ability to ask dangerous questions and dis-cover magical answers. We have no "givens" beyond that which is "other than": "deviant," "abnormal," "unnatural," "queer," false descriptions we begin with and cannot afford to forget. . . . The Lesbian Perspective makes it possible to challenge the accuracy of male consensus reality.

    I experienced an example of male consensus reality in action recently at an annual classics meeting. A good friend (male) congratulated me on my recent marriage. Hearing his words, I was excited and happy, since I had just lately entered into a long-term, committed relationship with a woman, and believed he referred to this. He then continued, "Yes, it is the talk of the conference, this new phase in your life, and we are all so pleased for you—and for Mr. Passman." I realized that he was referring to the fact that a few years ago I took back my birth name; however, many of my colleagues still knew me by the name "Nielson" until several articles appeared with the name Passman. This type of heteropatriarchal assumption (that the only reason a woman changes her name, i.e., her identity, is in marriage, and to a man) was particularly painful, embarrassing, and alienating, especially when coming from such a well-meaning person.

10. I am speaking as a white working-class Lesbian in academe and acknowledge that there are many unintentional racist and probably classist assumptions in my writing. I use the term radical/Lesbian in an attempt to be inclusive of other positions radical for mainstream academic feminism, such as Black feminisms and non-Western feminisms, recognizing that this effort is only one of recognition and does not sufficiently account for these positions. My understanding of racism, especially within the academy, owes a great deal to my friend and colleague, Shelley Haley.

11. Lerner (1986: 3–14) articulates this well in her introduction. Göttner-Abendroth (1991: 1) can serve as an example of the belief in the historical reality of the early matriculture, a view held by many writers cited herein.

12. Horizontal hostility works especially well when combined with outright discrimination. A woman of color has struggled for years in classics. After similar experiences of dismissal and lack of sensitivity from the majority of her colleagues, she has decided to leave our professional organization, the American Philological Association. A Jewish feminist classicist left the American Philological Association for similar reasons. She tells me she does not feel silenced or like a tolerated intruder when she participates in the MLA. As a Lesbian in the APA, and a member of the Women's Classical Caucus and the Lesbian/Gay Caucus, I can only say that without these caucuses, and the fleeting affirmation they provide, I would be unable to continue in the APA. It is an ongoing struggle to retain courage and optimism.

13. This is not to say that language is not of central concern in radical and feminist analyses of culture. Indeed, it is essential in the analysis of power relations within contemporary culture—for example, Daly (1987), Penelope (1990). I am speaking here of a thorough knowledge of ancient languages, and the related question of translation.

14. Unfortunately, the biography of Jane Harrison by Sandra Peacock is marred by outmoded psychologizing and patriarchal complicity; in the text she subverts and sacrifices the real and important strengths of her insights into Harrison's life and work. Works of use in contextualizing Harrison's life include her own *Reminiscences of a Student's Life* (Harrison 1926) and the work of her dear friend and student, Jessie Stewart (1959), *Jane Ellen Harrison: A Portrait from Letters*. Harrison also appears in the memoirs and reminiscences of her contemporaries, including Virginia Woolf, Lytton Strachey, Francis Cornford, and Gilbert Murray. See also Robert Ackerman (1991) and Robert Segal (1980a, 1980b) for the place of the Cambridge Ritualists in the development of myth theory.

15. Recent writings on the topic of women's spirituality derived from the "lost" goddesses of ancient Greece owe their basic arguments to the work of Harrison. These include Christ (1987), Daly (1978, 1984, 1987), Downing (1987, 1988, 1989), Goldenberg (1979, 1990), Orenstein (1990), Plaskow and Christ (1989), Reis (1991), Sjöö and Mor (1987), and Spretnak (1982, 1984). Contemporary feminist classicists, such as Arthur (1977, 1982, 1983), Bergren (1982, 1983), Passman (forthcoming 1993) and Zeitlin (1981, 1982), have enlarged upon Harrison's basic ideas through studies of language and ritual. This work fills in important gaps and explicates clearly the pre-Hellenic condition of women in the Mediterranean and the redefinition of pre-Hellenic women as they descended into patriarchy.

16. Joan Cocks (1989) discusses the importance of this "oppositional imagination" within social institutions in her work.

17. Charlene Spretnak first used these terms in 1982; Göttner-Abendroth (1991: 229–33) expands and adapts them.

Bibliography

Ackerman, Robert. 1991. *The Myth and Ritual School: J. G. Frazer and the Cambridge Ritualists*. New York: Garland.

Africa, Thomas W. 1991. "Aunt Glegg among the Dons or Taking Jane Harrison at Her Word." In Calder 1991, 21–35.

Allen, Jeffner, ed. 1990. *Lesbian Philosophies and Cultures*. Albany: SUNY Press.

Anzaldúa, Gloria, ed. 1990. *Making Face, Making Soul: Haciendo Caras. Creative and Critical Perspectives by Women of Color*. San Francisco: Aunt Lute Foundation Books.

Arthur, Marylin. 1977. "Politics and Pomegranates: An Interpretation of the Homeric Hymn to Demeter." *Arethusa* 10: 7–47.

———. 1982. "Cultural Strategies in Hesiod's *Theogony*: Law, Family, Society." *Arethusa* 15.1, 2: 63–82.

————. 1983. "The Dream of a World without Women: Poetics and the Circles of Order in the *Theogony* Proemium." *Arethusa* 16: 97–116.

Bachofen, J. J. 1967. *Myth, Religion, and Mother Right: Selected Writings of J. J. Bachofen*. Trans. by Ralph Manheim, with a preface by George Boas and an introduction by Joseph Campbell. Princeton: Princeton University Press. (From the German edition of 1954.)

Bergren, Ann L. T. 1982. "Sacred Apostrophe: Re-Presentation and Imitation in the Homeric Hymns." *Arethusa* 15.1, 2: 83–108.

————. 1983. "Language and the Female in Early Greek Thought." *Arethusa* 16: 69–95.

Bernal, Martin. 1987. *Black Athena: The Afroasiatic Roots of Classical Civilization*. Vol. 1: "The Fabrication of Ancient Greece 1785–1985." New Brunswick, N.J.: Rutgers University Press.

Bleier, Ruth. 1984. *Science and Gender: A Critique of Biology and Its Theories on Women*. New York: Pergamon Press.

Calder, William M., III, ed. 1991. *The Cambridge Ritualists Reconsidered*. Atlanta: Scholars Press.

Christ, Carol P. 1987. *Laughter of Aphrodite: Reflections on a Journey to the Goddess*. San Francisco: Harper and Row.

Cocks, Joan. 1989. *The Oppositional Imagination: Feminism, Critique and Political Theory*. New York: Routledge.

Daly, Mary. 1978. *Gyn/Ecology: The Metaethics of Radical Feminism*. Boston: Beacon Press.

————. 1984. *Pure Lust: Elemental Feminist Philosophy*. Boston: Beacon Press.

————. 1987. (In cahoots with Jane Caputi.) *Webster's First New Intergalactic Wickedary of the English Language*. Boston: Beacon Press.

Diop, Cheikh Anta. 1974. *The African Origin of Civilization: Myth or Reality*. Translated by Mercer Cook. Chicago: Lawrence Hill Books. (French edition 1955, 1967.)

Dobson, Marcia D.-S. 1992. "Ritual Death, Patriarchal Violence, and Female Relationship in the Hymns to Demeter and Inanna." *NWSA Journal* 4.1 (Spring): 42–58.

Downing, Christine. 1987. *The Goddess: Mythological Images of the Feminine*. New York: Crossroad Press.

————. 1988. *Psyche's Sisters: Re-Imagining the Meaning of Sisterhood*. San Francisco: Harper and Row.

————. 1989. *Myths and Mysteries of Same-Sex Love*. New York: Crossroad Press.

duBois, Page. 1982. *Centaurs and Amazons: Women and the Pre-History of the Great Chain of Being*. Ann Arbor: University of Michigan Press.

————. 1988. *Sowing the Body: Psychoanalysis and Ancient Representations of Women*. Chicago: University of Chicago Press.

Eisler, Riane. 1987. *The Chalice and the Blade: Our History, Our Future*. San Francisco: Harper and Row.

Foucault, Michel. 1970. *The Order of Things: An Archeology of the Human Sciences.* (Translator not cited.) New York: Pantheon. (French edition 1966.)

———. 1972. *The Archeology of Knowledge.* Translated by A. M. Sheridan Smith. New York: Vintage. (French edition 1969.)

French, Marilyn. 1985. *Beyond Power: On Women, Men, and Morals.* New York: Ballantine Books.

Freud, Sigmund. 1950. *Totem and Taboo.* Translated by James Strachey. New York: W. W. Norton.

George, Demetra. 1992. *Mysteries of the Dark Moon: The Healing Power of the Dark Goddess.* San Francisco: HarperCollins.

Gimbutas, Marija. 1982. *Goddesses and Gods of Old Europe: Myths and Cult Images.* Berkeley: University of California Press.

———. 1989. *The Language of the Goddess.* San Francisco: HarperCollins.

Goldenberg, Naomi. 1979. *Changing of the Gods: Feminism and the End of Traditional Religions.* Boston: Beacon Press.

———. 1990. *Returning Words to Flesh: Feminism, Psychoanalysis, and the Resurrection of the Body.* Boston: Beacon Press.

Göttner-Abendroth, Heide. 1987. "Matriarchal Religion in Former Times and Today." Translated with the author by Lise Weil. Crossing Pamphlet. Freedom, Calif.: Crossing Press.

———. 1991. *The Dancing Goddess: Principles of a Matriarchal Aesthetic.* Translated by M. T. Krause. Boston: Beacon Press. (German edition 1982.)

Graves, Robert. 1948. *The White Goddess.* New York: Noonday.

Hall, Nor. 1988. *Those Women.* Dallas: Spring Press.

Harrison, Jane Ellen. 1913. *Ancient Art and Ritual.* New York: Henry Holt and Co.

———. 1915. *Alpha and Omega.* London: Sidgwick & Jackson Ltd. (1973. New York: AMS Reprint.)

———. 1921. *Epilegomena to the Study of Greek Religion.* Cambridge: Cambridge University Press.

———. 1991 [1922]. *Prolegomena to the Study of Greek Religion.* Princeton: Princeton University Press. (From the 3rd edition.)

———. 1926. *Reminiscences of a Student's Life.* London: Hogarth Press.

———. 1912, 1927. *Themis.* Cambridge: Cambridge University Press.

Kermode, Frank. 1967. *The Sense of an Ending.* Oxford: Oxford University Press.

Lauter, Estella, and Carol Schreier Rupprecht, eds. 1985. *Feminist Archetypal Theory: Interdisciplinary Re-Visions of Jungian Thought.* Knoxville: The University of Tennessee Press.

Lerner, Gerda. 1986. *The Creation of Patriarchy.* Oxford: Oxford University Press.

Lorde, Audre. 1984. "The Master's Tools Will Never Dismantle the Master's House." In her *Sister Outsider,* 110–13. Trumansburg, N.Y.: Crossing Press.

McWilliams-Tullberg, Rita. 1977. "Women and Degrees at Cambridge University, 1862–1897." In Vicinus 1977, 117–45.

Mellaart, James. 1967. *Çatal Hüyük: A Neolithic Town in Anatolia.* New York: McGraw-Hill.

Morgan, Lewis Henry. 1963. *Ancient Society.* New York. (Reprint of 1877 ed.)

Nietzsche, Friedrich. 1967. *The Birth of Tragedy and the Case of Wagner.* Translated, with commentary, by Walter Kaufmann. New York: Vintage.

O'Barr, Jean F., ed. 1989. *Women and a New Academy: Gender and Cultural Contexts.* Madison: University of Wisconsin Press.

Orenstein, Gloria Feman. 1990. *The Reflowering of the Goddess.* New York: Pergamon Press.

Passman, Kristina. 1991. "The Classical Amazon in Contemporary Cinema." In Martin M. Winkler, ed., *Classics and Cinema,* 81–105. Lewisburg, Penn.: Bucknell University Press.

———. Forthcoming, 1993. "Re(de)fining Woman: Language and Power in the Homeric Hymn to Demeter." In Mary DeForest, ed., *Essays in Honor of Joy King.* Chicago: Bolchazy-Carducci.

Passman, Kristina, and Kathleen March. Forthcoming, 1993. "The Amazon in South America." In Wolfgang Hasse and Meyer Reinhold, eds., *The Classical Tradition in the Americas,* vol. 1. Leiden: Brill.

Peacock, Sandra J. 1988. *Jane Ellen Harrison: The Mask and the Self.* New Haven: Yale University Press.

———. 1991. "An Awful Warmth about Her Heart: The Personal in Jane Harrison's Ideas on Religion." In Calder 1991, 167–84.

Penelope, Julia. 1990. "The Lesbian Perspective." In Allen 1990, 89–108.

———. 1992a. *Call Me Lesbian: Lesbian Lives, Lesbian Theory.* Freedom, Calif.: Crossing Press.

———. 1992b. "Heteropatriarchal Semantics and Lesbian Identity." In Penelope 1992a: 78–97.

Phelan, Shane. 1989. *Identity Politics: Lesbian Feminism and the Limits of Community.* Philadelphia: Temple University Press.

Plaskow, Judith, and Carol P. Christ, eds. 1989. *Weaving the Visions: New Patterns in Feminist Spirituality.* San Francisco: Harper and Row.

Reed, Evelyn. 1975. *Women's Evolution: From Matriarchal Clan to Patriarchal Family.* New York: Pathway.

Reis, Patricia. 1991. *Through the Goddess: A Woman's Way of Healing.* New York: Continuum.

Schlesier, Renate. 1991. "Prolegomena to Jane Harrison's Interpretation of Ancient Greek Religion." In Calder 1991, 185–226.

Segal, Robert. 1980a. "The Myth-Ritualist Theory of Religion." *Journal of the Scientific Study of Religion* 19: 173–85.

———. 1980b. "In Defense of Mythology: The History of Modern Theories of Myth." *Annals of Scholarship* 1: 3–49.

Silk, M. S., and J. P. Stern. 1981. *Nietzsche on Tragedy*. Cambridge: Cambridge University Press.

Sjöö, Monica, and Barbara Mor. 1987. *The Great Cosmic Mother: Rediscovering the Religion of the Earth*. San Francisco: Harper and Row.

Skinner, Marilyn. 1987. "Classical Studies, Patriarchy and Feminism: The View from 1986." *Women's Studies International Forum* 10.2: 181–86.

Spelman, Elizabeth V. 1988. *Inessential Woman: Problems of Exclusion in Feminist Thought*. Boston: Beacon Press.

Spretnak, Charlene, ed. 1982. *The Politics of Women's Spirituality*. New York: Anchor.

———. 1984. *Lost Goddesses of Early Greece: A Collection of Pre-Hellenic Myths*. Boston: Beacon Press.

Starhawk. 1982. *Dreaming the Dark: Magic, Sex & Politics*. Boston: Beacon Press.

Stein, Diane. 1991. *Dreaming the Past, Dreaming the Future: A Herstory of the Earth*. Freedom, Calif.: Crossing Press.

Stewart, Jessie G. 1959. *Jane Ellen Harrison: A Portrait from Letters*. London: Merlin Press.

Stone, Merlin. 1976. *When God Was a Woman*. New York: Dial Press.

Trebilcot, Joyce. 1990. "Dyke Methods." In Allen 1990, 15–30.

Tylor, E. B. 1924. *Primitive Culture*. New York: Brentano (Originally 1871. 2 vols. London: Murray.)

Tyrrell, William Blake. 1984. *Amazons: A Study in Athenian Mythmaking*. Baltimore: Johns Hopkins University Press.

Vicinus, Martha, ed. 1977. *A Widening Sphere: Changing Roles of Victorian Women*. Bloomington: Indiana University Press.

———. 1985. *Independent Women: Work and Community for Single Women, 1850–1920*. Chicago: University of Chicago Press.

Walker, Alice. 1984. *In Search of Our Mother's Gardens*. San Diego: Harcourt Brace Jovanovich.

Wolkstein, Diane, and Samuel Noah Kramer. 1983. *Inanna—Queen of Heaven and Earth: Her Stories and Hymns from Sumer*. New York: Harper and Row.

Zeitlin, Froma I. 1981. "Travesties of Gender and Genre in Aristophanes' *Thesmophoriazousae*." *Critical Inquiry* 8.2: 301–27.

———. 1982. "Cultic Models of the Female: Rites of Dionysus and Demeter." *Arethusa* 15.1, 2: 129–57.

Epistemology and
Material Culture

9

The Case for Not Ignoring Marx in the Study of Women in Antiquity

Peter W. Rose

For Judith Hallett

There are at least two grounds for my hesitating to undertake the following effort and for the reader's justifiable skepticism in reading it. One is the questionable status of Marxism at this historical moment; the other is my questionable status as a male presuming to address issues predominantly addressed by women. I believe the two grounds are related.

For many months now, as I write, we have been hearing the triumphant proclamations of the final death of Marxism and socialism—and at the same time celebrations of the absolute equivalence between democracy, human liberation, and the free market. Since Desert Storm, however, and the proclamation of the New World Order, we have all had an important political lesson, though obviously not all of us read it in the same way. The most powerful capitalist country in the world has seen fit to incinerate or blast to pieces perhaps as many as 100,000 fellow human beings and inflict irreparable damage to the human ecosystem, not only to defend the privileges of a few American capitalists and a few feudal potentates in the Middle East, but to demonstrate to the rest of the third world its unmitigated ferocity against any defiance of its "right" to exploitation. Feminist classicists will no doubt have been particularly struck by the inspiring defense of the freedom of patriarchal Arabs to maintain "their" women in a state of forcibly imposed infantilization recalling the grimmest reconstructions of women's lot in fifth-century B.C.E. Athens. Socialism is not dead for the simple reason that the horrors of capitalism continually force us to reinvent socialism. Moreover, the readiness of capitalism to enlist age-old patriarchal patterns of oppressing women in its vampirish hunger for profits is a crucial factor in any potential alliance between socialism and feminism.

Since in the following discussion I will be arguing for a specifically Marxist version of standpoint theory or positionality, and since a number of theorists both male and female have raised serious questions about what has variously been dubbed "male feminism," "men in feminism," "femmeninism," or "critical cross-

211

dressing" (Jardine and Smith 1987), I owe it to my readers to offer some account of my own standpoint. Without denying the inevitable array of unconscious intentions regularly attributed to males who address feminist issues, I do not believe that my efforts here precisely fit any of the descriptive terms cited above, nor do I feel that I fit the terms of Teresa de Lauretis's devastating pun: I am not simply paying "hommage" to feminism (de Lauretis 1987: 21). As someone who has awkwardly juggled political activism and academic endeavors for some twenty-five years, my engagement with feminism as a political movement long antedates trying to come to terms with issues raised by feminists in the study of classical antiquity.

I am aware that I am likely to be "talking about things women feminists had been talking about for years," as Jardine characterizes most American male "ventures into feminism" (Jardine and Smith 1987: 245). Beyond the wish to add whatever support I can to the feminist renewal of the field of classics (Skinner 1989), my primary motive is a political one. As a socialist in a terrifying New World Order—one in which *The Handmaid's Tale* every day looks less like a paranoid fantasy and more like a blueprint—I am looking for allies. This does not mean, again in Jardine's terms, that I intend to do "the male leftist thing of saying: now let's move along to the bigger issues" (Jardine and Smith 1987: 242; compare Showalter's critique of Eagleton, *ibid.*, 117–18 and 127–30). I have learned painfully what the far right seems to have known all along, namely, that meaningful political transformation requires confronting the whole spectrum of oppositions. It is not a matter of hierarchizing two separate agendas, but opening up a "complicated map of contingencies"—to echo a formulation of Nancy Miller's (Jardine and Smith 1987: 142).

I understand a specifically feminist approach in classics to imply not just an interest in or concentration on women in antiquity, but an essentially *political* commitment to change the rules of the game, to intervene in and transform the discourse of classical scholarship—including its institutional forms—as part of a broader commitment to transform society in the direction of both greater equality and greater respect for difference. Mary-Kay Gamel's recently published account of struggles over the setting of the program at the annual APA meetings (Gamel 1990: 172–74) is a good example of what I mean by struggle over the *institutional* forms of classical scholarship. Opening up classical journals and conferences (Skinner 1989: 199 n.1; Hallett 1989) to sustained consideration of feminist work on Greek and Roman antiquity is a more obviously discursive form of what I at least call political action. It is a part of contesting the whole spectrum of discursive and institutional forms of oppression.

There are as well specificities of the field of classics that may render less otiose my "talking about things women feminists [have] been talking about for years." In classics at least, not very many men *have* been talking about feminism. Skinner's description of the field in 1986 seems to me fundamentally accurate today: "androcentrism seems crystallized there in its purest form: classics is certainly one of the most conservative, hierarchical and patriarchal of academic fields" (Skinner 1987: 181).[1] She points out that "fear of becoming too theoretical, too speculative, of going beyond the drastically limited evidence, is apparent in much mainstream research on antiquity; and the employment of non-standard methodologies and techniques—post-structuralist literary theory, current anthropological models, Jungian, Freudian and Marxist analysis—is regarded with deep suspicion by the editorial boards of our so-called 'better' journals" (Skinner 1987: 183).[2]

But while few readers might question the prima facie desirability of a male classicist addressing feminist issues, there are still grounds for skepticism about a male *Marxist* entering this dialogue. The earlier alliance of feminism and Marxism, in itself by no means unproblematic, seems—with only few exceptions (for example, Arthur 1973; duBois 1988)[3]—to have left no trace on the feminist study of antiquity, while the current political and intellectual climate within feminism seems in many respects distinctly hostile to a revived and reconceived version of that alliance. A recent dismissal of "Masculine Marx" is in many respects typical of the position of many former socialist feminists:

> There is general agreement among feminists that the Marxist categories of "production," "reproduction," "labor," "exploitation," and "class" fail to capture important dimensions of women's lives. . . . Marx's theory . . . is profoundly embedded within a masculine horizon of meaning and sensibility . . . it is part and parcel of a misogynous configuration of values, meanings, practices to which feminism stands opposed (Di Stefano 1991: 147).[4]

Ehrenreich's retrospective on the socialist feminism of the seventies suggests further grounds for today's skepticism about Marxism among feminists:

> In the mid-seventies . . . socialist-feminists were an embattled species. On the one hand there was cultural and/or separatist feminism, drifting off toward spirituality, Great Goddess worship, and socio-biological theories of eternal male perfidy. To these "radical" feminists, socialist-feminists were male-identified dupes of the left, which they always described as the "male left." On the other hand, there was the left, which featured at the time a flourishing Marxist-Leninist tendency, bent on self-proletarianization and the "rectification" of everyone else. To it, socialist-feminists were agents of the petite bourgeoisie on assignment to distract working-class women from the main event, the class struggle. The Marxist-Leninists and separatist feminists were extremes in a much wider radical context, but they helped define a political atmosphere in which socialist-feminism was hard put to establish that

it was neither an oxymoron nor a form of treason (Ehrenreich 1984: 49).[5]

At the same time, the final paragraph of Ehrenreich's essay, published in 1984, seems to me to hold out some promise beyond the hyphen, so to speak, of socialist-feminism:

> I still believe that if there is a vantage point from which to comprehend and change the world, our world today, it will be socialist and feminist. Socialist—or perhaps here I should say Marxist—because a Marxist way of thinking, at its best, helps us understand the cutting edge of change, the blind driving force of capital, the dislocations, innovations, and global reshufflings. Feminist because feminism offers our best insights into that which is most ancient and intractable about our common situation: the gulf that divides the species by gender and, tragically, divides us all from nature and that which is most human in our nature. This is our intellectual heritage, and I do not think we have yet seen its full power—or our own. (Ehrenreich 1984: 57)

Without attempting in very limited space to answer the important critiques of Marx by former socialist feminists, I will only say here that what I admire in the work of feminists who are fully conversant with Marxist discourse (for example, Spivak, Fraser, duBois) and find lamentably lacking in post-Marxists is the ongoing serious attempt to grasp the connections between capitalism and the oppression of women. With others it is as if an intellectually telling attack on Marx somehow facilitates the bracketing of any serious engagement with the critique of capitalism.

Quite apart from the specifically feminist critique of Marxism and the lessons drawn daily in the media from the welcome dismantling of the last vestiges of Stalinism, other critics have recently raised serious questions about classical Marxism—its epistemological assumptions, its deterministic base-superstructure model, its concomitant notions of ideology as false consciousness, and its apparently simple equation of the proletariat with the "subject" of history, just to name a few.[6] I must say that though I am a classicist by profession and still profess myself a Marxist, I am not exactly a *classical* Marxist. Though all labels are problematic in some contexts, I still prefer to call myself a Marxist with all the ambiguities that entails, rather than a post or ex-Marxist with the peculiar politics that entails. What I am learning to live with and trying to think through is the characteristic postmodernist turn toward a new acceptance of partiality, in several senses. This postmodernist turn eschews the sort of totalizing discourse that claims access to the whole of a truth, a discourse that claims to be "scientific," and, with respect to feminism, claims access to solid criteria by which to hierarchize the analytic value of such categories as gender, class, or race.

If, then, we give up these potentially oppressive traditional claims, I argue that there still remain a number of methodological themes of Marxism in the work of Marx himself and in contemporary post-Stalinist Marxists, which have by no means outworn their usefulness, but on the contrary retain a distinct power and striking relevance to feminism at this particular historical conjunction. No less are these themes relevant to a feminist examination of classical antiquity. While none of these themes, given the wide if usually unacknowledged influence of Marx, is necessarily unique to Marx, their combination and their centrality to what I at least see as Marxism, are part of why I still use that label. Rather than give the grounds in Marx or Marx-inspired texts for these elements, I will elaborate them as specifically Marxist alternatives or supplements to a number of non-Marxist models at work in feminist scholarship on antiquity.

Empiricism versus the Quest for Social Totality and the Critique of Essentialism

I'll begin with what I think remains the most pervasively hegemonic methodology in classics—traditional empirical historicism or what Hayden White has dubbed "doctrinal realism" (White 1973: 164)—though of course it rarely calls itself by any name since its only characteristic methodological claims are "rigor" and "truth." These claims are usually summed up in the master claim to "objectivity"—to an utter lack of "preconceptions."

In any analytic model there is always a tension between, on the one hand, a process of breaking up, separating out a specific set of phenomena and, on the other hand, the process that attempts to correlate and integrate those phenomena with other data in an "explanation"—an explanation that is presumed to be useful for some end. The traditional empiricist analytic model especially valorizes the first operation. It breaks up data into as many separate pieces as possible and is wary of the grounds on which the different sets of data are related to each other. It prefers, indeed, to believe that the "data speak for themselves." Thus empiricists sooner or later appeal to a "common sense" reading of the data or invoke an allegedly accessible *intention* of the original author as the only valid grounds for interpretation. The very notion that the past is "useful" for anything beyond the antiquarian joys of simply "knowing the past the way it really was" (Jameson 1979a) fills the true empiricist with scorn or anxiety. For Ranke (1795–1886), the father of empiricist historiography, the relation of objective data to each other is a fervently desired but virtually unattainable goal: as White paraphrases him, "the particulars of history must ultimately find their unity as parts of a whole . . . in the governance of a spiritual power" (White 1973: 165), that is, they are ultimately sorted out and have their truest existence only in the mind of God.

The persistence, the distressing durability of this empiricist mindset is obvious, for example, in the strategy of Jasper Griffin's recent disparaging review of work by David Halperin and John J. Winkler. (It is significant that controversial work by women classicists on equally "sensational"—i.e., sexual—issues [one thinks, for example, of Amy Richlin's *The Garden of Priapus*] does not get covered in the pages of the *New York Review of Books,* whereas this work by feminist-inspired males receives extensive and—despite the empiricist jabs of the reviewer—inevitably sales-enhancing coverage.)[7] Griffin complains of Halperin, for example, "He does not seem to me to succeed in disproving the *natural* reading of a number of Greek texts" (Griffin 1990: 8, col. b, my emphasis). Halperin's essays, we are told, "make interesting points, but . . . the reader feels at moments the tug of special pleading" (Griffin 1990: 9, col. a). For the confirmed British empiricist any analysis of data which reveals a concern about its implications for the present is by definition hardly worth listening to.

In sharp contrast, Marxist thought, though in common parlance it is most often characterized and disparaged as separating out and hypostatizing only *economic* phenomena, is in fact most profoundly focused, as Lukács repeatedly emphasized, upon the historically constructed *social totality,* on that temporally specific nexus of mutually interactive relationships that together constitute the true object of analysis (Lukács 1971 [1921]: 9–10). Marx and twentieth-century Marxists have produced a wide range of theoretical texts exploring modes of reading evidence and means of making useful connections between the multifarious dimensions of a historically specific social formation. Marx's own most influential analytic achievement, the major task he set himself in *Capital,* was a "Critique of Political Economy" (Marx's subtitle for *Capital*), that is, a critique of bourgeois economic theory—theory that was founded on a spurious severing of economic phenomena from their concrete historical coordinates, so that they might appear as simple facts of nature. Thus, for example, Marx argues that the formulae of bourgeois economic theory "bear stamped upon them in unmistakable letters that they belong to a [historically specific] state of society"; but, he continues,

> such formulae appear to the bourgeois intellect to be as much a self-evident necessity imposed by *Nature* as productive labour itself. Hence forms of social production that preceded the bourgeois form, are treated by the bourgeoisie in much the same way as the Fathers of the Church treated pre-Christian religions (Marx 1967: 80–81).

I want to stress the linkage in Marx between this pervasive critique of essentialism and his attempt to grasp the interconnections of a vast array of factors in a historically specific social situation. There is a clear parallel between Marx's project in the critique of political economy and what I take to be a central feature of the feminist project in history: both have conducted a full-scale assault on different essentialisms that have sought to justify the power and privileges of the present rulers of society by substituting an alleged nature for history—for specific and changing constructions of individual and collective identities (Alcoff 1988).[8]

Essentialism remains, however, one of the primary untheorized assumptions of hegemonic empiricism. To cite again as an example Griffin's review, he takes Winkler to task for suggesting that, in Longus's novel *Daphnis and Chloe,* there should have been sexual freedom for the female Chloe as much as for the male Daphnis. Declares Griffin, "the sympathetic reader sees that such questions simply *cannot* be asked" (Griffin 1990: 11, col. a, my emphasis) and he elaborates his point with the "fact that girls get pregnant, boys do not—a fact which remains virtually unmentioned in both these books on sexuality" (Griffin 1990: 11). Commonsense empiricism by virtue of the very fact that it assumes that the evidence—"objectively considered"—speaks for itself leads directly into a potentially oppressive biologistic essentialism. It is significant here that the present tense ("girls *get* pregnant") blandly effaces the historical particularity of a period in which the options for females in relation to pregnancy were radically different from what they are today. Winkler's contemporary focus on an oppressive ideology of a past era is measured against an implicitly transhistorical empirical reality. This smug essentialism of the male empiricist historian has little to do with the debates *within* feminism between those who have stressed the struggle for equality and those who have insisted on the specificity of the female body and the experience associated with that body as a locus of difference (Scott 1988). In somewhat different terms cultural feminists have insisted on a positive evaluation of traditionally female labor[9] and values while poststructuralist feminists have spelled out the mechanisms by which female identity is constructed in discourse (Alcoff 1988). This is a complex matter to which we must return, but empiricist essentialism will not help us sort it out.

Functionalist Anthropology versus the Dynamic of Change

As compared with the empiricist's unreflective and often arrogant posture of alleged objectivity, Marxism's explicitly partisan engagement in a struggle to transform the rules of the game—in part at least through a rigorous critique of the past—recommends it especially to feminism. The distinction between Marxism and empiricism is parallel, I believe, to the distinction between Marxism and much of what is often dubbed the anthropological approach, an approach either tacitly or explicitly at work in much feminist scholarship on ancient Greece. As a term, of course, "anthropology" embraces a wide range of methodologies. As Marvin Harris showed some time ago in his vast survey of anthropological theory (Harris 1968), there is, besides such familiar varieties as functionalist, structuralist, and British empiricist anthropology, even something called Marxist anthropology. More recently we have had the semiotic anthropology of Geertz (1973), symbolic anthropology (especially Victor Turner, for example, 1967), and what has been designated as "feminist anthropology" (for example, Moore 1988). Within this extensive body of thought there have certainly been sophisticated theorizations of the role of the observer in the process of observing (see Harris 1968: chap. 20; Clifford 1988). Moore's survey of specifically feminist

218 / PETER W. ROSE

anthropology details an array of impressive work—not least by Marxist feminist anthropologists, and it would be impertinent of me to attempt to characterize or summarize it. I will, however, quote Moore's summary statement from her last page: "In the final analysis, the contribution of feminist anthropology to contemporary feminism is simply to point to the value of comparison and to the importance of acknowledging difference" (Moore 1988: 198).

Unquestionably one of the prime liberatory potentialities of the study of women in classical antiquity is precisely its capacity to undermine contemporary claims about what is alleged to be "natural" for women by revealing the often radically different roles and stereotypes of women in a society often claimed as a warrant for our own. Broadly speaking, moreover, I would add that anthropology of all varieties appears to share with the more Lukácsian version of Marxism a focus on "the social totality." For example, Helene Foley's admirable analysis of Penelope's role as a temporary and strategic displacement of the normal confinement of females to the domestic sphere (Foley 1978) depends upon anthropological work which demonstrates that the point of temporary public empowerment of women in traditional societies is to reestablish the threatened "normal" hierarchy, i.e., the very structures that keep women confined to the domestic sphere. However, Foley herself (1981a) has subsequently offered an insightful critique of the stock anthropological polarities, nature and culture, domestic and public spheres. Such normative constructs tend to be used in ways that ignore the fact that these polarities are themselves the locus of ideological struggle. For most anthropologists the social totality tends to be conceived of in static terms. Unintentionally, this static perspective tends to reinforce the idea that the norms themselves are immutable.

For a Marxist, all struggles between unequals in power are related to a fundamental dynamic of *change* in society—a dynamic that may be held in check for very long periods in some societies, but is nonetheless part of a single, worldwide struggle for a more just society. The motor force of this dynamic is not, as it is sometimes understood, some posited primal will to conflict. Nor is it accurate, I think, to claim that a dogmatic Marxist faith in dialectic leads me to see conflict where there is none. The fact of exploitation and inequality in both the distribution of society's necessary work and the distribution of socially generated wealth— the subjective experiences of oppression—create an inherent and often traceable instability and potential energy for change in the overwhelming majority of known societies, at least since the urban-agricultural revolution (L. White 1959: chap. 12; Diamond 1967).[10]

The issue, moreover, is not simply the alleged imposition of irrelevant modern demands on a society long gone, but rather about situating the analysis of any society within an ever evolving and critically refined vision of what real liberation for women would be like. The more clearly we understand both the internal dynamics and destabilizing contradictions of other social arrangements from our own, the better equipped we are to envision and to struggle for that real liberation.

Thus, sketchy though Arthur's (1973) early treatment of the *Odyssey* was, it remains for me at least methodologically superior to both Foley's (1978; but see Foley 1981a: 150–51) and Winkler's (1990: 129–61), because Arthur attempts to situate the representation of women in the *Iliad, Odyssey,* and Hesiod within an exploration of broad shifts in the mode of production (from grazing to intensive farming), in the mode of political domination (from kin-based aristocratic warrior elites to the polis run by tyrants or hoplites), and in the social organization (from the kin-based warrior band to the polis conceived as a collection of nuclear households). While one might dispute this or that reading by Arthur of the available data, her implicit notion of the social totality is not solely concerned with the mechanisms and—to use Foucault's favorite term—technologies that *maintain* the status quo, but takes account as well of the unmistakable evidence that significant *changes* were taking place.

The Functionalism of Structuralism

The tremendous popularity of structuralist anthropology among feminist classicists is due far less to the direct influence of Lévi-Strauss than to the brilliant contributions of Jean-Pierre Vernant. In a trenchant essay on Greek tragedy Vernant defends himself against the charge that his earlier work in that area had invoked transhistorical categories incompatible with Marxism (Vernant and Vidal-Naquet 1988: 237–47). Relying on the famous early dictum of Marx that "The forming of the five senses is a labour of the entire history of the world down to the present" (Marx and Engels: vol. 3.302; Vernant and Vidal-Naquet 1988: 239–42), Vernant argues ingeniously that the sensibility constructed by the work of Greek tragedy becomes a permanent part of human consciousness as long as there is a cultural continuity with Greek tragedy sustained through history. Yet the line of argument here is symptomatic of the heavy emphasis, even in this most "Marxist" of structuralists, on elucidating structural relationships which are conceived in essentially static and often explicitly apolitical terms.

Nicole Loraux's apoliticism is far more typical of structuralist strategies. She surveys (Loraux 1990) the vast array of Greek and Latin data on the myths associated with Heracles and attempts to explain the implications of his specifically gendered relationships. She finds ultimately a structuralist homology between the reinforcement of Heracles's masculinity through transvestism and the reinforcement of Hera's femininity through Heracles's assaults on Hera's right breast, which Loraux argues—using medical and iconographic evidence—represents the "masculine" side of the female divinity. In passing, she dismisses politics as a serious object of analysis of this myth:

> It is essential to my interpretation that no Greek hero was more popular than Heracles. . . . But because no city was able to appropriate him definitively, the process of reevaluation took place not in the political

field, with its multiple identifications and inevitable distortions, but rather within the logic that presides over the Greek concept of the powerful hero (Loraux 1990: 23).

This false antithesis, which limits Greek "politics" to intercity rivalries, excludes the whole realm of class ideology and struggle with which "reevaluations" of this most popular hero were deeply integrated. In its place we are offered an idealist "logic" which preserves the status quo with neatly balanced homologies.

The aristocratic ideology most commonly associated with the figure of Heracles celebrates inherited excellence—the claim of ruling class males to have by birth an innate superiority ultimately derived from divine ancestry. This ideological theme is in turn an integral element in the whole array of social and legal institutions for the oppression of women in ancient Greece. The more profoundly human male worth is figured in terms of descent, the more obsessive becomes the desire to control the sexuality of women. The principle so succinctly stated in Roman law, *mater certa, pater incertus est,* becomes the nightmare of the Greek male citizen who is determined at all costs to reduce this incertitude to a minimum. An extraordinary array of components in the social totality of classical Athens can be traced to the operation of this obsession with inherited excellence. Gould (1980) and Ste. Croix (1970, 1981: 101–3), among others, have studied the complex laws of property at Athens regarding women—particularly heiresses— designed not only to keep the family property under the control of males but to insure the sexual reproduction of males in the same family line. Private orations— one thinks especially of Lysias's *On the Murder of Eratosthenes*—confirm the evidence of archaeology that the architectural and social conventions of Athens aimed directly at minimizing the social intercourse especially of upper-class Athenian women. The women's quarters were on the second floor and closed off with a door that could be locked. Grocery shopping was done by slaves or males to remove married women's opportunities for interactions outside the confines of the house. The whole panoply of misogynistic values recently surveyed brilliantly by Carson (1990: 135–69), and the elaborate mechanisms for reinforcing a heterosexual image for the most politically prominent of Athenians studied by Winkler (1990: 45–70), all depend not simply on the obsession with private property but on the more subjective ideological commitments to inherited excellence.

Already in the *Iliad* Heracles figures as the quintessential paradigm of human excellence, implicitly attributed in the poem to descent from the male patriarch Zeus, and brought to nought by the vicious machinations of Zeus's wife Hera (*Iliad* 18.117–19). For Pindar too Heracles is the supreme figure of "innate nature" (*phua,* Doric for *phusis,* "nature"), the embodiment of the principle of inherited excellence. Perhaps Pindar's most optimistic myth is the tale of how even as a newborn infant Heracles succeeded in strangling the terrifying, devouring serpents sent by Hera to destroy him (*Nemean* 1). The grimmest surviving representation of Heracles is perhaps Euripides's tragedy about the *Madness of Heracles,* in which the triumphant rescuing hero, suddenly driven mad by another visitation from the ever-hateful Hera, kills his own wife and children. The most progressive political moment in this play occurs when the hero, now returned to his senses, rejects the proffered consolations of Theseus by declaring that he, Heracles, the alleged son of Zeus, does not believe all those stories about gods mating with mortal women! This mind-boggling repudiation of the whole basis for the ideology of inherited excellence by its prime exemplar is surely not accidentally combined with perhaps the most brutal representation of the victimization of women in Greek literature.[11] Thus even if it is strictly true that no city succeeded in appropriating Heracles definitively, as Loraux argues, it does not follow even on this level that the most obviously *political* reevaluations of the hero are devoid of interest or can be safely ignored by feminists. This complex interface in the case of Heracles between myth, sexual ideology, law, custom, and sexual attitudes all contributing to the oppression of women is a small example of what can be missed by a structuralist anthropology ill at ease with politics and struggle.

Poststructuralism and Deconstruction versus the Focus on Institutions, the Totalizing Project, Standpoint Theory, and Utopia

I would like now to look briefly at Froma Zeitlin's potentially quite political use of structuralist and poststructuralist methodology. In general her work fairly bristles with polarities and mediating terms, with homologies, synchronies, and diachronies. Though I do not think her analysis of the dynamics of misogyny in the *Oresteia* (Zeitlin 1978) is necessarily the last word on that issue, this groundbreaking study offers a striking demonstration of what a Trotskyist might call "unequal development" and what Joan Kelly so brilliantly theorizes in "Did Women Have a Renaissance?" (Kelly 1984): namely, that an advance of male freedom during a particular historical epoch may well entail a homologous escalation of female unfreedom.

In any case, Zeitlin's work, particularly her more poststructuralist analysis (Zeitlin 1981) of *mimesis* in the *Thesmophoriazusae* of Aristophanes, which traces the association of the feminine with the ambiguities of representation itself, well illustrates the more politically progressive side of deconstruction's whole problematization of representation and its focus on textual strategies. Nonetheless, I suggest that the political value of this sort of analysis might stand out in sharper relief if it were situated within the framework elaborated by the Marxists Gramsci and Althusser, namely, the focus on ideological state apparatuses as sites of struggle. Zeitlin's focus on Aristophanes's multilayered deconstruction of genre and gender brilliantly demonstrates the struggles that took place within the chief ideological state apparatus of fifth-century Greece, namely, the state-supported dramatic festivals. The form wars between tragedy and comedy staged in the *Thesmophoriazusae* can be seen in this perspective as the locus where the oppressive gender stereotypes that sustain patriarchal hegemony are shown to be nothing more than "forms" themselves.

Skinner (1986), Culham (1986), and, somewhat earlier, Foley (1981a) have all called attention to the problems arising from the use of Greek tragedy as evidence about ancient Greek women—usually in terms of a dichotomy between "image" and "reality." Gramsci, Althusser, who proclaims himself the follower of Gramsci, and finally Jameson, who draws on both of these and the rich output of the Frankfurt School of Marxists, together offer a range of theoretical perspectives on power, ideology, and artistic representation uniquely valuable for the very reasons I have already suggested—because as Marxists they take for granted what other models deny or cannot see, namely, the reality of constant conflict and the necessity of taking sides. Gramsci (1971) argues that what maintains the status quo is not normally pure brute domination and the institutions of domination—the army, the police, the courts with the power of imprisonment and the threat of execution. He posits the concept of hegemony to designate that spontaneous acceptance—whether despairing or enthusiastic—inspired by the ruling class's version of reality (Gramsci 1971: 57). This version of reality is formulated and promulgated in institutions ranging from those directly under state control to nominally private institutions like the family. It constitutes most of what is neutrally called "culture" and affirms the values of those who hold power. As Said has pointed out, "Well before Foucault, Gramsci had grasped the idea that culture serves authority, and ultimately the national State, not because it represses and coerces but because it is affirmative, positive, and persuasive" (Said 1983: 171).

Althusser (1971) describes ideology as a "system of representations" and attempts to carry further Gramsci's exploration of how these representations work through social institutions to win that spontaneous acquiescence in our own oppression and exploitation. Althusser's notion of "interpellation"—the summons to acceptance of a certain definition of our identities through various practices associated with the ideological apparatuses of the state—offers an analytic framework for exploring precisely what we mean when we talk about the *social construction* of our class and sexual identities (Althusser 1971: 127–86). In particular, the problem (raised and dismissed by Culham 1990: 164) of understanding how images of women—designed by men to serve the interests of men—contribute to the construction of subjected female subjectivities is significantly illuminated by Althusser's concept of interpellation (see also de Lauretis 1987: 6–9). To be sure, as Barrett (1988) has rightly pointed out, the conscious and unconscious aspects of identity are not clearly worked out in Althusser, who himself ignores the question of gender, but I believe the model is still suggestive and productive—particularly to the extent to which we stress, with Smith (1988) and others, the designation of these ideological apparatuses as sites of struggle. When Culham speaks of "ideologically male, statist texts of the theatre" (Culham

1986: 16), she rightly points to the fact that in fifth-century Athens, drama constituted the ideological apparatus par excellence of the Athenian state. What merits further analysis is the fact that by virtue of the persuasive, contestatory character of hegemonic ideology, drama reveals not just the self-serving images of the dominant group, but the challenges to hegemony that it seeks to contain, distort, and dispel.

This model might help in explaining what Barbara McManus (1990) has recently pointed to: the congruence between the evidence of Greek tragedy for young women's terror of marriage and the evidence of Greek ritual, the evidence of Greek myth in the *Homeric Hymn to Demeter,* and the findings of contemporary comparative anthropology. McManus speaks of a "dialogue between different sources" (McManus 1990: 228) and seems primarily concerned to avoid "either-orism" (McManus 1990: 226), but I think the contemporary Marxist approach I have outlined above makes a useful framework for her findings. While it is clearly not in the direct interest of male authors of tragedy to reveal women's fear of marriage—if it is in any sense a social secret—this harmony of disparate sorts of evidence, of which some sorts are clearly more ideologically self-conscious than others, fits well with a conception of tragedy's ideological function as essentially rhetorical—as a persuasive effort to deal with contradictory realities by acknowledging their force even as it seeks to dispel potential resistance to the status quo. Such an approach might also offer a broader political framework for understanding Zeitlin's impressive subtleties (1981) in treating the representations of rebellious women and sexually ambiguous males in Aristophanic comedy. Similarly, a recent analysis of Euripides's *Hippolytus* (Rabinowitz 1986), though it invokes the name of Althusser on the first page, concentrates its insightful analysis exclusively on the poststructuralist thematics of speech, silence, and symbolic representation (coinage, the *deltos,* and the *pharmakos*—the figure of scapegoat/medicine so brilliantly analyzed by Derrida). Not only might fuller use of Althusser's notion of interpellation help clarify the mechanisms by which female characters are shown internalizing an ideology that oppresses them, but the broader role of the institution of Greek drama in the social totality of fifth-century Athens might be clarified as a site of struggle. At the same time, as Richard Johnson points out, feminism has "aided a more general turn from older kinds of ideological critique (which centered on maps of meaning and versions of reality) to approaches that centre on social identities, subjectivities, popularity and pleasure" (Johnson 1986/87: 40). Such approaches to the ideological dimension of Greek drama would broaden the project of grasping its function as an ideological state apparatus.

To be sure, the most thoroughgoing pursuit of deconstruction ultimately deconstructs any ground for political resistance or any resisting subjects. Thus the Marxist quest for the social totality is of course widely perceived as inherently incompatible with the postmodernist abandonment of the all-encompassing "master narrative" (for example, Lyotard 1984). Marxist totalizations of all sorts have recently come under serious attack from self-designated "post-Marxists"—who have been at pains to equate all totalization with totalitarianism. But not all totalization is necessary the same or necessarily "totalitarian."[12] Indeed, Jameson has recently dubbed this the "silliest of all puns" (Jameson 1988: 60), and related it to the systematic demarxification of France in which "what is staged as a principled fear of Stalinism is probably often little more than a fear of socialism itself. . . . Totality," Jameson argues, "is not in that sense, for Lukács, a *form* of knowledge, but rather a *framework* in which various kinds of knowledge are positioned, pursued and evaluated." Thus Lukács speaks of "an *aspiration* to totality"; and Jameson argues, "such a concept and a framework is not an *individual* matter but rather a *collective* project" (Jameson 1988: 60, my emphasis). Jameson proceeds to argue that this Lukácsian notion of an epistemology based on the *priority* of a particular social group—for Lukács the working class—finds its most relevant contemporary analogue in the standpoint theory of feminists Hartsock (1985), Harding (1986), and Jaggar (1988), two of whom acknowledge a debt to Lukács. Jameson sums up the presupposition as follows:

> owing to its structural situation in the social order and to the specific forms of oppression and exploitation unique to that situation, each group lives the world in a phenomenologically specific way that allows it to see, or better still, that makes it unavoidable for that group to see and to know, features of the world that remain obscure, invisible, or merely occasional and secondary for other groups (Jameson 1988: 65).

I alluded earlier to the debate within feminism over essentialism and social construction. Social construction theory, though it owes much to orthodox Marxism, replicates in its most rigorously poststructuralist forms the very determinism that seems to deny the possibility of human agency for change even as it denies the lived experience of women as women (Alcoff 1988). The alternative of positionality elaborated by de Lauretis (1984) and Alcoff (1988) shares with the more explicitly Marxist standpoint theory an epistemology that makes experience and the struggle against oppression central elements without falling into a universalizing essentialism so vulnerable to rightist appropriation. There is a vast political difference, for example, between, on the one hand, valorizing the specific experience, knowledge, and struggles associated with being a mother and, on the other, speaking as if the reproductive capacity of a female human being constituted her only relevant essence.[13] Studies of women in antiquity (for example, Pomeroy 1975; Keuls 1985) which have focused on the distinctly diverse roles fulfilled by women help to dispel the implicit essentialism of a primary emphasis on the ancient mother. Nonetheless, an explicit theorization of the complexities of positionality or standpoint theory might be clarifying. Most obviously, for example, the perspective on childbearing of the noncitizen female prostitute in classical Athens would have been radically different from that of the citizen wife, whose primary social function was to produce a legitimate male heir. But the chief attraction of standpoint theory in the study of women in antiquity is its theorization of the validity of contemporary women scholars taking their own experience and epistemological standpoint as a valid ground for posing the sorts of questions of the ancient evidence that are unlikely to occur to male scholars. Again it is not a matter of imposing the answers on the data. Indeed, one could well argue that contemporary women scholars of antiquity have—because of their feminist standpoint—a greater stake in getting at the truth of the past than males, who have until recently been quite content with a version of ancient history that left the female half of the species entirely out of the picture. Precisely to the extent that an accurate critique of the past is a key component in envisioning a more tolerable future, women have a special stake in the "thickest" possible description of the situation of women in antiquity.[14]

Jameson moves from his Marxian defense of feminist standpoint theory to his characteristic concern for the utopian movement in this process:

> Such an analysis is finally not complete until the identification of the "moment of truth" of group experience—itself negative and positive all at once, an oppressive *restriction* which turns into a *capacity for new kinds of experience* and for seeing features and dimensions of the world and of history masked to other social actors—is prolonged by an epistemological articulation that translates such experience into *new possibilities* of thought and knowledge (Jameson 1988: 70, my emphasis).

I think this deep linkage of a standpoint epistemology with a quest for new options is among the most central affinities between Marxist and feminist methodology. Pure critique stripped of a mobilizing vision of a better world can simply reinforce acquiescence in an intolerable status quo by spelling out the subtlety of the mechanisms of oppression (Alcoff 1988: 418–19). Donna Haraway's cyborg essay, for example, which repeatedly critiques the oppressive naivety of old quests for a single origin or a master narrative, is itself the best example I have encountered recently of just the sort of strategic totalization Jameson has in mind. Haraway offers a dazzling if always provisional assessment of what are the real forces at work in the contemporary world—in all sorts of science, information theory, social theory, literary theory, feminist theory—consistently focused on the real conditions of possibility for envisioning an enabling myth for an alternative future. It is not then surprising that she characterizes her point of departure as a kind of socialist feminist blasphemy—where the point of "blasphemy" is precisely that it takes orthodoxy seriously.[15]

Image and Reality versus Ideological Critique

This totalizing from a critical standpoint implies a mode of reading evidence radically different from the mode of either the antiquarian empiricist, the enlightened cultural anthropologist, or the poststructuralist. Marx in the *German Ideology* already offered the most cutting assault on the empiricist and idealist dogma that elucidating the author's own intentions and in general the self-conception and self-presentation of a given historical period are the only legitimate aspirations of a historian—just the point where Griffin chides Halperin and Winkler. Marx writes,

> Whilst in ordinary life every shopkeeper is very well able to distinguish between what somebody *professes* to be and what he really *is,* our historiography has not yet won this trivial insight. It takes every epoch at its word and believes that everything it says and imagines about itself is true (Marx and Engels: vol. 5, 62).

Jameson has elaborated in earlier work the implications of Marx's own mode of reading evidence, which Jameson (borrowing from Ricoeur) dubbed a *double hermeneutic* (Jameson 1971: 118–21). More recently, in *The Political Unconscious,* without abandoning the double hermeneutic, he elaborates a *symptomal* (Jameson 1981: 56–57) reading that owes much to Althusser's pupil Macherey (1978). The "negative" side of the hermeneutic operation in assessing cultural data focuses on all the ways they perpetuate and reinforce the oppressions, the multiple injustices of the status quo. These complicities may involve simple distortions, but most often they involve a "structured silence," a major omission of some troubling reality that nonetheless leaves symptoms. Thus for example, the Homeric poems—especially the *Iliad*—give the surface impression that the only source of material wealth worth discussing is war, rapine, murder, or deadly male games. Peasant agricultural production (in which women and children participated) and productive female work within the household are thus largely a "structured silence"; but they leave symptomal traces in passing allusions to weaving, in the similes, and in the sustained description of Achilles's shield (see especially *Iliad* 18.555 and 567–68). But beyond this *negative* hermeneutic operation, cultural data must also be sifted for the *positive* element they contain or adumbrate—all the factors, including formal innovation, that affirm or point to a utopian aspiration toward more just and humanly gratifying social organization.

I will venture two brief illustrations of how a double hermeneutic might be applied to classical works—one Greek, one Roman. Some years ago a feminist classicist posed the problems of Plato's discourse on women in the *Republic* in terms of the paradoxical title, "Plato: Misogynist, Paedophile, and Feminist" (Wender 1973). The article is a model of subtle learning deployed with high wit. The fundamentally psychoanalytic answer Wender offers to the paradox with which she has confronted us merits serious consideration in any comprehensive account of the aetiology of Plato's proposals about women. But the choice of a fundamentally individual explanation comes after a tantalizing glance at a political analysis. "Clearly," she notes, "something was going on about women in the last part of the fifth century" (Wender 1973: 83). Something was also going on about the claims of the old aristocracy of birth to continued hegemony in democratic Athens and in Greece at large. A negative hermeneutic would explore all the ways in which Plato's proposals about women represent the simultaneous effort to respond to and contain more radical ideas about general liberation of women— ideas of which we get persistent if grotesquely distorted evidence in Aristophanes's late comedies—and at the same time project a new ground for establishing the old prestige of specifically inherited excellence, a value overwhelmingly of interest to males and, as I have suggested above, deeply intertwined with a whole array of factors oppressing women in ancient Greece.

Aristophanes's *Lysistrata* (411 B.C.E.) portrays a rebellion of women against the long war of Athens against the Spartan alliance. Mixed in with lots of sexual and sexist joking is a poignant protest against the real deprivations that the war has caused women and, more significant for a reading of Plato, an insistence that the total exclusion of women from participation in political decisionmaking was scarcely justified either by the performance of men in that area or by the intelligence level of women. Eva Keuls has even suggested that allusions in the text of this play to the women's festival of the Adonia in conjunction with protests against the Sicilian expedition (*Lysistrata* 387–98) fit with an allusion in the same play to men's fears of the "herm choppers" (*Lysistrata* 1093–94): she concludes that women may have been responsible for the mysterious incident in which statues of the god Hermes were deprived of their usual phallic excrescences (Keuls 1985: 387–95). She goes on to suggest that it is probable that "a certain feminism was in the air" in Athens in the late fifth century and relates it directly through Socrates to the radical proposals of Plato, whom she dubs "the Western world's first feminist" (Keuls 1985: 402).

Nearer to Plato's *Republic* in date, Aristophanes's *Ecclesiazousae* (*Women in Assembly,* c. 393–91 B.C.E.) depicts an actual takeover of the Athenian political assembly by women. Though most readers find this later play less than sympathetic to women's political aspirations, it is a reasonable inference that an idea that seemed to provoke such savage irony from the male comic poet was not sheer invention but represents a response to real women's expressed discontents and aspirations to full political equality. Thus a negative hermeneutic of the *Republic* would take account of the ways in which the proposals about women may seek to contain broad demands for restructuring the democracy to include all Athenian female citizens. Certainly Plato is at pains to stress the general inferiority of women as a category to men as a category, while focusing on the exceptional women who, he acknowledges, distinctly surpass many males (*Republic* 5.455c4–d5). His entire project aims at solving the crisis of the Athenian (and Greek) aristocracy by a program of rigorous eugenics and totalitarian control of education to produce a new super race of rulers. Such rulers would be a living refutation of the demonstrated incapacity—underlined by the sophists— of aristocrats consistently to produce offspring fit to rule. They would also supersede the sophistic attempt to supplant aristocratic "breeding" by education as the decisive factor in political ability.

It is primarily as worthy breeders for this ruling class that Plato opens education and political power to those few women who meet his criteria and could survive the elaborate testing he imposes. The key vehicle by which Plato introduces his radical proposals about women is the analogy of dog breeding which he has already used to stress the specialness of the male military elite he seeks to create. Perhaps precisely because of the severe questions which the sophists' critique of the aristocracy had raised about the efficacy of breeding alone—breeding unsupplemented by the proper nurture and education—Plato dare not ignore the possibility that the rearing and training of female hunting dogs contributes directly to the quality of their offspring. Accordingly, women who are to breed the master-race must receive the same rearing and education as men (*Republic* 5.451d4–e6). The analogy of dog breeding so fully exploited in Plato's argument looks back to a reactionary aristocratic line of argument at least as old as Theognis (183–92 West). As suggested earlier apropos of Heracles, the aristocratic obsession with inherited excellence goes a long way toward explaining the whole set of institutional practices aimed at controlling and policing female sexuality. Plato's proposals in many respects escalate and further systematize that controlling activity, at the same time clarifying its exclusive class-based function by confining control apparently only to women in the guardian class. Moreover, while essentializing women as breeders, the whole thrust of the proposals for the socialization of ruling-class women is to efface totally the "otherness" of women qua women (Irigaray 1985).

A positive hermeneutic would point to what Wender articulates so clearly: "Plato . . . advocated more liberation and privilege for [women] than any man in history had ever done, so far as we know" (Wender 1973: 82). The utopian leap by which the ideologue attempts to confront and answer threats to his class's position opens up a liberatory space because the persuasive character of ideological struggle requires some acknowledgement—in however distorted a form—of the very threats and demands that are the ideologue's target. The audience for this effort at persuasion is free to respond to the acknowledgement (in this case, the acknowledgement of the oppression of women) and refuse the proffered solution (a totalitarian breeding system that would permit a small elite of women to do all the types of work normally restricted to ruling-class males). Moreover, a whole set of liberatory inferences can be drawn from Plato's own arguments that radically exceed his own efforts at ideological closure on a narrow set of reforms. If, for example, the superiority of some women to some men has to be acknowledged by Plato, then no philosophically valid basis for institutionalized inequality in any sphere of life is left intact. If some women would make better rulers than some men, it would be foolish to exclude women qua women from all politics. If the logic of ruling class women exercising nude with ruling class men is defended, then the utter arbitrariness of the whole set of conventions controlling both the covering and the display of the female body in Greek society and art is implicitly acknowledged. A double hermeneutic of the *Republic* might thus elucidate both its circumscribing, controlling gestures and its substantial opening up of a utopian space where the logic of full liberation for women first makes its way into the public sphere.[16]

Vergil's *Aeneid* is in many respects a remarkably misogynist text. The systematic deployment throughout the narrative of emotionally unstable, potentially vindictive, and destructive female characters—for example, Juno, Dido, Allecto, Amata—suggests that some essential female evil is at the bottom of all the troubles in history. This evil associated with the sexual and reproductive aspects of women is, in typical misogynistic terms, itself emblematic of the disaster that the text seems to associate with all passion. To the best of my knowledge, one of the first explicitly feminist texts to take on the misogyny of the *Aeneid* was duBois's analysis of Dido as a *pharmakos*/scapegoat (duBois 1976). The telling evidence she cites for the politically motivated misogyny played out in the narrative treatment of Dido perfectly constitutes what I would call a negative hermeneutic of the poem—a spelling out of the text's complicity in sustaining an oppressive political, economic, and sexual order. At the same time, a number of the very elements which most compellingly confirm the ideological thrust of Dido's narrative function—the symbolic parallel to Carthage and to Cleopatra, the multiple levels on which Dido represents a threat to all that is figured in the poem as essentially "Roman"—are also data for any positive hermeneutic of the poem. Female rule as exemplified by the parallel of Cleopatra may be "an inversion, according to Augustan propaganda" (duBois 1976: 22); but the haunting echo of *dux femina facti* ("a woman was leader of the action," *Aeneid* 1.364) insists along with the narrative of her heroic achievements as a leader of a colony that women are fully credible in roles systematically denied them. The superb image of the efficient and humane queen at the end of Book 1, who "not unacquainted with misfortune, [is] learning to come to the aid of the wretched" (*non ignara mali miseris succurrere disco, Aen.* 1.630), similarly insists on a utopian fusion of the traditional stereotyped males' "arts of rule" with what the text marks as a specifically female modesty and generosity of spirit. The aura of shabbiness and insensitivity that clings to the departing Aeneas of Book 4 acknowledges the utter bankruptcy of the Augustan status quo, the defense of which seems to demand such intolerable sacrifices.

Moreover, the text's strongly positive investment in the Amazon type, the desexualized female warrior, does not simply confirm the pervasive fears of sexuality. It also opens up a utopian space that negates the whole world of male politics. In the iconography of fifth-century and fourth-century Greece the Amazons represent figures analogous to the Persian barbarians and the bestial centaurs: they are everything the male world of the polis is not, and, as such, are compulsively shown in defeat. The presence of the hunter goddess Artemis in battle against these alien forces confirms the founding hierarchies of the Greek polis (duBois 1982: 64–67). Vergil, however, fuses the female huntress with the female warrior figure in terms that celebrate the purity and freedom of the countryside against the complexities and political machinations of the overwhelmingly male world of the city. Aeneas in Book 1 is aided by his mother disguised as a Carthaginian huntress, who is in turn associated with the image of a Spartan or a Thracian maiden—figures that violate all the stereotypical roles for women in antiquity, but are represented in sympathetic and appealing terms (*Aeneid* 1.314–20). Aeneas immediately associates her with the goddess Diana, Rome's analogue of Artemis (*Aen.* 1.329), the same goddess with whom the poet soon associates Dido (*Aen.* 1.498–504). But first Aeneas views the representations of the Trojan War on the temple of Juno. The climactic figure among these images that first soothed his fear and stirred his hope (cf. *Aen.* 1.450–52) is the Amazon queen Penthesilea—not a monster, but an ally of the Trojans who, though a "maiden, dared to clash with men" (*Aen.* 1.493). One function of these images is to anticipate figures in the later Italian "replay" of the Trojan War (Troilus, for example, anticipates Pallas). The Amazon queen here looks forward to the figure of Italian Camilla in Book 12, a virgin devoted to Diana, a brave warrior slain deviously by a cowardly male. The text of the *Aeneid* celebrates these images of strong, independent women in imagery that links them with the whole range of pastoral repudiation of the male world of politics. Together the positive image of Dido as leader and queen and these images of warrior virgins who escape the impositions of the "normal" world ruled by men effect a dramatic, utopian negation of the more obvious misogynistic ideology in the poem.

In the case of Plato, the application of a double hermeneutic makes no assumptions about the personal, individual motives of the ideologue beyond the presumed intention of countering a presumed threat. So too in the case of the *Aeneid* there is no necessity to psychologize the author in order to explain the mixed message of the text. The ideological function, which Jameson once described as "psychic horsetrading" (Jameson 1979b: 141), inevitably pursues its persuasive function by raising impossible desires that the status quo cannot finally satisfy. Yet there is no barrier to exploring whatever additional factors contribute to the overwhelming impression of so many readers of the *Aeneid* that the constantly deferred and frustrated dream of peace, quiet, love—of some final personal gratification—is more emotively compelling that the vision of achieved empire (compare Wiltshire 1989).

I am well aware that the foregoing analyses may be too brief or too selective to be entirely compelling. In asserting the continued value and relevance to feminist approaches of the analytic methods of Marx and of authors clearly in the Marxian tradition, I have tried to emphasize the complementary role such analytic perspectives might play—not only to work already being done in the field of classics but to the significant theoretical work carried on by contemporary feminism. Marxism can play that role indeed only to the extent that it is itself recast and renewed by feminist theory.

Notes

I would like to thank, in addition to the editors, Page duBois, Phyllis Culham, Judith de Luce, Valerie French, Judith Hallett, Susan Jarratt, Diana Robin, Marilyn Skinner, and Bella Zweig for helpful and honest criticism of earlier drafts. I regret that I am far from being able to respond adequately to all the valid questions they have raised.

1. For a more sanguine view of the openness of the field of classics to feminist approaches see Hallett 1983: 25.

2. *Arethusa, Ramus, Arion,* and (ignoring, but not forgiving, some egregious crimes in the past) *Helios* have been notable exceptions. *Arethusa* certainly holds pride of place, but its all but unique distinction in this regard only confirms the general truth of Skinner's observation.

3. In addition to duBois's explicit use of Marx in her recent work (1988: 12–13, 22), she participated in a panel at the December 1989 meeting of the Modern Language Association, where she expressed her sense of the continuing compatibility and mutual benefit of Marxism and feminism. Her most recent book, *Torture and Truth* (1991), though it makes no explicit reference to Marx, seems, to me at least, unthinkable without her serious engagement in a full range of Marxist discourses.

4. Though the specific grounds are often different, there is a similar tone of disillusionment and categorical repudiation in Zillah Eisenstein's most recent pronouncement on the relation of Marxism and feminism (1989). She earlier (1979, reprinted in Hansen and Philipson 1990) articulated one of the more compelling cases for socialist feminism. For another recent dismissal of Marx see Nicholson 1987. Barrett, at the 1989 MLA meeting, expressed her sympathy for the post-Marxist positions of Laclau and Mouffe (1985); but I personally find *Women's Oppression Today* (Barrett 1988 [1980]) one of the best statements of the case for socialist feminism. Another "classic" personal favorite is Juliet Mitchell's "Women: The Longest Revolution," reprinted in Hansen and Philipson (1990). Nancy Fraser is one of the few contemporary theorists of whom I am aware who uses the term "socialist-feminist" without apology. She calls for a "Struggle over Needs" and offers an "Outline of a Socialist-Feminist Theory of Late Capitalist Political Culture" (Fraser 1989: 161–87). My own perception of the work of bell hooks is that—despite her sustained critique of the various labels put upon or assumed by feminism—it represents perhaps the richest vein of contemporary socialist feminism. See hooks 1984, 1989, 1990. Gayatri Spivak—whose very "essence," so to speak, as a critic is to avoid being labeled—regularly engages Marxist discourses, particularly in her feminist criticism (see Spivak 1987: 77–92, 134–53). A footnote from 1982 nicely captures the militant indirection of her relationship to Marx: "I should add that the absence of Marxist issues in this paper signifies nothing that cannot be explained by the following conviction: as women claim legitimation as agents in a society, a congruent movement to redistribute the forces of production and reproduction in that society must also be undertaken. Otherwise we are reduced to the prevailing philosophy of liberal feminism: 'a moralistically humanitarian and egalitarian philosophy of social improvement through the re-education of psychological attitudes' (Charnie Guettel, *Marxism and Feminism* [Toronto: Women's Press, 1974], p. 3). As a deconstructi-

vist, my topic in the present essay is—can deconstruction help? That should not imply that I am blind to the larger issues outlined here" (Spivak 1982: 192).

5. For a fuller and perhaps even more depressing account of the relationship between socialist feminism and radical feminism during this period see Echols (1989: 103–37).

6. Among the more influential post-Marxist critics are Jean Baudrillard (1975), André Gorz (1982), François Lyotard (1984), and the teams of Hindess and Hirst (1975) and Laclau and Mouffe (1985).

7. In focusing on a review of work by two male classicists, I do not intend simply to replicate the androcentrism of which Skinner speaks. Rather I consider the lengthy treatment of this work in such a forum as a striking instance of that very androcentrism. To the best of my knowledge, major controversial work by female classicists does not make it into the pages of *The New York Review*. Bernard Knox, a frequent contributor to the *NYR* on classical subjects, did, to be sure, publish a rather disparaging, brief review of Eva Keuls's *The Reign of the Phallus* in the *Atlantic* (reprinted in Knox 1989: 110–15).

8. I am well aware that there is a strong current of essentialism in varying degrees *within* feminism. Di Stefano's critique of "Masculine Marx," for example, comes perilously close to asserting that no male brought up in a Western-style bourgeois family is capable of other than a misogynistic posture directed simultaneously at the domination of "nature" and of all women, since both are emblems of the engulfing mother. In addition to Alcoff and subsequent arguments in the text, see Fuss (1989). The feminist journal *differences* has a special issue devoted to the problem, "The Essential Difference: Another Look at Essentialism" (1989). Personally I find Spivak's notion of strategic essentialism (1987: 205) attractive as a "transcendence" of a seemingly impossible bind, but see her subsequent qualifications of the concept (Spivak 1989: 124–54).

9. One of Di Stefano's strongest points against Marx is Marx's failure to theorize the specificity of female reproductive and nurturing labor (Di Stefano 1991: 152–56), a point made earlier by Spivak (1987: 80–81) among others.

10. Di Stefano's harsh indictment (1991: 152, 156) of Marx's account of the emergence of human history and his alleged disparagement of the female role in human reproduction misses, I think, Marx's attempt to theorize the transition from simple food-gathering societies to those which emerged only after human beings succeeded in gaining substantial control over food production. That this revolution permanently altered the relationship of human beings to nature is indisputable. That theorizing this difference entails only a ruthlessly exploitative relationship to nature is another question. See Merchant (1980) and the introductory essay by Marxist economist James O'Connor in the new journal of socialist ecology *Capitalism, Nature, Socialism* (O'Connor 1989).

11. This is scarcely the place to attempt a full interpretation of this extraordinarily complex play. I would only say here that I suspect that the representation of the dark, misogynist psychopathic side of the hero so fully associated with his descent from Zeus in the first portion of the play is "structurally homologous"—to ape the terminology being questioned here—with the repudiation of the ideology of inherited

excellence as Heracles gropes his way in the latter portion of the play toward a notion of human excellence as a purely human construct.

12. Alcoff, following de Lauretis, effects a nice reversal by accusing most anti-essentialist analyses of the "totalization of language or textuality" of ignoring the role of habits and practices in the construction of meaning (Alcoff 1988: 431). The whole analysis she offers here of self-reflective experience and practice has fascinating affinities with the traditional Marxist concept of *praxis* (see entry in Bottomore 1983).

13. Gayatri Spivak counters this reproductive essentialism with an emphasis on the clitoris as the metaphor "woman-in-excess" (Spivak 1987: 151–53), but see also her discussion of the womb as a "workshop" (Spivak 1987: 80–81).

14. In speaking of "thick description" I am borrowing the terminology of anthropologist Clifford Geertz (1973: 3–30).

15. It is perhaps symptomatic of the creative renewal rather than outright rejection of socialist feminism in Haraway's piece that it has recently been reprinted as the final essay in the massive collection by Hansen and Philipson subtitled *A Socialist-Feminist Reader* (1990: 580–617).

16. This approach to the *Republic* is elaborated in the final chapter of my *Sons of the Gods* (Rose 1992: 351–69).

Bibliography

Alcoff, Linda. 1988. "Cultural Feminism versus Post-Structuralism: The Identity Crisis in Feminist Theory." *Signs* 13, no. 3 (Spring): 405–36.

Althusser, Louis. 1971. "Ideology and Ideological State Apparatuses." In his *Lenin and Philosophy and Other Essays*. Translated by Ben Brewster. New York: Monthly Review Press.

Arthur, Marylin B. 1973. "Early Greece: The Origins of the Western Attitude toward Women." *Arethusa* 6, no. 1 (Spring): 7–58.

Barrett, Michèle. 1988 [1980]. *Women's Oppression Today: The Marxist/Feminist Encounter*. Rev. ed. London: Verso.

Baudrillard, Jean. 1975. *The Mirror of Production*. Translated by Mark Poster. St. Louis: Telos Press.

Bottomore, Tom, et al., eds. 1983. *A Dictionary of Marxist Thought*. Cambridge, Mass.: Harvard University Press.

Carson, Anne. 1990. "Putting Her in Her Place: Woman, Dirt, and Desire." In Halperin et al. 1990, 135–67.

Clifford, James. 1988. *The Predicament of Culture: Twentieth-Century Ethnography, Literature, and Art*. Cambridge, Mass.: Harvard University Press.

Culham, Phyllis. 1986. "Ten Years after Pomeroy: Studies of the Image and Reality of Women in Antiquity." *Helios* 13, no. 2: 9–30.

———. 1990. "Decentering the Text: The Case of Ovid." *Helios* 17, no. 2: 161–70.

Culham, Phyllis, and Lowell Edmunds, eds. 1989. *Classics: A Discipline and Profession in Crisis?* Lanham, Md: University Press of America.

de Lauretis, Teresa. 1984. *Alice Doesn't: Feminism, Semiotics, Cinema.* Bloomington: Indiana University Press.

———. 1987. *Technologies of Gender.* Bloomington: Indiana University Press.

Diamond, Stanley. 1967. "Primitive Society in Its Many Dimensions." In Kurt H. Wolff and Barrington Moore, Jr., eds., *The Critical Spirit: Essays in Honor of Herbert Marcuse,* 21–30. Boston: Beacon Press.

Di Stefano, Christine. 1991. "Masculine Marx." In Mary Lyndon Shanley and Carole Pateman, eds., *Feminist Interpretations and Political Theory,* 146–63. University Park: The Pennsylvania State University Press.

duBois, Page. 1976. "The *pharmakos* of Virgil: Dido as Scapegoat." *Vergilius* 22: 14–22.

———. 1982. *Centaurs and Amazons: Women and the Pre-History of the Great Chain of Being.* Ann Arbor: University of Michigan Press.

———. 1988. *Sowing the Body: Psychoanalysis and Ancient Representations of Women.* Chicago: University of Chicago Press.

———. 1991. *Torture and Truth.* New York: Routledge.

Echols, Alice. 1989. *Daring to Be Bad: Radical Feminism in America 1967–1975.* Minneapolis: University of Minnesota Press.

Ehrenreich, Barbara. 1984. "Life without Father: Reconsidering Socialist-Feminist Theory." *Socialist Review* 73, vol. 14, no. 1 (January–February): 48–57. Reprinted in Hansen and Philipson 1990, 268–76.

Eisenstein, Zillah. 1979. "Developing a Theory of Capitalist Patriarchy and Socialist Feminism." In Zillah Eisenstein, ed., *Capitalist Patriarchy and the Case for Socialist Feminism,* 5–40. New York: Monthly Review Press. Reprinted in Hansen and Philipson 1990, 114–45.

———. 1989. "Rejecting 'Precise' Marxism for Feminism." *Rethinking Marxism* 2, no. 4 (Winter): 79–81.

Foley, Helene P. 1978. " 'Reverse Similes' and Sex Roles in the *Odyssey*." *Arethusa* 11: 7–26.

———. 1981a. "The Concept of Women in Athenian Drama." In Foley 1981b, 127–68.

———, ed. 1981b. *Reflections of Women in Antiquity.* New York: Gordon and Breach Science Publishers.

Fraser, Nancy. 1989. *Unruly Practices: Power, Discourse, and Gender in Contemporary Social Theory.* Minneapolis: University of Minnesota Press.

Fuss, Diana. 1989. *Essentially Speaking: Feminism, Nature, and Difference.* New York: Routledge.

Gamel, Mary-Kay. 1990. "Reading 'Reality.' " *Helios* 17, no. 2: 171–74.

Geertz, Clifford. 1973. *The Interpretation of Cultures.* New York: Basic Books.

Gorz, André. 1982. *Farewell to the Working Class: An Essay on Post-Industrial Socialism*. Translated by Michael Sonenscher. Boston: South End Press.

Gould, John. 1980. "Law, Custom and Myth: Aspects of the Social Position of Women in Classical Athens." *Journal of Hellenic Studies* 100: 38–59.

Gramsci, Antonio. 1971. *Selections from the Prison Notebooks*. Edited and translated by Quintin Hoare. New York: International Publishers.

Griffin, Jasper. 1990. "Love and Sex in Greece." Review of Halperin 1990 and Winkler 1990. *The New York Review of Books* 37, no. 5 (March 29): 6–12.

Hallett, Judith P. 1983. "Classics and Women's Studies." Working Paper No. 119, Wellesley College Center for Research on Women. Wellesley, Mass.

————. 1989. "The Women's Classical Caucus." In Culham 1989, 339–50.

Halperin, David M. 1990. *One Hundred Years of Homosexuality and Other Essays on Greek Love*. New York: Routledge.

Halperin, David M., John J. Winkler, and Froma Zeitlin, eds. 1990. *Before Sexuality: The Construction of Erotic Experience in the Ancient Greek World*. Princeton: Princeton University Press.

Hansen, Karen, and Ilene J. Philipson, eds. 1990. *Women, Class, and the Feminist Imagination: A Socialist-Feminist Reader*. Philadelphia: Temple University Press.

Haraway, Donna. 1985. "A Manifesto for Cyborgs." *Socialist Review* 80, vol. 15, no. 2 (March–April): 65–108.

Harding, Sandra. 1986. *The Science Question in Feminism*. Ithaca: Cornell University Press.

Harris, Marvin. 1968. *The Rise of Anthropological Theory: A History of Theories of Culture*. New York: Crowell.

Hartsock, Nancy C. M. 1985. *Money, Sex, and Power: Toward a Feminist Historical Materialism*. Boston: Northeastern University Press.

Hindess, Barry, and Paul Q. Hirst. 1975. *Pre-Capitalist Modes of Production*. London: Routledge and Kegan Paul.

hooks, bell. 1984. *Feminist Theory: From Margin to Center*. Boston: South End Press.

————. 1989. *Talking Back: Thinking Feminist, Thinking Black*. Boston: South End Press.

————. 1990. *Yearning: Race, Gender, and Cultural Politics*. Boston: South End Press.

Irigaray, Luce. 1985. *Speculum of the Other Woman*. Translated by Gillian C. Gill. Ithaca: Cornell University Press.

Jaggar, Alison M. 1988 [1983]. *Feminist Politics and Human Nature*. Totowa, N.J.: Rowman & Littlefield.

Jameson, Fredric. 1971. *Marxism and Form: Twentieth-Century Dialectical Theories of Literature*. Princeton: Princeton University Press.

————. 1979a. "Marxism and Historicism." *New Literary History* 10, no. 1 (Autumn): 41–74.

————. 1979b. "Reification and Utopia in Mass Culture." *Social Text* 1: 130–48.

————. 1981. *The Political Unconscious*. Ithaca: Cornell University Press.

————. 1988. "*History and Class Consciousness* as an Unfinished Project." *Rethinking Marxism* 1, no. 1 (Spring): 49–72.

Jardine, Alice, and Paul Smith, eds. 1987. *Men in Feminism*. New York: Methuen.

Johnson, Richard. 1986/87. "What Is Cultural Studies Anyway?" *Social Text* 16: 38–80.

Kelly, Joan. 1984. *Women, History, and Theory*. Chicago: University of Chicago Press.

Keuls, Eva. 1985. *The Reign of the Phallus: Sexual Politics in Ancient Athens*. New York: Harper and Row.

Knox, Bernard. 1989. *Essays Ancient and Modern*. Baltimore: The Johns Hopkins University Press.

Laclau, Ernesto, and Chantal Mouffe. 1985. *Hegemony and Socialist Strategy: Towards a Radical Democratic Politics*. Translated by Winston Moore and Paul Cammack. London: Verso.

Loraux, Nicole. 1990. "Heracles: The Super-Male and the Feminine." In Halperin et al. 1990, 21–52.

Lukács, Georg. 1971 [1921]. *History and Class Consciousness*. Translated by Rodney Livingston. Cambridge: MIT Press.

Lyotard, Jean-François. 1984. *The Postmodern Condition: A Report on Knowledge*. Translated by Geoff Bennington and Brian Massumi. Minneapolis: University of Minnesota Press.

Macherey, Pierre. 1978. *A Theory of Literary Production*. Translated by Geoffrey Wall. London: Routledge and Kegan Paul.

Marx, Karl. 1967 [1867]. *Capital: A Critique of Political Economy*. Translated by Samuel Moore and Edward Aveling. New York: International Publishers.

Marx, Karl, and Frederick Engels. 1975ff. *Collected Works*. New York: International Publishers (in progress).

McManus, Barbara F. 1990. "Multicentering: The Case of the Athenian Bride." *Helios* 17, no. 2: 225–35.

Merchant, Carolyn. 1980. *The Death of Nature: Women, Ecology, and the Scientific Revolution*. New York: Harper.

Moore, Henrietta L. 1988. *Feminism and Anthropology*. Minneapolis: University of Minnesota Press.

Nicholson, Linda. 1987. "Feminism and Marx: Integrating Kinship with Production." In Seyla Benhabib and Drucilla Cornell, eds., *Feminism as Critique*, 16–30. Minneapolis: University of Minnesota Pres.

O'Connor, James. 1989. "Political Economy of Ecology." *Capitalism, Nature, Socialism: A Journal of Socialist Ecology* no. 3 (November): 5–14.

Pomeroy, Sarah B. 1975. *Goddesses, Whores, Wives and Slaves*. New York: Schocken Books.

Rabinowitz, Nancy. 1986. "Female Speech and Female Sexuality: Euripides' *Hippolytos* as Model." *Helios* n.s. 13, no. 2: 127–40.

Richlin, Amy. 1992. *The Garden of Priapus: Sexuality and Aggression in Roman Humor*. New York: Oxford University Press. Revised edition of 1983, New Haven: Yale University Press.

Rose, Peter W. 1992. *Sons of the Gods, Children of Earth*. Ithaca: Cornell University Press.

Said, Edward W. 1983. *The World, the Text, and the Critic*. Cambridge, Mass.: Harvard University Press.

Scott, Joan Wallach. 1988. *Gender and the Politics of History*. New York: Columbia University Press.

Skinner, Marilyn, ed. 1986. *Rescuing Creusa: New Methodological Approaches to Women in Antiquity*. (*Helios* n.s. 13, no. 2.)

———. 1987. "Classical Studies, Patriarchy, and Feminism: The View from 1986." *Women's Studies International Forum* 10, no. 2: 181–86.

———. 1989. "Expecting the Barbarians: Feminism, Nostalgia, and the 'Epistemic Shift' in Classical Studies." In Culham and Edmunds 1989, 199–210.

Smith, Paul. 1988. *Discerning the Subject*. Minneapolis: University of Minnesota Press.

Spivak, Gayatri. 1982. "Displacement and the Discourse of Woman." In Mark Krupnick, ed., *Displacement, Derrida, and After*, 169–95. Bloomington: Indiana University Press.

———. 1987. *In Other Worlds: Essays in Cultural Politics*. New York: Routledge.

———. 1989. "In a Word: Interview." *differences* 1, no. 2 (Summer): 124–54.

Ste. Croix, G. E. M. de. 1970. "Some Observations on the Property Rights of Athenian Women." *Classical Review* 20: 273–78.

———. 1981. *The Class Struggle in the Ancient Greek World*. Ithaca: Cornell University Press.

Turner, Victor. 1967. *The Forest of Symbols*. Ithaca: Cornell University Press.

Vernant, Jean-Pierre, and Pierre Vidal-Naquet. 1988. *Myth and Tragedy in Ancient Greece*. Translated by Janet Lloyd. New York: Zone Books.

Wender, Dorothea. 1973. "Plato: Misogynist, Paedophile, and Feminist." *Arethusa* 6, no. 1: 75–90.

White, Hayden. 1973. *Metahistory: The Historical Imagination in Nineteenth-Century Europe*. Baltimore: The Johns Hopkins University Press.

White, Leslie A. 1959. *The Evolution of Culture: The Development of Civilization to the Fall of Rome*. New York: McGraw-Hill.

Wiltshire, Susan Ford. 1989. *Public and Private in Vergil's Aeneid*. Amherst, Mass.: University of Massachusetts Press.

Winkler, John J. 1990. *The Constraints of Desire: The Anthropology of Sex and Gender in Ancient Greece*. New York: Routledge.

Zeitlin, Froma I. 1978. "The Dynamics of Misogyny: Myth and Mythmaking in the *Oresteia*." *Arethusa* 11, nos. 1, 2: 149–84.

———. 1981. "Travesties of Gender and Genre in Aristophanes' *Thesmophoriazousae*." In Foley 1981b, 169–217.

10

Feminist Research in Archaeology: What Does It Mean? Why Is It Taking So Long?

Shelby Brown

Lewis Binford, a famous proponent of scientific archaeology, labels a feminist argument concerning archaeological gender bias "nonsense" (Binford 1989: 4). Ian Hodder, an opponent of "narrow scientism" in archaeology, emphasizes the importance of a "feminist perspective" (Hodder 1991: xiv, 168). Such divisiveness stems from deep conflicts about what archaeology is and how one can or should conduct archaeological inquiry. Neither author discusses a feminist approach to archaeology in any detail; rather, each uses feminist research as an example of what is wrong, or right, with recent developments in the field. A consciously feminist approach to archaeology has only emerged in the past decade, despite a quarter-century of feminist research in related disciplines of the humanities and social sciences, especially anthropology (Conkey and Gero 1991: 3–4; di Leonardo 1991a: 6–10).

Margaret Conkey and Janet Spector published the first feminist criticism of prehistoric Mediterranean and New World archaeology as late as 1984, with little effect on their peers, and no noticeable influence at all on classical archaeologists (Conkey and Spector 1984). Joan Gero and Margaret Conkey edited the first collection of feminist essays on gender research in prehistoric Mediterranean and New World archaeology in 1991 (Gero and Conkey 1991b; see also Walde and Willows 1991). The very notion of a feminist archaeology is not yet widely acknowledged or understood, and feminists are still in the process of defining their goals. What *is* a feminist approach to archaeology today? Why does archaeology seem unresponsive to feminism? And why do classical archaeologists rarely hear the word "feminist" at all?

This essay is a classical archaeologist's attempt to answer such questions about Mediterranean and New World archaeology. Much of what follows is intended for feminists and classicists; classical and prehistoric archaeologists have expressed many of these thoughts elsewhere, but usually only to one another. Feminists, classicists, and archaeologists are often unaware of each other's publications, or unprepared to evaluate each other's work fully when they do read it. This mutual ignorance is illustrated, for example, in the ongoing debates about the existence and significance of an all-powerful Mother Goddess in early Greek and Balkan religion. The interpretation of prehistoric figurines by the archaeologist Marija Gimbutas is crucial for the Goddess theories of both academic and so-called popular feminists, yet the response of professional archaeologists to her work is largely unknown outside the field. Meanwhile, archaeologists are often unaware of the positive impact of Gimbutas's theories in other academic fields, including classics.

I surveyed archaeological friends and colleagues about what they thought a "feminist archaeology" would be, and found their answers instructive. They generally agreed that feminist theory is primarily concerned with women and women's issues, and therefore with the interests of a "special interest" group, albeit a large one; that feminists can be aggressive in pointing out male bias and searching for information specifically about women; that this aggression is in itself not necessarily bad, but can make others uncomfortable and is no more valid than an undue focus on men; and, finally, that the term "gender studies" clearly includes men as well as women, and so is more balanced (i.e., less exclusive) than "feminist studies" or "women's studies." These reactions reflect what has been called the "ghettoization" of women's studies in the 1970s and 1980s, and the transition to a more inclusive terminology in the 1990s. The archaeologists I surveyed were uncomfortable with the adjective "feminist" and its association with an unpleasant kind of "me-tooism" (di Leonardo 1991a: 5) and negativism. I realized belatedly how embarrassed I myself felt about mentioning any of my own negative experiences as a woman in archaeology to any but the closest of friends.

The archaeological literature of the past decade that calls itself "feminist" can indeed be actively opposed to male bias in the field. Authors, male and female, vigorously take issue with many of the common attitudes toward interpreting the past. They stress the study of women and endorse a view of the ancient world incorporating women's experiences today. In the introduction to *Engendering Archaeology*, Gero and Conkey note the "appalling absence of concepts that tap women's experience" (Conkey and Gero 1991: 3). Nevertheless, archaeologists writing from a consciously feminist perspective clearly define the goals of feminist research more broadly than my survey of other archaeologists indicated, and have moved well beyond the stage of just "adding women and stirring" (Conkey and Williams 1991: 124; Wylie 1991: 39). The history of feminist debate within anthropology has taught that women, like feminists, are not a monolith, and vary in "racial, ethnic, class, sexual, age, regional, and national identities" (di Leonardo 1991a: 18). Gender is "necessarily embedded within other cultural and historical social institutions and ideologies such as status, class, ethnicity, and race" (Conkey and Gero 1991: 9). The study of gender relations in archaeology, as in other fields, therefore goes beyond evaluations of just the activities or positions of women to include other subordinated groups (Flax 1987: 622–23; Hodder 1991: 168–72).

Two major feminist goals emerge from the archaeological literature. The first is to reevaluate the biases of excavators regarding both the fixity of gender roles through time, and the greater importance of male activities or of artifacts (supposedly) made by men, for understanding past cultures. The second is to identify the intended viewers, buyers, or users of art and artifacts, and to consider what their values were and are. The analysis helps to show how the norms of society are maintained—and for whose benefit, and with what effect on others, particularly the less powerful. Both these feminist goals are linked to a broader tendency in archaeology to reflect generally on the relationship of a judging researcher and a subordinated subject.[1] In a feminist framework, one such subject would be "prehistoric women."

In his foreword to *Domination and Resistance*, Peter Ucko describes the inclusion in a World Archaeological Congress held in England in 1986 of nonacademics from varied backgrounds, who were "accustomed to being treated as 'subjects' of archaeological and anthropological observation," and had never before been admitted as "equal participants in the discussion of their own (cultural) past or present." Ucko stresses archaeology's "special responsibility in the creation and dispossession of identity" (Ucko 1989: ix). Such statements are an acknowledgment that archaeologists often function as external judges of what is meaningful within other cultures. We do so on two levels when carrying out our fieldwork: while excavating the remains of ancient cultures, we usually live as outsiders within modern societies. Many of us have gained field experience supervising the excavation of a trench by local workmen with whom we could hardly communicate. Often our allegiance is clearly to the ancient society and not the modern one, which sometimes even impedes our "progress into the past" with its present odd customs and rules.

My own introduction to feminist theory came about through reading feminist art history rather than feminist archaeology. At the time, my research was not even on women, but on the Roman arena. I contributed a chapter on arena-mosaics to a collection of essays on Greco-Roman antiquity, in which all the authors applied feminist theory in various ways to their subjects of study (Brown 1992; Richlin 1992). The study of gladiators, and an earlier interest in human sacrifice in the Mediterranean, had made me reflect on who was the assumed spectator or judge of others' behavior and images of that behavior. Feminist "gaze theory," often applied to representations of women intended for a male audience, was especially relevant to my research.[2] The various approaches to viewing more recent art illuminated ways of seeing ancient images from outside the viewpoint of their intended viewer, and outside his/her idea of that viewpoint as the only or the natural one.

In the Greek sense of theory as "looking at," a "watching of spectacles" (duBois 1988: 9), feminist theory was for me a "way of viewing" ancient images. The goal was to identify the assumptions and expectations of dominant spectators about themselves, and also their attitudes—often narrow, condescending, or abusive—toward the other, less powerful people around them. The "others" in my research were slaves, foreigners, outsiders, criminals, children, nonconformists, and troublemakers of various kinds. What made this "way of viewing" feminist was its foundation in women's experiences of "otherness"; its critical stance (in unmasking it also undermined the view that subordination of others is inherently logical or right); and its tacit admission that the researcher is not untouched by the subject and truly objective, but affected by the attitudes uncovered by his/her study. Such an approach is clearly relevant to many traditional subjects of classical art-historical study, such as Greek vase painting (in which roles of dominance and submission are regularly depicted) or Roman imperial sculpture (in which the enhancing of an emperor's image and the diminishing of an enemy's is a key theme).

From my initiation into "gaze theory," I progressed to reading everything I could find that associated the word "feminist" with archaeology. I discovered that female archaeologists simply do not discuss in public, either in print or in public talks, their problems as women in the field. The feminists who have recently challenged the field to review and abandon its androcentric practices concern themselves only with research. They do not reveal their personal experiences as students, teachers, or excavators, although these would show androcentrism in action on a daily basis, and perhaps help explain it. Their silence is surely not an indication that women archaeologists have no problems resulting from their gender. Although archaeology is in some ways unusually open to women, who make up a large proportion of those working on some aspect of ancient material culture, the discipline can also be very conservative in its unvoiced attitudes toward women in the field. Women succeed as dig directors, as tenured professors, and even as presidents of the Archaeological Institute of America (AIA), but many of them have had to put up with a great deal to get where they are, and have often faced problems different from the usual ones academic women confront.

Female archaeologists seem to take their problems for granted and to weigh them against the genuine love of the field, and especially of excavating, that so many of us feel. People who are willing to abandon reality every summer and go live in the middle of nowhere, often under difficult conditions, in order to get up at 5 A.M. and broil in the hot sun all day, are already on a different wave length. Diggers are alternately enthusiastic and discouraged, but generally united by the sheer love of solving puzzles about the past. Excavation is a great leveler, in that everybody gets hot, dirty, and sweaty. The ethos is definitely a "manly" one— love of hard work, hardship, roughing it—and a peculiar, hardy, "deal-with-it-or-get-out" mentality is generated.[3] This attitude does make sense, since archaeologists usually work under severe time pressure and with insufficient funds. Some directors do not want to spend money on luxuries, or even comfort, if it can be avoided. Yet even "rough and tough" female excavators and staff face problems on excavations that are rarely acknowledged.

The "dirt" archaeologists see themselves as better, on some level, than the "house" archaeologists and specialists who clean, restore, catalogue, draw, and analyze classes of artifacts. The field staff are, after all, out there on the real frontier, doing the sweaty work. In my experience, there are more women among the house staff, generally, than men. Those members of a dig who cross between the two spheres have to readjust their sources of self-esteem in small ways. On some excavations, I have served alternately as draftsperson and field supervisor, and although the shift in allegiance is minor and rarely deep, it is real. The photographers and architects who cross regularly between the two spheres are almost inevitably male. And the upper level dig "management" is still usually male. All of this is changing with time, of course. And does the primacy of a male ethos or power-structure really make a difference in the treatment of women? It can make a lot of difference.

Many directors are uncomfortable with women to some extent (although they may have favorite female students) with the inevitable result that they favor men. I have participated on digs where men were given better or more prestigious work to do, or could get away with extreme behavior—rudeness, drunkenness—that women would simply not have engaged in. Female complaints of male behavior came across as prudish. I have excavated at many different sites in western Europe, the Aegean, North Africa, and the Levant for the sake of the variety and the experience, and have at the beginning often been unfamiliar with what I was digging. Some male colleagues have felt free to come see and discuss my trench without consulting me, or have even made such a visit a test of my knowledge rather than an opportunity to share their information. This is a sort of excavation power playing that women seem more often to bear the brunt of than men. There is also sometimes a competitive element of digging illustrated by a need to "prove" oneself in fighting for tools or workmen, or by exhibiting knowledge, that can make many women uncomfortable. The further problem for women of supervising men who often do not want to be under the control of females is a fact of life on excavations that is rarely addressed. It is not insurmountable, since women in control can be accepted as honorary men. When I supervised a trench on an excavation in Egypt in the late 1970s, the workmen who were uncomfortable with female supervisors called us "Mister." "Male" is the norm, and women conform to it.

I have participated in excavations where the sexual relationships of the director or his friends with young students were taken as a matter of course. The "harem" effect of a largely female house staff has also at times intruded into women's desire for a professional relationship with a director who could not see his way past the gender of all those "dependent" females. The paucity of child care on excavations contributes to the "harem" effect by blocking out the real world of children. The few (if any) women with young children on digs are usually the wives of excavators, not excavators themselves. Female excavators with infants generally stop digging for some time, or leave their children at home. Husbands of professional archaeologists and other female contributors to excavations also rarely accompany them on excavations, whether to keep them company, watch the children, or participate in menial dig tasks. Wives more often join their husbands and contribute to the excavation as "house" staff by washing potsherds, cataloguing, or performing other jobs with low prestige.

Such experiences and observations of mine are validated by other women, but also accepted and balanced against the very real rewards of excavating and teaching archaeology. Perhaps astonishingly, we hardly ever discuss the problems, although they are the backdrop to the few feminist studies in archaeology published in the last ten years. The Archaeological Institute of America has never even had an internal organizational counterpart of the Women's Classical Caucus within the American Philological Association. Female archaeologists have apparently never deemed it necessary or appropriate to have a separate women's organization or newsletter within the larger Institute. In 1993, for the first time, the AIA has the opportunity to join forces with the WCC in a panel entitled "Feminist Approaches to Classical Art and Archaeology." This will again be a forum for the discussion of research strategies, not personal experiences. Why have women archaeologists been so reticent about sexist behavior in their everyday lives, and so slow even to note problems with androcentric research?

One explanation for women's silence about personal experiences is possibly that these are difficult to quantify and summarize in suitably objective archaeological language. Most of us are thoroughly trained to present ideas in neutral or "scientific" terms and to avoid sounding emotional about anything, except perhaps a glorious piece of classical sculpture or someone else's simplistic or subjective conclusion. Feelings and complaints also do not fit in with the archaeological ethos of "hardiness." Finally, despite any personal experiences to the contrary, women archaeologists tend to think of the field as one that does not discriminate against women, even if certain individuals do. Eastern women's colleges educated women in the subjects of ancient art history and archaeology from the late nineteenth century on (Donohue 1985: 4 n.5). My own undergraduate training in archaeology at Bryn Mawr College provided strong female role models who were well-known in their specialties. Famous female scholars have contributed to the field almost from its inception (Williams 1981). Many examples spring to mind, from the Cretan excavator Harriet Boyd Hawes (Allsebrook 1992) to the female scholars who dominated certain areas of Greek research in the early-to-mid-twentieth century, such as Lucy Shoe Meritt (architectural moldings) and Gisela Richter (Archaic sculpture, especially). But these women, and others working outside Greece, were exceptions to the male norm, and do stand out because they are female. A glance at the lists and photographs of the chairmen of the managing committee and the directors of the American School of Classical Studies in the course of this century—all male but for Mabel Lang—makes this clear for Greek archaeology (Meritt 1984: 300, 304, plates 10–12).

Archaeology's slow response to feminist research in related disciplines is perhaps easier to understand. It must be partly due to the field's fragmented interests and goals. There is an unfortunate but historically entrenched split in Mediterranean archaeology between prehistory and classical archaeology/art history. In particular, the traditions of scholarship within classical archaeology have discouraged new approaches to research on topics outside traditionally studied classes of objects, architecture, and sites. The two branches of Mediterranean archaeology are further separated within different academic disciplines to which they are subordinated. As a result, archaeology has had difficulty defining and criticizing its goals and sharing new ideas internally. These facts have limited the field's absorption of feminist theory.

Archaeological Schizophrenia and Feminist Theory: Whose Field Is This?

Most archaeologists who recognize the existence of feminist theory are working with (or as) anthropologists on the archaeology of the New World or on the prehistoric archaeology of the Old World and the Mediterranean. In this country, the Old World prehistory of western Europe is separated from so-called Mediterranean prehistory, including Greece, Italy, the Balkans, the Aegean islands, and Anatolia. Occasionally, a department of classics or classical studies with a strong focus on archaeology teaches both classical and prehistoric archaeology (of either the Old World or the Mediterranean, or both). More often, anthropology departments teach the prehistoric archaeology of the Old World along with that of the New World, leaving out the prehistoric archaeology of the Mediterranean.

Departments of classics or art history cover classical archaeology and sometimes Mediterranean prehistory. The Bronze Age may be included with either the Neolithic, under prehistory, or with the Iron Age, under classical archaeology. Anthropology departments do not teach Bronze Age or classical archaeology, and art history departments do not include prehistoric archaeology (although they may discuss artifacts labeled "prehistoric art" in certain courses). Also complicating matters is the designation of anthropology—since it includes physical anthropology—as a social science, and of classics and art history as humanities. Furthermore, so-called Near Eastern archaeology, including Egypt, the Levantine coast, western Phoenician colonies, Mesopotamia (and other Arab states) is further segregated into separate programs or included within departments of biblical studies. Thus, despite cross-cultural interaction of all sorts within the Mediterranean and between east and west, related fields are cut off from one another.

Archaeologists traditionally associated with anthropology have been introduced, through feminist anthropology, to developing feminist theories about how one can or should analyze culture. In the absence of ancient literary sources, many have also been drawn to ethnographic research for help in understanding their data. Through ethnography they encounter varied research subjects, often still alive and talking rather than fixed forever in text. This exposure sometimes seems to make it easier to remember that real people are involved and that there may be more than one side to a story. Prehistoric Mediterranean and New World archaeologists have mainly been the ones to reconsider excavation strategies from a feminist perspective and to evaluate a wide variety of excavated artifacts, including those sometimes defined as having artistic value. Classical archaeologists have focused primarily on certain classes of Greek and Roman art.

The two most reasonable sources of information about feminist theory for classical archaeologists are classics and art history. Classicists and classical archaeologists have many problems with communicating, however, despite their shared interests. James Wiseman's quotation from "one of this century's most distinguished professors of Greek" comes to mind: "Archaeologists are Classicists whose brains have sunk to their feet" (Wiseman 1980: 279). In turn, archaeologists often scorn classicists in a friendly fashion as "book-bound" types who cannot picture the physical world in which their subjects of study operated. Archaeologists generally do not understand literary criticism, and classicists cannot judge primary sources of archaeological data, and so rely on syntheses that "sound right" to them (such as Gimbutas's publications on Goddess figurines). Classical archaeology's tie with traditional art history and collecting has meanwhile worked against its absorption of recent feminist art criticism. Feminist analyses of ancient art undertaken in the past decade have appeared in volumes edited by classicists, anthropologists, and art historians rather than by classical archaeologists.

Classical archaeology developed from a Renaissance interest in Greek and Roman texts, which expanded to include classical art and architecture. Aristocratic European collectors of classical antiquities were spurred on in the eighteenth century by the treasure-hunting excavations carried out at Pompeii and Herculaneum. Research into antiquity functioned to provide a glorious past for European aristocrats, especially Italians (Trigger 1989: 35–36). The field is thus linked to the ideologies of certain classes of men, and historically has involved the relegation of women to the sidelines. C. M. Hinsley describes European archaeology of the second half of the nineteenth century as concerned with "notions of colonial power and appropriation, technological prowess, and male presentation of treasures to metropolitan females" (Hinsley 1989: 88). Women participated as "audience, helpmates, or preservators," forecasting the prominence of women on the staffs of archaeology museums today, although not often in the highest positions (Hinsley 1989: 94).

In its inception in the plundering of tombs and sites in Italy, archaeology was the collecting arm of antiquarianism and what was eventually to become classical art history. Classical archaeology has been tied ever since to the collecting and displaying of "good art" and the value judgments that accompany the identification of "art" as well as the definition of "good" (hence the traditional focus, for example, on fine wares rather than household ceramics, and patrician or imperial rather than plebeian imagery).[4] From early antiquarianism was born a role of classical and, often, Bronze Age archaeology as validator of textual information (Troy really did exist), promoter of the great works of famous men (Praxiteles really was a great sculptor), and arbiter of the aesthetic works of highly "civilized" cultures (McNally 1985: 2). Definitions of what constitutes good art or a good artist have often effectively shut out women from the art historical canon, even when women have produced art. They have also led us to accept unquestioningly the natural artistic superiority or value of certain types of images (Nochlin 1988: 145–75; Salomon 1991: 223–27).

Many collectors of classical antiquities were also interested in other ancient objects of less clear origin, such as stone tools and fossils. Gradually, antiquarians recognized that some of these curiosities were material evidence for the existence of early, so-called primitive peoples. Without the aid of written records, however, it seemed impossible to order the earlier, nonclassical finds chronologically, except as pre-Roman. The first chronology of archaeological artifacts that did not rely on ancient written evidence—although it did go back to ancient ideas of cultural stages—was established in 1816. On the basis of biblical evidence and some data from excavation, Christian Thomsen carefully ordered a national collection of Danish antiquities into three rough chronological ages: Stone, Bronze, and Iron (Renfrew 1980: 287; Trigger 1989: 78). Thomsen's technique for relative dating was largely ignored elsewhere in Europe. There, developments in geology and evolutionary biology revealed the possibility of uncovering a long and changing human past through examination of a stratified material record. These fields had a tremendous impact on what eventually became the separate discipline of prehistoric archaeology (Trigger 1989: 87–94).

In the third quarter of the nineteenth century, recognition of the chronological significance of stratigraphy was a major breakthrough, permitting consideration of excavated artifacts as more than a meaningless jumble. A related emphasis on major stages of evolution and human "progress," however, was a product of the intellectual climate of the times, which continues to influence archaeological research. Just as the interests of classical archaeologists tended to obscure women, so the judgmental, macroscale focus of prehistory on a progression of assumed male achievements helped make women invisible and gender issues seem irrelevant in archaeology.[5] To oversimplify: prehistorians became increasingly goal oriented (specifically, interested in human origins and stages of development through time); classical archaeologists continued to focus on identifying and classifying good art, largely for its own sake, or on finding and excavating famous places. The goals of classical and Bronze Age archaeologists overlapped when the latter were motivated to discover sites, such as Troy, immortalized in texts.

This historical division between classical and prehistoric Old World and Mediterranean archaeology is paralleled by a split between the archaeology of the Old World and the New (the Americas). Prehistorians studying ancient societies were united with anthropologists studying modern cultures in their focus on "primitive" peoples. In the United States, New World archaeology and anthropology merged (McNally 1985: 3). American archaeologists were not researching their own ancestors, but rather those of contemporary peoples generally regarded as inferior. As Walter Taylor succinctly put it in 1948 in his book about American archaeology, "The point upon which the archaeological stream is observed to split is the literacy, the 'primitiveness,' and perhaps the artistic quality of its subject cultures" (Taylor 1948: 22).

The stated interests of the Archaeological Institute of America, founded in 1879, included classical and biblical studies and both Old and New World archaeology (Donohue 1985: 3–4). Nevertheless, the AIA's primary focus was classical archaeology. The first annual report of the AIA in 1880 stated: "The study of American archaeology relates, indeed, to the monuments of a race that never attained to a high degree of civilization . . . whose intelligence was for the most part of a low order. . . . From what it was or what it did nothing is to be learned that has any direct bearing on the progress of civilization" (cited in Renfrew 1980: 291). In contrast, study of the Greek and Roman past supposedly contributed to the understanding of our own civilization's origins and goals. Classical archaeologists claimed "a special position for themselves as the interpreters of an especially important civilization" (Dyson 1989: 131).

Despite its perceived role in preserving a noble past, classical archaeology in the United States suffers from an inferiority complex "reinforced by the regular importation of European professors throughout the history of the discipline," which has helped to keep the subfield conservative and to segregate it from "more dynamic branches of archaeology" (Dyson 1989: 130–31). Not so surprisingly, these imported professors are usually male. The essentially conservative, monolithic nature of classical archaeology is illustrated by the fact that the *American Journal of Archaeology* (the professional journal of the AIA) showed little interest as late as 1985 in innovative approaches to archaeology as compared with the anthropological journal *American Antiquity* (Dyson 1985); and "a 1985 AIA program was not materially different from one in 1935" in either format or paper topics (Dyson 1989: 133). Another source of conservatism in classical archaeology has been the existence of traditional, hierarchical archaeological academies overseas (the American School of Classical Studies in Athens; the American Academy in Rome), which influence the interests and excavation strategies of archaeologists and are invested in maintaining the archaeological/ art historical status quo (Dyson 1981: 9–11, 1989: 134; Small 1992: 164).

Finally, field archaeology's traditional role as a technique for supplying data is another problem related to the fragmentation of the discipline and archaeologists' divergent interests. As the so-called handmaiden of history and other fields (Cole

1985: 50), archaeology has in the past been treated as a method of excavation either divorced from theoretical concerns, or borrowing them from others as needed. Of course, excavators have always operated on the basis of theoretical concerns, whether or not they think about them or make them explicit. In classical archaeology the unstated assumption was often that uncovering a temple was simply a good thing to do, or that establishing the nature of stylistic change in marble sculpture was worthwhile in and of itself (Manning 1990: 257). New World and prehistoric Mediterranean archaeologists have addressed the question, "What should the goals of archaeology be?" in numerous ways over the last half-century, although classical archaeologists have not learned a great deal from their debates. The problem for feminists and others interested in issues of gender has been that both the unarticulated and the explicitly stated assumptions and goals of archaeologists have often either left questions about gender unanswered or defined culture in terms of male roles and values.

From Static Present to Dynamic Past:
The Archaeology of Men and Genderless People?

Many of the goals of archaeology as practiced today in the United States were heavily influenced by a revolution of sorts which took off in the early 1960s at the hands of a group of anthropologists, New World archaeologists, and prehistorians of varied interests (Gibbon 1989: 61–90).[6] This revolution, labeled the "New" Archaeology, in many ways deflected archaeologists' attention from the study of gender relations and other feminist issues. In the early 1970s, when feminist anthropologists began to discuss the problem of male bias in reporting on and interpreting human culture, many archaeologists' attention was focused on the debates about the new approaches.

One of the chief forces behind the New Archaeology was an anthropologist, Lewis R. Binford. As a New World archaeologist, Binford defined archaeology as anthropology, and was dissatisfied with how little archaeology was contributing to what he identified as anthropology's aims: "to explicate and explain the total range of physical and cultural similarities and differences characteristic of the entire spatial-temporal span of man's existence" (Binford 1972a: 93). While granting that the archaeology of the past 50 years had greatly advanced knowledge of the "diversity which characterizes the range of extinct cultural systems," Binford thought that it had failed to explain the "operation and structural modification" (or "processual" or "systemic" change) of total cultural systems, which included people's adaptation to the environment (Binford 1972a: 93, 101). He also focused attention on a serious problem in archaeology, namely the inability of many excavators to state their theoretical goals (Binford 1972b: 160). Binford stressed the desirability of framing hypotheses and testing predictions based on them, rather than simply drawing conclusions based on unstated assumptions, and then assuming that they were right. New Archaeology modeled its inquiries after those of the hard sciences and developed its own terminology. Perhaps most important, the New, scientific archaeology seemed to hold forth the possibility of establishing neutral, predictive truths about people in the past who reacted passively and predictably in the aggregate to external stimuli.[7]

Put simply, the goal of archaeology was either to derive objective, scientific explanations for cultural processes and changes mainly in group behavior, as Binford wanted to do; or to develop more ambiguous, relative, contextual explanations for the cumulative effects of individual actions, as more "culture-historical" archaeologists wanted to do (Sabloff 1981: 4). The still ongoing debate is often adversarial (Wylie 1991: 48)[8] and simplistically polarized in its struggle between objectivism and relativism (Manning 1990: 262), despite the existence all along of varied approaches to archaeological data and multiple labels to cover them (New Archaeology is most often called "processual," and subsequent, different, or opponent approaches "postprocessual").[9] Kent Flannery summed up the essence of the debate of the 1960s as "whether archaeology should be the study of culture history or the study of cultural process," defining the concern of the process theorist as not ultimately "with 'the Indian behind the artifact' but rather with the system behind both the Indian and artifact" (Flannery 1972: 105; Hodder 1985: 7). Feminists, who not only wanted to see Indians, but specifically male and female Indians, found themselves in the camp of the culture historians.

A focus on the "system" did not preclude an interest in gender, yet a lack of interest was one result of systems-theory (Conkey and Spector 1984: 22; Wylie 1991: 35). To those interested in macroscale processes, gender seemed irrelevant; the terms "people" or "Indians" were clear enough. Even classical archaeologists were influenced to borrow some of the resources of natural science, perform quantitative and statistical analyses, and look beyond Great Works to "nameless human beings in groups" (William McDonald, cited in Wilkie and Coulson 1985: xvi). Systems-theorists in particular focused on changes in the environment and in technology as more knowable and causal of cultural change than social or symbolic factors; and they then tended to define "technologies" (of stone tools, for example) in terms of presumed male achievements and activities (Conkey and Williams 1991: 108–10; Gero 1991: 168–69). Archaeologists newly in search of methodological rigor now also questioned the possibility of deducing gendered behavior at all from ambiguous material evidence (as opposed, for example, to more easily identifying the physiological sex of skeletons or statues).

No archaeologist can ignore the limitations of excavation (Renfrew 1984: 3–4; Salomon 1982: 40). Excavators are directly concerned with material remains and their contexts rather than with people and their relationships. The remains reflect human behavior in the past, but the link between an artifact in a particular context in the ground and the social role and the conscious and unconscious thoughts, feelings, and intentions of a person who made or used it is tenuous. There are also inevitable gaps in the preserved record, and archaeologists rarely have enough time, money, or inclination to excavate all of what does remain.

Excavation itself is furthermore a destructive process. In uncovering artifacts one destroys their contexts—their vertical and horizontal relationships with other objects, structures, and natural features—which help establish their meaning. When archaeologists fail to notice or record information, it is often lost forever. The question of what we can meaningfully ask about the "dynamic" past (Sabloff 1981: 3) from its "static," unsatisfactory remains, and how to go about finding the answers, is therefore crucial in archaeology.[10]

I would argue that, while it is often true that gender relations and activities cannot be securely identified in the physical record of the past, that is no reason to ignore them. Archaeologists regularly try to interpret other social and cultural constructs (aspects of status, for example) from data equally removed from those constructs. They have not attempted to develop theoretical and practical strategies for uncovering gender mainly because they have not considered it important or relevant. The interests of excavators, together with the prohibitive expense of excavation, often result in a focus on "special" artifacts and monumental architecture or on evidence for progress, change, and "firsts" (origins). Classical archaeologists may focus on large-scale architecture and public spaces (temples, fora), which they discuss in terms of their aesthetic qualities or as loci of male activities. Prehistorians, especially in the absence of "impressive" architecture, may attempt "complete coverage" by digging vertically. They search for small amounts of information about change in stages, from many layers, in deep trenches dug if possible to the bottom of a site (to sterile soil or bedrock). Women often either did not play, or are not seen as having played, a significant role in stages of aesthetic or technological "progress" as traditionally measured. Horizontal excavation of public places and vertical excavation of deep trenches also limit the broad search for "local, internal structuring principles" (Wylie 1991: 34), or for information about the microscale organization of households (Tringham 1991: 125), in which women clearly took part and are perhaps more difficult to ignore. Feminist authors, however, cite the increasing body of evidence for gender as a crucial factor in the structuring of social relations, and hence of material culture, on both the macro- and microscale (Conkey and Spector 1984: 19–21). How then can archaeologists engender the physical record of the past on both these levels?

Whose Past? Approaches to Engendering Archaeology

The first publication to view archaeology explicitly "through the lens of feminist criticism" was an article in the journal *Advances in Archaeological Method and Theory*. In it, Margaret Conkey and Janet Spector highlighted the lack of an archaeological framework for "conceptualizing and researching gender and . . . social roles" and deplored archaeology's role in "substantiating contemporary gender ideology" (Conkey and Spector 1984: 1–2). In spite of archaeologists' claims of objectivity, Conkey and Spector showed that researchers had been neither objective nor inclusive but had adhered to a particular "gender mythology," and that the approaches and goals of science had tended to reenforce male bias rather than provide objective, deductive purity in collecting and interpreting data.[11]

Conkey and Spector illustrated some of archaeology's androcentric, ethnocentric assumptions about gender roles as fixed, and they documented the field's acceptance of a male subject's or researcher's view of his society as the representative one. Their survey included literature on "the entire temporal span of human existence" from early hominids through contemporary gatherer-hunters (Conkey and Spector 1984: 6). The archaeological response to this essay was minimal. Margaret Ehrenberg only briefly noted its existence in her useful but atheoretical book, *Women in Prehistory* (1989), which generally assumed "womanness" as a "cross-cultural given" (Bender 1991: 213). In *Engendering Archaeology*, published in 1991, Conkey and Joan Gero observed that archaeologists continued to make the same "troublesome assumptions about gender" identified by Conkey and Spector in 1984 (Gero and Conkey 1991a: xi).

As one familiar example of androcentrism in archaeology, Conkey and Spector cited the well-known man-the-hunter model of human evolution, which rigidly defines gender roles and emphasizes the activities presumed to be male. The result of this bias for the interpretation of the archaeological record is the assumption that certain artifacts are inevitably linked with one gender (projectile point—male, pot—female: Conkey and Spector 1984: 7, 10; Conkey and Williams 1991: 111; di Leonardo 1991a: 7). Archaeologists hardly ever describe the female half of this model, woman-the-gatherer, in the same detail, or consider stages or supposed revolutions in human development in terms of the contributions of women (Conkey and Williams 1991: 115–17). In a similar vein, Gero notes the biases archaeologists reveal in their analyses of stone tools. Male archaeologists' experimental programs for testing tool use emphasize "male activities" such as hunting. In contrast, women experiment with using tools for tasks such as nutting and leatherworking. The same dichotomy occurs in modern experiments with making stone tools, since flintknapping is recognized as "publicly male territory." Ethnographers describing toolmakers and users in action focus on males, even when females also make and use tools, and emphasize a narrow range of activities. In these ways, "constructs of archaeological interpretation interact with modern gender ideology" (Gero 1991: 167–68).

How *can* one associate artifacts with behavior, much less gendered behavior, especially in the absence of written evidence? Even if researchers do question their own present-day assumptions, and decide to evaluate archaeological data on the basis of parallels with modern ethnographic or ancient-historical evidence, is this a real improvement? Archaeologists have tackled the problem of engendering the prehistoric or ahistoric past in a variety of ways. Several authors have shown that a traditionally rigorous methodology of excavation and artifact analysis can be applied in an innovative way to reveal, rather than disguise, gender and document it as a variable, complex social process. Before teaming up with

Conkey, Spector had been evaluating an approach to testing ethnographic evidence for gendered behavior against the archaeological record.[12] This kind of testing is a necessary precursor to building general theory, one of the goals of processual archaeology.[13] Spector's strategy was similar to one used by Binford himself when he compared the butchering practices of contemporary Eskimo hunters with the animal remains they left behind, in order to understand better the distribution patterns of bones on archaeological sites.

Using ethnographic data, Spector studied the task organization of the Hidatsa men and women of the Great Plains, considering "spatial, temporal, and material dimensions" of their execution of tasks. Her assumption was that patterns of activity would be reflected in "the frequency, variability, and distribution of material remains and the spatial arrangements and physical characteristics of structures and facilities," permitting her to make a correlation between dynamic, gendered behavior and the archaeological record.[14] Her main concern was with the role gendered behavior could play in shaping the responses of populations to changes in their social or natural environments (Spector 1983: 78–79). Elizabeth Barber documented a more direct, geographically broader association of gendered behavior with specific physical remains. She consistently linked a wide variety of evidence (including archaeological) for Neolithic and Bronze Age cloth and non-prestigious textile-making equipment with female spinners and weavers. Barber suggests that we now have a way to follow the movements of women and whole families, rather than just warriors or traders, by tracking "invasions" of textile equipment (Barber 1991: 283–98).

Increasingly, however, feminists resist the idea that the study of gender depends upon the absolute association of particular material remains with one sex or the other. They illustrate that even the process of asking questions, from a perspective that views women as integrated participants in human history, results in a substantial improvement both in research strategies and in the awareness of alternative interpretations of the past (Conkey and Gero 1991: 11–12; Wylie 1991: 32). Many of the authors publishing in *Engendering Archaeology* suggest new ways of viewing the material record to illuminate possible female roles, but without assuming that their models of antiquity necessarily represent "the" correct answer. Ironically, both sides of the still ongoing processual-postprocessual debate are equally concerned with the problem of the researcher's subjective biases and his/her conscious or unconscious reliance on personal views of what is right.

Lewis Binford believes that his kind of archaeology involves the development of reliable means to justify inferences, while the postprocessual kind embodies the identification of "products" of archaeologists as "good" or "bad" based on their personal, contemporary values (Binford 1989: 4). He cannot see how becoming "self-aware" can help matters (although many of us might ask, how can it not?). Binford views one result of feminist-inspired awareness as the "trivial" replacement of neutral words for offensive words ("humankind" for "mankind"), rather than any growth in knowledge. For him the only solution to bias is reliable (scientific) methodology. From the feminist perspective, Binford's scientific approach can also be viewed as biased and subjective for many reasons, including its establishment of the archaeologist as the empowered possessor of a special insight, and its assumption that objective facts can be obtained from approaches still invented today largely by the same people who were inventing them in the nineteenth century, namely upper-middle-class, European and Anglo-Saxon males, often legitimizing the ideals of the modern technocratic West, and operating as colonialist interpreters of their subjects of study (Hodder 1985: 20–22, 1991: 166–68; Trigger 1989: 380).

In feminist archaeological publications, the admitted subjectivity of the researcher emerges as perhaps the most significant and defining issue (Engelstad 1991: 512; Wylie 1992: 17). It is related to the relativist contention that archaeologists cannot discover scientific "truth," and so must analyze their own motivations and attitudes. Although most of the archaeologists publishing in *Engendering Archaeology* use ethnographic or historical information to associate women with particular activities or materials, they do so guardedly, wary of accepting inappropriate models for the past (Conkey and Gero 1991: 17–18). Many are well-trained in the methodologies emphasized within New Archaeology, and methodological rigor is very much a part of the studies presented. Nevertheless, the book's "position statement" is that archaeology is more interpretive than positivist, and that subjective constructs and relationships affect both the social processes of the past and the research strategies of the present (Conkey 1991: 81–83; Tringham 1991: 118–19; Wylie 1991: 46, 49).

A desire for a new way of seeing past prevalent models of prehistory, which claim to be empirical and yet are based on gender bias, has resulted in some dramatic feminist departures from the norm of publishing archaeological evidence. Several authors employ "alternative narratives" that consciously subvert traditional standards of rigor by admitting subjectivity. Spector herself undertakes this radical enterprise in her chapter in *Engendering Archaeology*. In carrying out research on the nineteenth-century Eastern Dakota people at Little Rapids in Minnesota, she became discouraged by "dull, tedious, boring, hard-to-grasp" male archaeological publications of the 1970s and 1980s. These works heavily featured description, categorization, an unconscious ranking of artifacts according to Western male notions of importance, and depersonalized narratives focusing on objects rather than people (Spector 1991: 402–3).

Spector "returned to the core issue in feminist criticism: the ramifications of excluding groups from the production and distribution of knowledge" (Spector 1991: 389). This problem is reflected in more traditional, "objective" studies focusing on aspects of culture that the research subjects themselves might find amusing or incomprehensible. Spector was strongly influenced by ethnographic studies as well as by the insights she gained from talking with modern Dakota people about their lives and their view of the past. What is really unusual about her sample narrative in *Engendering Archaeology* (Spector 1991: 397–401), and the one she plans to publish as the centerpiece of her proposed book on Little Rapids, is that they are a kind of interpretive, historical fiction. Her sample narrative focuses on a particular find, an inscribed awl handle, and brings to life its user and her thoughts and feelings. Spector contrasts this account with a more traditional, de-peopled discussion of awls by another archaeologist.

Ruth Tringham, too, became uncomfortable with genderless descriptions; she appends a brief narrative, entitled "Fantasy > Fact," to the end of her consideration of the evidence for the burning, abandonment, and relocation of houses in Neolithic southeastern Europe. Her conventional text concludes with a reference to recent ethnographic and non-Western architectural studies describing the impact on the people involved of processes we tend to describe "coldly and objectively." Her fantasy text then adds emotion (Tringham 1991: 124). In a separate, less radical departure from the norms of archaeological argumentation, Tringham also includes within her text an imaginary radio interview with four well-known archaeologists (including herself and Marija Gimbutas) who have different perspectives. She thereby presents in a more accessible, readable, and visibly subjective form than usual the "alternative historical trajectories" one can associate with the data (Tringham 1991: 99).

The problems of biased archaeological writing will probably not be solved for most archaeologists by a shift from one end of the narrative spectrum to the other: from dry descriptions that omit some facts and all emotion to ones that omit other facts and include fictionalized emotion. There is an intermediate path between pseudo-scientific, supposedly objective descriptions and interpretations, and the emotion- and thought-laden narratives usually labeled as literature and not social science. Nevertheless, these alternative approaches are interesting, thought-provoking, and (unheard of!) fun to read. The texts are not meant to stand alone, but rather to accompany more conventional sources of information; they are not historical fiction in the same way Mary Renault's novels about the ancient world are. These feminist narratives, consciously crafted to reveal information subjectively, are carefully presented within a framework that permits the validation of facts and the consideration of alternatives.

The approaches of these explicitly feminist archaeologists contrast with those of Marija Gimbutas, whose publications on the material evidence for a supposedly prepatriarchal Goddess cult have had a tremendous impact in both popular and academic feminism (especially Gimbutas 1982, 1989, 1991; see Orenstein 1990). Gimbutas does not present herself as either a feminist or a postprocessualist, although others have taken her to be both. It is ironic that what many see as archaeology's major contribution to feminist theorizing has to date hardly been acknowledged within the field. In their introduction to *Engendering Archaeology*, Conkey and Gero mention the Goddess theories, but not Gimbutas; they contrast the "tiny smattering" of archaeological literature which notes even "the *existence* of women in prehistory" with the popular "but essentially unsubstantiated" idea outside archaeology of powerful Neolithic goddesses (Gero and Conkey 1991a: xi; see also Cole 1985: 50–51; di Leonardo 1991a: 8).

According to Gimbutas in *The Goddesses and Gods of Old Europe*, Old European society was peaceful, agricultural, and dominated by women in the period before waves of pastoral proto-Indo-Europeans infiltrated and imposed a patriarchal, stratified culture. People worshipped a "Goddess incarnating the creative principle as Source and Giver of All" (Gimbutas 1982: 9). More recently, in *The Civilization of the Goddess*, Gimbutas asserts that the civilization of Old Europe "was, in the main, peaceful, sedentary, matrifocal, matrilinear, and sex-egalitarian," until aggressive male invasions ended the earth-centered, "gylanic" culture (Gimbutas 1991: xx–xxi). Gimbutas's work in particular convinced early academic feminists of the existence of a prehistoric pansocietal Goddess "culture" (Broude and Garrard 1982b: 3),[15] and contributed to the popular view of a peaceful golden age of female power in the past (Eisler 1987; Gadon 1989; Reis 1991; Woolger and Woolger 1987). Yet most archaeologists, including feminists, do not accept Gimbutas's methodology. Ruth Tringham notes that Gimbutas has interpreted her data "to her own satisfaction," whereas others have criticized it "for its inconsistencies and hasty inferences" (Tringham 1991: 96–97). In fact, Gimbutas is working within an old-fashioned, "establishment" epistemological framework of polar opposites, fixed gender roles, brutish invaders, and cultural stages now generally considered naive (Tringham 1991: 115–16).

Gimbutas has revived a century-old notion of a European Mother Goddess, often associated with the later Near Eastern goddess Ishtar cited in texts, and assumed to be connected with deities from as far away as India. This Goddess is identified largely through the existence of figurines and other illustrations, supposedly of women, found in a variety of contexts dating from the Paleolithic period through the Neolithic. The images vary enormously in appearance and span both thousands of years and thousands of miles. Until the late 1960s they were nevertheless interpreted as if spatially and temporally homogeneous. This problem was finally addressed by Peter Ucko, who summarized both the archaeological evidence and the history of thought about the figurines (Ucko 1968: 409–43; Talalay 1991; see also Ehrenberg 1989: 66–76).

Ucko identified a number of problems with the then-current, generalizing theories about the Goddess (Ucko 1968: 412–19). Archaeologists reiterate many of his criticisms when they evaluate Gimbutas's work: she illustrates material that validates her assertions, rather than presenting reasoned arguments; she uncritically selects objects from scattered sources, regardless of era, geography, or context, eliminating those that do not "fit"; and she ignores alternative explanations for the images she cites, including ones not at all clearly associated with a Great Goddess (Barnett 1992; Fagan 1992; Renfrew 1991: 222–23; Talalay 1991: 47). A review of *The Language of the Goddess* by Colin Renfrew illustrates the

common association of "soft" (less-than-rigorous) archaeology and postprocessual methodologies, at least in the minds of many archaeologists influenced
by the processual school. Renfrew praises Gimbutas's thorough publication of
her various excavations, and somewhat patronizingly admires her book's
"charms" and her "energy." Rather than directly attacking her work, he relates her
approach to the unsatisfactory interpretive methods of postprocessual colleagues
(Renfrew 1991: 223).

Professional disagreement with Gimbutas's view of a powerful gynocentric
past is largely expressed through silence. Gimbutas is an "insider" with an
impressive record of excavation and publication, and she does not threaten the
archaeological status quo by criticizing her colleagues. The field has reacted
much more vocally to Martin Bernal, an "outsider" trained in Chinese studies,
who is aggressive in his recreation of a more powerful past for prehistoric (in
terms of Greek history) and later Levantine, Phoenician, and Egyptian "others"
of the ancient world.[16] In Bernal's first two volumes of *Black Athena*, he presents
and documents his theories about the origins and nature of Greek civilization and
about a prevalent "Aryan Model" of interpreting the past, which specifically
suppresses and denies Semitic and Egyptian influence on Greek culture (Bernal
1987, 1991). Bernal suggests that we must not only "rethink the fundamental
bases of 'Western Civilization' but also recognize the penetration of racism and
'continental chauvinism' into all our historiography" (Bernal 1987: 2). Whether
archaeologists have responded to Bernal with friendliness or thinly veiled hostility, they have uniformly criticized him for many of the same methodological
failings as Gimbutas: using his evidence selectively, conflating data, making
simplistic assumptions, and working within a model he deplores. At the same
time, authors only briefly mention Bernal's message about our biased historiography, either denying its truth or its relevance, or acknowledging it while assuming
that any problem does not rest with them.

The uncomfortable fact remains that archaeologists do seem more likely to
ignore or deny models of the past when these create mythologies of dominance
for women (see Tina Passman in this volume); and they often do see "our" cultural
heritage as European. We generally accept the essentially negative Greek and
Roman view of "others" such as the Phoenicians, even when we acknowledge
their contributions to classical civilization. The Phoenicians have recently become
a popular subject of research, and archaeologists now view them more favorably
than in past decades. Even so, authors still sometimes describe them in derogatory
terms, or explain away, from a Western perspective, their moral, cultural, or
aesthetic failings (Brown 1991: 75, 149; Brown 1991b: 21, sidebar). Archaeologists also tend to assume that "our" ancestors are Caucasian. Conkey and Williams
cite the telling cover illustration on an issue of *Newsweek* which illuminates "our
Ice Age heritage" with the image of a white male resembling Rembrandt (Conkey
and Williams 1991: 120, fig. 5). Such imagery in nonprofessional publications
does not appear out of nowhere. Many renditions of the evolution of man as a

series of striding men begin with "the swarthy and 'dark' australopithecines" and move through "the increasingly hairless and 'light' early *Homo* to modern 'man' " (Conkey and Williams 1991: 117). Simplistic interpretive models do seem to be more readily tolerated if they are centered in the views of white men. Like people of color asking, "Whose flesh?" of beige products labelled "flesh"-toned, feminists and others are now asking of white men, "Whose past?"

What Is a Feminist Approach to Classical Archaeology?

How do classical archaeologists address the issues raised by feminist prehistorians and New World archaeologists? For the most part, they do not discuss them at all. Classical archaeology first took note of androcentric research bias in 1975 when Sarah Pomeroy, a classicist, published *Goddesses, Whores, Wives, and Slaves: Women in Classical Antiquity* (Pomeroy 1975). Her book highlighted the lack of studies of ancient women, and many other publications and collections about women and gender from the Bronze Age through the Roman period have followed, many including physical evidence.[17] Few classical art historical or archaeological publications, however, have been based on explicit feminist theory (but see duBois 1988; Richlin 1992), or even on a view of gender as a complex social process involving dynamics of power, status, and other variables within a specific cultural context (recently, Kampen 1991).

Prehistorians must sometimes rely on later ethnographic and historical evidence, perhaps even from completely different cultures, in attempting to explain their data. Classical archaeologists can instead often use informative, contemporary texts to clarify issues of gender and illuminate women's lives. These texts usually themselves relegate women to the sidelines, and they reinforce many modern notions about gender. In relying on such sources, many archaeologists have tended to assume that "femaleness" and gender roles are a cross-cultural given, that we already understand male and female roles in the classical world sufficiently well, and that these roles make a certain, natural kind of sense. One aim of feminist archaeology, as defined within the context of prehistoric Mediterranean and New World studies, has been to move beyond "naming" sexual difference (Gilchrist 1991: 499) to explaining it. Classical archaeologists sometimes just note the presence or activities of women and "name differences" between male and female roles. The study of women is also often relegated to the sidelines as a special topic within the subfield "Women in Antiquity."

Some feminist authors have summarized the development of feminist academic research in stages, starting with criticism of male bias (stage one), then moving on to the study of women where they have been ignored (but often still seeing the evidence from a traditionally male viewpoint; stage two), and, finally, progressing to a broader methodological/theoretical inquiry into the dynamics of gender relations and social constructs (stage three; Conkey and Spector 1984: 17–18; Wylie 1991: 30–31). This is a simple but useful framework within which to view classical archaeological publications on women and gender. In general, classical archaeologists have largely avoided stage one (criticizing "the field" for androcentrism or other biases) and stage three (using feminist theory to explain gender relations and structures of power). Classical archaeologists often simply provide useful physical evidence of the ways in which women were "there" in a "man's world" (Havelock 1982 on vase painting; Walker 1983 on domestic architecture). Sometimes they describe the female lot in life as polarized—either "bad," or "better than one might have expected"—or discuss women in terms of only two main male responses to them, "low" responses to improper females, and "high" responses to respectable females (Williams 1983).

The sources of information on both women and gender roles in the Bronze and Iron Ages are vast. Women are depicted in a variety of contexts in art, both public and private, in many media. Images of mythological females, divinities, and real women of different classes exist in stone, bronze, and terracotta statues, figurines, and reliefs; wall paintings and frescoes; mosaics; vase paintings; bronze and ceramic lamps and vessels; carved gemstones and ivories; metal jewelry; coins; and more. Artifacts such as loom weights and particular kinds of toiletries, clothing, jewelry, vases, and many other objects can be more or less clearly linked with patterns of female behavior through descriptions in literature, depictions in art, and associations of artifacts with women in burials sexed by inscriptions as well as skeletal remains. Classical archaeologists have not always used these resources to answer complex questions about gender, or even other social relation-ships, partly because of their training in traditional approaches to their research. They often study one medium or class of art, sometimes only from one area or one chronological period (for example, Attic vase painting, Hellenistic portraiture, Archaic bronze figurines, Republican coinage, Imperial reliefs of the Julio-Claudians). Within each category, traditional topics of study are long established and aesthetic standards set.

As a result, classical archaeologists have often tended to consider stylistic and typological changes in isolation, rather than to analyze art "as a phenomenon within its culture" (duBois 1988: 50). In general, prehistorians have been more likely than classical archaeologists to note problems both with accepting andro-centric and other biases in art history and with analyzing images outside their cultural context. This is partly because the identification of artifacts as "art," and even as "images" (Davis 1987: 116), is especially problematic in many prehistoric contexts (Conkey and Williams 1991: 119–21; Handsman 1991: 332–34). A recent book on Hellenistic sculpture illustrates a traditional, "connoisseur's" analysis of nude female statues and unwittingly reveals the field's need for self-criticism. Andrew Stewart considers the appeal and significance of Hellenistic female nudes, analyzing them according to a low/high view of female sexuality. According to him, the sculpture Praxiteles shows in the Knidian Aphrodite a perfect beauty matched by an equally perfect modesty. The Knidia's "gracefully instinctive gesture" of covering her pubis, and other ways of distancing herself from a male gaze, reduce the male spectator "to the ignominious role of a Peeping Tom" (Stewart 1990: 78). Although female nudity normally indicates a context of violence against women and reconfirms female subservience, here it supposedly elevates the goddess.

Aphrodite's appropriate rejection of the male gaze apparently emphasizes her status as proper female, while her instinctive gracefulness increases the viewer's sense of his own good taste. Needless to say, the Peeping Tom, although humbled, fully enjoys his peep. Stewart describes later, less modest, nude Aphrodites as if they were real women, using negative terms such as "trivially coquettish" and "overripe" (Stewart 1990: 52). In essence, a naked woman's reaction to sexual vulnerability is a source of intense aesthetic pleasure within Stewart's traditional art history, and the less coquettish or inviting her response is, the more elevated and enjoyable the image is for the discerning viewer. The polar opposites, "lady" and "whore," are implicitly invoked here with no consideration of their significance for gender relations in either Hellenistic Greek or modern society. Stewart apparently accepts a male view of a polarized female sexuality as natural and eternal, requiring no examination or explanation in its context. In another recent book, R. R. R. Smith does place such images within the art historical context of women as objects of ideal composition and male voyeurism, but nevertheless sees them as expressing a wholly positive view of female sexuality (Smith 1991: 81–82).

Despite classical archaeologists' tendency toward connoisseurship and their sometimes simplistic approach to gender issues, several authors have been pioneers in the study of gender in classical art, starting in the early 1980s. They have considered gender as one of many variables fundamental to understanding the past, and have even evaluated the role of the classical patron (the viewer) in creating appropriate images of men and women within the limits of established cultural norms.[18] Others, too, have noted the value of considering factors such as age, rank, and social context in analyzing past gendered behavior in art (nonfeminist authors include Davis 1986; Marinatos 1987). In general, classical archaeology is becoming increasingly interested in the social and symbolic dimensions of art, and aware of the existence of an ancient spectator with a point of view. Recent studies of Roman domestic architecture and related art link the social dynamics of such cultural phenomena as status and patronage with artistic and architectural forms of spatial demarcation (Clarke 1992; Gazda and Haeckl 1991; Wallace-Hadrill 1988; see also Leach 1992: 555–57).

Unfortunately, recognition of the social and symbolic significance of art and architecture has generally not led archaeologists to focus on gender relationships, even when their subject is women's roles, nor on modern research epistemologies, even when their subject is ancient ways of viewing women. The increasing interest of classical archaeologists in social context does, however, create an environment in which feminist theoretical approaches could flourish. Classical archaeologists, with all sorts of literary, epigraphical, historical, and artistic evidence to draw from in answering questions about the past, are often in a better position than prehistorians to analyze gendered behavior in all its complexity as a significant aspect of human culture. The presence and activities of women within a classical world governed by a male social norm have been amply and usefully documented in the past fifteen years. Where does a feminist approach lead from here? The few classical archaeologists and art historians who have published explicitly feminist evaluations of art illustrate the enormous potential of feminist theory for the field.

A feminist art historian's analysis of classical nude sculpture, for example, is in striking contrast to that of the androcentric norm. Nanette Salomon utilizes both a "stage one" and "stage three" feminist approach in her brief analysis of the nudes within the larger context of an androcentric art history. Formal, modern art history texts "treat the male and female nudes in ways that prevent conscious consideration of them as dynamic components in establishing power relations that are expressed in sexual terms." Salomon points out that the female gesture of covering the pubis, generally described as a gesture of modesty, has been "naturalized" within our culture, as it was in antiquity; we no longer "connect" with the fear the gesture can represent. She describes the transformation of viewer into voyeur as s/he looks at the naturalistic image of a woman who does not want to be seen. Male heterosexuals are encouraged to translate that desire into "socially sanctioned public acts" (Salomon 1991: 233). In our society, these can include the appreciation of female nudes (in high culture) and the harassment of women by men in groups (in low culture). Such an evaluation of a Greek image is unusual and tantalizing. Salomon establishes a statue type as the product of specific gender relationships in the past, and documents its role today within the "mental template" of a male art history.

As an example of a feminist analysis of vase painting, H. A. Shapiro and Robert Sutton's studies of Attic vases document the complicated interrelationship of age, social status, and gender of Greek men and women in their erotic encounters within a changing political climate (Shapiro 1992; Sutton 1992). Both authors also use literary and other artistic evidence to help them explain the images and to illuminate the attitudes of both makers and users of the vessels about "appropriate" male and female, homosexual and heterosexual roles in different contexts. The paintings both reflect and reinforce changing standards of gendered sexual behavior and illustrate the relative power of men and women of different classes in their sexual and romantic relationships. The approach of these feminist authors to seeing the classical past with new eyes parallels that of feminist prehistorians. They neither assume that present-day reactions to images are the "right" ones nor accept that gendered behavior is eternal and cross cultural. As well, they are methodologically rigorous in seeking explanations for vase paintings within their ancient context.

The underlying, "feminist" assumption behind such analyses of classical art, as in a feminist prehistory, is simply that attitudes toward gender have complex and significant effects on the ways societies structure themselves, and that gendered behavior both reflects and determines real and symbolic power from the micro- to the macroscale. Classical archaeologists have not yet applied feminist theory to the study of Greek and Roman architecture, although recent feminist studies of modern architecture evaluate space as a locus of negotiation for gendered power and status (Colomina 1992; Spain 1992). A feminist approach to classical domestic architecture might move beyond the validation of textual information about women's and men's quarters (Walker 1983) to the documentation of relative male and female access to information or resources, or to the consideration of their spheres of power beyond the usually cited categories of "domestic" and "public/political" (see Small 1991).

Wherever a feminist archaeology leads, and whether it is classical or prehistoric, Old or New World archaeology, it seems to require two ideological positions. First, feminist archaeologists accept the premise that archaeological research is at least partly, and perhaps largely, a subjective, relative ("postprocessual") enterprise. This does not, however, make it any easier for them to talk about their own subjective experiences in archaeology, especially when these might be taken as complaints. All members of the fragmented field of archaeology could nevertheless benefit from reconsidering unstated, unquestioned assumptions about women and "natural" gender roles that affect both daily life and research. Second, feminist archaeologists agree that gender is an essential factor in human culture that we cannot afford to ignore. There is, however, no one archaeological approach to engendering the past. The material resources of classical archaeology make feminist "gaze theory" particularly valuable as a research tool for identifying viewer subjectivity—ancient and modern. Prehistorians will continue to rely on ethnographic and historical comparisons for interpreting much of their data, without assuming that they can obtain "truth," but with the goal of seeing women as meaningful participants in the history of "man."

Despite their willingness to interpret the past in new ways, feminist archaeologists are acutely aware of the problems with interpreting physical evidence and bridging the chronological and interpretive gulf between "us" and "them." They acknowledge their tie to the realities of an often ambiguous material evidence. Although sometimes angry at current archaeological approaches to research, and often excited about new ways to envision and interpret the past, explicitly feminist archaeologists have therefore not contributed, so far, to feminist revisionist histories; they are usually not sympathetic to broad, generalizing Goddess theories or feminist visions of a past pansocietal matristic culture, however much these may serve as useful models for nonarchaeologists. Archaeological visions of an engendered antiquity are more specific and factual than emotional or mythological. In fact, feminist archaeology at this early stage of its development sometimes seems to influence us toward contradictory goals: to become self-aware, but remain silent about our personal experiences; and to be objective and rigorous in our research methodologies, but subjective and imaginative in our interpretations. A feminist archaeology must still address this dilemma and integrate its two halves.

Notes

Once again, many thanks to Amy Richlin for intellectual stimulation, helpful prodding, and general encouragement. I am grateful to my archaeological colleagues Jeremy Rutter, Ernestine Elster, and Claire Lyons for their help, and to Nancy Sorkin Rabinowitz for perspective. Special thanks to Paul Sandberg for editing and other assistance beyond the call of duty. Lauren Talalay was very generous with her insights, especially into Goddess research, and freely shared her knowledge of Mediterranean prehistory. Finally, I am enormously grateful to Tracey Cullen, who patiently provided invaluable suggestions, criticisms, bibliographical references, editorial comments, and moral support, at my convenience rather than hers.

1. The trend is reflected in Miller, Rowlands, and Tilley 1989; Stone and MacKenzie 1990; and McGuire and Paynter 1991. Hodder explicitly links feminism in archaeology with "anti-colonialist" awareness of the dynamics of domination in various forms (Hodder 1985: 22, 1991: 168); Spector and Wylie do so less directly (Spector 1991: 398, 402–3; Wylie 1992: 17).

2. The bibliography is extensive, but good starting points include: Alpers 1982; Berger 1972; Betterton 1987; Broude and Garrard 1982a; Hess and Nochlin 1972; Kappeler 1986; Kent 1985; Kendall and Pollock 1992; Nochlin 1988; Salomon 1991; Tickner 1988.

3. See Redfield 1991: 6, on the sweaty, "macho" aspects of anthropological fieldwork. Redfield's imagery often clearly applies to males. Gero (1985: 344) also notes archaeologists' "masculine" and "active" self-images. She suggests that women are awarded National Science Foundation grants more readily when they apply to do non–field-related archaeological research than the "manly" kind (Gero 1985: 347).

4. See William McDonald's list of the standards by which classical archaeologists generally measured accomplishments in the field in 1981 (Wilkie and Coulson 1985: xiv).

5. Kehoe describes the three-stage system as an instrument of ideology, fitting a "white mythology" of dominant males, and privileging technology (Kehoe 1989: 105–6). See also Hinsley 1989: 80, on the perceived stages within a male history of archaeology. Wylie (1991: 31–32), and Conkey and Williams (1991: 113–14), stress problems of male bias in the search for origins and developmental milestones in the past.

6. Useful overviews of the history of archaeology or of recent intellectual approaches to excavating, interpreting, and presenting evidence include: Dyson 1981, 1985, 1989, 1993; Engelstad 1991; Evans 1981; Gero and Conkey 1991b; Gibbon 1989; Gilchrist 1991; Manning 1990; McNally 1985; Renfrew 1980, 1984; Renfrew and Bahn 1991; Sabloff 1981; Taylor 1948: 9–22; Trigger 1989; Walde and Willows 1991; Wilkie and Coulson 1985; Wiseman 1980; Wylie 1992.

7. For negative views of New Archaeological approaches to understanding group

behavior through science, see Handsman 1991: 330; Hodder 1985: 1–2; Manning 1990: 258; Wylie 1991: 35–38 (also note Hill and Gunn 1977, who focus on the individual).

8. Stephen Dyson irreverently describes the panic of a typical classical archaeologist when confronted with New Archaeological theorists (Dyson 1981: 7).

9. New Archaeology has been called, among other terms, "processual," "systems-theoretical," "deductive," "logical-positivist/empiricist," "materialist," "behavioral," and "nomothetic." Different or opponent approaches are labeled, variously, "postprocessual," "normative," "structural," "contextual," "symbolic," "cultural," "historical," "inductive," "Marxist," "realist," and "feminist," among other terms (Binford 1989: 3; Manning 1990: 257). Erika Engelstad has pointed out that postprocessualists can be just as sexist in their assumptions as processualists (Engelstad 1991: 511–12).

10. Patrik 1985 provides an outsider's (philosopher's) perspective both on defining the "archaeological record" and on understanding processual and postprocessual approaches to archaeology.

11. See also Conkey and Gero 1991: 20, 22; Engelstad 1991: 503–6; Harding 1986: 82–110; Kelley and Hanen 1988: 44–59, 281; McNally 1985: 12; Wylie 1985: 87–88. The orderly, reductionist aspects of many processual models ignore ambiguity and complexity (Sperling 1991: 224 discusses this point with regard to primatology).

12. On the significance of and problems with ethnographic analogy in archaeology, see Conkey and Gero 1991: 18; Kelley and Hanen 1988: 378; Wylie 1985.

13. Jeremy Sabloff's description of one approach to successful theory-building can serve as a paradigm for a New Archaeology-influenced, scientific approach to ethnography to compare with Spector's, since her strategy was based on such a paradigm (Sabloff 1981: 4; Conkey and Spector 1984: 24–27; Spector 1983; Spector 1991: 390–91).

14. Liv Gibbs also established an association between sex/gender and material culture in burials and figurines from Denmark (Gibbs 1987: 89).

15. Broude and Garrard accepted the Goddess theory without question in 1982, although it had been under attack within archaeology since 1968 (Broude and Garrard 1982b: 3). They included in their collection of feminist essays a chapter on architecture, first published in 1962, in which Vincent Scully sought to relate Minoan building plans and locations to the cult of the Great Goddess (Scully 1982).

16. For archaeological responses to Bernal, see in particular the special issue of *Arethusa* (1989); the *Journal of Mediterranean Studies* 3 (1990); Vermeule 1992; Coleman 1992; and Weinstein 1992.

17. Among others, Broude and Garrard 1982a; Cameron and Kuhrt 1983; Davis 1986; Ehrenberg 1989; Foley 1981; Havelock 1982; Kampen 1981, 1982, 1991; Keuls 1983, 1985; Marinatos 1987; Peradotto and Sullivan 1984; Pomeroy 1991; Richlin 1992; Shapiro 1981, 1992; Sissa 1990; Sutton 1981, 1992; Walker 1983; Williams 1983.

18. For example, duBois 1982, 1988; Kampen 1981, 1982, 1991; Shapiro 1981, 1992;

Sutton 1981, 1992. See Trembley 1992 for relevant quotations from Gloria Pinney about her research on women in Greek vase painting.

Bibliography

Allsebrook, Mary. 1992. *Born to Rebel: The Life of Harriet Boyd Hawes*. Oxford: Oxford University Press.

Alpers, Svetlana. 1982. "Art History and Its Exclusions." In Broude and Garrard, *Feminism and Art History: Questioning the Litany*, 183–200.

Barber, E. J. W. 1991. *Prehistoric Textiles: The Development of Cloth in the Neolithic and Bronze Ages with Special Reference to the Aegean*. Princeton: Princeton University Press.

Barnett, William. 1992. Review of Marija Gimbutas, 1989, *The Language of the Goddess*. In *American Journal of Archaeology* 96: 170–71.

Bender, Barbara. 1991. Review of Margaret Ehrenberg, 1989, *Women in Prehistory*. In *Proceedings of the Prehistoric Society* 57: 213–14.

Berger, John. 1972. *Ways of Seeing*. Harmondsworth and London: British Broadcasting Company.

Bernal, Martin. 1987. *Black Athena: The Afroasiatic Roots of Classical Civilization. I: The Fabrication of Ancient Greece 1785–1985*. New Brunswick: Rutgers University Press.

———. 1991. *Black Athena: The Afroasiatic Roots of Classical Civilization. II: The Archaeological and Linguistic Evidence*. New Brunswick: Rutgers University Press.

Betterton, R., ed. 1987. *Looking On: Images of Femininity in the Visual Arts and Media*. New York: Pandora.

Binford, Lewis R. 1972a. "Archaeology as Anthropology." In Leone, *Contemporary Archaeology. A Guide to Theory and Contributions*, 93–101.

———. 1972b. "A Consideration of Archaeological Research Design." In Leone, *Contemporary Archaeology. A Guide to Theory and Contributions*, 158–77.

———. 1989. *Debating Archaeology*. London: Academic Press.

Broude, Norma, and Mary D. Garrard, eds. 1982a. *Feminism and Art History: Questioning the Litany*. New York: Harper and Row.

———. 1982b. "Introduction: Feminism and Art History." In Broude and Garrard, *Feminism and Art History: Questioning the Litany*, 1–17.

Brown, Shelby. 1991a. *Late Carthaginian Child Sacrifice and Sacrificial Monuments in their Mediterranean Context*. (JSOT/ASOR Monograph Series 3.) Sheffield: Sheffield Academic Press.

———. 1991b. "Perspectives on Phoenician Art." *Biblical Archaeologist* 55: 6–24.

———. 1992. "Death as Decoration: Scenes from the Arena on Roman Domestic Mosaics." In Richlin, *Pornography and Representation in Greece and Rome*, 180–211.

Cameron, Averil, and Amélie Kuhrt, eds. 1983. *Images of Women in Antiquity*. Detroit: Wayne State University Press.

Christenson, Andrew, ed. 1989. *Tracing Archaeology's Past: The Historiography of Archaeology*. Carbondale and Edwardsville: Southern Illinois University Press.

Claassen, Cheryl, ed. In press. *Explorations in Archaeology and Gender*. Madison, Wisc.: Prehistory Press.

Clarke, John R. 1992. *The Houses of Roman Italy, 100 B.C.–A.D. 250: Ritual, Space, and Decoration*. Berkeley: University of California Press.

Cole, Susan Guettel. 1985. "Archaeology and Religion." In Wilkie and Coulson, *Contributions to Aegean Archaeology: Studies in Honor of William A. McDonald*, 47–59.

Coleman, John E. 1992. "The Case against Martin Bernal's *Black Athena*." *Archaeology* 45: 49–52, 77–81.

Colomina, B., ed. 1992. *Sexuality and Space*. (Princeton Papers on Architecture.) Princeton: Princeton University Press.

Conkey, Margaret W. 1991. "Contexts of Action, Contexts of Power: Material Culture and Gender in the Magdalenian." In Gero and Conkey, *Engendering Archaeology: Women in Prehistory*, 57–92.

Conkey, Margaret, and Joan Gero. 1991. "Tensions, Plurality, and Engendering Archaeology: An Introduction to Women and Prehistory." In Gero and Conkey, *Engendering Archaeology: Women in Prehistory*, 3–30.

Conkey, Margaret W., and Janet D. Spector. 1984. "Archaeology and the Study of Gender." *Advances in Archaeological Method and Theory* 7: 1–38.

Conkey, Margaret W., with Sarah W. Williams. 1991. "Original Narratives: The Political Economy of Gender in Archaeology." In di Leonardo, *Gender at the Crossroads of Knowledge: Feminist Anthropology in the Postmodern Era*, 102–39.

Davis, Ellen N. 1986. "Youth and Age in the Thera Frescoes." *American Journal of Archaeology* 90: 399–406.

Davis, Whitney. 1987. "Replication and Depiction in Paleolithic Art." *Representations* 19: 111–47.

di Leonardo, Micaela. 1991a. "Introduction: Gender, Culture and Political Economy: Feminist Anthropology in Historical Perspective." In di Leonardo, *Gender at the Crossroads of Knowledge*, 1–48.

———, ed. 1991b. *Gender at the Crossroads of Knowledge: Feminist Anthropology in the Postmodern Era*. Berkeley: University of California Press.

Donohue, A. A. 1985. "One Hundred Years of the *American Journal of Archaeology*: An Archival History." *American Journal of Archaeology* 89: 3–30.

duBois, Page. 1982. *Centaurs and Amazons: Women and the Pre-History of the Great Chain of Being*. Ann Arbor: The University of Michigan Press.

———. 1988. *Sowing the Body: Psychoanalysis and Ancient Representations of Women*. Chicago: The University of Chicago Press.

Dyson, Stephen L. 1981. "A Classical Archaeologist's Response to the 'New Archaeology.' " *Bulletin of the American Schools of Oriental Research* 242: 7–13.

————. 1985. "Two Paths to the Past: A Comparative Study of the Last Fifty Years of *American Antiquity* and *American Journal of Archaeology.*" *American Antiquity* 50: 452–63.

————. 1989. "The Role of Ideology and Institutions in Shaping Classical Archaeology in the Nineteenth and Twentieth Centuries." In Christenson, *Tracing Archaeology's Past: The Historiography of Archaeology*, 127–35.

————. 1993. "From New to New Age Archaeology: Archaeological Theory and Classical Archaeology—A 1990s Perspective." *American Journal of Archaeology* 97, no. 1. In press.

Ehrenberg, Margaret. 1989. *Women in Prehistory*. London: British Museum Publications.

Eisler, Riane. 1987. *The Chalice and the Blade*. San Francisco: Harper and Row.

Engelstad, Erika. 1991. "Images of Power and Contradiction: Feminist Theory and Post-processual Archaeology." *Antiquity* 65: 502–14.

Evans, John D. 1981. "Introduction: On the Prehistory of Archaeology." In John Evans, Barry Cunliffe, and Colin Renfrew, eds., *Antiquity and Man: Essays in Honor of Glyn Daniel*, 12–18. London: Thames and Hudson.

Fagan, Brian. 1992. "A Sexist View of Prehistory." *Archaeology* 45: 14–18, 66.

Flannery, Kent. 1972. "Culture History vs. Cultural Process: A Debate in American Archaeology." In Leone, *Contemporary Archaeology: A Guide to Theory and Contributions*, 102–7.

Flax, J. 1987. "Postmodernism in Gender Relations in Feminist Theory." *Signs: Journal of Women in Culture and Society* 12: 621–43.

Foley, Helene P., ed. 1981. *Reflections of Women in Antiquity*. New York: Gordon and Breach Science Publishers.

Gadon, Elinor W. 1989. *The Once and Future Goddess: A Symbol for Our Time*. New York: Harper and Row.

Gazda, Elaine K., and Anne E. Haeckl, eds. 1991. *Roman Art in the Private Sphere: New Perspectives on the Architecture and Decor of the Domus, Villa, and Insula*. Ann Arbor: University of Michigan Press.

Gero, Joan M. 1985. "Socio-politics and the Woman at Home Ideology." *American Antiquity* 50: 342–50.

————. 1991. "Genderlithics: Women's Roles in Stone Tool Production." In Gero and Conkey, *Engendering Archaeology: Women in Prehistory*, 163–93.

Gero, Joan M., and Margaret W. Conkey. 1991a. "Preface." In Gero and Conkey, *Engendering Archaeology: Women in Prehistory*, xi–xii.

————, eds. 1991b. *Engendering Archaeology: Women and Prehistory*. Cambridge, Mass.: Basil Blackwell.

Gibbon, Guy. 1989. *Explanation in Archaeology*. New York: Basil Blackwell.

Gibbs, Liv. 1987. "Identifying Gender Representation in the Archaeological Record: A Contextual Study." In Ian Hodder, ed., *The Archaeology of Contextual Meanings*, 79–101. Cambridge: Cambridge University Press.

Gilchrist, R. 1991. "Women's Archaeology? Political Feminism, Gender Theory and Historical Revision." *Antiquity* 65: 495–501.

Gimbutas, Marija. 1982. *The Goddesses and Gods of Old Europe, 6500–3500 B.C.: Myths and Cult Images*. London: Thames and Hudson.

———. 1989. *The Language of the Goddess*. San Francisco: Harper and Row.

———. 1991. *The Civilization of the Goddess: The World of Old Europe*. New York: Harper Collins.

Handsman, Russell G. 1991. "Whose Art Was Found at Lepenski Vir? Gender Relations and Power in Archaeology." In Gero and Conkey, *Engendering Archaeology: Women and Prehistory*, 329–65.

Harding, Sandra. 1986. *The Science Question in Feminism*. Ithaca: Cornell University Press.

Hartman, Joan E., and Ellen Messer-Davidow, eds. 1991. *(En)gendering Knowledge: Feminists in Academe*. Knoxville: The University of Tennessee Press.

Havelock, Christine Mitchell. 1982. "Mourners on Greek Vases: Remarks on the Social History of Women." In Broude and Garrard, *Feminism and Art History: Questioning the Litany*, 44–61.

Hess, Thomas B., and Linda Nochlin. 1972. *Woman as Sex Object: Studies in Erotic Art, 1730–1970*. (Art News Annual 38.) New York: Macmillan.

Hill, J. N., and J. Gunn, eds. 1977. *The Individual in Prehistory*. New York: Academic Press.

Hinsley, C. M. 1989. "Revising and Revisioning the History of Archaeology: Reflections on Region and Context." In Christenson, *Tracing Archaeology's Past: The Historiography of Archaeology*, 79–96.

Hodder, Ian. 1985. "Postprocessual Archaeology." *Advances in Archaeological Method and Theory* 8: 1–26.

———. 1991. *Reading the Past. Current Approaches to Interpretation in Archaeology*. Cambridge: Cambridge University Press.

Kampen, Natalie. 1981. *Image and Status: Roman Working Women in Ostia*. Berlin: Gebrüder Mann Verlag.

———. 1982. "Social Status and Gender in Roman Art: The Case of the Saleswoman." In Broude and Garrard, *Feminism and Art History: Questioning the Litany*, 63–77.

———. 1991. "Between Public and Private: Women as Historical Subjects in Roman Art." In Sarah Pomeroy, ed., *Women's History and Ancient History*, 218–48. Chapel Hill: University of North Carolina Press.

Kappeler, Susanne. 1986. *The Pornography of Representation*. Minneapolis: University of Minnesota Press.

Kehoe, Alice B. 1989. "Contextualizing Archaeology." In Christenson, *Tracing Archaeology's Past: The Historiography of Archaeology*, 97–106.

Kelley, Jane H., and Marsha P. Hanen. 1988. *Archaeology and the Methodology of Science*. Albuquerque: University of New Mexico Press.

Kendall, Richard, and Griselda Pollock, eds. 1992. *Dealing with Degas: Representations of Women and the Politics of Vision.* London: Pandora Press.

Kent, Sarah. 1985. "Looking Back." In Sarah Kent and Jacqueline Morreau, eds., *Women's Images of Men,* 55–74. London: Writers and Readers Publishing.

Keuls, Eva. 1983. "Attic Vase-Painting and the Home Textile Industry." In Warren G. Moon, ed., *Ancient Greek Art and Iconography,* 209–30. Madison: The University of Wisconsin Press.

Keuls, Eva C. 1985. *The Reign of the Phallus: Sexual Politics in Ancient Athens.* New York: Harper and Row.

Leach, Eleanor Winsor. 1992. "Reading Signs of Status: Recent Books on Roman Art in the Domestic Sphere." *American Journal of Archaeology* 96: 551–57.

Leone, Mark P., ed. 1972. *Contemporary Archaeology: A Guide to Theory and Contributions.* Carbondale and Edwardsville: Southern Illinois University Press.

Manning, Sturt. 1990. "Frames of Reference for the Past: Some Thoughts on Bernal, Truth and Reality." *Journal of Mediterranean Archaeology* 3: 255–74.

Marinatos, Nanno. 1987. "Role and Sex Division in Ritual Scenes in the Aegean." *Journal of Prehistoric Religion* 1: 23–34.

McGuire, R. H., and R. Paynter, eds. 1991. *The Archaeology of Inequality.* Oxford: Basil Blackwell.

McNally, S. 1985. "Art History and Archaeology." In Wilkie and Coulson, *Contributions to Aegean Archaeology: Studies in Honor of William A. McDonald,* 1–21.

Meritt, Lucy Shoe. 1984. *History of the American School of Classical Studies at Athens, 1939–1980.* Princeton, N.J.: American School of Classical Studies at Athens.

Miller, Daniel, Michael Rowlands, and Christopher Tilley, eds. 1989. *Domination and Resistance.* London: Unwin Hyman.

Nochlin, Linda. 1988. *Art, Women and Power and Other Essays.* New York: Harper and Row.

Orenstein, Gloria Feman. 1990. *The Reflowering of the Goddess.* Elmsford, New York: Pergamon Press.

Patrik, Linda E. 1985. "Is There an Archaeological Record?" *Advances in Archaeological Method and Theory* 8: 27–62.

Peradotto, John, and J. P. Sullivan, eds. 1984. *Women in the Ancient World: The Arethusa Papers.* Albany: State University of New York Press.

Pomeroy, Sarah B. 1975. *Goddesses, Whores, Wives, and Slaves: Women in Classical Antiquity.* New York: Schocken Books.

———, ed. 1991. *Women's History and Ancient History.* Chapel Hill: University of North Carolina Press.

Redfield, James. 1991. "Classics and Anthropology." *Arion* (third series) 1.2: 5–23.

Reis, Patricia. 1991. *Through the Goddess: A Woman's Way of Healing.* New York: Continuum.

Renfrew, Colin. 1980. "The Great Tradition versus the Great Divide: Archaeology as Anthropology?" *American Journal of Archaeology* 84: 287–98.

———. 1984. *Approaches to Social Archaeology*. Edinburgh: Edinburgh University Press.

———. 1991. Review of Marija Gimbutas, 1989, *The Language of the Goddess*. In *Proceedings of the Prehistoric Society* 57: 222–23.

Renfrew, Colin, and Paul Bahn. 1991. *Archaeology: Theories, Methods and Practice*. London: Thames and Hudson.

Richlin, Amy, ed. 1992. *Pornography and Representation in Greece and Rome*. New York: Oxford University Press.

Sabloff, Jeremy A. 1981. "When the Rhetoric Fades: A Brief Appraisal of Intellectual Trends in American Archaeology during the Past Two Decades." *Bulletin of the American Schools of Oriental Research* 242: 1–6.

Salmon, Merrilee H. 1982. *Philosophy and Archaeology (Studies in Archaeology)*. New York: Academic Press.

Salomon, N. 1991. "The Art Historical Canon: Sins of Omission." In Hartman and Messer-Davidow, *(En)gendering Knowledge: Feminists in Academe*, 222–36.

Scully, Vincent. 1982. "The Great Goddess and the Palace Architecture of Crete." In Broude and Garrard, *Feminism and Art History: Questioning the Litany*, 33–43.

Shapiro, H. A. 1981. "Courtship Scenes in Attic Vase-Painting." *American Journal of Archaeology* 85: 133–43.

———. 1992. "Eros in Love: Pederasty and Pornography in Greece." In Richlin, *Pornography and Representation in Greece and Rome*, 53–72.

Sissa, Giulia. 1990. *Greek Virginity*. Translated by Arthur Goldhammer. Cambridge, Mass.: Harvard University Press.

Small, David B. 1992. Review of Bruce Trigger, 1989, *A History of Archaeological Thought*. In *American Journal of Archaeology* 96: 163–64.

———. 1991. "Initial Study of the Structure of Women's Seclusion in the Archaeological Past." In Walde and Willows, *The Archaeology of Gender*, 336–42.

Smith, R. R. R. 1991. *Hellenistic Sculpture*. London: Thames and Hudson.

Spain, D. 1992. *Gendered Spaces*. Chapel Hill: University of North Carolina Press.

Spector, Janet D. 1983. "Male/Female Task Differentiation among the Hidatsa: Toward the Development of an Archaeological Approach to the Study of Gender." In Patricia Albers and Beatrice Medicine, eds., *The Hidden Half: Studies of Plains Indian Women*, 77–99. Lanham, Md.: University Press of America.

———. 1991. "What This Awl Means: Toward a Feminist Archaeology." In Gero and Conkey, *Engendering Archaeology: Women in Prehistory*, 388–406.

Sperling, S. 1991. "Baboons with Briefcases vs. Langurs in Lipstick: Feminism and Functionalism in Primate Studies." In di Leonardo, *Gender at the Crossroads of Knowledge: Feminist Anthropology in the Postmodern Era*, 204–34.

Stewart, Andrew. 1990. *Greek Sculpture: An Exploration*. New Haven: Yale University Press.

Stone, Peter, and Robert MacKenzie. 1990. *The Excluded Past: Archaeology in Education*. Boston: Unwin Hyman.

Sutton, Robert F., Jr. 1981. *The Interaction between Men and Women Portrayed on Attic Red-figure Pottery*. Ann Arbor: University Microfilms.

———. 1992. "Eros in Love: Pederasty and Pornography in Greece." In Richlin, *Pornography and Representation in Greece and Rome*, 3–52.

Talalay, Lauren. 1991. "Body Imagery of the Ancient Aegean." *Archaeology* 44(4): 46–49.

Taylor, William W. 1948. *A Study of Archaeology*. (American Anthropological Association Memoir Series 69.) Carbondale and Edwardsville: Southern Illinois University Press.

Tickner, Lisa. 1988. "Feminism, Art History, and Sexual Difference." *Genders* 3: 92–128.

Trembley, J. T., ed. 1992. "In and Out of Our Times: New Avenues in Art, Archaeology, Architecture." *Bryn Mawr Alumnae Bulletin* (Spring): 2–5.

Trigger, Bruce G. 1989. *A History of Archaeological Thought*. Cambridge: Cambridge University Press.

Tringham, Ruth. 1991. "Households with Faces: The Challenge of Gender in Prehistoric Architectural Remains." In Gero and Conkey, *Engendering Archaeology: Women in Prehistory*, 93–131.

Ucko, Peter J. 1968. *Anthropomorphic Figurines of Predynastic Egypt and Neolithic Crete with Comparative Material from the Prehistoric Near East and Mainland Greece* (Royal Anthropological Institute Occasional Paper 24). London: Andrew Szmidla.

———. 1989. "Foreword." In Miller, Rowlands, and Tilley, *Domination and Resistance*, ix–xiv.

Vermeule, Emily. 1992. "The World Turned Upside Down." *The New York Review of Books* 39 (6): 40–43.

Walde, Dale, and Noreen Willows, eds. 1991. *The Archaeology of Gender: Proceedings of the 22nd Annual Chacmool Conference*. Calgary: Calgary University Press.

Walker, Susan. 1983. "Women and Housing in Classical Greece: The Archaeological Evidence." In Cameron and Kuhrt, *Images of Women in Antiquity*, 81–91.

Wallace-Hadrill, A. 1988. "The Social Structure of the Roman House." *Papers of the British School at Rome* 56: 43–97.

Weinstein, J. M. 1992. Review of Martin Bernal, 1991, *Black Athena II*. In *American Journal of Archaeology* 96: 381–83.

Wilkie, Nancy, and William Coulson, eds. 1985. *Contributions to Aegean Archaeology: Studies in Honor of William A. McDonald*. Minneapolis: Center for Ancient Studies, University of Minnesota.

Williams, B. 1981. *Breakthrough: Women in Archaeology*. New York: Walker.

Williams, Dyfri. 1983. "Women on Athenian Vases: Problems of Interpretation." In Cameron and Kuhrt, *Images of Women in Antiquity*, 92–106.

Wiseman, James. 1980. "Archaeology in the Future: An Evolving Discipline." *American Journal of Archaeology* 84: 279–85.

Woolger, J. B., and R. J. Woolger. 1987. *The Goddess Within*. New York: Fawcett Columbine.

Wylie, Alison. 1985. "The Reaction against Analogy." *Advances in Archaeological Method and Theory* 8: 63–111.

———. 1991. "Gender Theory and the Archaeological Record: Why Is There No Archaeology of Gender?" In Gero and Conkey, *Engendering Archaeology: Women in Prehistory*, 31–54.

———. 1992. "The Interplay of Evidential Constraints and Political Interests: Recent Archaeological Research on Gender." *American Antiquity* 57: 15–35.

11

The Ethnographer's Dilemma and the Dream of a Lost Golden Age

Amy Richlin

Every oppressed group needs to imagine through the help of history and mythology a world where our oppression did not seem the pre-ordained order. Aztlan for Chicanos is another example. The mistake lies in believing in this ideal past or imagined future so thoroughly and single-mindedly that finding solutions to present-day inequities loses priority, or we attempt to create too-easy solutions for the pain we feel today.
—Cherríe Moraga, "From a Long Line of Vendidas" (1986: 188–89)

Optimists and pessimists

Why does anyone study the past? That is, what are people's motives for doing this, and what are the possible results? Looking forward to the panel from which this book began, Marilyn Skinner wrote to me, "We ought to see some wonderful battles between the optimists and the pessimists." I have been thinking about this accurate but odd division ever since. How mysterious: what is there to be hoped for, or despaired of, in the past? Do these hopes relate to our own progress in knowledge? Scholars often talk in terms of "getting somewhere," as if all learning were a quest with a grail at the end of it, or a series of metamorphoses, with a last glorious transformation at the end. Reflecting on the history of a field of scholarship, people tend to divide it into developmental stages, implying "We were dumb before, but we're smart now." (Thus the volume you hold in your hands might define itself as the new, improved version of women in antiquity; really the different kinds of thinking are interdependent.) "Beyond X" is a common title: after structuralism comes poststructuralism; after modernism, postmodernism. Like Mr. Ramsay in Virginia Woolf's *To the Lighthouse*, thinkers are obsessed with getting past Q to the next letter of the alphabet, and so finally to some ultimate Z. Or does our optimism or pessimism relate to our actions in the present and our goals for the future? The problem is that the focus on hope or despair, the focus on getting to Z, has obscured political goals and divided writers more and more from any audience outside the academy. As Cherríe Moraga suggests, it is not good to get distracted from what needs to be done.

I myself am a gloomy writer, included among the pessimists in Marilyn Skinner's assessment. My research began with Roman satire and invective, texts now rarely read outside the field of classics. Here is an example of what I read (*Priapea* 46; my translation):

272

O girl no whiter than a Moor,
but sicker than all the queers,
shorter than the pygmy who fears the crane,
rougher and hairier than bears,
looser than the pants that Medes or Indians wear:
[why don't you go away?]
for though I might seem ready enough,
I'd need ten handfuls of [Spanish fly]
to be able to grind the cracks of your groin
and bang the swarming worms of your cunt.

This comes from the *Songs of Priapus*, a group of lyric poems in which the ithyphallic god who watched over Roman gardens threatens to rape intruders. But there is a great deal of material like this in Latin, and indeed in Greek, in later European cultures, and in non-European cultures. The more I looked, the more I found; I soon began to hypothesize that such texts went along with basic social formations, and not only in Rome. This coincided with my growing awareness of violence against women in my own culture, on my own campus, on my own street. Three months after my book *The Garden of Priapus* first came out, the woman who had captained the Princeton crew with me was raped and murdered; she was barely thirty years old.

So I write in anger, and I write so that oppression is not forgotten or left in silence. Yet I know this is not the only way to write. I once team-taught a course with Walter Williams, the historian of gender, whose work has emphasized the freedom of sexual identity within Native American and other non-European cultures. He used to tell me that the glass is half full, and that my gloomy views derive from the cultures I have chosen to study. I know that other feminists in my discipline do find positive things in those cultures. I also know that it is not part of the traditional practice of classics to care so much about the social implications of texts. As we read Latin and Greek, we distance ourselves, muffling the meaning with layers of grammar, commentary, and previous scholarship. We skip things. I think that is not a responsible or honest way to read, and that reading should be socially responsible; this is one reason classicists need feminist theory—our old way of reading keeps us cut off. As a woman, a feminist, and a scholar, I want to know what relation scholarship can have to social change. This question seems to me to necessitate serious thought about the attitudes we bring to our work—our optimism or pessimism—and their relation to action.

Thinking about optimists and pessimists and their arguments with each other within the academy, I have evolved a taxonomy in order to describe them. Sandra Joshel, whose work on Roman slavery figures below, and who is always a sharp critic, objects that my oppositional categories obscure overlaps and exclude other possibilities: life is not either-or. You will have to imagine her saying "But . . ." at the end of each paragraph. The making of such a taxonomy is itself characteristic of one of its own main categories, and her objection is characteristic of the other. I would argue that my neat categories describe something that is really there and needs to be addressed in this sort of orderly way; but I concede the overlaps, which indeed give the system its paradoxical energies, and make it possible for us to talk to each other. The chart below groups theorists at two levels: according to their assumptions about knowledge, and according to their feelings about what they study. For feminist theorists, these divisions are already well-known; the consideration of feeling as a motive for theory may be new. I think it is important to be conscious of this web of attitudes for several reasons. It forms a background of unexamined assumptions to every current discussion; it distracts from clear thinking about the political uses of scholarship; and it some-times camouflages scholarship as activism. Our energy is directed to arguments about theory rather than to action or solidarity. For classicists, these ideas are important because we have hardly as yet become aware of the whole argument, much less worked out its implications for us.

The first split lies at the level of epistemology: the question of what is knowable, of how we know what we know. Some people believe in what is called "grand theory," a kind of theory which claims validity across history and cultures. I would call this an optimistic epistemology, since it takes a sanguine attitude toward the ability of a human subject to view a huge mass of information and express it in a meaningful order. Other people pooh-pooh grand theory and work on tracing local-historical differences instead. I would call this a pessimistic epistemology, since it takes a negative attitude: huge masses of information are chaotic ("complex," "shifting"), and human efforts to reduce them to "order" are futile and self-deluding (because necessarily solipsistic). Thus this group de-scribes the efforts of the first group as "reductionist," and condemns its theories as "totalizing theories."[1] The optimists stress similarities, the pessimists stress difference. Though some optimist groups (for example, Marxists) do make histori-cal change part of their model, the pessimist groups tend to accuse the optimist groups of being ahistorical and stress their own "historicizing" of phenomena. Often models that posit very slow change—in terms of millennia—seem to register with their opponents as no-change models.

The second split lies at the level of attitude. Optimists see in the past, or in other cultures, good things to be emulated; pessimists see bad things that determine or elucidate our own ills. This split depends on personality as much as on politics, and implies an infinite number of fruitless arguments. Writers accentuate either the positive or the negative, usually to make a larger point; then the larger point is forgotten or obscured by the dueling details of the positive/negative picture. Optimists and pessimists tend to annoy each other and quarrel: those who celebrate "women's culture" are attacked as romantic; the cheerful, upbeat, and inventive Foucauldians are critiqued as politically naive; the glum chroniclers of patriarchy are in turn dismissed for their use of grand theory. What is important is what is getting lost, the larger point at stake, the "so what." "See? Women can be

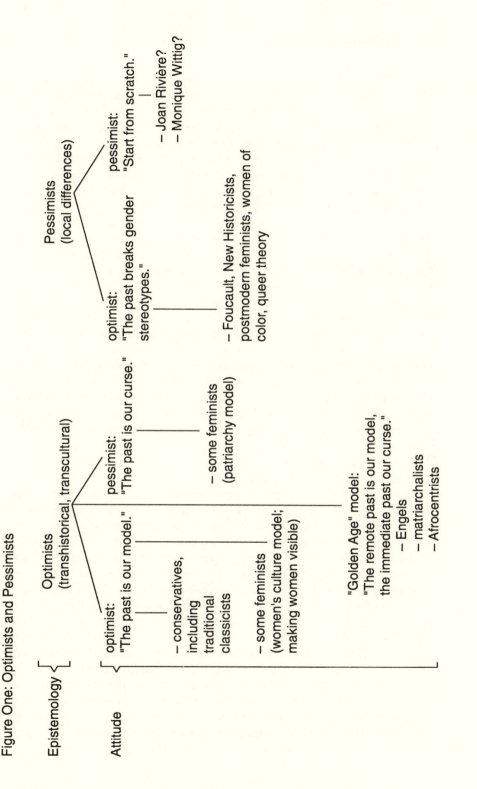

Figure One: Optimists and Pessimists

Epistemology

Optimists
(transhistorical, transcultural)

Pessimists
(local differences)

Attitude

optimist:
"The past is our model."

– conservatives,
including
traditional
classicists

– some feminists
(women's culture model;
making women visible)

pessimist:
"The past is our curse."

– some feminists
(patriarchy model)

"Golden Age" model:
"The remote past is our model,
the immediate past our curse."

– Engels
– matriarchalists
– Afrocentrists

optimist:
"The past breaks gender
stereotypes."

– Foucault, New Historicists,
postmodern feminists, women of
color, queer theory

pessimist:
"Start from scratch."

– Joan Rivière?
– Monique Wittig?

275

powerful" vies with "See? Women have always been oppressed." The implied "Then . . ." that connects to action usually remains implicit; whole social programs hover—unexpressed—behind articles on Belgian mine workers or ancient Greek pederasty. Sometimes it is hard to tell the players apart; as the chart shows, an optimistic epistemology often goes with a pessimistic tone, and vice versa. To avoid confusion in what follows, I will use "Optimist" and "Pessimist" to refer to epistemologies, "optimist" and "pessimist" to refer to attitudes.

Feminists in the academy are currently engaged in a running argument about grand theory (see de Lauretis 1990 for overview; Rose in this volume). In this case, the issue is cast as "essentialism"—the belief that something (woman, patriarchy, sexuality) exists as an abstract entity that would be recognizably the same across time and cultures. Feminist theorists in the 1970s built their political analysis on the idea of patriarchy (gender asymmetry in which power tends to reside in males over females), which they saw as universal, or nearly so. Moreover, whereas a long tradition in Western thought held that women were essentially different from men and inferior to them (Aristotle, Aquinas, Freud), and some feminists countered this by arguing for the equality/sameness of women and men, other feminists countered by arguing that women are essentially different from men and superior to them (Mary Daly, Adrienne Rich). These feminist essentialists stress qualities like nurturance, warmth, kindness as inherently female. But the 1980s saw the rise of postmodernist theory, which is generally hostile to grand theory, and the rising consciousness of differences among women themselves across class, race, sexual, and geopolitical lines. "Difference" for women of color means the assertion of identity; in contrast, postmodernist theory, despite its emphasis on the particular and on local-historical differences, rejects the idea of the "subject"—the independent individual; instead, each person represents an intersection of fluctuating currents of power, so that the whole culture makes up a sort of network. Recent anti-essentialist arguments assert that the female (for example) would have a different meaning in any given culture, even that the category "woman" is meaningless; and indeed that some constructs in culture A would not exist as such in culture B (for example, Michel Foucault's claim that "homosexuality" is a nineteenth-century idea [1978: 43]). The strength of the anti-essentialist reaction seems to come partly from a feeling of revulsion against an idea that was for so long used against women; partly from a feeling that totalizing theories involve the theorist in speaking for other people, preempting them (a feeling that can result in aphasia, see Alcoff 1991; hooks 1990:26); and sometimes also from the belief that all totalizing theory is invalid. Thus some feminists have claimed both that the essentialist concept of gender is a trap for women and that it is not in fact valid. It is important to note that these are separate claims; too often the first ("trap for women") is asserted as if it were the second ("not valid"). I will refer to this assertion as the "wrong because depressing" argument; it has been the source of numerous detours and breakdowns. Long duration does not preclude change, and we have ample evidence that nature itself is a historical entity.

Postmodern ideas have been met by some feminist theorists with interest, by others with indignation.[2] Without the category "woman," some wonder, how can we have feminism? The disappearance of the subject, they point out, also neatly makes disappear the material existence of oppression, of agency and responsibility; this critique often takes the form of what I have called (1991: 161) the "just-when" argument: "Just when women (people of color, colonial people) finally begin to claim subjecthood, Western elite theorists claim there is no such thing."[3] Still, "essentialist" is now a bad word, something no one wants to be, while feminism shatters into feminisms. Each side claims confidently that its methodology points the way to women's future, and will usher in profound social change. Fine: how?

The title of our volume, *Feminist Theory and the Classics*, invites the question of what contribution feminists in classics can make to feminist theory in other fields. How you answer this question depends very much on where you stand in relation to grand theory. If you are interested in a construct like "patriarchy" and want to test how long it has gone on, it is helpful to have as much information as you can get about cultures two thousand years in the past. If you are not, the value of classics changes. If we abandon a model that charts a pattern over long periods of time, if each culture is distinct, then time collapses into space and classics becomes a branch of anthropology, investigating its cultures. Nor can classics offer a special method; whereas anthropology, for example, not only finds out as much as it can about individual cultures but postulates rules for how cultures work, classics stops at finding out as much as it can about two cultures within a set period (c. 1500 B.C.E. to c. 500 C.E.). The rules we have generated have to do with how to find things out more efficiently. Our only special claim was that Greece and Rome themselves were somehow important, either because of their intrinsic worth or because of their putative status as the origin of Western culture. When such claims are abandoned or rejected, what does classics have to offer? One answer seems to be that, to those who stress difference within our culture, it has been important to stress difference in the Western past. And those who want to prove that the modern period is different in kind from earlier periods need to know something about them. The glamor of antiquity is slow to evaporate. Arguments both optimistic and pessimistic often depend on having (or not having) an understanding of what happened in the ancient Mediterranean.

The Ethnographer's Dilemma and the Dream of a Lost Golden Age

The division into Optimist and Pessimist has taken two special forms within the disciplines of anthropology and history. (1) Feminist and postmodernist anthropology have, for some years now, been increasingly involved with what I call the ethnographer's dilemma. For example: radical feminists early on decried crimes against women, and gave genital mutilation (clitoridectomy) as a prime instance (Daly 1978: 153–77; Barry 1979: 189–92).[4] They Optimistically assumed their values applied to all cultures. But feminist anthropologists began to wonder whether it is really incumbent upon Western scholars to view other cultures in light of our own values, among which they placed feminism. Suppose that Other women derive pride and satisfaction from practices we find abhorrent ("oppressive")? This principle also applies to less extreme examples, like division of labor (women take pride in weaving, potmaking, tubergathering) or religious segregation (the menstrual hut as source of solidarity, even primacy). Where an old-fashioned Marxist analysis would have called pride in clitoridectomy "false consciousness," feminists are now uneasy about labeling other people's values false, preferring that each should speak for herself. On the other hand, anthropologists generally have become conscious that the observer cannot escape her own values; we see through the eyes socially constructed for us. For a feminist, the combination of these realizations produces an epistemological double bind (we should try to see things through the Other's eyes, but we can't) and brings into question the whole purpose of the anthropological project. Maybe the West should stop being so nosy. Maybe we should just stay home. But what about home? Does this mean it's all right for women to have cosmetic surgery? And what about false consciousness—should we learn to respect clitoridectomy? Are values ever transferable?

The bogging down of the ethnographer coincided with the rise of the field of postcolonial theory and subaltern studies. During the 1980s, theorists' attention turned to the aftermath of the invasion and occupation of many parts of the world by Europeans in the modern period. Now that these occupations are officially over, or fading, the people who live in those parts of the world, or who returned to the "mother country," have begun writing about what it means to them to have two languages and two cultures, or a mixed culture. The title of Gayatri Spivak's noted article, "Can the Subaltern Speak?" (1988), refers to the problem of finding a voice for those who are outside the structures of power and language in colonial systems (for example, the title character in Mahasweta Devi's story "Draupadi"). In what language should s/he speak? What gives people the power to speak? These issues, long recognized in feminist theory (see Gal 1991 for a review), take on a new dimension when race, gender, and class combine with a colonial history. The voices speaking out of the colonies have turned the ethnographer's monologue into a conversation and remind us whose dilemma it is. For the ancient world, the problem is that we do have many "native" voices; but we have to scramble to find the voices of women, of slaves, and of those who were literally colonized within that world.[5] Since our conversation has to be one-sided, our dilemma rarely troubles us.

One way out of the ethnographer's dilemma has been suggested by anthropologist Lila Abu-Lughod. In "Can There Be a Feminist Ethnography?" (Abu-Lughod

1990: 26–27), she talks of the practice of anthropology by indigenous anthropologists and "halfies," people of mixed cultural background: "Their agony is not how to communicate across a divide but how to theorize the experience that moving back and forth between the many worlds they inhabit is a movement within one complex and historically and politically determined world." Women working on women, she says, do break down the self/other divide, to a degree. But, unless just being a woman in our field is enough, feminists in classics can never be "halfies." We cannot even be participant observers. We suffer all the drawbacks of being "colonizers" of the past—thousands of years of skewed sources, invasion into cultures that did not ask us to come—without the advantage of actually being able to go there. On the other hand, we do speak the language; and there is no one to resent us, nor is Messallina here to tell her own story.

(2) At the same time that anthropologists have been getting nervous about what we do when we look else*where*, historians have been redefining what they think they are doing when they look else*when*. Postmodernist historians, at least, have produced a version of history writing that is closely aligned with anthropology and exhibits the same paradoxes (see Veeser 1989 on the New Historicism). Michel Foucault has inspired a school of critics who look for local differences in stretches of the past, mapping a terrain of ideas and social mores.[6] The epistemological problem on which they focus was formulated by Louis Montrose (1989: 20) as "the textuality of history, the historicity of the text." That is, as past events are only actually knowable to us through a screen of texts—rather, the screen of texts is all that is knowable to us of the past—so each text must be located in its historical context and can only be understood within that context. This leaves the historian in much the same position as the anthropologist in her dilemma, able at best to appreciate and understand; value judgments are not part of this method (see Newton 1988 for a feminist critique).

However, ironically, and maybe because appreciation *is* still part of the method, this school of history writing falls into what I would call the dream of a lost golden age. Societies in the past, especially precapitalist societies, are privileged; the strangeness of their customs is admired, their emotions seen as free of the dread hand of Freud. This optimistic attitude shows up, to give a classical example, in the work of the Foucauldian John J. Winkler, who often sets up what he calls "ancient Mediterranean" cultures in favorable contrast to what he calls "NATO cultures" (Winkler 1990: 13, 27, 73, 93). We see here how the elsewhere and elsewhen can be combined.

But it is not only the postmodernist historians who look to the past for something to admire. Other kinds of historians want to use past cultures as a means to redeem the present, or claim the distant past as a charter for future social change. This desire can be seen as a form of what is called in religion studies "chronological dualism"—a belief that there was once a time when everything was wonderful, then there was a Fall so that we have the long expanse (including now) when everything is terrible, but someday there will again come a time when everything will be wonderful. Models like this combine optimism with pessimism, in stages. The theorists who have chosen this model make odd companions. (1) Some feminist historians and archaeologists have looked to the past for instances of matriarchy, high valuation of women, or goddess worship; the implication is that if such a state of things existed once, it can exist again. (This can be seen to be similar to the feminist anthropologist project of finding models else*where*: if there is gender equality among the !Kung San, we can have it, too. As anthropologist Micaela di Leonardo points out, this move was partly justified by first claiming that cultures elsewhere represented "primitive" societies, living remnants of the elsewhen [di Leonardo 1991a: 15].) Most of the scholars looking for matriarchy in the past focus on pre-Indo-European cultures and the traces of their survival; but some have even looked to the Greco-Roman world. Bella Zweig and Tina Passman in this volume make forceful arguments along these lines.

(2) A second and increasingly active group of historians seek to put the rest of the Mediterranean world back into our picture of antiquity, turning to African and Semitic cultures from their Greek and Roman neighbors (see Shelley Haley in this volume); for Afrocentrists, this forms part of a political program of reclaiming a great past. (3) An early and influential chronological-dualism model was produced by Engels, who was a contemporary of the early anthropological writers on matriarchy; in *Origin of the Family, Private Property, and the State*, he posited what he called the "world historical defeat of women," a time in the distant past when egalitarian societies gave way to male-dominated ones. This time began with the rise of states and would come to an end with revolution in the means of production. Engels's influence on feminist theory in the 1970s was considerable.[7] (4) Finally, and oddly enough, the romantic view of the golden past also seems to be responsible for the politically conservative discipline of classics itself: viz. the name. You wouldn't think that the august male philologists Wilamowitz and Gildersleeve had much in common with Merlin Stone or Cheikh Anta Diop or Engels, but all of their projects are determined by a belief that certain pasts are especially worthy of study and that such study empowers the student. This leaves us with a sad argument for the arbitrary nature of the historical endeavor, since all these romantics have sallied forth into the past and returned with completely different trophies. If we agree that all the trophies were there to be found, along with others, there is still wide disagreement about which ones are worth looking for, and how to establish criteria.

It is my goal here to set out for the reader an array of feminist theorists in anthropology, history, and classics, both (O)ptimist and (P)essimist, ending with some illustrations from ancient material culture. I have picked these disciplines and these illustrations in order to stress materialities as much as possible, to maintain a focus on women's lives. The debate over grand theory—whether framed in terms of essentialism, the ethnographer's dilemma, or the dream of a lost golden age—strikes me as having served its purpose and run its course. It has raised the consciousness of scholars, and makes for less naive analyses, but its focus on particulars gets to be paralyzing, and it is the source of feuds among people who need to form political coalitions. As will be seen, some theorists in the fields to be covered are arriving at the same conclusion: we need to acknowledge our differences, but we can work together. My own preference is for an Optimistic epistemology that maps a real reality and then does something about it; difference is a part of reality, not a sign of its demise.

Anthropology, History, Women in Antiquity

Anthropology

The ethnographer's dilemma and the dream of a lost golden age were being discussed in feminist anthropology by the early 1980s, and the most recent discussions in part reproduce what was being said ten years ago. In an excellent overview, Judith Shapiro (1981: 119) divided feminist anthropological work into two types, one seeking "to affirm the universality of male dominance and to seek ways of accounting for it without falling into biological determinism. Another [denies] the generality of the pattern by producing cases to serve as counterexamples . . . showing how sexual differentiation may imply complementarity as well as inequality." Bella Zweig applies a complementarity model to ancient Greece in this volume; contrast Eva Keuls's depiction of Athens as phallocracy (Keuls 1985). The perception of the division Shapiro outlined as a choice between grand theory and local-historical differences has driven postmodernist feminist anthropologists into quandaries, for example, Henrietta Moore in *Feminism and Anthropology*, who begins from the premise that "the concept 'woman' cannot stand" (Moore 1988: 7). Moore is then defensive about doing "feminist" anthropology, and states outright that "the basis for the feminist critique is not the study of women, but the analysis of gender relations," dismissing earlier work (Moore 1988: vii, 6). In this, she is anticipating a trend, in which women per se have gone out of fashion; a new collection of essays in feminist anthropology, intended (di Leonardo 1991b: vii) as an update on the classic *Woman, Culture and Society* (Rosaldo and Lamphere 1974), is titled *Gender at the Crossroads of Knowledge*, underscoring the retreat of some feminist scholarship from "women" to "gender" (Modleski 1991: 3–22).

The ethnographer's dilemma is a specialized form of this grand-theory issue. Judith Shapiro sums up the problem (Shapiro 1981: 117):

> Marxist idealizations of sex-role differentiation in small-scale societies bring us back to the Noble Savage; what we are seeing is an attempt to seek a charter for social change in the myth of a Golden Age. This approach is also a way of avoiding one of the thornier problems that recent sex-role studies have raised for the field of anthropology, which is the question of how we can go about adopting a critical perspective

> on societies very different from our own. . . . If we engage in a critique
> of other cultures . . . do we risk engaging in what we have generally
> seen as the opposite of anthropology—missionization? . . . Do we
> operate with a theoretical double standard: a critique of society for us
> and functionalism for the natives?

Micaela di Leonardo, in her recent survey of feminist anthropology, notes that anthropologists have had to contend with actual complaints from third world women about "uninformed Western feminist deprecation of non-Western gendered practices" (di Leonardo 1991a: 11). Again, the problem throws Moore into self-reproach: feminist anthropology, by trying to be inclusive, practiced exclusion; anthropologists were pre-empting third world women, and thereby being not just ethnocentric but racist (Moore 1988: 191). Di Leonardo devotes a whole section of her overview to the dilemma, which she calls "ethnographic liberalism and the feminist conundrum," and which she sets in the context of anthropology's political relation to its object of study (di Leonardo 1991a: 10): "how could we analyze critically instances of male domination and oppression in precisely those societies whose customs anthropology was traditionally pledged to advocate?" Her formulation points to a way in which this issue is relevant for classics: classicists are trained to feel a strong love for the ancient world, a duty to cherish its memory. Thus her words bear a significant resemblance to the way in which the ancient historian Judith Hallett posed the problem in a recent paper (Hallett 1992: 7): "How are we to foster a debate about ancient Greek and Roman constructions of sexuality which acknowledges the shortcomings of Greek and Roman societies?" The cultural separation of anthropologists from the cultures they study, and the cultural continuities between antiquity and the present that are part of the self-definition of classics, both leave the feminist in a position that makes it hard to justify her own critique.

Golden age models and origins theories attempt to escape the ethnographer's dilemma via the past. A great deal of attention is taken up in anthropology and archaeology by the question of who is responsible for human civilization, man-the-hunter or the new contender woman-the-gatherer; some want to find woman-centered cultures in the remote past, others at least to make Neolithic women visible (Gero and Conkey 1991). Michelle Rosaldo's often-cited "The Use and Abuse of Anthropology" duly includes a section on the search for origins and universals (Rosaldo 1980: 390–96; cf. O'Brien and Roseberry 1991). Best known herself as a formulator of grand theory (so described in di Leonardo 1991a: 13), she nonetheless directs a frown at origins theories, on the grounds that they depict gender systems as "essentially unchanging" (Rosaldo 1980: 392–93). This is a version of the "wrong because depressing" argument; note also here the way "long-lasting" or "slow to change" is read as "unchanging." On the other hand, Rosaldo more or less concedes that "sexual asymmetry" is a universal, and calls ignoring it "romantic" (Rosaldo 1980: 396). A good word to choose: surely these arguments about the most distant human past exhibit clearly the mythopoeic impulse driving scholarly endeavors—the rewriting of Genesis.

The discipline emerges as a battleground for Optimist and Pessimist epistemologies, incorporating optimist and pessimist attitudes. Di Leonardo lists six solutions theorists have posed to solve the "feminist conundrum": various types of grand theory, including Engels's Marxist model; various optimistic models, in which women are either said to enjoy high status in a given culture, or the power of their separate sphere is stressed. Her favorites are the *Verstehen* model associated with Weber, in which the investigator tries to get into the mindset of the ones investigated, and a sort of feminist Marxist theory that stresses the study of political economy. She rejects postmodernist theory (di Leonardo 1991a: 17–27) as nihilistic, incapable of political commitment, and points out that it is possible to see problems in language without throwing the material world overboard. Even Moore (1988: 10–11) posits a kind of feminist postmodernism that will hang on to real women's real experiences, rather than just listing their varieties.

These issues matter to classicists because we, too, have to worry about dealing with cultures not our own. We need a theory that can define our relation to the people we are studying: what is a writer supposed to do who studies cultures buried in the past, who reads "dead" languages? If the goal of feminist anthropology is to replace monologue with conversation, we have still to decide what the equivalent would be for speech about the past. We, too, have to examine our reasons for writing (about) the past; we need a theory that spells out the relation between "antiquity" and ourselves. Moreover, as we pore over our fragmentary evidence, it is useful to us to make comparisons with other cultures. Ongoing work in Mediterranean anthropology (for example, Dubisch 1986, Herzfeld 1985, Brandes 1981) has seemed particularly pertinent (as in Winkler 1990), but comparative method is not limited by geography; to explain Roman obscene humor, I use comparanda ranging from Africa to Mexico to Turkey to Hollywood (Richlin 1992a). So we need a theory that can justify such comparisons.[8]

But, as feminists, we all need to remind ourselves of why we are doing this in the first place. If the idea originally was to find a charter for social change someplace else, we should not let arguments about how to find the charter keep us from working on the social change. We should not wind up talking about women extremely remote from us in time and space, in language extremely remote from the everyday, so that we never have time to talk in everyday words with women close to us. We should hold on to the reality of what we are doing.[9]

History

Feminist theory in history has come to focus on problems in dealing with the elsewhen much like those anthropologists have found in dealing with the elsewhere. Moreover, there is a surprising degree of agreement among feminist historians of various political persuasions. To begin with, it is repeatedly stated that the goal of writing women's history is social change. Gerda Lerner begins *The Creation of Patriarchy* (Lerner 1986: 3) with the words, "Women's history is indispensable and essential to the emancipation of women." Judith Newton emphasizes the point in her materialist critique of postmodern theory (Newton 1988: 94); more surprising, Joan Scott also talks of "feminist commitments to analyses that will lead to change" in her essay "Gender: A Useful Category of Historical Analysis" (Scott 1989: 83). These same critics are willing to begin from the premise that history is mythmaking (Lerner 1986: 35–36; Newton 1988: 92). Lerner both acknowledges the human need for myth and calls on feminists to abandon "the search for an empowering past . . . compensatory myths . . . will not emancipate women in the present and the future" (Lerner 1986: 36).

But historians are left in an uncomfortable position with regard to grand theory other than golden age-models. Accepting the hortatory function of writing history involves a steady reluctance to hear bad news, and more versions of the "wrong because depressing" argument. Thus a model that posits the transhistorical existence of patriarchy is said by its opponents to be ahistorical (i.e., wrong), because it involves something that does not change over time (or has not changed yet; or has not changed for as long as we have records). To Joan Scott, patriarchy watchers are pessimists: "History becomes, in a sense, epiphenomenal"; against varieties of grand theory, she sets "my hopeless utopianism" (Scott 1989: 86–87, 91), an interesting oxymoron. More resourcefully, Gerda Lerner suggests that totalizing theory can comprehend change: "anatomy *once was* destiny" (Lerner 1986: 52–53, her emphasis). Such a position seems to me to be both more productive and more sensible than the wholesale rejection of grand theory. Here classics has something to contribute: a long view. We are used to noting trends over the two thousand year period which is our own domain, along with the fifteen hundred years that came after. In this perspective, capitalism is a flash in the pan. On such a large scale, local-historical differences do not seem so significant, or so different. Rather than serving as an end in themselves, surely their best use is to modify grand theory, not vitiate it.

To solve their problem, historians express a desire for a combined model that will let them describe both women's oppression and their agency—the fact that women were not always just victims (Lerner 1986: 4; Newton 1988: 99; Fiorenza 1989: xv, 25, 85–86). These two concepts, "oppression" and "agency," correspond with "pessimistic" and "optimistic" expectations on the part of scholars. Linda Gordon (1986: 23–24) sketches three similar pessimist/optimist oppositions: between "domination" and "resistance" models; among Marxists, between structure and agency; and, among feminists, between political history and social history. The social historians who recover women's culture are accused by the gloomy political historians of "romanticization of oppression." Here we have a historical version of the ethnographer's dilemma: is women's separate culture, women's special world, a thing of beauty or a grinding oppression? This is where the category "woman" begins to vanish down the rabbit hole. To reconstruct Greek or Roman women's separate culture requires years of painstaking research and putting together tiny fragments; we long to know more; and yet almost everything we get is filtered through male texts and a culture that favored the male. A combined model would take into account the male nature of the sources while keeping a firm grip on the women hidden behind them.

An approach like this would be able to test the model of the "world historical defeat of women" tied to the rise of states by Engels, which should be of special interest to classicists. Rome in particular developed from a small-scale pastoral culture to a large-scale empire, turning other small-scale cultures into colonies as it went along. We might look at Irene Silverblatt's work on the Inca (Silverblatt 1991), in which she takes a strongly optimistic view of women's position; Judith Hallett's work on Roman elite women leads in a similar direction (Hallett 1984a, 1989a). The problem, for all periods of history, is to avoid restricting our gaze to the elite, or adopting a strong identification with or admiration of the studied culture. In many cases *Verstehen* all has been to forgive all.

The ethnographer's dilemma is noted by historians as a problem also for modern women looking into the past; there is the same Self/Other difference, the same imbalance of power between observer and observed. Here, where elsewhere and elsewhen merge, so do the ethnographer's dilemma and the dream of a lost golden age. As in Judith Shapiro's remarks about the use of the noble savage in anthropology, the distance between now and an imperfectly known then allows for all sorts of wishful projections. And the search for validation in the past haunts even those writers who are critical of such searches. Nazife Bashar, arguing against the usefulness of the concept "the status of women" cross-culturally (Bashar 1984), surveys a group of English historians of women, all of whom structure their history as a progression—or regression: the bad old days or the golden age. Yet Bashar concludes that, without a golden age, "the future looks dismal."[10] Those who seek matriarchy in the past have come under attack by historians (Lerner 1986: 16, 26–35, 146–48), archaeologists (see Brown, Passman, Zweig in this volume), and historians of religion (Fiorenza 1989: 18, 21–31). Yet all these in turn are themselves seeking validation in the past. Lerner's history is a search for a charter: if patriarchy has a historical beginning, it can have a historical ending. The archaeologists just substitute woman-the-gatherer for the Goddess. Church historians are looking for some church mothers. The mythmaking function of history seems inescapable.[11]

But possibly there are other functions. For a classicist, an exciting, and surprising, extra set of motivations comes from Elizabeth Schuessler Fiorenza's *In Memory of Her*, a feminist history of the early church that devotes three lengthy chapters to theory. There is no doubt in Fiorenza's mind as to why the study of the first century c.e. is relevant; to her, the Bible is a living document. Most classicists pay no attention to Christians, the Moonies of the Roman empire, or to Jews; yet, all the time, flourishing beside us, large numbers of feminist historians of religion are writing about the periods we think of as our own, and by necessity writing about non-elite culture. Feminist biblical scholars often think in terms of salvage, of finding women in the sacred text, but Fiorenza recognizes the operation as dangerous: "the source of our power is also the source of our oppression" (Fiorenza 1989: xviii, 35). Feminists in classics might think here of our problematic relation to our own canonical texts, and of the controversies over "reappropriating" beloved male authors (*Helios* 17.2 [1990]). And Fiorenza also makes a claim for writing history as activism: remembering the sufferings of women in the past is a reclaiming of them; it "keeps alive the suffering and hopes of Christian women in the past but also allows for a universal solidarity of sisterhood with all women of the past, present, and future" (Fiorenza 1989: 31, cf. xix–xx; hooks 1990: 43, 215). In this optimistic model, we are helping, not hurting, when we speak for these dead others. We are actually doing something for them.

Women in Antiquity

If anthropology and history are perhaps overly embroiled in epistemological questions, the study of women in antiquity has been preoccupied with empirical ones. What can we find out from our material? Feminists in classics are only too familiar with the textuality of history, and have made a business out of reading gaps and silences. We can attest that studying gender doesn't mean not studying women. The nature of our sources has forced us to think in terms of gender systems from the outset; feminists in classics began working on gender, the body, and sexuality in the late 1970s.[12] Most ancient women are outside literary texts; we have asked, is history a more feminist project than literary criticism? But, in our work, we have rarely paused to worry about the ethnographer's dilemma, and have until recently taken grand theory for granted.

A new interdisciplinary collection presents the reader with the unusual sight of a feminist epistemologist commenting on a survey of feminist work in classics (Harding 1991, on Gutzwiller and Michelini 1991). Sandra Harding (1991: 103) asks:

> what are the feminist assumptions that permit contemporary women to identify with other women across two millennia, across the vast cultural differences between Antigone's culture and ours, across the class, race, and sexual identity differences between contemporary female feminist readers and the imagined female audiences for these literatures.[13]

Harding uses our praxis to suggest that the ethnographer's dilemma can be overcome, that all kinds of difference can be bridged. But it's a good question: what *are* our assumptions, anyway? And why do we study the past?

A look at major surveys written in the field of women in antiquity shows a narrow range of motives and assumptions, among which it is hard to find Harding's question. The field may be dated to a conference at SUNY Buffalo that resulted in a special issue of the classical journal *Arethusa* in 1973. Surveys and collections followed: Sarah Pomeroy's *Goddesses, Whores, Wives, and Slaves* (1975) is the best known outside the field, but during the 1980s waves of brave pioneers pushed the frontiers onward (see list in appendix). In accord with the empiricist bent of classics, some of these justify themselves by the modest claim to be presenting new research results to the reader. Most also refer to the basically optimistic women's studies goal of making women visible in history; Mary Lefkowitz and Maureen Fant (1982), in the most stripped-down version, stop with these two assertions. However, from the beginning a tacitly pessimistic grand theory justification from origins is present; thus Pomeroy (1975: xii):

> The story of the women of antiquity should be told now, not only because it is a legitimate aspect of social history, but because the past illuminates contemporary problems in relationships between men and women. Even though scientific technology and religious outlook clearly distinguish ancient culture from modern, it is most significant to note the consistency with which some attitudes toward women and the roles women play in Western society have endured through the centuries.

Similarly Helene Foley (1981: xii): "In studying these literary texts carefully we examine, in effect, the origins of the Western attitude towards women." John Peradotto and J. P. Sullivan open with an explicitly gloomy version (Peradotto and Sullivan 1984: 1):

> Prejudice against women . . . goes back to the very beginning of western culture . . . we are prone to idealize [Greek and Roman] cultures. . . . Without belittling their achievements and their contributions, however, we ought not to blind ourselves to the seamier legacies they left us.

They go on to say in so many words that they are writing a history of gender oppression, likening the history of women to "the history of slavery and the origins of racial prejudice"(Peradotto and Sullivan 1984: 4).

The field has looked for patterns rather than differences. A striking instance is the statement by Averil Cameron and Amélie Kuhrt (1983: ix): "although the societies under discussion vary greatly . . . the questions which suggest themselves are remarkably constant." (Their table of contents is broken down into the following sections: Perceiving Women, Women and Power, Women at Home, The Biology of Women, Discovering Women, The Economic Role of Women, Women in Religion and Cult.) This seems odd in a collection that includes articles on Greek, Persian, Assyrian, Egyptian, Hittite, Celtic, Hurrian, Hebrew, and

Syrian women, from cuneiform tablets and hieroglyphics, papyrus and codex; many of these cultures are not Indo-European; and the time span covered within antiquity is greater than that between the late antique and today. A postmodernist might argue that the remarkable consistency of the questions that "suggested themselves" belonged to the Ancient History Seminar of the University of London rather than to the cultures studied. A fan of grand theory would counter that the consistency inhered in the cultures themselves, and was discovered, not invented.

A similar faith in unified theory is manifested by Ross Kraemer in her sourcebook on women in ancient religions (Kraemer 1988:4):

> I approach the sources primarily as a feminist historian of religion: I seek to recover and understand the religious beliefs of women and to integrate that knowledge into a revised, enriched appreciation of human religion. . . . The texts here . . . are where we must begin to reconstruct women's religion in antiquity, to inquire about the differences between women's religion and men's as well as about the similarities, and to revise our models and theories accordingly.

That is, while she recovers an immense amount of particular knowledge about particular cultures, Kraemer's project involves the categories "women's religion," "men's religion," and "human religion," and the ancient religions studied form part of these possible transhistorical entities.

In the teeth of these disciplinary, epistemological, and political appeals to grand theory, and of her own oath of fealty to "the basic postulates of feminist theory" including a belief in patriarchy, Marilyn Skinner (1986: 4) suggests there has been a "far-reaching intellectual shift within our own discipline," which she calls "postclassicism":

> . . . most readily characterized . . . by its denial of the *classicality* of the ancient cultural product, its refusal to champion Greco-Roman ideas, institutions and artistic work as elite terrain, universally authoritative and culturally transcendent, and therefore capable of only one privileged meaning. Instead, it subscribes to the idea of all cultural artifacts and systems as broadly accessible "texts" open to multiple and even conflicting readings.

The move here conceals a step which undercuts grand theory much in the way outlined in the discussions of essentialism and of history above: some grand theory is repugnant, therefore grand theory itself is bad. Skinner is talking about refusing the privilege accorded to Greco-Roman ideas by conservatives, those on the political right (Allan Bloom, Camille Paglia). Because of the history of right-wing, anti-woman use of Greece and Rome in grand theory, Skinner, and others, want to de-privilege Greece and Rome. There is more than one way to do this:

the feminist grand-theory approaches listed above make Greece and Rome the origin of something bad rather than of all things good. Skinner describes an alternate way, which pulls the rug out from under the right by doing away with grand theory altogether.

Similarly, David Konstan and Martha Nussbaum, in a collection influenced by Foucault and focusing on sexuality rather than on women, reject the tendency of grand theory to see (or construct) patterns (Konstan and Nussbaum 1990: iii): "The appropriation of classical Greece and Rome as origins and models of a so-called "Western" tradition has helped to obscure some of the deep differences between ancient and modern societies." This is the same move made by Marilyn Skinner. In order to reject a right-wing claiming of Greece and Rome as full of things the right wing likes, this group chooses to say not "those things were there but they're bad" but "those things were not there—different things were there." Things, as it turns out, that *we* like: different sexualities, different attitudes toward knowledge, women writers.[14] Greece and Rome remain models, sources of inspiration, for "postclassicists" just as they were for conservatives. The difference is that the postclassicists look to the past for liberatory models rather than ones that preserve the status quo.

Two recent collections go back to grand-theory assumptions. *Stereotypes of Women in Power* (Garlick, Dixon, and Allen 1992) raises the question of why the same kinds of negative images are used against politically powerful women across cultures and time (see Dixon's "Conclusion," *ibid.*, 209–25). The collection traces what it names as a single phenomenon through Egyptian, Roman, Byzantine, medieval Scandinavian, Ming Dynasty, Renaissance Italian, Victorian, and modern Australian cultures. A related premise initiated *Pornography and Representation in Greece and Rome* (Richlin 1992c), which applies modern feminist theory on the pornographic to ancient cultures. Both collections share a focus on images that are arguably harmful to women, some extremely harsh.

But between the pessimistic grand-theorists and their more optimistic opponents, Harding's question—what are our assumptions?—has been left a little in shadow. Both sides have been drawn instead into a simpler version of the optimist/pessimist battle, a variety of what Micaela di Leonardo dubs "the 'native women better off' argument" (di Leonardo: 1991a: 11): the question is reduced to "how bad was it for women in antiquity, really?" And, due to the relative inaccessibility of ancient women and the insistent presence of the calendar boys of the canon, the battle has receded to an argument over telling the "good guys" from the "bad guys" (cf. Rose 1992: 8, 33–42); this may sound familiar to critics working on other periods. Reading against the text, reading for a subversive text (see Gold, Zweig in this volume), became popular for beloved great authors like Homer. The argument is most strongly substantiated for the plays of Euripides, as recently summarized in Gutzwiller and Michelini 1991; his heroines are well-known to the nonclassicist, but Gutzwiller and Michelini (1991: 75) also make a claim for the Hellenistic age and the poet Callimachus. In a similar way, many have argued for a feminine persona or feminist sympathies in the Roman poets Catullus (Skinner forthcoming), Horace (Oliensis 1991), Ovid (Hemker 1985, Cahoon 1988), and the elegist Propertius (Hallett 1984b, Gold in this volume). Yet a strong and diametrically opposite argument has been made about these same authors, claiming their work to be marked by extreme machismo, by violence against women, and by repeated fantasies of rape (Rabinowitz 1986, 1992, 1993 on Euripides; Richlin 1984, 1992a, 1992b). Sandra Joshel argues that Roman men's imaginings of woman structure their imagining of empire (Joshel 1992a).

So, at a controversial panel of the Women's Classical Caucus in 1985, the ancient historian Phyllis Culham argued that a feminist project on women in antiquity would stop spending time on the panel's proposed theme: "Reappropriating Male Texts: The Case of Ovid" (Culham 1990, with responses). A questioner in the audience that day asked whether this meant "counting the steps to the fountain house"; Culham replied "yes," and backed this up with a call for a renewed commitment to the recovery of women's lived experience, using a feminist empiricism informed by theory (Culham 1986). Indeed the quarrel over how to read literary texts becomes meaningless—arbitrary—unless seen in the context of gender norms in the culture as a whole. Such an ability to dolly back from texts produced Judith Hallett's innovative and provocative model (Hallett 1989a): here she claims for women in elite Roman culture a simultaneous status as "Same" and "Other," foregrounding some positive statements about Roman women ("in her, her father's talents lived again") that previous models had dismissed or elided. Students of Greece and Rome often feel that Roman women were relatively well off (see Gardner 1986: 257–66), but studies of ancient ideology have tended to lay out repetitions in misogyny. Hallett here points to a kind of kin-based pride in women that does seem characteristically Roman. Her move here and in her earlier work on the Roman family (Hallett 1984a) recalls the search by feminist historians to recover women's agency along with their oppression.[15] The trick will be for us as scholars to view ancient women as both "Same" and "Other"; we may be seeing them too much as us.

We need to interrogate not only the received epistemology of our discipline but the epistemology within which we have been working on women in antiquity. The ethnographer's dilemma has hardly touched feminist writing in classics; where other disciplines have had too much of it, we could perhaps stand to have more. Many categories have grown blurry: "Greece and Rome" is used interchangeably with "the ancient Mediterranean" (excluding Africa and Asia); fifth-century B.C.E. Athens is often made representative of all antiquity; "Greece" is used when only "Athens" is meant; "Rome" is used without much consideration of the hugeness and ethnic variation of the empire; the Iron Age cultures of northern Europe are left to archaeologists. Most of all, though feminists have worked hard to correct the old bias whereby "Romans" meant "Roman men," a focus on literary texts has often led scholars into a nebulous, class-free world in which they can say "women" and mean "free citizen women." Even David

Schaps's useful *Economic Rights of Women in Ancient Greece* just writes off slaves and prostitutes in the introduction (Schaps 1979: 2), despite his title. Such a prefatory disclaimer has been much disparaged by theorists of difference.[16] Just as critiques by women of color and postcolonial women have changed the face of feminist theory, so new work on women in antiquity should aim for the incorporation of the subjectivity of slave and colonized women. Sandra Joshel's work on Roman slave child-nurses (Joshel 1986) serves as a model here, and Madeleine Henry's work on prostitutes opens up another vista (Henry 1985, 1992). The critiques of classics for its exclusion of Africa have not dealt with gender; this work is just beginning (see Haley in this volume). And we need to be conscious that many of the ancient women we know best—some themselves not freeborn—owned slaves, and participated in the colonizing of the ancient world.

Pliny's Brassiere: Still Life with Absent Objects

Here are some examples of how (O)ptimism and (P)essimism are played out in the study of ancient material culture. I will present to the reader a range of items that have to do with the lives of Roman women. They might be used to show the longevity of patriarchy, or the ability of women to resist by means of their own culture. They might be used to show the horrors of the Roman colonial system, or to recover the voices of the colonized. The tone of the picture depends on the attitude of the painter.

To stress difference, an anthropologist or historian will often stress the strangeness of the studied culture (Darnton 1984: 3–7). Hence the subtitle of this section, which refers to one of the many strange flashes of Roman culture available in the writings of the elder Pliny, an upper-class scientist of the first century C.E. Pliny's voluminous *Natural History* is full of recipes for medicines, many to be made from the secretions of humans and other animals. And at one point Pliny says: "I find that headaches are relieved by tying a woman's brassiere (*fascia*) on [my/ the] head" (Pliny *HN* 28.76). Now, this example exemplifies also the problem of transhistorical interpretation. The word *fascia* is conventionally translated "breast-band" (*Oxford Latin Dictionary* s.v. 2.a), a word with no connotations in English. The oddity of Pliny's behavior is lessened or intensified depending on whether we translate "breast-band" or "brassiere." Really to understand how a Roman would have seen this act, we would have to know more about Roman attitudes toward women's breasts, and check out the usage of the word *fascia* (does it appear in Roman dirty jokes? No). The picture of the dignified polymath laboring away late into the night at the *Natural History* with a brassiere on his head can serve the modern reader in different ways. For a New Historicist, it is a reminder of the uniqueness of Roman culture, and a corrective for earlier, homogenized pictures of the Romans. For a feminist, it raises many questions about the significance of the female body in Roman ideology. Are you an optimist?

Pliny valorizes the female body by using it to cure himself: there is no limit to it, he says (Pliny *HN* 28.77). Are you a pessimist? This is part of an ideology in which the female body is colonized for male use (look back at that poem from the *Priapea*); or monstrous—elsewhere in Pliny, we find discussions of the fearful powers of menstrual blood.

Pliny also confides in us (*HN* 22.45) that Roman women chewed gum. The feminist, rummaging happily through the volumes of Pliny and other encyclopedists, picks up here and there more indicators that Roman women had what ethnographers call "foodways." They are said to have preferred certain sweet drinks, *muriola* and *passum* (sweet wine and raisin wine, Paulus ex Festo 131L, Varro in Nonius 551M); again, we can translate this into Diet Coke and white wine spritzers, or we can refuse to be so misled, and *Verstehen* further, constructing a map of Roman women's foodways. Optimistically celebrating women's culture, we can connect foodways with other indicators that Roman women had a subculture of their own: a special way of talking (evidence discussed in Hallett 1989a: 62), special modes of transport (Paulus ex Festo 225L, 282L), and of course a clearly marked dress code (Paulus ex Festo 112L). The texts—not only elite literary texts but laws, anecdotes, and inscriptions—tell us plenty about Roman women's active lives in public and private (Gardner 1986; Hallett 1989a; Forbis 1990). Maybe Roman women had a group identity!

Pessimistically, we might ask whether this is identity or the face of oppression. Roman lesbians are lost behind a screen of invective (Hallett 1989b), and Roman women's sexuality in general is very hard to recover. Furthermore, we would have to pull back and remind ourselves that these "women" are not all women, and that most of the scraps culled from our rummaging probably describe free citizen women, in Italy. Nevertheless we do not have to fall back on what might be our version of the old feminist bogey: "add slaves and stir." It is indeed possible to recover a women's culture that cut across class lines, which alas turns out to be, as far as we can tell, structured by the institutionalized abuse of slave women by free women. This shows up, for example, in Roman rituals like the festival of Mater Matuta, in which *matronae* drove a slave woman out of a sacred enclosure by slapping her; and in many other rites which divide women according to their sexual accessibility. (So is this a "women's culture"? We still have a top-down view.)[17] Similar distinctions seem to have held in Greek cultures as well; the whole point of the prosecution of Neaira, for example, which tells us so much about the miseries of a prostitute's life in classical Greece, is that she had tried to pass her daughter off as fit to carry out certain ritual roles.[18] (For an optimist's rendition of Greek women's subjectivity, see Zweig in this volume.) In Theocritus's *Idyll* 15, from Hellenistic Egypt, two happy, bourgeois housewives go off to the queen's festival, abusing their maids and leaving the baby home with the nanny. This poem is often read in courses on women in antiquity to show how the power of the Hellenistic queens raised the status of women in Hellenistic culture; but we might compare Black theorist Audre Lorde's criticism of white bourgeois feminists whose attendance at feminist conferences depends on household work by women of color (1984).[19] The ancient tchatchke industry, which produced huge masses of terracotta figurines, seems to have included old nurses along with pretty girls (and old men, dwarves, actors) as suitable decorative objects; shades of the Aunt Jemima salt shaker. The pessimist will find further examples of interclass oppression in art, like the three female attendants who stand around a woman seated in a wicker chair in a stone funerary monument from Roman Gaul (published in Kampen 1982: fig. 15); one holds a mirror to her mistress's face. Satire (should we believe it?) gleefully describes such mistresses stabbing their hairdressers with hairpins and causing them to be flogged (Ovid *Ars Amatoria* 3.239–42; Juvenal *Satire* 6.487–507). Here is a good test case for the ongoing debate on the validity of Engels's theory of the world historical defeat of women with the rise of the state: certainly the institutions of imperialism and slavery are better for some women than for others.

The optimist, nothing daunted, can turn around and begin to construct a subjectivity for the women of the underclasses, about whom the literary texts give us such a small and biased view. The article by Natalie Kampen from which I abstracted the Gallic altar begins with a full-page photograph of a relief sculpture from Ostia, showing a woman selling vegetables, facing the viewer, her hand extended in what is known as the "speaker's gesture" (Kampen 1982: 62). Whether she is saying, "Buy some asparagus," or "I'm the best darn vegetable-seller in the Forum Holitorium," this woman made her mark, and had the money to do it. Sandra Joshel (1992b) has in a large-scale study reconstructed a voice for the freed slaves of Rome from the inscriptions they placed, usually on their tombs, that talk about their occupations; here we see men, women, kin networks, the interrelationships between owner and owned.

Outside of Italy, there are papyrus letters from Hellenistic and Roman Egypt that often speak to and for women (we cannot always be sure whether they were written by a scribe); these have much to tell us about women's lives. For example, a soldier's letter home to his wife calmly advises her to keep the baby if it is a boy, and to cast it out if it is a girl. Another letter gives an account of how a peasant woman arrested a bathman who had scalded her with hot water. One gives what seems to be a woman's shopping list.[20] Texts in Latin are harder to come by, but one turned up recently—a letter from the Roman frontier fort of Vindolanda in the north of Britain (Bowman and Thomas 1987: 137–40); here we have a shred of the life of a colonizing woman, an officer's wife inviting another to her birthday party.

All these "texts" serve the postcolonial theorist's program of locating the subaltern's speech (Spivak 1988), a program with huge implications for classics, since the ancient world was a flourishing and multilingual site of slavery and imperialism. The implications of Rome's status as an empire (a status, it must be noted, also held at various times by some Greek, Asian, and African cities) are only starting to be explored in postcolonial terms. Athenian ideology of Self versus barbarian Other has been dealt with, and Page duBois established the intersection of this version of Self/Other with that of gender (duBois 1982). A field day for the pessimistic historian lies ahead, as the vast ethnographic writings of the Romans unroll their record of atrocities. These records, moreover, constitute in themselves an argument for the transhistorical nature of the colonial mind (*colonia* is a Roman word, though in fact colonies were established by Greeks and Carthaginians while the Romans were herding cattle). For that matter, they establish the pedigree of the involvement of ethnography with empire.

Yet the seeker for difference between ancient and modern can find it here. It is hotly debated whether the concept of "race" existed in antiquity (see Haley in this volume); the Greeks and Romans were certainly xenophobic, but is this racism? The amused Foucauldian can ponder with interest the amply attested Roman contempt for northern Europeans, described in terms of physical stereotypes as huge, stupid, lazy, and barbarous (Sherwin-White 1967).

Beyond Optimism and Pessimism

In the end, I come back to my original question, Why study the past? If feminists—optimists and pessimists alike—are all really hoping for better days ahead, how can we best use our study of the past to make that dream come true?

The one thing of which I am sure is that we cannot contribute to a revolution if we speak only to each other and in very difficult language.[21] Nor is it likely that such writing will change any laws or feed anyone. Arguments, even schisms, over issues like essentialism take energy and attention away from action. Looking into the past or far away, some people accentuate the positive and some the negative, and a lot of that is just personal preference—though I would never let the history of oppression be denied. But nobody is ever going to get to Z. Meanwhile, many people outside the academy do want to know about the past; we can write for them. If we do not, the followers of Allan Bloom will. Meanwhile, we cannot make change contingent on myths of the past.

What are we trying to do? Describe truth? Contribute to a revolution? Achieve immortality through the brilliance of our scholarship? Get tenure? Prove that we're right and the other people are wrong? Sometimes I think that scholarship is just an art form, a weird esoteric art form that often plays to an audience of one or two people. But then I think that this is the ultimate pessimistic epistemology.[22] Sometimes I think that scholarship is just a job, like plumbing or typing: something we do all day, in our radical or conservative way. Revolutionary activity mostly happens outside our working hours, assuming we leave time for it; and most revolutionary activity is carried on by people who are not scholars. But sometimes I do think that there is something revolutionary about knowing the past; that when we recover long-gone women from oblivion we are really shifting some balance; that what is taught in the classroom, what is written in the history books, makes a difference. This cheers me up. Still, I think the future of feminist theory lies in proving what the connection is between the scholarly journals and the streets. bell hooks writes: "We must actively work to call attention to the importance of creating a theory that can advance renewed feminist movements, particularly highlighting that theory that seeks to further feminist opposition to sexist oppression" (hooks 1992: 81). What would this mean for classics? What can we do to make a difference?

Notes

Many thanks to Nancy Sorkin Rabinowitz and Sandra Joshel for hours on the telephone. This essay owes much to ongoing conversations with Sheryl Conkelton, Judith Hallett, Micaela Janan, Ellen Olmstead, and Diana Robin, and to the extraordinary resources of Dennis Johnson and the Occidental College Bookstore. Special thanks to Gregory Thalmann, and to Shelby Brown and David Small for talking about archaeology. Lon Grabowski continues to give me hope for life after patriarchy, always nice for a natural pessimist. For S.V.R., with all my love.

1. See, for example, Butler 1992, where totalizing theory is identified with racism and blamed for the U.S. war on Iraq; in general, see the overview presented in the introduction to Butler and Scott 1992, where "poststructuralism" itself is seen as a totalizing term. For comments on such claims, see Rose in this volume. The division I outline is usually historicized as one between the Western humanistic tradition and postmodernism; for a lucid introduction, see Nicholson 1990: 1–4. I am, in part, oversimplifying; but the anti-grand-theory ideas of postmodernism can be found in the past, for example in the sophistic tradition of the fifth century B.C.E. For a model similar to mine, comparing various theories of writing history to big-bang versus steady-state theories, see Golden 1992. On the intersection of nineteenth-century schools of historiography with the study of women in antiquity, see the analysis by Josine Blok (1987). Her division into positivism and idealism corresponds in many ways to mine between Optimism and Pessimism, and provides important and erudite historical context. For a helpful overview that includes the middle ground of standpoint epistemology, see Harding 1987: 181–90; further remarks are in the introduction to Richlin 1992a.

2. Collections that take a primarily positive attitude toward Foucault or postmodernism include Diamond and Quinby 1988; Weed 1989. Nicholson 1990 includes two especially critical pieces, by Nancy Hartsock and Susan Bordo; to which add Pierce 1991; Modleski 1991. For a critique of postmodernism in anthropology, see Mascia-Lees et al. 1989. Butler 1992 is framed as a response to such critiques, which she refers to as "the chant of antipostmodernism" (Butler 1992: 17); for the volume in which her essay appears, the editors indeed posed a useful set of questions critical of postmodernism for the contributors to respond to (Butler and Scott 1992: xiv–xvii). Contrast hooks 1990: 23–33. For an introduction to the current state of feminist theory, see Hirsch and Keller 1990; a good basic introduction to feminist theory is Tong 1989, which however does not cover literary theory.

3. To instances in Richlin 1991, add Hartman and Messer-Davidow 1991: 4; Harding 1991: 112. The argument is discussed by hooks 1990: 26–29, and specifically

countered by Butler 1992: 14–15. For a lively, reader-friendly, and strong critique of essentialism as a problem in feminist theory, including chapters on Plato and Aristotle, see Spelman 1988.

4. Compare the recent case of Aminata Diop of Mali, whose case prompted the French Commission for Appeals of Refugees to become "the first judicial body to recognize genital mutilation as a form of persecution under the terms of the Geneva Convention," reported in *Ms.* (January/February 1992), 17. Alice Walker's recent novel, *Possessing the Secret of Joy* (Harcourt Brace Jovanovich, 1992), focuses on clitoridectomy as a central issue.

5. The bibliography in postcolonial studies is enormous and growing. A good place to start might be Michelle Cliff's two essays in Rick Simonson and Scott Walker, eds., *The Graywolf Annual Five: Multi-Cultural Literacy* (St. Paul: Graywolf Press, 1988: 57–81); Cliff's training in the classical tradition makes these pieces especially resonant for a classicist. For a sampling of the field to date, see Mohanty et al. 1991; Parker et al. 1992. Works by Trinh T. Minh-ha and Gayatri Spivak are important, but much more difficult.

6. On Foucault, see bibliography in Diamond and Quinby 1988; for a critique of the "hagiographical industry" writing about him, Bersani 1985.

7. See Tong 1989: 47–51, 274–78, for a brief discussion and introductory bibliography.

8. The relationship between classics and anthropology is an old one; see Finley 1975, Humphreys 1978, Culham 1986: 9–14, Redfield 1990, and Passman and Zweig in this volume. Page duBois (1988: 24–29) gives an elegant account of the implications of the ethnographer's dilemma for her own work on Greek culture.

9. On the political of theoretical language, see hooks 1990: 23–33; hooks 1992: 80, "It is evident that one of the uses of theory in academic locations is in the production of an intellectual class hierarchy where the only work deemed theoretical is abstract, jargonistic, difficult to read, and containing obscure references. It is easy to imagine different locations, spaces outside academic exchange, where such theory would not only be seen as useless, but would be seen as politically nonprogressive." For a striking example, see Alcoff 1991, which is actually *about* achieving dialogue among all kinds of women, and praises Barbara Christian's "The Race for Theory," which attacks the very kind of language Alcoff uses in her piece.

10. This essay appears in an extremely useful workbook, ideal for teaching, consisting as it does of short essays on basic problems of theory, interspersed with case studies on the history of preindustrial women. The book is also hard to find; write to: Women's History Group, P.O. Box 4, Canberra, ACT 2601, Australia.

11. See Gordon 1986 for a sharp and balanced discussion.

12. For feminist work on ancient sexuality, see Richlin 1991, 1992a, including bibliography; on the female body in ancient medicine and philosophy, see Dean-Jones 1992, with bibliography.

13. Note the use here of "Antigone," a character in a play by Sophocles, apparently to mean "an ancient woman." Feminist work on antiquity has tried to disentangle such constructs, among others; see Rabinowitz in this volume.

14. See, for example, Halperin 1990 on Greek pederasty; Winkler 1990 on ancient interpretation of dreams, magical practices, and women's culture. Foucauldian accounts of antiquity amount to a submerged chronological dualism, in which, for example, greater sexual freedom is imputed to the Greeks (the Romans remain vague), with the suggestion that our own culture could profit by the example. This is unfortunately in large part wishful thinking; see Richlin 1991, 1993 for further critique.

15. Work on family history in antiquity is generally relevant to feminist concerns. See esp. the work of Suzanne Dixon; in her book on the Roman mother (1988) she distinguishes between Roman and modern definitions of motherhood, considers slave motherhood, tries to recover feelings as well as facts, and considers children as well as parents. See also work by Keith Bradley, Valerie French, Beryl Rawson on Rome; Mark Golden on Greece.

16. See Spelman 1988: 2, 37–56, on women, slave women, and Aristotle. Sarah Pomeroy made this issue a focus of the introduction to her 1975 social history; it has tended to fade since then. Cross-class studies include Dixon 1988, Gardner 1986, Kampen 1982. For a critique of the disclaimer tactic, see Lugones 1991: 38; Alcoff 1991: 25; and, in general, Spelman 1988.

17. See Kraemer 1992 for an account of Roman women's religion. Compare María Lugones (1991), who uses Lorraine Bethel's "What Chou Mean *We*, White Girl?" to start her discussion of difference among feminists.

18. The speech *Against Neaira* (*In Neairan*, mid-4th c. B.C.E.), attributed to Demosthenes but probably not by him, may be found in translation in the Loeb series (*Demosthenes: Private Orations*, trans. A. T. Murray, vol. 3 [Cambridge and London: Harvard/Heinemann, 1939], pp. 347–451). For a brief discussion, see Keuls 1985: 156–58.

19. Cf. Gutzwiller and Michelini 1991: 75, and n.45.

20. The Loeb series provides a large and convenient collection of nonliterary papyri in translation (*Select Papyri*, vols. 1–2, ed. A. S. Hunt and C. C. Edgar [Cambridge and London: Harvard/Heinemann, 1932, 1934]). On infanticide, vol. 1, no. 105; on the bathman, vol. 2, no. 269; the shopping list, vol. 1, no. 186. For an introduction to work on women in papyri, see Pomeroy 1984.

21. On the disconnection between postmodernism and revolution, see Graff 1989: 174.

22. For a discussion of the co-optive force of the academy on feminists, see Bordo 1990; Fiorenza 1989: 6. For the postmodern *reductio ad artem*, see di Leonardo 1991b: 22–23, on Hayden White, and, in anthropology, on what she calls the "ethnography-as-text school," who "focus . . . away from the ethnographic experience, onto an analysis of ethnographic texts themselves."

Bibliography

Abu-Lughod, Lila. 1990. "Can There Be a Feminist Ethnography?" *Women & Performance* 5.1: 7–27.

Alcoff, Linda. 1991. "The Problem of Speaking for Others." *Cultural Critique* 12: 5–32.

Barry, Kathleen. 1979. *Female Sexual Slavery*. New York and London: New York University Press.

Bashar, Nazife. 1984. "Women and the Concept of Change in History." In Dixon and Munford 1984, 43–50.

Bersani, Leo. 1985. "Pedagogy and Pederasty." *Raritan* 5.1: 14–21.

Blok, Josine. 1987. "Sexual Asymmetry: A Historiographical Essay." In Josine Blok and Peter Mason, eds., *Sexual Asymmetry: Studies in Ancient Society*, 1–57. Amsterdam: J. C. Gieben.

Bordo, Susan. 1990. "Feminism, Postmodernism, and Gender-Scepticism." In Nicholson 1990, 133–56.

Bowman, Alan K., and J. David Thomas. 1987. "New Texts from Vindolanda." *Britannia* 18: 125–42.

Brandes, Stanley. 1981. "Like Wounded Stags: Male Sexual Ideology in an Andalusian Town." In Sherry B. Ortner and Harriet Whitehead, eds., *Sexual Meanings*, 216–39. Cambridge: Cambridge University Press.

Butler, Judith. 1992. "Contingent Foundations: Feminism and the Question of 'Postmodernism.' " In Butler and Scott 1992, 3–21.

Butler, Judith, and Joan Scott, eds. 1992. *Feminists Theorize the Political*. New York and London: Routledge.

Cahoon, Leslie. 1988. "The Bed as Battlefield: Erotic Conquest and Military Metaphor in Ovid's *Amores*." *Transactions of the American Philological Association* 118: 293–307.

Cameron, Averil, and Amélie Kuhrt, eds. 1983. *Images of Women in Antiquity*. Detroit: Wayne State University Press.

Culham, Phyllis. 1986. "Ten Years after Pomeroy: Studies of the Image and Reality of Women in Antiquity." *Helios* n.s. 13.2: 9–30.

———. 1990. "Decentering the Text: The Case of Ovid." *Helios* n.s. 17.2: 161–70.

Daly, Mary. 1978. *Gyn/Ecology: The Metaethics of Radical Feminism*. Boston: Beacon Press.

Darnton, Robert. 1984. *The Great Cat Massacre*. New York: Basic Books.

Dean-Jones, Lesley. 1992. *Women's Bodies in Classical Greek Science*. New York: Oxford University Press.

de Lauretis, Teresa. 1990. "Upping the Anti (sic) in Feminist Theory." In Hirsch and Keller 1990, 255–70.

Diamond, Irene, and Lee Quinby, eds. 1988. *Feminism & Foucault*. Boston: Northeastern University Press.

di Leonardo, Micaela. 1991a. "Introduction: Gender, Culture and Political Economy: Feminist Anthropology in Historical Perspective." In di Leonardo 1991b, 1–48.

———, ed. 1991b. *Gender at the Crossroads of Knowledge*. Berkeley: University of California Press.

Dixon, Suzanne. 1988. *The Roman Mother*. Norman: Oklahoma University Press.

Dixon, Suzanne, and Theresa Munford, eds. 1984. *Pre-Industrial Women: Interdisciplinary Perspectives*. Canberra: Australian National University Printery.

Dubisch, Jill, ed. 1986. *Gender and Power in Rural Greece*. Princeton: Princeton University Press.

duBois, Page. 1982. *Centaurs and Amazons: Women and the Pre-History of the Great Chain of Being*. Ann Arbor: The University of Michigan Press.

———. 1988. *Sowing the Body: Psychoanalysis and Ancient Representations of Women*. Chicago: University of Chicago Press.

Finley, M. I. 1975. "Anthropology and the Classics." In his *The Use and Abuse of History*, 102–19. New York: Viking Penguin.

Fiorenza, Elizabeth Schuessler. 1989. *In Memory of Her: A Feminist Theological Reconstruction of Christian Origins*. New York: Crossroad.

Foley, Helene P., ed. 1981. *Reflections of Women in Antiquity*. New York and London: Gordon and Breach Science Publishers.

Forbis, Elizabeth P. 1990. "Women's Public Image in Italian Honorary Inscriptions." *American Journal of Philology* 111: 493–512.

Foucault, Michel. 1978. *The History of Sexuality*. New York: Vintage.

Gal, Susan. 1991. "Between Speech and Silence: The Problematics of Research on Language and Gender." In di Leonardo 1991b, 175–203.

Gardner, Jane F. 1986. *Women in Roman Law and Society*. Bloomington: Indiana University Press.

Garlick, Barbara, Suzanne Dixon, and Pauline Allen, eds. 1992. *Stereotypes of Women in Power*. Westport: Greenwood Press.

Gero, Joan, and Margaret Conkey, eds. 1991. *Engendering Archaeology*. Oxford: Blackwell.

Golden, Mark. 1992. "Continuity, Change and the Study of Ancient Childhood." *Échos du Monde Classique/Classical Views* 36, n.s. 11: 7–18.

Gordon, Linda. 1986. "What's New in Women's History." In Teresa de Lauretis, ed., *Feminist Studies/Critical Studies*, 20–30. Bloomington: Indiana University Press.

Graff, Gerald. 1989. "Co-optation." In Veeser 1989, 168–81.

Gutzwiller, Kathryn J., and Ann Norris Michelini. 1991. "Women and Other Strangers: Feminist Perspectives in Classical Literature." In Hartman and Messer-Davidow 1991, 66–84.

Hallett, Judith P. 1984a. *Fathers and Daughters in Roman Society: Women and the Elite Family*. Princeton: Princeton University Press.

———. 1984b. "The Role of Women in Roman Elegy: Counter-Cultural Feminism." In Peradotto and Sullivan 1984, 241–62.

———. 1989a. "Women as *Same* and *Other* in the Classical Roman Elite." *Helios* 16:1: 59–78.

———. 1989b. "Female Homoeroticism and the Denial of Roman Reality in Latin Literature." *Yale Journal of Criticism* 3.1: 209–27.

———. 1992. "Ancient Greek and Roman Constructions of Sexuality: The State of the Debate." Paper presented at the symposium "Sexualities, Dissidence, and Cultural Change," April 10, University of Maryland at College Park.

Halperin, David M. 1990. *One Hundred Years of Homosexuality*. New York and London: Routledge.

Harding, Sandra, ed. 1987. *Feminism and Methodology*. Bloomington: Indiana University Press.

———. 1991. "Who Knows?: Identities and Feminist Epistemology." In Hartman and Messer-Davidow 1991, 100–115.

Hartman, Joan E., and Ellen Messer-Davidow, eds. 1991. *(En)Gendering Knowledge: Feminists in Academe*. Knoxville: The University of Tennessee Press.

Hartsock, Nancy. 1990. "Foucault on Power: A Theory for Women?" In Nicholson 1990, 157–75.

Hemker, Julie. 1985. "Rape and the Founding of Rome." *Helios* 12: 41–47.

Henry, Madeleine. 1985. *Menander's Courtesans and the Greek Comic Tradition*. Frankfurt: Peter Lang.

———. 1992. "The Edible Woman: Athenaeus's Concept of the Pornographic." In Richlin 1992c, 250–68.

Herzfeld, Michael. 1985. *The Poetics of Manhood: Contest and Identity in a Cretan Mountain Village*. Princeton: Princeton University Press.

Hirsch, Marianne, and Evelyn Fox Keller, eds. 1990. *Conflicts in Feminism*. New York and London: Routledge.

hooks, bell. 1990. *Yearning: Race, Gender, and Cultural Politics*. Boston: South End Press.

———. 1992. "Out of the Academy and into the Streets." *Ms*. 3.1 (July/August): 80–82.

Humphreys, Sally. 1978. *Anthropology and the Greeks*. London: Routledge and Kegan Paul.

Joshel, Sandra R. 1986. "Nursing the Master's Child: Slavery and the Roman Child-Nurse." *Signs* 12.1: 3–22.

———. 1992a. "The Body Female and the Body Politic: Livy's Lucretia and Verginia." In Richlin 1992c, 112–30.

———. 1992b. *Work, Identity, and Legal Status at Rome: A Study of the Occupational Inscriptions*. Norman: Oklahoma University Press.

Kampen, Natalie Boymel. 1982. "Social Status and Gender in Roman Art: The Case of the Saleswoman." In Norma Broude and Mary Garrard, eds., *Feminism and Art History: Questioning the Litany*, 62–77. New York and London: Harper & Row.

Keuls, Eva C. 1985. *The Reign of the Phallus*. New York: Harper and Row.

Konstan, David, and Martha Nussbaum, eds. 1990. "Sexuality in Greek and Roman Society." *differences* 2.1 (special issue).

Kraemer, Ross S[hepard], ed. 1988. *Maenads, Martyrs, Matrons, Monastics*. Philadelphia: Fortress Press.

————. 1992. *Her Share of the Blessings: Women's Religion among Pagans, Jews, and Christians in the Greco-Roman World*. New York: Oxford University Press.

Lefkowitz, Mary R., and Maureen B. Fant, eds. 1982. *Women's Life in Greece and Rome*. Baltimore: The Johns Hopkins University Press.

Lerner, Gerda. 1986. *The Creation of Patriarchy*. New York and London: Oxford University Press.

Lorde, Audre. 1984. "The Master's Tools Will Never Dismantle the Master's House." In her *Sister Outsider*, 110–13. Trumansburg, N.Y.: Crossing Press.

Lugones, María C. 1991. "On the Logic of Pluralist Feminism." In Claudia Card, ed., *Feminist Ethics*, 35–44. Lawrence: University Press of Kansas.

Mascia-Lees, Frances E., Patricia Sharpe, and Colleen Ballerino Cohen. 1989. "The Postmodernist Turn in Anthropology: Cautions from a Feminist Perspective." *Signs* 15: 7–33.

Modleski, Tania. 1991. *Feminism without Women: Culture and Criticism in a "Postfeminist" Age*. New York and London: Routledge.

Mohanty, Chandra Talpade, Ann Russo, and Lourdes Torres, eds. 1991. *Third World Women and the Politics of Feminism*. Bloomington: Indiana University Press.

Montrose, Louis. 1989. "Professing the Renaissance: The Poetics and Politics of Culture." In Veeser 1989, 15–36.

Moore, Henrietta L. 1988. *Feminism and Anthropology*. Minneapolis: University of Minnesota Press.

Moraga, Cherríe. 1986. "From a Long Line of Vendidas: Chicanas and Feminism." In Teresa de Lauretis, ed., *Feminist Studies/Critical Studies*, 173–90. Bloomington: Indiana University Press.

Newton, Judith. 1988. "History as Usual?: Feminism and the 'New Historicism.'" *Cultural Critique* 9: 87–121.

Nicholson, Linda J., ed. 1990. *Feminism/Postmodernism*. New York and London: Routledge.

O'Brien, Jay, and William Roseberry. 1991. "Introduction." In their *Golden Ages, Dark Ages: Imagining the Past in Anthropology and History*, 2–18. Berkeley: University of California Press.

Oliensis, Ellen. 1991. "Canidia, Canicula, and the Decorum of Horace's *Epodes*." *Arethusa* 24.1: 107–38.

Parker, Andrew, Mary Russo, Doris Sommer, and Patricia Yaeger, eds. 1992. *Nationalisms and Sexualities*. New York: Routledge.

Peradotto, John, and J. P. Sullivan, eds. 1984. *Women in the Ancient World: The Arethusa Papers*. Albany: State University of New York Press.

Pierce, Christine. 1991. "Postmodernism and Other Skepticisms." In Claudia Card, ed., *Feminist Ethics*, 60–77. Lawrence: University Press of Kansas.

Pomeroy, Sarah B. 1975. *Goddesses, Whores, Wives, and Slaves*. New York: Schocken Books.

———. 1984. *Women in Hellenistic Egypt*. New York: Schocken Books.

Rabinowitz, Nancy S[orkin]. 1986. "Female Speech and Female Sexuality: Euripides' *Hippolytos* as Model." *Helios* n.s. 13.2: 127–40.

———. 1992. "Tragedy and the Politics of Containment." In Richlin 1992c, 36–52.

———. 1993. *Anxiety Veiled: Euripides and the Traffic in Women*. Ithaca: Cornell University Press.

Redfield, James. 1991. "Classics and Anthropology." *Arion* (third series) 1.2: 5–23.

Richlin, Amy. 1984. "Invective against Women in Roman Satire." *Arethusa* 17.1: 67–80.

———. 1991. "Zeus and Metis: Foucault, Feminism, Classics." *Helios* 18.2: 160–80.

———. 1992a. *The Garden of Priapus: Sexuality and Aggression in Roman Humor*. New York: Oxford University Press. (Rev. ed. of 1983, New Haven: Yale University Press.)

———. 1992b. "Reading Ovid's Rapes." In Richlin 1992c, 158–79.

———, ed. 1992c. *Pornography and Representation in Greece and Rome*. New York: Oxford University Press.

———. 1993. "Not before Homosexuality: The Materiality of the *Cinaedus* and the Roman Law against Love between Men." *Journal of the History of Sexuality* 3.4: 523–73.

Rosaldo, M[ichelle] Z[imbalist]. 1980. "The Use and Abuse of Anthropology: Reflections on Feminism and Cross-cultural Understanding." *Signs* 5.3: 389–417.

Rosaldo, Michelle Zimbalist, and Louise Lamphere, eds. 1974. *Woman, Culture and Society*. Stanford: Stanford University Press.

Rose, Peter W. 1992. *Sons of the Gods, Children of Earth: Ideology and Literary Form in Ancient Greece*. Ithaca and London: Cornell University Press.

Schaps, David M. 1979. *Economic Rights of Women in Ancient Greece*. Edinburgh: Edinburgh University Press.

Scott, Joan W. 1989. "Gender: A Useful Category of Historical Analysis." In Weed 1989, 81–100.

Shapiro, Judith. "Anthropology and the Study of Gender." In Elizabeth Langland and Walter Gove, eds., *A Feminist Perspective in the Academy: The Difference It Makes*, 110–29. Chicago and London: The University of Chicago Press.

Sherwin-White, A. N. 1967. *Racial Prejudice in Imperial Rome*. Cambridge: Cambridge University Press.

Silverblatt, Irene. 1991. "Interpreting Women in States: New Feminist Ethnohistories." In di Leonardo 1991b, 140–71.

Skinner, Marilyn. 1986. "Rescuing Creusa: New Methodological Approaches to Women in Antiquity." *Helios* n.s. 13.2: 1–8.

———. Forthcoming. "*Ego Mulier*: The Construction of Male Sexuality in Catullus." *Helios*.

Spelman, Elizabeth V. 1988. *Inessential Woman: Problems of Exclusion in Feminist Thought*. Boston: Beacon Press.

Spivak, Gayatri Chakravorty. 1988. "Can the Subaltern Speak?" In Cary Nelson and Lawrence Grossberg, eds., *Marxism and the Interpretation of Culture*, 271–313. Urbana and Chicago: University of Illinois Press.

Tong, Rosemarie. 1989. *Feminist Thought: A Comprehensive Introduction*. Boulder and London: Westview Press.

Veeser, H. Aram, ed. 1989. *The New Historicism*. New York and London: Routledge.

Weed, Elizabeth, ed. 1989. *Coming to Terms: Feminism, Theory, Politics*. New York and London: Routledge.

Winkler, John J. 1990. *The Constraints of Desire: The Anthropology of Sex and Gender in Ancient Greece*. New York: Routledge.

Appendix: Short Bibliographies on Feminist Theory and on Women in Antiquity

Feminist Theory

There are many kinds of feminist theory, which have different and interesting applications in classics. The list here is not at all a comprehensive one—that would be many pages long—but is meant to give readers a way in, and includes both landmark work and new directions. All the works cited here have bibliographies of their own, which will take you further. For more on specific areas (anthropology, archaeology, art, class, film theory, history, mythology, race) see chapter bibliographies above.

Abel, Elizabeth, and Emily K. Abel, eds. 1983. *The Signs Reader: Women, Gender and Scholarship*. Chicago: University of Chicago Press. A group of classic essays: interdisciplinary.

Anzaldúa, Gloria, ed. 1990. *Making Face, Making Soul/ Haciendo Caras: Creative and Critical Perspectives by Women of Color*. San Francisco: Aunt Lute. Non-conventional format includes essays, poems, and scholarly writing.

Broude, Norma, and Mary Garrard, eds. 1982. *Feminism and Art History: Questioning the Litany*. New York: Harper and Row. Chronological; includes several essays on ancient art.

de Lauretis, Teresa, ed. 1986. *Feminist Studies/ Critical Studies*. Bloomington: Indiana University Press. Interdisciplinary.

Fuss, Diana, ed. 1991. *Inside/Out: Lesbian Theories, Gay Theories*. New York and London: Routledge. Includes work on literature, film, and culture.

Harding, Sandra, ed. 1987. *Feminism and Methodology*. Bloomington: Indiana University Press. Interdisciplinary, with focus on science and epistemology.

Hirsch, Marianne, and Evelyn Fox Keller, eds. 1990. *Conflicts in Feminism*. New York and London: Routledge. Interdisciplinary.

Hull, Gloria, Patricia Bell Scott, and Barbara Smith, eds. 1982. *All the Women Are White,*

All the Blacks Are Men, But Some of Us Are Brave: Black Women's Studies. Latham, N.Y.: Kitchen Table Press. Helpful early essays on Black women's studies.

Mohanty, Chandra Talpade, Ann Russo, and Lourdes Torres, eds. 1991. *Third World Women and the Politics of Feminism*. Bloomington: Indiana University Press. Postcolonial theoretical essays on the intersections of gender, race, and sexuality.

Moraga, Cherríe, and Gloria Anzaldúa, eds. 1983. *This Bridge Called My Back: Writings of Radical Women of Color*. Latham, N.Y.: Kitchen Table Press. One of the first anthologies of the writings of women of color.

Nicholson, Linda J., ed. 1990. *Feminism/Postmodernism*. New York and London: Routledge. Pro and con.

Rosaldo, Michelle Zimbalist, and Louise Lamphere, eds. 1974. *Woman, Culture, and Society*. Stanford: Stanford University Press. Classic essays in anthropology, much debated over the years.

Tong, Rosemarie. 1989. *Feminist Thought: A Comprehensive Introduction*. Boulder and London: Westview Press. A good general introduction to the political spectrum within feminism; does not cover literary theory.

Warhol, Robyn R., and Diane Price Herndl, eds. 1991. *Feminisms: An Anthology of Literary Theory and Criticism*. New Brunswick: Rutgers University Press. A reader, covering the past fifteen years; among a wide range of topics, includes classic essays in French feminism, film studies, and reading the romance.

Women in Antiquity/Feminism in Classics

Again, a comprehensive list of what has been published in the field would be enormous; listed here are collections of articles, special issues of journals, sourcebooks, and broad surveys. All include bibliographies that can open the way into the intricacies of publication in the field, of special interest for comparative work in art, history, law, literature, philosophy, religion, sexuality, and much else.

Blok, Josine, and Peter Mason, eds. 1987. *Sexual Asymmetry: Studies in Ancient Society*. Amsterdam: J. C. Gieben. Theoretical and anthropological approaches to the study of ancient women.

Cameron, Averil, and Amélie Kuhrt, eds. 1983. *Images of Women in Antiquity*. Detroit: Wayne State University Press. Unique range of cultures studied, from Hittite to Celtic (no Rome).

Foley, Helene P., ed. 1981. *Reflections of Women in Antiquity*. New York and London: Gordon and Breach Science Publishers. Greek/Roman.

Gutzwiller, Kathryn J., and Ann Norris Michelini. 1991. "Women and Other Strangers: Feminist Perspectives in Classical Literature." In Joan E. Hartman and Ellen Messer-Davidow, eds., *(En)gendering Knowledge*, 66–84. Knoxville: The University of Tennessee Press. Most recent survey.

Konstan, David, and Martha Nussbaum, eds. 1990. "Sexuality in Greek and Roman Society." *differences* 2.1 (special issue). Postmodernist/Foucauldian.

Kraemer, Ross S., ed. 1988. *Maenads, Martyrs, Matrons, Monastics*. Philadelphia: Fortress Press. Sourcebook on women's religion in antiquity.

Lefkowitz, Mary R., and Maureen B. Fant, eds. 1982. *Women's Life in Greece and Rome*. Baltimore: The Johns Hopkins University Press. Sourcebook.

Peradotto, John, and J. P. Sullivan, eds. 1984. *Women in the Ancient World: The* Arethusa *Papers*. Albany: State University of New York Press. Includes some art history.

Pomeroy, Sarah B. 1975. *Goddesses, Whores, Wives, and Slaves*. New York: Schocken Books. The first textbook in the field.

————, ed. 1991. *Women's History and Ancient History*. Chapel Hill: University of North Carolina Press. Greek/Roman; some art history.

Richlin, Amy, ed. 1992. *Pornography and Representation in Greece and Rome*. Uses feminist theory on the pornographic.

Scafuro, Adele, and Eva Stehle, eds. 1989. "Studies on Roman Women." *Helios* n.s. 16.1–2 (two special issues).

Skinner, Marilyn. 1986. "Rescuing Creusa: Women in Antiquity." *Helios* n.s. 13.2 (special issue).

Snyder, Jane McIntosh. 1989. *The Woman and the Lyre: Women Writers in Classical Greece and Rome*. A good general overview.

See also: *Helios* n.s. 17.2 (1990). Discussion by seven feminist classicists of Phyllis Culham's "Decentering the Text."

Index

Walker, Alice: 186, 296 n.4
Washington, Mary Helen: 26
Weaving: 10, 169–70, 252
Weedon, Chris: 129
Wender, Dorothea: 226–27, 228
Williams, Patricia: 24
Williams, Walter: 273
Winkler, John J.: 279
Wittig, Monique: 7, 79–80
Women
    as audience for male-authored texts, 7–8,
        91, 94–95n.7
    Black women in classics, 25–26
    controlled by men in Athenian culture, 220,
        227
    employment in field of classics, 5
    importance of women and the female in
        Greek culture, 164–71
    importance of women and the female in Na-
        tive American culture, 153–60

importance of women in Roman culture,
    290
in archaeology, 241–44, 245, 247
philosophers, Greek, 162–63
Women in antiquity (subfield): 8–11, 28, 31–
    32, 37, 224–25, 257–62, 286–91
Women's Classical Caucus: 8, 76, 243, 290
Women's culture and texts: 14–15, 56, 57, 59,
    61, 76, 128–29, 130–38, 145–46, 154–
    57, 161–66, 167, 168, 250, 251–52, 292,
    293
Woolf, Virginia: 6, 139 n.4, 272
Wyke, Maria: 63, 77, 93, 93 n.1, 94 n.10, 95
    n.21

Zeitlin, Froma: 57, 221–22, 223
Zweig, Bella: 57, 280, 281

Contributors

SHELBY BROWN is a classical archaeologist who has published on the Roman gladiatorial games and on Phoenician child sacrifice. She has excavated in Greece, Italy, North Africa, Portugal, Tunisia, and Israel.

BARBARA K. GOLD, Professor of Classics at Hamilton College, has published widely on Augustan Latin poetry; she is known especially for her *Literary Patronage in Greece and Rome* (Chapel Hill: The University of North Carolina Press, 1987). She is now at work on a commentary on Juvenal's Sixth Satire "On Women," and on female patrons in antiquity and the Renaissance.

SHELLEY P. HALEY, Associate Professor of Classics at Hamilton College, has written extensively on gender and race in Roman history and is currently writing a book entitled *Amor Parentis: Parental Expression of Affection in the Age of Cicero*. Her recent research focuses on the interrelationships between nineteenth-century African-American women and the classics.

JUDITH P. HALLETT is Associate Professor of Classics at the University of Maryland, College Park. Her publications include *Fathers and Daughters in Roman Society* (Princeton: Princeton University Press, 1984), as well as numerous articles on Latin literature, women in Greco-Roman antiquity, ancient sexuality, and the study of classics in the United States.

TINA PASSMAN is Associate Professor of Classics at the University of Maine, Orono. She has written on Greek myth and its applications to modern feminist concerns, and in Chicana and multicultural studies. She is now at work on Jane Ellen Harrison and is producing a sourcebook on Amazon narratives.

NANCY SORKIN RABINOWITZ, Professor of Comparative Literature, teaches at Hamilton College and has written on a wide range of authors (Charlotte Brontë, Margaret Drabble, Adrienne Rich, Aeschylus). She uses psychoanalytic, structuralist, and poststructuralist forms of feminism in her book, *Anxiety Veiled: Euripides and the Traffic in Women* (Ithaca: Cornell University Press, 1993).

AMY RICHLIN is Associate Professor of Classics and Women's Studies at the University of Southern California. Her recent publications include an edited volume, *Pornography and Representation in Greece and Rome* (New York: Oxford University Press, 1992), and the revised edition of *The Garden of Priapus: Sexuality and Aggression in Roman Humor* (New York: Oxford University Press, 1992). Her work in progress includes a study of Roman witches.

DIANA ROBIN is chair of the Department of Foreign Languages and Literatures at the University of New Mexico, Albuquerque. As a film theorist, she considers her work on Latin writers of the Italian Renaissance as a form of cultural critique; she has written one book, *Filelfo in Milan* (Princeton: Princeton University Press, 1991), and is at work on another on humanist Cassandra Fedele.

PETER ROSE is Professor of Classics at Miami University of Ohio. He is best known for his Marxist analyses of Homer and Pindar and is the author of *Sons of the Gods, Children of Earth: Ideology and Literary Form in Ancient Greece* (Ithaca: Cornell University Press, 1992).

MARILYN B. SKINNER is Professor of Classics and head of the Department of Classics at the University of Arizona. She has published numerous articles on the female poetic tradition in ancient Greece, focusing on Sappho and her successors Corinna, Erinna, and Nossis. She has also published widely on Roman constructions of gender and sexuality, especially in the poetry of Catullus, and is now co-editing a collection of essays on Roman sexuality.

BELLA ZWEIG, Senior Lecturer in Humanities at the University of Arizona, is interested in multiculturalism in the ancient and modern worlds. Her study of Greek drama and poetry, women in ancient Greek religion, and the status of women in antiquity is informed by multi-ethnic and women's studies and by direct learning from Native American peoples. Her 1992 Innovative Teaching Award recognized her work in multi-ethnic curricular development.